Reading French in the Arts and Sciences

Fourth Edition

Edward M. Stack
North Carolina State University

Houghton Mifflin Company   **Boston**

Dallas   Geneva, Illinois   Lawrenceville, New Jersey   Palo Alto

Cover design by Richard Hannus

Copyright © 1987 by Houghton Mifflin Company. All rights reserved.

No part of this work may be reproduced or transmitted in any form or by any means, electronic or mechanical, including photocopying and recording, or by any information storage or retrieval system, except as may be expressly permitted by the 1976 Copyright Act or in writing by the Publisher. Requests for permission should be addressed to College Permissions, Houghton Mifflin Company, One Beacon Street, Boston, Massachusetts 02108.

Printed in the U.S.A.
Library of Congress Catalog Number: 86-80905
ISBN: 0-395-35968-6
      N - QP/F 02 01 00

Contents

3

Past Participles   Adverbs   Attributes   Present Tense

4

Subject Pronouns   Reflexive Verbs   *dont*   Multiple Modifiers
Participle-Preposition Linkage   Infinitives   Impersonal Verbs

Essential Word Review I (Chapters 1–4)

5

Negative Forms of Verbs   *ne . . . que   tenir*

6

Personal Pronouns Used as Subjects   Present Tense
Recognition of Future and Conditional System

Structures:

Readings:

7

Special Future and Conditional Stems of Irregular Verbs   Past Tenses
Translation of the Imperfect Tense   *avoir*

Structures:

Readings:

8

Object Pronouns   Compound Tenses and *être*

Structures:

Essential Word Review II (Chapters 5–8)   83

9

Present Participles   Comparisons   *celui   prendre   faire*

Structures:

10

Inverted Word Order   Causative *faire   mettre   savoir   voir   pouvoir*

Structures:

Readings:

11

Supplemental Auxiliary Verbs   *lequel   en   vouloir   devoir   aller*

Structures:

Readings:

12

Past Definite Tense   Expressions of Time   *venir*   Immediate Past

Structures:

Readings:

13

Relative Pronouns   Gender as It Affects Meaning   *tout*   *ouvrir*

Structures:

Readings:

14

Adjectives with Variable Meanings   Possessive Adjectives   *y*   Conjunctions

Structures:

Readings:

15

Disjunctive Pronouns   Imperatives   *aussi*

Structures:

16

Subjunctive Mood   Possessive Pronouns   *partir* and *se servir de*

Structures:

Essential Word Review IV (Chapters 13–16)

17

Reflexive Verbs   Interrogatives   *ne* without *pas*   Dictionary Use

Structures:

Supplementary Readings:

Appendices

Preface

The purpose of *Reading French in the Arts and Sciences, Fourth Edition* is to provide students with an effective way to learn to read and translate French. The method assumes no previous knowledge of French or grammatical terminology, and since the text aims to teach reading, no exercises in composition or conversation are included. The success of *Reading French in the Arts and Sciences* over the three previous editions lies in its straightforward, pragmatic approach to the teaching of reading skills.

Proficiency in understanding a foreign language, like any other skill, is attained by persistent application of a systematic method. Such a method is described in the Introduction to this book and is applied in the succeeding chapters. Learning time is shortened through the introduction of special strategies governing verb tenses and word-order problems and through the omission of discussion of and practice in matters important only for composition or conversation.

Organization

Each chapter begins with simple explanations of grammar, followed by translation exercises using sentence fragments and isolated sentences. These sentence-fragment exercises give students a chance to apply the principles they have learned and to become aware that there are often several possible ways to translate any given fragment. Full sentences and longer readings then enable students to test the various possibilities to find the one that fits a particular context.

The reading selections are heterogeneous so as to call the attention of students in the sciences and technical fields to the values of literature and philosophy, as well as to make students of the humanities aware of the method and precision of scientific literature. In teaching reading, scientific and technical passages provide a good starting point because of the many cognates and the rigorous march of logic. Literary passages are usually more difficult because of the wider-ranging vocabulary and the intervention of the imagination, which often makes it impossible to predict the sequence of ideas. Thus, in this book, early readings are short passages on familiar scientific topics, and more technical and literary topics are saved for presentation until later, when students are more comfortable using the techniques needed to read them.

Key Features

The most important feature of this book is its systematic approach. The systematic presentation of grammar, along with concise explanations and examples, emphasizes forms used in writing rather than speaking; students learn only the grammar necessary for comprehending and translating texts. Vocabulary recognition techniques such as comparison of English and French vocabulary, including cognates and false cognates, allow students to expand their vocabulary rapidly. Included in every chapter are translation exercises which progress gradually from cognates to phrases to entire sentences and paragraphs, easing students into reading.

Another important feature is the footnotes; vocabulary is placed in footnotes so students need not waste time referring incessantly to an end vocabulary. Whenever possible, footnotes are used to provide a *guide* to the solution of problems, rather than to provide outright translations. Footnoted items are not labeled in the exercises and readings, in order to encourage students to try to figure meanings out on their own before they resort to checking the footnotes for a hint. When students encounter an unknown word, they should look first at the context and spelling to see whether they can deduce the meaning. Only when this does not help should they look for the word in the footnotes. If they do not find it, they will know that either it has already been footnoted earlier in the text, it appears in the end vocabulary, or they *should* be able to deduce the meaning from context or spelling. Emphasis in the text is on basic vocabulary common to all fields and on conversion of French to English structure. Since eventually the student will need to use a dictionary, dictionary techniques are introduced. The optional unglossed readings at the end of the book can be used for practice in using the dictionary.

End matter contains the supplementary readings, hints on translation, models and lists of regular and irregular verbs, an explanation of numbers, a list of suggested dictionaries, a reference list of false cognates, integrated tests for each chapter, a French-English end vocabulary, and a comprehensive index.

In addition to many features of the third edition, the fourth edition contains substantial improvements. About one-third of the readings are new; they have been added to provide fresh material and up-to-date topics. Other selections from past editions have been shortened or deleted so as to provide less complex readings for students not familiar with specific technical fields. New supplementary readings without footnotes at the end of the book challenge students to put their reading skills into practice. Instructors can choose to use the supplementary readings either at the course's end, as periodic tests, or as replacements for readings in the chapters. With the main text, several new grammar topics have been added, grammar explanations have been simplified throughout, and vocabulary review sections have been added after every fourth lesson to aid students in studying words that recur frequently in the reading material. Exercise content has been improved to make exercises more relevant to topics in the chapter readings and more representative of modern French style. Footnotes have been shortened and simplified. Lastly, a new design has dramatically improved readability and modernized the appearance of the text.

For careful review of the previous edition and for numerous helpful suggestions for this fourth edition, I am very grateful to Professors Suzanne Chamier of the University of Missouri at Rolla, Lionel Friedman of the University of Washington, Jeanine M. Goldman of the State University of New York at Stony Brook, Lisa Long of Drew University, and Donald Stone, Jr. of Harvard University. My thanks also go to the numerous students whose letters have brought encouragement in their expressions of accomplishment.

My sincere appreciation for the editing, design, and production of this edition is extended to the staff at Houghton Mifflin Company.

Raleigh, North Carolina   Edward M. Stack

Introduction

To the Student

This textbook differs from most French texts in that it is designed solely to teach you to *read* and *translate*. Much grammar and other instructional material that is usually included—but is only necessary if the purpose of the book is to teach composition and conversation in addition to reading—has been omitted, saving you time and energy. This, then, is a book in which the grammatical information is very selective; only what you actually need to accomplish your goal has been retained.

Three main tasks lie ahead of you: (1) learning a vocabulary, (2) learning the structural organization of French (that is, word-order), and (3) learning to discriminate among verb tenses. There is a method for accomplishing each of those tasks; that method is outlined below and incorporated into the instructional material of the book.

Organization of the Book

This text has seventeen lessons, each calculated to be approximately a week's work in class (not counting outside preparation). The rate of progress will depend on your instructor's estimate of the situation, of course; you may spend more or less time as he or she sees fit. Each lesson contains explanations, with examples; short translation exercises using sentence fragments to fix the principles explained; longer sentences; and connected readings. For each lesson there is one (or two, in the case of the first few lessons) Integrated Test at the back of the book. Your instructor may assign this test as homework or may actually use it as a test. In any case you should try the exercises in the tests, because they contain material that will make your mental wheels grind into action and cause some creative thinking—not just memory work.

Like most books, this one is equipped with a storehouse of reference material: the Appendices. Get into the habit of referring to them for verb forms and other information. Use the Index to locate material that you have already covered but need to recheck. A small dictionary (called End Vocabulary) is also at the back of the book. Use it to find the meaning of French words for which you have tried but failed to "invent" a probable meaning.

Vocabulary

Learning new words is a feat involving both memory and the imaginative ability to deduce the probable meaning of a word from the *context* (the surroundings) in which it is found. The lessons begin with easy French words called cognates, which cause little difficulty because they resemble their English equivalents. Soon, however, the text introduces words that you will be explicitly asked to memorize.

Memorization of frequently used words is part of the spadework of language learning, just as learning the multiplication table is a necessary prelude to performing simple arithmetical functions. It is not very exciting, but it can lead to amazing results if properly done.

Vocabulary Cards.   How should you memorize the words you are called upon to recognize time after time? A good method is to use vocabulary cards, which you can make yourself.

Use index cards or cut a number of slips of paper of equal size. On one side write the French word you wish to learn; on the other side, its English equivalent. (You should start this system at once, so that you do not have too great a number of cards to make all at the same time.) In choosing words to put on vocabulary cards, concentrate on the lists in the text marked to be learned, as well as the words in the Essential Word Review lists.

Now pile the cards in a single pile, French words up. Glance at the first word, tell yourself its English equivalent, and then turn the card over to check your accuracy. At this point you begin placing used cards in two piles: Pile A is where you place cards you have correctly identified, and Pile B is where you place those cards you got wrong or hesitated over. Go through the entire pile, sorting the cards into piles A and B as you give the English meanings.

Next time through, concentrate on pile B, and see if you can get some of the cards into pile A. Continue as long as possible in this fashion. WARNING: Always shuffle the cards in a pile before you start through them; if you do not, you may learn the *sequence* of words, rather than the words themselves.

Review pile A once every two or three days, or the words in that pile may sneakily revert to B status. Keep them in A condition by frequent review. Carry a few B cards around with you, and go through them at odd moments, such as while you're loafing between classes or waiting for the bus.

Vocabulary by Logical Deduction.   Before even attempting a translation, read a whole sentence or paragraph entirely through. This first "rough" reading will orient you to the general subject matter, even though you do not get all the details.

Next reread the first sentence of the paragraph. Now that you know the general orientation of the whole paragraph, the first sentence will fit into a definite scheme of meaning that will aid you in deducing the meaning of any words you do not definitely know. It is at this point that you are *emphatically encouraged to make an educated guess* at the probable meaning.

Let's take an example. Suppose that the rough reading of the paragraph you are to translate indicates that it is about the solar system. You can translate the first sentence readily, except for one word, as follows:

The planets revolve around **une étoile** . . .

WARNING! Don't stop just because you don't know the meaning of **une étoile**; don't bother to look in the vocabulary. Read on! You may get a clue! You read

The planets revolve around **une étoile** called the Sun.

Now reflect for a moment and deduce logically what that unknown French word must be. Did you say *a cigar? a doghouse?* What, then? Of course, it is *a star*. It takes only a small acquaintance with the subject to deduce meaning, and you probably do it all the time in reading English, to save trips to the dictionary.

Cognates.   The first lesson deals with French words you already know, like *nation, observation*, and *résumé*. You will not need to make vocabulary cards or deduce meanings for these, as they are already part of your working vocabulary.

False Friends.   The "false friends" *look* as if you knew them, but they are often traitors, meaning something else. They are marked with a dagger (†) on their first few appearances, just to warn you. They should be placed on vocabulary cards and their correct meanings learned.

An example is the word **vase**: see it in action in the sentence

John slipped and fell in **la vase**.

Logical deduction tells us that it is unlikely that John fell into a piece of ceramic pottery. However, as John could have fallen into almost anything from a vat of sulphuric acid to Niagara Falls (unless we are given more context), there is no way to know that **la vase** means *mud*. False friends must be memorized.

Footnote Vocabulary

New words are given in the form of footnotes, in the order in which they appear on the page. The key to the footnotes is the number in brackets at the beginning of the sentence or paragraph you are reading. If a new word is not listed, either (a) you should already know it, as it has appeared before, or (b) you are expected to make a clever logical deduction of the meaning. In either case you may find the word in the end vocabulary—but only as a last resort!

Study Methods

It is important that you practice French regularly and frequently. Try to do some reading *every* day. It has been very definitely proved that a little every day is more effective than a lot on just one day. In other words, an hour every day is better than seven hours one day a week.

Method of Presentation of Material

The structure of the French language is presented in definite stages in this text.

The core of *noun-adjective groups*, or basic units of thought, is a noun and its article.

la nation   *the nation*

These noun groups 'are built into larger units through the addition of adjectival modifiers.

la nation **américaine**   the *American* nation
la **grande** nation **américaine**   the *great American* nation
cette nation à géographie diverse   *this* nation *with diversified geography*

The noun-adjective group is converted into a prepositional phrase by placing a preposition in front.

de la nation américaine   *of* the American nation

Sentence or clause groups are formed by inserting a *verb* between two familiar noun-adjective groups.

La nation américaine **possède** un gouvernement démocratique.
The American nation *possesses* a democratic government.

Adverbs are introduced to give more subtle distinctions.

Cette **assez** grande nation possède **déjà** un gouvernement **complètement** démocratique.
This *rather* large nation *already* possesses a *completely* democratic government.

Other slight variations are introduced systematically, and finally the time-relationship is varied through the verb *tense*.

Translations

An English translation of a French passage must have the following characteristics:

It must be in natural sounding English, devoid of traces of French word order. It should sound as if you composed it originally in English. There need not be an English word for every French word.

It must present the entire idea of the French passage. You must read each French sentence, and then provide an English one that conveys the same idea in English. It must not add any ideas (or interpretations) or omit any.

It must not change the time (verb tense) of the French (with a few exceptions explained later), as this would be a mutilation of an important part of the idea.

Your command of English will be taxed in the selection of the exactly appropriate word. The writing of a translation is a creative act which is separate from and more difficult than merely reading and understanding French. You should soon develop the ability to read through a French passage and tell the general meaning without attempting a sentence-by-sentence translation.

The kind of so-called literal translation that results from a word-for-word substitution of English for French is a poor translation. After arriving at a rough translation, try to free yourself from the French for a moment and visualize the situation as it would exist in the arena of your own experience. Then simplify and rearrange the *idea* of the French as much as necessary to convey the situation perfectly in English, leaving no ideas out. For example, in reading a letter from a French business firm, you find at the end the following sentence:

Veuillez agréer, Monsieur, l'expression de nos sentiments distingués.

A literal translation of this is

Kindly accept, Sir, the expression of our distinguished sentiments.

This way of ending a letter is obviously hilarious in English, but the intent of the French writer was quite serious. He was merely using the customary final formula. The proper translation of the long French formula is the English phrase that serves the same purpose in a letter—*Yours truly.*

In summary, then, attack the job ahead seriously and conscientiously. Use vocabulary cards for words that you find recurring frequently and for those in special lists marked for you to learn. Be bold in deducing meanings by context, shunning reliance on the End Vocabulary. Don't be afraid to make mistakes —they are fine in the learning process, and they make the classroom cheerful. Beware of the false friends, and take comfort in the cognates. The method is readymade, so just follow the book and use your instructor's comments as a means of improving what you are doing; after all, you are solely responsible for your progress.

To the Instructor

In the first class meeting it is a good idea to give an explanation of the noun-construct method described in the Introduction (which you may wish to assign as review after the first class) and a drill on the first exercise.

You may also want to explain the French division of words into syllables and demonstrate how stress is placed on the final syllable of each sense-making group. The class exercise then proceeds as follows:

1. The instructor says the French item (for example, "**numéro un. le directeur**").
2. The class repeats the words in French.
3. A designated individual repeats the words in French and translates.

This procedure is carried out for each word in the exercise.

Although teaching pronunciation is not an aim of the text, this approach provides a way for the students to identify words they wish to discuss and makes them feel more comfortable with the material. Since the first lesson deals nearly exclusively with cognates, you can concentrate on pronunciation while ostensibly working on translation. Words should be pronounced aloud as part of the translation practice when time allows, at least for the early lessons.

When the class has advanced to lessons having longer readings, you have the option of assigning either whole readings or particular numbered sections of readings. A longer reading may be divided among groups of students so that the whole reading can be translated in class.

The unglossed supplementary readings enable you to monitor the students' use of dictionaries. They can serve as a transition to independent reading, or they can be used as replacements for readings in the chapters if you wish to give students dictionary practice throughout the course.

Reading French
in the Arts
and Sciences

1

Structures

1. French Vocabulary

The main task in gaining a reading knowledge of French, at the outset, is to learn the words that will appear most often in the material you plan to read. This stock of words, or vocabulary, consists of two types: (1) words common to all kinds of writing, regardless of the subject matter, and (2) words peculiar to a particular field of study, such as psychology or chemistry.

Clearly, the first type of vocabulary is important to everyone, and so in this text stress is placed on commonly used vocabulary and structure. You can quickly build a specialized vocabulary in your own field of interest after the groundwork has been done. The explanation of technical terms like **isotope** and **décibel**, which you will encounter in the readings, would fall within the scope of a course in physics. Here you will merely be expected to read and supply English equivalents, leaving to the specialists in a class the explanation of these and other such terms.

Fortunately, you already possess a fairly large French vocabulary. There are many French words that have the same (or almost the same) spelling and meaning as English words. These words, called *cognates*, may safely be translated by their English equivalents. On the other hand, there are other French words called "false friends" (**faux amis**) that look like English words but have important differences in meaning from their English counterparts. When you encounter one of these false friends, you must allow for more than one possibility. The best way to avoid difficulties is to be forewarned and to learn thoroughly the different meanings of these words. The French word **expérience,** for instance, looks like a cognate but does not always mean "experience." Indeed, it is a word of prime importance to scientists, with its meaning of *experiment*.

2. Cognates

These French words closely resemble English ones and may usually be translated by the English words they look like. Many terms pertaining to science, architecture, law, music, society, and military organization came into English from the French.

A. **Exact cognates.**   These are words that are spelled exactly like their English equivalents. They may ordinarily be translated by the English cognate, although some have *additional* meanings in French.

table	village	train
résumé	colonel	auto
fiancé	lieutenant	boulevard
amateur	général	dose
restaurant	sabotage	édifice
plan	capture	danger
rare	architecture	influence

B. **Cognates ending in -*ion*.**   Almost all English words ending in -*ion* are exact cognates of French words (all feminine gender).

construction	pénétration	décoration
agitation	bifurcation	confusion
déviation	diffraction	direction
distribution	émission	introduction
investigation	possession	complication

C. **Cognates ending in -*ie*.**   Many French nouns may be recognized in their English form by substituting -*y* for the -**ie** ending.

géographie	géométrie	géologie
énergie	psychologie	sociologie
théorie	océanographie	photographie

D. **Cognates ending in -é.**   Some French words ending in -**é** may be recognized in their English form by substituting -*y*.

beauté   identité   obscurité

E. **Cognates ending in -*ique*.**   Many French words ending in -**ique** correspond to English words ending in -*ic*, -*ics*, or -*ical*.

-**ique** → -*ic*	électrique	Atlantique	magnétique
	spécifique	géométrique	dynamique
	métallique	cosmique	énigmatique
-**ique** → -*ics*	linguistique	dynamique	politique
-**ique** → -*ical*	optique	mécanique	physique
	symétrique	mathématique	identique

F. Cognates with a circumflex accent [ˆ]. In some French words a written circumflex accent replaces the letter s, which was originally part of the word. Knowledge of this fact is helpful in recognizing the meaning of many words spelled with a circumflex accent.

> forêt   hôpital   île

3. False Friends (†)

False friends are words that look like English but must not be translated as cognates in most cases. Here are a few important ones to learn at once. (Related words are given in parentheses.) A more complete list is in Appendix F.

French	*Meaning*
actuel, actuelle	present-day, current
actuellement	currently, at present
(en réalité)	(actually, in reality)
apparition, une	appearance
axe, un	axis
but, le	purpose, goal
car	for, because
commodité, la	convenience
court, courte	short
davantage	more
demander	to ask for, to request
éditeur, un	publisher
(rédacteur, le)	(editor)
esprit, un	mind, spirit
éventuel, éventuelle	possible, potential
évidemment	obviously
expérience, une	experiment
important, importante	large
inconvénient, un	disadvantage
journée, une	day
large	wide
(grand, grande)	(large, big)
lecture, la	reading
(conférence, la)	(lecture, conference)
librairie, la	bookstore
(bibliothèque, la)	(library)
misère, la	poverty, misery
partie, la	part
phrase, la	sentence
(locution, la)	(phrase)
physicien, le	physicist
(médecin, le)	(physician, doctor)
prétendre	to claim
sensibilité, la	sensitivity
tour, la	tower

French	*Meaning*
tour, le	turn, tour
ville, la	city
(village, le)	(village)
vase, la	mud
(vase, le)	(vase)

4. Gender of Nouns

All French nouns are classified as masculine or feminine in grammatical gender. A few nouns have either gender (e.g., **enfant,** *child*). Nouns designating persons usually, but not always, correspond to the sex of the person. (**Le professeur** can refer to either a man or a woman teacher.) The gender of most nouns designating things or concepts cannot be deduced. There are a few clues, however, that are helpful: the endings **-tion** and **-ie** tell us that a noun is feminine, and the endings **-ment, -eur,** and **-ien** that the noun is masculine.

5. Definite Articles *le, la, l', les* (the)

All four words **le, la, l',** and **les** correspond to *the.* The first three (**le, la, l'**) are used with singular nouns; **les** is used with plural nouns. The article is generally omitted in English if the noun refers to a thing in general rather than to a specific object: thus, *the* would be omitted in translating **J'aime le golf,** *I like golf.*

Here are the forms of the definite article in French.

le is used before a masculine noun	le médecin
la is used before a feminine noun	la tour Eiffel
l' is used before any vowel sound (*m.* or *f.*)	l'arbre
les is used before any plural noun (*m.* or *f.*)	les médecins
	les arbres

In translating, remember: you must decide whether a noun is to be taken in a general sense or whether it refers to a specific thing or idea.

General: **Les vitamines** sont essentielles.
             Vitamins are essential.

Specific: **Les vitamines** dans ce groupe sont essentielles.
             The vitamins in this group are essential.

As a reader, you may need to know the gender of French nouns in order to decide whether some other word in the text—an adjective, for example—applies to a specific noun. Therefore, you should be aware of signals, such as articles, that show gender.

Exercises

Series A (Sections 1–5)

These exercises will assist you in developing skill in reading. Each series of exercises is accompanied by footnotes containing special remarks and numbered according to the exercise item number. Thus the first note is 6, because it refers to exercise item 6, **le ministre.**

Give the English equivalents. In Exercises A and D, give the gender of each noun. (Since l' could represent either **le** or **la**, you will need to look up nouns preceded by l' in a French dictionary.) Omit the translation of the definite article when appropriate, as in **le coton**. In this exercise, false friends are marked with a dagger (†), but this assistance will be discontinued later.

A.
1. le directeur
2. le colonel
3. le secrétaire
4. la technique
5. la capitale
6. le ministre†
7. la sociologie
8. le caporal
9. le capitaine
10. l'arbre
11. la nation
12. l'architecte
13. le musicien
14. la cathédrale
15. l'édifice
16. le coton
17. l'animal
18. la théorie
19. la quantité
20. l'extrémité
21. la condition
22. le but†
23. l'expérience†
24. la science
25. l'élément
26. l'océan
27. la possibilité
28. l'hémisphère
29. la géologie
30. l'inconvénient†

B.
31. caractéristique
32. catastrophique
33. électronique
34. énigmatique
35. cylindrique
36. géométrique
37. physique
38. identique
39. fantastique
40. métallique
41. historique
42. économique
43. biologique
44. astronomique
45. sociologique
46. atomique
47. magnifique
48. mathématique

C.
49. les physiciens†
50. les médecins†
51. les arbres
52. les nations
53. les probabilités
54. les économistes

---

6. **ministre**† *m.* government minister 15. **édifice** *m.* (Although *edifice* is a correct English equivalent, you should try to find a synonym in common use)

55. les musiciens	61. les sciences
56. les théories	62. les océan
57. les éditeurs†	63. les possibilités
58. les buts†	64. les inconvénients†
59. les machines	65. les médicaments
60. les expériences†	66. les axes†

D. 67. l'empereur	88. la correction
68. la journée†	89. plastique
69. spécifique	90. la beauté
70. l'agitation	91. extérieur
71. élégant	92. la misère†
72. la patience	93. la nature
73. la série	94. l'éditeur†
74. actuel†	95. la commodité†
75. les mathématiques	96. actuellement†
76. la fête	97. cosmique
77. les expériences†	98. la radiation
78. la difficulté	99. large†
79. la partie	100. le cap†
80. le but†	101. la météorologie
81. théorique	102. le désordre
82. la pharmacie	103. l'attraction
83. les conférences†	104. la comète
84. la densité	105. les comètes
85. les circuits	106. la solution
86. la hâte	107. la proportion
87. les corrections	108. la variation

Test 1A, page 211

Structures

6. Indefinite Articles *un, une, des* (a, an, some)

The words **un** and **une** mean *a* or *an*. Un appears before masculine singular nouns, **une** before feminine singular nouns. Des means *some*, but it is not usually needed in a translation.

un moyen	*a* means	**des** moyens	(some) means
un plan	*a* plan	**des** plans	(some) plans
une raison	*a* reason	**des** raisons	(some) reasons

In questions, **des** means *any*: **Avez-vous des livres?** *Do you have any books?*

---

88. **correction**† *f.* (In addition to having the obvious meaning, this word also means *correctness*)   89. **plastique** *adj.* (Since there is no accompanying article, this is an adjective rather than the name of a material)

7. Regular Plurals of Nouns

A. General.   Normally nouns are made plural by adding -s to the basic singular form found in dictionaries.

un fait	a fact	des faits	(some) facts
le jour	the day	les jours	the days

B. Special cases.   Some nouns in their singular form already end in -s, -x, or -z. They look like plurals in the singular form, and the plural form remains the same. When you see such a noun, check the accompanying article to determine whether it is singular or plural.

le cas   the case (*s.*)   **les** cas   the cases (*pl.*)

Here are some common nouns whose singular form already carries a plural-like ending.

le cas	the case	**les** cas	the cases
le fils	the son	**les** fils	the sons
le poids	the weight	**les** poids	the weights
le gaz	the gas	**les** gaz	the gases
le nez	the nose	**les** nez	the noses
le choix	the choice	**les** choix	the choices

8. Irregular Plurals of Nouns

Nouns ending in -s, -x, and -z are usually plural; those listed in Section 7 are exceptions. When in doubt, check to see whether the accompanying article is plural (that is, ends in -s).

A.   Although most nouns are made plural simply by adding -s, it is quite usual for nouns ending in **-au** and **-eu** to take the old form of the plural, -x.

le niveau	the level	les niveaux	the levels
un niveau	a level	des niveaux	(some) levels
(le) le rameau	the branch	les rameaux	the branches

B. Nouns ending in **-al** are usually made plural by changing the **-l** to **-u** and adding **-x**.

un animal	an animal	des animaux	(some) animals
un journal	a newspaper	des journaux	(some) newspapers
le minéral	the mineral	les minéraux	the minerals

C. Totally different plurals occur in a few cases.

un œil	an eye	des yeux	eyes

9. Prepositions

The following prepositions indicating position should be memorized.

dans	in (contained within)
sur	on (on the surface of)
sous	under
devant	in front of, before
derrière	behind
à côté de	beside

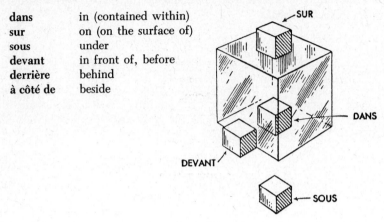

Exercises

Series B (Sections 6–9)

Give the English equivalent of the following noun structures.

A.
1. un directeur
2. un général
3. un secrétaire
4. une capitale
5. une armée
6. une théorie
7. des théories
8. un fait
9. des faits
10. des buts†

11. des médecins†
12. des généraux
13. des musiciens
14. une cathédrale
15. des cathédrales
16. des arbres
17. des journaux
18. des poids
19. un poids
20. un niveau

21. des conditions
22. une quantité
23. des expériences†
24. une science
25. des sciences
26. des niveaux
27. une possibilité
28. des possibilités
29. un inconvénient†
30. des inconvénients†

B.
31. derrière le garage
32. sur la table
33. sous une table
34. devant les tables
35. sur l'océan
36. dans l'océan
37. à la condition
38. dans la solution
39. à côté de l'éditeur†
40. à côté des machines

41. derrière la cathédrale
42. devant le fait
43. dans le cas
44. dans les cas
45. dans les journaux
46. dans le journal
47. sous un poids
48. sous des poids
49. sous le poids
50. sur un rameau

C. 51. à côté des musiciens
   52. sur les extrémités
   53. sous des conditions
   54. derrière l'édifice
   55. devant un choix
   56. des fils
   57. un fils
   58. les fils
   59. dans la nature
   60. dans les expériences
   61. une perception
   62. des perceptions
   63. un événement
   64. des équations
   65. un moyen
   66. des moyens
   67. le moyen
   68. les moyens
   69. la correction
   70. des attractions
   71. l'attraction
   72. les attractions
   73. dans le gaz
   74. dans un gaz
   75. dans les gaz
   76. dans des gaz
   77. un résumé
   78. des résumés
   79. dans le résumé
   80. des villages
   81. dans les villages
   82. le week-end
   83. les week-ends
   84. un week-end
   85. le golf
   86. le football
   87. une complication
   88. un coefficient
   89. des concepts
   90. le concept
   91. le médecin†
   92. les médecins†
   93. des professeurs
   94. un ingénieur
   95. une opération
   96. des opérations
   97. un œil
   98. des yeux
   99. un téléphone
   100. la télévision
   101. des influences
   102. sous des influences
   103. le flux
   104. un orchestre
   105. des orchestres
   106. derrière l'orchestre
   107. sur le podium
   108. dans les autos
   109. des théâtres
   110. à côté du théâtre
   111. sur le boulevard
   112. devant l'édifice
   113. dans le train
   114. dans la tour

Test 1B, page 213

---

55. **devant un choix** (Translate using some assumed context, such as *He found himself* **devant un choix**)   59. **la nature** (Decide whether **la** should be translated; it is always helpful to think of a context)   65. **moyen** *m.* way (**Le moyen-âge** means *the Middle Ages*)   85. **le golf** (Use the word in a sentence to determine whether to use the article in English)   86. **football** *m.* soccer (U.S. *football* is **le football américain**)   94. **ingénieur** *m.* engineer

2

Structures

10. Adjectives

An adjective is a word whose chief function is to limit and define more precisely the meaning of a noun. This function is demonstrated by the progressive limitation in the following series. (Refer to the squares in the adjoining figure.)

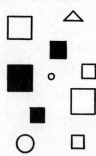

1. Look at the squares. (You look at all of them as an entity when the noun is used alone.)

2. Look at the *white* squares. (When one adjective is used, your attention is already greatly concentrated.)

3. Look at the *small white* squares. (A second adjective further defines which squares you should observe.)

4. Look at the *top small white* square. (Just one of the seven squares requires your attention.)

11. Position of Adjectives

In French, most adjectives normally follow the noun they describe. In translating, we restore English order by skipping over the noun to the adjective, then returning to read the noun.

une	méthode	**moderne**		a	*modern*	method
1	3	2		1	2	3

le	plateau	**continental**		the	*continental*	plateau
1	3	2		1	2	3

Certain common short adjectives usually precede the noun. (See below, Sections 14 and 15.)

12. Agreement of Adjectives

Adjectives agree in gender and number with the noun they qualify. The basic form of an adjective listed in vocabularies is masculine singular. This form is made feminine by adding **-e**; either the masculine or the feminine form may be made plural by adding **-s**. Hence most adjectives have four possible forms.

	singular	*plural*
masculine	grand	grands
feminine	grande	grandes

The reader need not be able to form these agreements, as the work has already been done by the French writers. Note, however, that the correspondence of gender and number helps show to what noun an adjective applies.

un fait intéressant (*m.s.*)	des faits intéressants (*m.pl.*)
une hypothèse intéressante (*f.s.*)	des hypothèses intéressantes (*f.pl.*)

A. Adjectives ending in -*e* in the basic form.   Some adjectives like **magnifique, autre** (other), and **jeune** (young) end in an unaccented **-e**; these do not add another **-e** for the feminine: both *m.* and *f.* singular are the same, and both *m.* and *f.* plural are the same.

un plan magnifique	des plans magnifiques
une table magnifique	des tables magnifiques

B. Adjectives ending in -*s* or -*x* in the basic form.   These adjectives already have a plural-like ending in the masculine singular, and do not change in the masculine plural.

un homme **heureux**	des hommes **heureux**
une femme heureuse	des femmes heureuses

Note that when an adjective ends in **-x** the **-x** is changed to **-s** before the characteristic feminine ending **-e** is added: **heureux** (*m.*), **heureuse** (*f.*) happy.

13. Prepositions

Learn the following prepositions.

avec	with	**à**	to, at, in
sans	without	**de**	of, from
par	by, through		(**d'** before a vowel or mute *h*)
vers	toward	**pour**	for
entre	between	**contre**	against
en face de	opposite		

Exercises

Series A (Sections 10–13)

Translate into English. Find the words you do not know in the vocabulary at the back of the book. Helpful remarks appear in the footnotes, whose numbers correspond to the item numbers. Look there first.

A.   1.   une possibilité historique   *a historic possibility*
     2.   des possibilités historiques   *some historic possibilities*
     3.   un but utile   *a useful goal*
     4.   des buts utiles   *some useful goals*
     5.   des cas pathologiques   *some pathological cases*
     6.   la programmation linéaire   *a linear programming*
     7.   un disque magnétique   *a magnetic disk*
     8.   un plan géométrique
     9.   une cathédrale gothique
    10.   une machine automatique
    11.   des machines automatiques
    12.   une expérience physique
    13.   un économiste énigmatique
    14.   un cas identique
    15.   un tube cylindrique
    16.   un programme assembleur
    17.   des minéraux métalliques
    18.   une théorie contradictoire
    19.   une conséquence naturelle
    20.   un système informatique
    21.   un ordinateur américain
    22.   des difficultés énormes
    23.   un diamètre critique
    24.   des cas extrêmes
    25.   des contrastes fréquents
    26.   un fait intéressant
    27.   un moyen efficace
    28.   un programme compilateur
    29.   une structure compliquée
    30.   la théorie musicale
    31.   des théories politiques
    32.   la musique classique
    33.   l'Institut national

---

6. **programmation** *f.* programming   8. **plan** *m.* plan (also a *cross-section*, or a *city map*)
20. **informatique** *adj.* data-processing   21. **ordinateur** *m.* computer   28. **compilateur** (*noun used as an adj.*) compiler (type of computer program)

34. la construction extérieure
35. les théories actuelles
36. un plan pratique

B. 37. par la science nucléaire
38. de l'hypothèse newtonienne
39. de l'architecture byzantine
40. par des moyens politiques
41. sans erreurs mathématiques
42. à la collection complète
43. avec une pression verticale
44. des choix difficiles
45. par l'informatique
46. sans indications précises
47. pour ou contre les examens
48. de l'état naturel
49. dans le mouvement scientifique
50. des cellules photoélectriques
51. de l'océan Atlantique . . .
52. . . . vers l'océan Pacifique
53. de la forme ancestrale
54. pour le guidage des fusées
55. à la fois
56. pour des calculs techniques
57. de Rome à Paris / entre Paris et Berlin
58. des résultats variables
59. de la première loi de Kepler
60. sans résultat satisfaisant
61. avec la révolution politique
62. sans argent
63. dans les molécules organiques
64. la partie active de la solution
65. contre le parti communiste
66. pour les nouveaux partis
67. le poids atomique
68. par un moyen empirique
69. à côté de la bibliothèque
70. la partie supérieure† de l'édifice

Test 2A, page 215

---

54. **guidage** *m.* guidance; **fusée** *f.* rocket, missile   55. **fois** *f.* time (recurrence of an event); **à la fois** at the same time, simultaneously   62. **argent** *m.* (*Hint:* What does the chemical symbol "Ag" represent?) silver, money

Structures

14. Preceding Expressions

Although most adjectives follow the noun in noun-adjective groups (Sec. 11), there are some that habitually precede the noun (Sec. 15). Certain other expressions ordinarily are also found before the noun and can be translated in the order in which they appear: expressions of quantity such as *many, several, some* (Sec. 16), possessive adjectives such as *my, your, our* (Sec. 17), and numbers (Sec. 18).

Sometimes an adjective not normally preceding will be placed before the noun for stylistic or emphatic purposes; but this should cause no difficulty in translation, as all adjectives in a group must be translated before the noun anyway.

Preceding Adjective:	une **nouvelle** machine	a *new* machine
Expression of Quantity:	beaucoup de café	a *lot of* coffee
Possessive Adjective:	ma machine à écrire	*my* typewriter
Number:	trois machines à écrire	*three* typewriters

15. Normally Preceding Adjectives

The following adjectives usually appear in front of the noun in a noun-adjective group. They should be learned because they are frequently encountered. In the list, the basic masculine singular form is given, followed by a hyphen and the letters added to form the feminine singular. The plurals are formed by adding -s.

bon, -ne	good	**long, -ue**	long
mauvais, -e	bad	**haut, -e**	high
grand, -e	large, big	**jeune**	young
petit, -e	small	**autre**	other
joli, -e	pretty	**même**	same

Four adjectives that generally precede the noun have two masculine forms.

vieux, vieil; vieille	old
beau, bel; belle	beautiful, fine, handsome
nouveau, nouvel; nouvelle	new
ce, cet; cette	this

The masculine forms **vieil, bel, nouvel,** and **cet** are used before singular nouns beginning with a vowel sound.

un nouveau livre	un **nouvel** avion	une nouvelle maison
ce livre	**cet** homme	cette maison

The plural of these adjectives is formed according to normal rules (Sec. 12).

Note that although all feminine adjectives end in -e, there are also masculine forms that end in -e (**jeune, autre, rouge,** etc.). The only conclusion that can be reached regarding endings is that if an adjective does not end in -e, it cannot be feminine (**intéressant, petit, vieil, cet, charmant**).

16. Expressions of Quantity

Learn the following expressions of quantity.

plusieurs	several	**assez de**	enough
quelques	a few	**trop de**	too much, too many
la plupart de	most (of)	**peu de**	very few, very little
bien des	many, much, lots of	**plus de**	more
beaucoup de	many, much	**moins de**	less, fewer

17. Possessive Adjectives

Learn the following third-person possessive adjectives.

adjective	*each means*
son, sa, ses	his, her, its
leur, leurs	their

The possessive adjective in French is selected not on the basis of the sex of the owner, as in English, but rather on the basis of the gender and number of the noun modified. Thus **son** is used before a masculine singular noun (or a feminine singular noun beginning with a vowel sound), **sa** before a feminine singular noun, and **ses** before any plural noun. Only the context tells who the possessor is.

son poids (*m.*)	his weight, her weight, its weight
sa table (*f.*)	his table, her table, its table
ses tables (*f.*)	his tables, her tables, its tables
leur plan (*m.*)	their plan
leurs théories (*f.*)	their theories

18. Numbers 1–10, 100, 1000

The following numbers should be learned.

Cardinal		*Ordinal*	
un, une	one	**premier, première**	first
deux	two	**second, deuxième**	second
trois	three	**troisième**	third
quatre	four	**quatrième**	fourth
cinq	five	**cinquième**	fifth
six	six	**sixième**	sixth
sept	seven	**septième**	seventh
huit	eight	**huitième**	eighth
neuf	nine	**neuvième**	ninth
dix	ten	**dixième**	tenth
cent	one hundred	**centième**	one-hundredth
mille	one thousand	**millième**	one-thousandth

The numbers in the first group are called *cardinal numbers;* those in the second group, since they indicate order, are *ordinal numbers.* Most ordinal numbers are distinguished by the ending **-ième.** (See Appendix D for a more complete list.)

19. Contractions

The prepositions **à** (*to, at*) and **de** (*of, from*) combine with the articles **le** and **les** as follows.

au (à + le)	to the, at the	**du** (de + le)	of the, from the
aux (à + les)	to the, at the	**des** (de + les)	of the, from the

When **des** means *of the* or *from the,* translate it; when it means *some,* do not translate it.

Exercises

Series B (Sections 14–19)

The purpose of these exercises is to allow you to gain a repertory of meanings, probably only one of which will fit a given context. Later on, you may have to try several possibilities to fit the context you are faced with.

Translation Aid: When **de** (or **d'**) *directly precedes an adjective,* disregard it in translation (see, for example, Exercise A–5).

A. Give English equivalents. In phrases beginning with **des,** give three possibilities.

>   ***Example:***
>   **des idées**   (1) *ideas,* (2) *of the ideas,* (3) *from the ideas*

1. cette grande ville†   *this large town*
2. le nouveau style   *the new style*
3. du nouveau programme   *of the new program*
4. des ordinateurs   *of the computers, some computers*
5. de longs programmes
6. de nouveaux développements   *of new developments*
7. de la troisième équation   *of the 3rd equation*
8. ce nouveau projet   *this new project*
9. ce vieil homme   *this old man*
10. cet avion supersonique   *this supersonic plane*
11. des médicamments
12. beaucoup de disques   *lots of disks*
13. trop de conférences†   *seminar topic*

14. trois beaux arbres
15. le sixième édifice
16. un long boulevard
17. plusieurs résultats intéressants
18. quelques petites fautes   *a few small mistakes*
19. trop d'énergie
20. moins de diffraction   *less diffraction*
21. moins d'arbres   *fewer trees*
22. une belle ville
23. une rue large†
24. un autre cas   *another case*
25. une autre théorie   *another theory; some other theory*
26. trois autres expériences   *3 other experiments*
27. une longue leçon
28. de longues histoires† intéressantes
29. une vieille voiture   *an old car*
30. un ministre habile   *a skillful minister*
31. des éléments chimiques
32. sept petits animaux   *7 small animals*
33. cinq siècles de progrès   *5 centuries of progress*
34. de petites librairies†
35. un bel arbre
36. un bel homme
37. du danger imminent   *of imminent danger*
38. des bâtiments importants
39. des obstacles naturels
40. la même longue rue
41. au même niveau intellectuel
42. cet édifice important†
43. cet autre édifice contemporain
44. aux États-Unis d'Amérique
45. de l'état actuel†
46. par les étoiles fixes
47. une limite fixe
48. des presses hydrauliques
49. de grandes presses automatiques
50. d'autres programmes compilateurs
51. de l'univers physique
52. des poèmes lyriques
53. de la nouvelle édition
54. de nouvelles expériences

---

18. **faute** *f.* fault, mistake, error   28. **histoire** *f.* story (as well as *history*)   33. **siècle** *m.* century   36. **bel** *adj.* (not translated the same way in 35 and 36)   38. **bâtiment** *m.* building (also *ship*)   43. **contemporain** *adj.* contemporary   45. **état** *m.* state   46. **étoile** *f.* star

55. aux nouveaux états chimiques
56. du moyen-âge
57. de la grande attraction
58. de hautes tours
59. de la partie active de l'air
60. des crises industrielles

B. The individual noun group may have more than one meaning when it stands alone, but in a context its meaning becomes stabilized. Try the various possibilities to see which one fits in the following contexts. Read the entire sentence in English, replacing the French phrase by the appropriate English equivalent.

61. (There are) **des ordinateurs** (in each building).
62. (The maintenance) **des ordinateurs** (is highly technical).
63. (These chips were taken) **des ordinateurs** (on the first floor).
64. (The sides) **des pyramides** (at Gizeh are rough).
65. (Moving away) **des pyramides,** (we came to the Sphinx).
66. (What do you think) **du nouveau style?**
67. (The trend is away) **du style gothique.**
68. (Let's examine this description) **du système économique.**
69. (People derive many benefits) **du système actuel.**
70. (The indicators) **des instruments** (are broken).
71. (There are) **des instruments** (for measuring diffraction.)
72. (The students are returning) **du théâtre.**
73. (The stage) **du théâtre** (is circular).
74. (Tonight we are going) **au théâtre.**
75. (We enjoy an evening) **au théâtre.**
76. **Des lignes sinueuses** (represent rivers on this map).
77. (I am referring) **aux phénomènes isolés** (of a single experiment).

C. *Expressions of quantity and numbers.* Translate.

78. plusieurs romans policiers   several ~~novels~~
79. beaucoup de romans historiques
80. assez de programmes linéaires   enough linear programs
81. moins d'éléments caractéristiques   fewer characteristic elements
82. une quantité importante   a ~~large~~ sizeable quantity
83. bien des livres   lots of books
84. beaucoup de livres techniques   a lot of technical books
85. peu d'argent
86. un peu d'argent
87. la plupart des expériences   most of the experiments
88. la neuvième théorie

---

55. **chimique** *adj.* chemical   76. **ligne** *f.* line   77. **isolé** *pp.* isolated   78. **roman** *m.* novel; **policier** *adj.* pertaining to the police (You must find the English equivalent, which is not *police novel*)   84. **technique** *adj.* technical

89. huit jours†   *8 days*
90. la huitième symphonie de Beethoven
91. sept mois agréables
92. quinze jours†   *15 days*
93. trois plumes rouges   *3 red pens*
94. quatre roses   *4 roses*
95. deux cent dix pages   *210 pages*

D. *Possessive adjectives.* Translate.

96. Einstein: ses théories physiques
97. Mme Curie: ses théories physiques
98. l'eau: son état solide
99. la presse: sa pression verticale
100. ces architectes: leur concept moderne
101. les auteurs: leurs buts littéraires
102. les généraux: leur but stratégique
103. la société Westinghouse: son ordinateur
104. le ministre: son parti politique
105. les étudiants: leurs études avancées
106. les vendeurs: leurs échantillons
107. Jean-Paul: sa petite maison
108. Mendelssohn: sa quatrième symphonie
109. les soldats: leur action inattendue
110. la vieille dame: son appartement

Test 2B, page 217

---

89. **huit jours** a week (The day one is presently on is counted; the French phrase **quinze jours**, *15 days*, designates *two weeks, a fortnight*) 93. **plume** *f.* feather 97. **Mme** (abbrev. of **Madame**) Mrs. 98. **eau** *f.* water 103. **société** *f.* corporation 105. **étude** *f.* study 106. **vendeur** *m.* salesman; **échantillon** *m.* sample 109. **inattendu, -e** *adj.* unexpected (The prefix **in-** often indicates an antonym; see Appendix A, Sec. 10)

3

Structures

20. Verb Listings

Verbs, which indicate some kind of action, are listed in dictionaries in the infinitive form (for example, **examiner**, *to examine;* **développer,** *to develop*). The characteristic feature of the English infinitive is that it is preceded by the word *to.*

A. Infinitive types. There are three main types of regular French infinitives. They are classified by the ending of the infinitive as (1) **-er** type; (2) **-ir** type; and (3) **-re** type. The first type is by far the most common.

1) **arriv/er**   to arrive; to happen
2) **fin/ir**   to finish
3) **vend/re**   to sell

B. Verb parts. A verb form consists of a stem and an ending. Remove the infinitive ending; the stem remains.

Stem   *Ending (infinitive)*

arriv / er

The stem of a regular verb is found in all forms of the verb and provides a sure means of identifying it. (Irregular verbs usually have changing stems and must be learned more thoroughly.)

21. Past Participles

Past participles of verbs are used in all compound tenses (to be examined later) and may be used as adjectives. To determine the English meaning of a past participle, say to yourself "I have..." and the form of the verb in question that naturally fits this phrase. For example, to determine the past participle of *to sell* (an infinitive), say "I have...sold." *Sold* is the past participle of *to sell.* (We shall use the abbreviation *pp.*)

A. Formation of the past participle.   Drop the infinitive ending of the verb, and replace it with the corresponding past participle ending.

verb type	add past participle ending
1) -er	-é
2) -ir	-i
3) -re	-u

Examples:

1) observ/er	to observe	observé	observed
2) bât/ir	to build	bâti	built
3) rend/re	to render	rendu	rendered

B. Past participle as adjective.   Observe the form of these past participles used as adjectives. Like all other adjectives, they follow the rule of agreement (Sec. 12).

un fait observé	an observed fact
la méthode perfectionnée	the perfected method
les faits observés	the observed facts
les méthodes perfectionnées	the perfected methods

C. Past participle as predicate adjective.   In the following sentences the past participle is used as a predicate adjective after **est** (*is*) and **sont** (*are*). Note agreement with the subject: an **-e** is added to form the feminine, and an **-s** to form the plural.

Le fait est observé	The fact is observed.
Les faits sont observés.	The facts are observed.
La méthode est perfectionnée.	The method is perfected.
Les méthodes sont perfectionnées.	The methods are perfected.

This arrangement may occur with any verb (such as **paraît**, *appears*) that takes a predicate adjective.

Cette méthode paraît perfectionnée.

Exercises

Series A (Sections 20–21)

A. *Past participles.* Give the English equivalent of the following past participles, and indicate the gender and number of each.

1. arrivé (2 meanings)	6. développée	11. accéléré
2. finie	7. bâties	12. pénétrées
3. vendu	8. rendu	13. accompagné
4. vendues	9. rendue	14. diminuées
5. examinés	10. perfectionnées	15. enrichie

B. *Past participles as adjectives.* Translate the phrases and sentences.

Translation Aids: Note the difference between a (no accent, meaning *has*) and à (grave accent, meaning *to*). The verbs to be noted are **est** (*is*), **c'est** (*he is, she is, it is*), **sont** (*are*), and two forms of *to have:* **a** (*has*), **ont** (*have*).

16. Le directeur est occupé.
17. L'accident est observé.
18. La construction est finie.
19. Cette maison est vendue.
20. Ces voitures sont vendues.
21. Les résultats sont examinés.
22. Des circuits sont développés.
23. des circuits compliqués
24. une désintégration accélérée
25. un mélange enrichi
26. un échantillon composé
27. des phénomènes isolés
28. un programme compliqué
29. le béton armé
30. un effort concentré
31. une particule désintégrée
32. Cette résistance est éliminée.
33. cette hypothèse compliquée
34. La désintégration des atomes est très accélérée.
35. Ce programme compilateur est perfectionné.
36. Cet homme a beaucoup d'hypothèses compliquées.
37. Deux sortes de programmes sont utilisées.
38. L'ordinateur a des circuits intégrés.
39. C'est un ordinateur bâti aux États-Unis.
40. Le médecin est occupé.
41. C'est un mélange enrichi de gaz.
42. C'est un architecte distingué.
43. La physique nucléaire est de la plus grande importance.
44. La Terre a un axe incliné.
45. C'est un médecin admiré de tout le monde.
46. C'est une hypothèse actuellement éliminée.
47. Le nez de Cléopâtre a un intérêt historique.
48. Les comètes ont des orbites allongés.
49. La littérature française est très variée.
50. L'accélérateur linéaire est complété.
51. L'accélération des particules est observée.

---

20. **voiture** *f.* car, automobile; vehicle 25. **mélange** *m.* mixture 26. **échantillon** *m.* sample 29. **béton** *m.* concrete (material); **armé** *pp.* reinforced 44. **Terre** *f.* Earth 45. **admiré de** (Translate **de** as *by*); **tout le monde** everybody 49. **très** *adv.* very

52. La particule a un mouvement accéléré dans le synchrotron.
53. Un triangle isocèle a deux côtés égaux.
54. Les symphonies de Beethoven sont souvent exécutées à Paris.
55. Le grand Sphinx de Gizèh est énigmatique.
56. La plupart des cathédrales en Europe sont gothiques.

C. Before translating the following sentences, divide each one into sense-making noun groups by placing parentheses around (a) nouns with their articles and adjectives and (b) prepositional phrases.

> *Example:*
>
> (La difficulté énorme) (**de** la distribution générale) (**de** ce produit) est (un inconvénient considérable).

The words in **boldface** type are prepositions, indicating the beginning of a prepositional phrase. Only the verb **est** is left out of the groups. Now it is easy to translate each noun group separately as you have done in previous exercises, but this time a complete sentence will emerge.

> The enormous difficulty of general distribution of this product is a considerable disadvantage.

57. Le but de ces expériences est la résolution de quelques problèmes compliqués.
58. La lecture de la documentation technique est une étude indispensable aux ingénieurs.
59. Ce bâtiment moderne au centre de la ville est bâti en béton armé.
60. Le terrain choisi pour le nouvel immeuble est extrêmement défavorable à la construction désirée.
61. Dans les symphonies, les mouvements lents sont gâtés dans une salle de concert trop grande.
62. La cybernétique est une nouvelle science qui traite des machines automatiques.
63. La sociologie est l'étude scientifique des institutions sociales et de leur évolution.
64. Un domaine compliqué de la science physique est la physique nucléaire.
65. Les premières applications des piles nucléaires intéressent la propulsion des sous-marins.
66. Les opéras de ce compositeur allemand unissent poésie et musique.
67. Les personnages principaux de ce roman historique ont un caractère dynamique.

Test 3A, page 219

---

53. **côté** *m.* side   54. **souvent** *adv.* often   60. **immeuble** *m.* apartment house; **défavorable** (The prefix **dé-** corresponds to the English prefix *un-* or *dis-*; see Appendix A, Sec. 10)   61. **lent** *adj.* slow; **gâtés** spoiled; **salle de concert** *f.* auditorium   62. **traite de** deals with   65. **pile** *f.* reactor; **intéressent** concern; **sous-marin** *m.* submarine   66. **allemand** *adj.* German; **unissent** unite   67. **personnage** *m.* character (of a play, novel, etc.); **caractère** *m.* character (moral, social)

Structures

22. Adverbs

A. Use.   Adverbs have already been used in the exercises to qualify verbs and adjectives.

un mouvement **très** accéléré	a *very* (much) accelerated movement
un terrain **extrêmement** défavorable	an *extremely* unfavorable site

Adverbs are placed (1) before an adjective or (2) after a verb. Many adverbs ending in **-ment,** like English adverbs ending in *-ly,* are placed almost anywhere.
   Learn the following important adverbs.

très	very	**plus**	more
bien	well, very	**moins**	less
trop	too	**tant**	so, so much
assez	rather	**à peu près**	approximately
beaucoup	very much		

Note the effect of adverbs on the meaning of adjectives.

un grand animal	a big animal
un **très** grand animal	a *very* big animal
un cas intéressant	an interesting case
un cas **assez** intéressant	a *rather* interesting case
un nombre réduit	a reduced number
un nombre **considérablement** réduit	a *considerably* reduced number
l'eau profonde	deep water
l'eau **moins** profonde	shallower water ("*less* deep")

B. Comparison of adverbs.   When **plus** (*more*), **moins** (*less*), or **aussi** (*as*) appears before another adverb, the comparative form is being used. The following **que** is equivalent to *than* after **plus** or **moins,** and to *as* after **aussi.**

Mon auto marche **vite.**
My car goes *fast.*

Ton auto marche **plus vite que** mon auto.
Your car goes *faster than* my car.

L'auto de Paul marche **aussi vite que** ton auto.
Paul's car goes *as fast as* your car.

For example, the comparative of **lentement** (*slowly*) would be

plus lentement **que**	*more* slowly *than* (slower *than*)
moins lentement **que**	*less* slowly *than*
aussi lentement **que**	*as* slowly *as*

There are two common adverbs that have irregular comparative forms.

bien	well	**mieux**	better
mal	badly	**pire**	worse

For example,

Il parle **bien**.	He speaks *well*.
Il parle **mieux que** Jean.	He speaks *better than* John.

When **le** immediately precedes any of the comparative forms, you have a superlative construction.

Mon auto marche **le plus vite**.	My car goes *the fastest*.
Robert travaille **le mieux**.	Robert works *the best*.

C. Adverb *peu* creates antonym.   The adverb **peu** is sometimes a signal to translate the following adjective by its antonym; the translation *not so (adj.)* may also apply.

l'eau profonde	deep water
l'eau **peu** profonde	*shallow* water
un événement important	an important event
un événement **peu** important	an *unimportant* event
un animal **peu** féroce	*not so* ferocious an animal

23. Attributes: à and de Phrases

Prepositional phrases beginning with **à** or **de**, or with a contraction of one of these (Sec. 19), often translate as a single adjective with a noun.

des moteurs **à pétrole**	*gasoline* motors
une lampe **à huile**	an *oil* lamp
une machine **à écrire**	a typewriter ("a machine *for writing*")
un animal **à quatre pattes**	a *four-footed* animal
un bateau **à vapeur**	a *steam*boat
une galerie **de tableaux**	an *art* gallery
une salle **de réunion**	a *meeting* room
le hall **de réception**	the *reception* hall

24. Materials: en and de

To indicate the material of which an object is made, a prepositional phrase beginning with **en** or **de** is often used after the name of the object.

une maison **en briques**	a *brick* house
une montre **en or**	a *gold* watch
un bâtiment **en béton armé**	a *reinforced-concrete* structure
des planchers **de béton**	*concrete* floors

25. Regular Verbs, Present Tense (Third Person)

Actions in the present are described using the present tense of a verb. The present tense is formed by taking the stem (Sec. 20B) and adding the present-tense endings. Only the third person forms are taken up at this point. The third person pronouns are **il** (*he, it*), **elle** (*she, it*), **ils** and **elles** (*they*). The following table shows the endings and examples.

	endings for		
type infinitive	*il*	*ils*	*examples*
-er (arriv/er)	**-e**	**-ent**	il arriv**e** *he is arriving, he arrives* ils arriv**ent** *they are arriving, they arrive*
-re (vend/re)	—	**-ent**	il vend *he is selling, he sells* ils vend**ent** *they are selling, they sell*
-ir (fin/ir)	**-it**	**-issent**	il fin**it** *he is finishing, he finishes* ils fin**issent** *they are finishing, they finish*

Notice that the second (one-word) translation on each English line is used only if habitual action is indicated. Note the following distinctions.

Action in Progress:

Maintenant il **finit** la leçon.
Now he *is finishing* the lesson.

Habitual Action:

D'habitude il **finit** la leçon à neuf heures.
Usually he *finishes* the lesson at nine o'clock.

The use of **maintenant** (**à présent, en ce moment**, etc.) indicates that you should use the two-word translation ("present progressive" in English); the appearance of the word **d'habitude** (**toujours, tous les jours**, etc.) means that you should use the one-word English equivalent. (The French makes no distinction between the two concepts in selecting the verb.)

When you wish to express in English a French verb used in the present tense, first try the progressive form (two words), since this is the correct English form for expressing an action in progress. If that does not sound right, or if there is an indicator that the action is habitual, use the one-word translation.

Exercises

Series B (Sections 22–25)

A. *Various noun structures.* Give the English equivalents.

Translation Aid: If **plus** appears before an adjective, use *more* plus the adjective.

un livre **plus important**	a *more important* book
un homme **plus célèbre**	a *more famous* man
une **plus longue** poésie	a *longer* poem

If **le plus** (**la plus, les plus**) appears, use the superlative (*the most* or its equivalent).

l'homme **le plus célèbre**	the *most* famous man
le plus grand bâtiment	the *largest* building

1. un gaz raréfié / un gaz très raréfié / plusieurs gaz raréfiés
2. un programme assez compliqué / des programmes plus compliqués / plusieurs programmes moins compliqués
3. dans un milieu différent / des milieux légèrement différents / au milieu du lac Supérieur
4. pour la partie essentielle de la dissertation / sans la partie la plus essentielle / contre le parti socialiste
5. par des vibrations / par des vibrations rapides / par des vibrations extrêmement rapides
6. un élément chimique / un élément répandu dans la nature / des éléments plus répandus dans la nature
7. la plupart des minéraux / bien des minéraux / plusieurs minéraux
8. une partie active / une grande partie des éléments / la plus grande partie des acides
9. un polygone irrégulier / une figure plane / une courbe assez régulière
10. cette évaluation exacte / ces évaluations assez exactes / plusieurs évaluations peu exactes
11. quatre arrangements possibles / cinq arrangements également possibles / cet arrangement impossible
12. un globe sphérique / un globe à peu près sphérique / plusieurs globes sphériques
13. la comète de Halley / la célèbre comète de Halley / la comète la plus célèbre
14. une variation importante / des variations plus importantes / quelques variations peu importantes

---

3. **milieu** *m.* environment, medium, milieu; **légèrement** *adv.* slightly (Note that adverbs ending in -ment end in English in -*ly*) 4. **sans** *prep.* without 5. **extrêmement** *adv.* (See note 3) 6. **répandu** *pp.* widespread 7. **minéraux** (plural of **minéral**) *m.* 9. **irrégulier** *adj.* (derived from **régulier, régulière**); **courbe** *f.* curve 11. **également** *adv.* (from **égal, égale** *adj.* equal; see note 3) 12. **à peu près** *adv.* approximately 13. **célèbre** *adj.* famous, renowned, well-known

15. plusieurs systèmes différents / plusieurs systèmes entièrement différents / quelques systèmes légèrement différents
16. tant d'auteurs / plusieurs auteurs célèbres / quelques auteurs d'articles scientifiques
17. une section étroite / plusieurs sections étroites / bien des sections assez étroites
18. un pays industriel / des pays agricoles / plusieurs petits pays sous-développés
19. une décision complexe / des décisions moins complexes / trop de décisions peu importantes
20. l'eau profonde / de l'eau moins profonde / de l'eau peu profonde

B. *Attributes and materials.* Translate.

21. deux bateaux à vapeur
22. trois machines à écrire
23. une machine à écrire électrique
24. les premiers ordinateurs à transistors
25. une pile à neutrons intermédiaires
26. un plancher de béton
27. une grande salle à manger
28. la salle de réunion
29. l'uniforme à culottes rouges
30. une dent en or
31. un vase de porcelaine
32. la machine à calculer
33. des horloges à pendule
34. la mémoire à grande capacité d'un ordinateur
35. la ville aux coupoles dorées
36. d'élégantes villas de briques et de marbre
37. un bassin d'argent
38. une fusée à trois étages
39. des torrents de métal liquéfié
40. des relais d'une extrême sensibilité†
41. une étoile à dimensions colossales
42. une pile à neutrons intermédiaires
43. une symphonie de style classique a quatre mouvements
44. une symphonie à trois mouvements
45. cet homme aux cheveux noirs
46. cet homme a les cheveux noirs

---

16. **auteur** *m.* author   17. **étroit, -e** *adj.* narrow   18. **pays** *m.* country (political division)
25. **intermédiaire** *adj.* intermediate   26. **plancher** *m.* floor   29. **culottes** *f.* trousers; **rouge** *adj.*
red   30. **or** *m.* gold   33. **horloge à pendule** *f.* pendulum clock   35. **coupole** *f.* cupola, dome; **doré,
-e** *adj.* gilded, gilt   36. **villa** *f.* (Cognate—do not confuse with **ville**); **marbre** *m.* marble
37. **bassin** *m.* platter, tray, basin   40. **sensibilité†** *f.* sensitivity   43. **a** (Do not confuse with **à**)
45. **cheveux** *m.pl.* hair; **noir, -e** *adj.* black   47. **papier** *m.* paper (material); (An academic paper is
une communication)

47. du papier à lettres
48. un ordinateur à usage commercial et scientifique

C. *Verbs in the present tense.* In the following sentences, distinguish between general and specific statements. In the translation of general statements, use one-word verb forms and omit the article *the.* For example,

> **General:**
>
> Les mathématiciens **examinent** des problèmes de logique.
> Mathematicians *examine* problems in logic.
>
> **Specific:**
>
> Ces mathématiciens **examinent** des problèmes de logique.
> These mathematicians *are examining* problems in logic.

49. Les astronomes observent les étoiles au moyen de télescopes.
50. Cet astronome observe les étoiles au moyen d'un radiotélescope.
51. Les physiciens trouvent ce cas bien compliqué.
52. La construction des instruments de musique repose sur les propriétés vibratoires de l'air.
53. Le cultivateur fournit de l'azote au sol sous forme d'engrais.
54. Maintenant ce cultivateur fournit de l'azote au sol sous forme d'engrais.
55. L'oxygène forme la partie active de l'air atmosphérique.
56. Un auteur écrit des livres.
57. Cet auteur écrit un roman policier.
58. Les mathématiciens classent l'algèbre dans le domaine des mathématiques pures.
59. La géométrie est une science qui mesure l'étendue de l'espace.
60. Le géomètre est un technicien qui mesure l'étendue de l'espace.
61. Un musicien compose de la musique. Ce musicien compose de la musique en ce moment.
62. Les psychologues étudient les faits psychologiques.
63. La psychologie est l'étude des faits psychologiques.
64. Les ingénieurs bâtissent des édifices, des ponts et des machines.
65. Cet ingénieur bâtit un radiotélescope moderne.
66. Les agents de police protègent le grand public.
67. Les détectives recherchent des personnes dangereuses ou suspectes.
68. Ce détective recherche une personne suspecte.
69. Les chimistes sont des scientifiques qui pratiquent la chimie.
70. La chimie est une science exacte qui étudie la nature des corps.

Test 3B, page 221

---

49. **au moyen de** by means of   51. **trouver** to find; **bien** *adv.* (before an adj.) very   52. **reposer sur** to be based on, to depend on   53. **cultivateur** *m.* farmer; **fournir** to furnish; **azote** *m.* nitrogen; **sol** *m.* soil; **engrais** *m.* fertilizer   54. **maintenant** *adv.* now   56. **livre** *m.* book   59. **qui** *rel. pron.* that, which; who; **étendue** *f.* area, extent   64. **pont** *m.* bridge   66. **protègent** (from **protéger,** *to protect*); **le grand public** (What is the English equivalent?)   67. **rechercher** to search for, to hunt for; **suspect, -e** *adj.* suspected   69. **chimiste** *m.* chemist; **scientifique** *m.* scientist; **pratiquer** to practice, to work with   70. **corps** *m.* body, substance

4

Structures

26. Subject Pronouns *il, elle, on*

A. General. The third-person forms of pronouns are as follows.

il	he, it (replaces a masculine singular noun)
elle	she, it (replaces a feminine singular noun)
on	one, they (unspecified)
ils	they (masculine plural)
elles	they (feminine plural)

Examples:

Voilà une maison. **Elle** est grande.
There is a house. *It* is large.

Ma voiture est une Fiat. **Elle** est petite.
My car is a Fiat. *It* is small.

Les Brésiliens? **Ils** parlent portugais.
The Brazilians? *They* speak Portuguese.

B. The pronoun *on*. When **on** plus a verb is followed by a noun structure (direct object), translate the noun structure first, then the verb in the passive form.

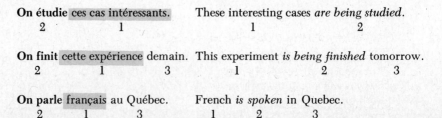

On étudie ces cas intéressants.　　These interesting cases *are being studied.*
　2　　　　　1　　　　　　　　　1　　　　　　　　2

On finit cette expérience demain.　This experiment *is being finished* tomorrow.
　2　　　1　　　　　3　　　　　1　　　　　　2　　　　　3

On parle français au Québec.　　French *is spoken* in Quebec.
　2　　1　　　3　　　　1　　2　　　3

When **on** plus a verb is followed by a **que** clause, it may be necessary to use the more literal *one* or *they* for **on,** or *It is* plus the past participle.

> **On dit que** l'expérience est finie.
> *It is said that* the experiment is finished.
> *They say that* the experiment is finished.

27. Reflexive Verbs

A. **General.**   Certain verbs are classified as reflexive, meaning that the action indicated is reflected back upon the doer. These verbs are listed in dictionaries with the pronoun **se** (for example, **se laver,** *to wash oneself*). Certain verbs are always reflexive; others, like **laver,** *to wash,* may be made reflexive. In this sentence **laver** is used nonreflexively.

> Cet homme **lave** sa voiture.   This man *is washing* his car.

The action here is performed on the car, not on the man. However, with the reflexive pronoun added, the sentence has quite a different meaning.

> Cet homme **se lave.**   This man *is washing himself.*
> Cet homme **se lave la figure.**   This man *is washing his face.*

In these last two examples, the man is performing the washing action upon himself. These are reflexive uses, and the presence of the reflexive pronoun *se* confirms this.

B. **Translation of reflexive verbs.**   With many reflexive structures, a simple solution is to translate **se** as a form of *to be* (*is, are*) and the verb itself as a past participle.

> La lumière **se propage**...   Light *is propagated*...
> Il **s'intéresse** aux timbres.   He *is interested* in stamps.

Certain other verbs must be treated as ordinary present tense verbs.

> se trouver   to be (located)
> se dépêcher   to hurry
> s'amuser   to have a good time

For example,

> La Bibliothèque nationale **se trouve** à Paris.
> The Bibliothèque Nationale *is* in Paris.
>
> Il **se dépêche** de lire le journal.
> He *hurries* to read the newspaper.
>
> Les étudiants **s'amusent.**
> The students *are having a good time.*

28. The Relative Pronoun *dont* (of which, of whom, whose)

The relative pronoun **dont** introduces a clause of a parenthetical nature within a sentence. Such a clause begins with **dont** and usually ends immediately before a verb. Isolate the **dont** clause, and read the rest of the sentence first to determine the main thought.

> Le monsieur (**dont** ils parlent) est médecin.
> The gentleman (*of whom* they are speaking) is a doctor.

There are three basic rules for the translation of **dont**.

> ### Rule 1: **dont** [+ numeral] = [numeral +] *of which*

If **dont** is followed by a numeral, translate the numeral first.

> Voici un mélange de gaz **dont** deux sont très dangereux.
> Here is a mixture of gases, two *of which* are very dangerous.

> ### Rule 2: **dont** [+ noun] = *whose* [+ noun] or *of which* [+ noun]

If **dont** is followed (either directly or a few words later) by a noun structure including **le, la, l'**, or **les**, translate **dont** as *whose* and follow at once with the noun; then continue translation of any words skipped after **dont**.

> La maison, **dont la construction** est finie, est magnifique.
> The house, *whose construction* is finished, is magnificent.

> *Remote Noun:*
> La dame (**dont** vous désirez faire **la connaissance**) est une actrice célèbre.
> The lady *whose acquaintance* you wish to make is a famous actress.
> The lady you would like to meet is a famous actress.

> Ces effets (**dont** nos professeurs attribuent **l'invention** à Mozart) sont admirables.
> These effects, *whose invention* our professors attribute to Mozart, are admirable.

> ### Rule 3: Other cases: **dont** = *of which*

If neither rule 1 nor rule 2 applies or results in a sense-making translation, use the meaning *of which*, and follow the word order used in the French sentence.

> Le livre **dont** il s'agit est bien compliqué.
> (The book *of which* it is a question is very complicated.)
> The book in question is very complicated.

> Le lac **dont** Rousseau parle se trouve en Suisse.
> (The lake *of which* Rousseau speaks is in Switzerland.)
> The lake Rousseau speaks about is in Switzerland.

Exercises

Series A (Sections 26–28)

A. *Subject pronouns*. Translate the following noun phrases and sentences.

1. la leçon: elle est finie
2. la littérature française: elle est intéressante
3. un triangle équilatéral: il a trois côtés égaux
4. la Terre: elle a un axe incliné
5. les symphonies de style classique: elles ont quatre mouvements
6. les physiciens nucléaires: ils finissent leur expérience
7. ces musiciens: ils exécutent une œuvre de musique de chambre
8. les professeurs: ils expliquent des problèmes
9. ces bâtiments: ils sont construits en béton armé
10. cette maison particulière: elle est bâtie en bois
11. On finit cette expérience.
12. On observe la désintégration des particules.
13. On trouve de l'oxygène dans la constitution des végétaux.
14. On trouve une solution à ce problème.

B. *Reflexive verbs*. Translate these sentences.

15. L'atmosphère se compose de plusieurs gaz.
16. La lumière se propage en ligne droite.
17. Cette règle se déduit de nos observations.
18. Ces cas se divisent en deux catégories.
19. Un rayon lumineux se réfléchit dans une direction unique.
20. Parmi les éléments présents dans l'atmosphère se trouvent le néon, le krypton et l'hélium.
21. La plupart des substances minérales se présentent sous forme cristalline.
22. La surface du globe se compose de grandes masses de terres qu'on appelle des continents.
23. La lumière, dont la vitesse est de 300.000 kilomètres par seconde, se propage en ligne droite.
24. L'oxygène existe dans l'air, dont il forme à peu près un cinquième en volume.
25. Les sous-marins à propulsion nucléaire dont parle l'amiral utilisent des neutrons lents.
26. Voilà trois boîtes dont une contient une machine électronique.
27. Un quadrilatère dont deux des côtés sont inégaux et parallèles est un trapèze.

---

3. **égaux** *adj. m.pl.* equal   10. **particulier, particulière†** *adj.* private   22. **appeler** to call   23. **lumière** *f.* light   24. **à peu près** approximately; **cinquième** fifth   25. **lent, -e** *adj.* slow   26. **voilà** there is, there are; **boîte** *f.* box; **contient** (present tense of **contenir***, *to contain*)   27. **inégaux** *adj.* unequal (The prefix **in-** indicates an antonym)

28. Le problème est plus simple si l'on divise les cas en deux catégories.
29. Le compositeur dont on célèbre l'anniversaire s'appelle Mozart.
30. Les données dont Paul examine la valeur sont exactes.

Test 4A, page 223

Readings

La Lumière

[31] La lumière se propage en ligne droite avec une vitesse de 300.000 kilomètres par seconde. [32] Un rayon lumineux qui tombe sur un miroir se réfléchit dans une direction unique. [33] Grâce à cette réflexion, le miroir donne l'image des objets placés devant lui.

[34] Un rayon lumineux change de direction lorsqu'il passe d'un milieu à un autre; on dit qu'il *se réfracte*. [35] C'est à cause de la réfraction qu'un bâton plongé dans l'eau paraît brisé.

[36] Le Son

[37] Le son est produit par des vibrations qui résultent de la compression de l'air. [38] Il parcourt l'air avec une vitesse de 340 mètres par seconde; dans les liquides et surtout dans les solides, sa vitesse est plus grande. [39] Lorsque le son rencontre un obstacle, il est réfléchi et produit un écho.

[40] La construction des instruments de musique à cordes repose sur les propriétés vibratoires des cordes tendues et de l'air.

L'Air

[41] L'air est un mélange de gaz dont les principaux sont: l'oxygène et l'azote. [42] L'oxygène est un élément qui forme la partie active de l'atmosphère. [43] Ce gaz, désigné par le symbole chimique «O», entretient les combustions et, par

---

28. **plus simple** (comparative of **simple**) simpler   30. **donnée** *f.* data; **examine la valeur** (This expression can be replaced by a single verb in English)   31. **300.000** (In French numbers, a period is used to set off thousands, and a comma is used as a decimal point; thus π is 3,1416)   32. **tomber** to fall; **miroir** *m.* mirror   33. **grâce à** thanks to, because of; **lui** [to] it   34. **lorsque** (synonym of **quand**) when; **milieu** *m.* medium; **on dit** (from **dire***, *to say*) one says, it is said   35. **à cause de** because of; **bâton** *m.* stick; **brisé** (from **briser**, to break)   36. **son** *m.* sound   38. **parcourt** (from **parcourir***, *to travel through*); **surtout** especially   39. **rencontrer** to meet, to encounter   40. **repose sur** (from **reposer†**, *to depend*) depends on, is determined by; **tendu, -e** *adj.* stretched   43. **entretient** (from **entretenir***, *to support*)

conséquent, la respiration. [44] L'azote, au contraire, modère l'action de l'oxygène et n'entretient ni la combustion ni la respiration, quoiqu'il entre pour 78,03 pour cent dans la composition de l'air. [45] Le poids atomique d'oxygène est de 16,000; celui d'azote est de 14,008.

[46] L'air est indispensable aux êtres vivants. [47] En outre il est le véhicule du son. [48] Parmi les autres éléments qui se trouvent dans l'air sont le néon, le krypton, l'hélium et des traces d'un certain nombre d'autres gaz. [49] On y trouve aussi du gaz carbonique et de la vapeur de l'eau.

[50] *Les Psychologues au travail*

[51] Les étudiants demandent souvent si la psychologie est une science. [52] Comparé aux sciences comme l'astronomie, la géologie, la physique, la chimie ou la biologie, le sujet d'étude de la psychologie paraît bien différent et bien préoccupé de lui-même. [53] En outre, les problèmes psychologiques ont été pendant si longtemps étudiés du point de vue philosophique et non scientifique qu'on a des doutes bien naturels au sujet du caractère scientifique de la psychologie. [54] Même dans les universités la psychologie est parfois classée parmi les humanités et parfois parmi les sciences sociales. [55] Le caractère scientifique de la psychologie, comme de toute autre science, naturelle ou sociale, repose sur ses méthodes et non pas sur son objet. [56] Ses méthodes sont essentiellement les mêmes que celles des autres sciences naturelles, mais la nature de ses matières appelle des problèmes méthodologiques qui ne se posent pas pour les autres sciences. [57] Les psychologues utilisent des variantes des méthodes suivantes: 1° observation directe; 2° méthode clinique; 3° expérimentation. Une autre méthode qui peut être employée pour analyser et interpréter les résultats obtenus par une de ces trois méthodes est 4° la méthode statistique.

---

44. ne [+ verb] ni...ni (Leave verb positive, translate ni...ni as *neither...nor*); quoique *conj.* although; pour cent percent   45. poids *m.* weight; celui that (in the sense of *the one*)   46. être* *m.* being (A few infinitives can be used as nouns, in which case they are accompanied by an article—for example, le pouvoir, *power;* le devoir, *duty;* le savoir, *knowledge*)   47. en outre moreover   48. parmi *prep.* among   49. aussi *adv.* also; gaz carbonique *m.* carbon dioxide; vapeur *f.* vapor (also *steam*)   50. psychologue *m.* psychologist; travail *m.* work   51. étudiant *m.* student; souvent *adv.* often   52. bien (synonym for très); lui-même itself   53. été (from être, *to be*) been (Note that été should be followed by the next past participle; skip ahead to it, then retrace the skipped words pendant si longtemps, *for such a long time*); point de vue (The adjectives philosophique and non scientifique modify point de vue)   54. même *adv.* (at the beginning of a clause) even; parfois *adv.* sometimes   55. comme *adv.* like; tout, -e *adj.* every; non pas not   56. celles those; appelle raises, calls to mind   57. suivant, -e *adj.* following; 1°, 2°, 3° *adv.* 1st, 2nd, 3rd; peut être can be; obtenu (past participle of obtenir*, *to obtain*)

Structures

29. Two or More Adjectives Qualifying a Single Noun

Several adjectives may qualify a single noun, making a rather large noun-adjective group. Many adjectives follow the noun in French, and must be restored to a position before the noun for good English style. It is a good idea to practice seeing a noun-adjective group as a whole—allowing the eye to take in this entire unit at once. Then, as you translate, say (or write) all the adjectives in the group before mentioning the noun itself.

> **une** machine **compliquée**
> *a complicated* machine

> **un autre** machine **compliquée**
> *another complicated* machine

If *two* adjectives follow the noun, translate them in reverse order:

> **une autre** machine **automatique compliquée**
> *another complicated automatic* machine

Two adjectives following a noun are often joined by **et** (*and*) or **mais** (*but*); move them as a single unit.

> **une autre nouvelle** machine **compliquée** et **lourde**
> *another new, complicated* and *heavy* machine   (not best English order)
> *another complicated* and *heavy new* machine   (slightly rearranged)

> **beaucoup de nouvelles** machines **compliquées** mais **utiles**
> *many complicated* but *useful new* machines

30. Participles or Adjectives Followed by a Prepositional Phrase

We have seen participles used as adjectives (Sec. 21B). If a participle or an adjective is immediately followed by a preposition, read straight through in French word order. Compare

les données **observées**	the *observed* data
les données **observées dans** ce cas	the data *observed in* this case
des routes **commodes**	*convenient* highways
des routes **commodes pour** les voitures	highways *convenient for* vehicles

31. Infinitives

A. **Ignoring à, de, or pour before an infinitive.**   Infinitives usually appear after a preposition. When the preposition is **à**, **de**, or **pour**, ignore the preposition and translate the infinitive in the regular *to* [*do something*] form.

Il commence à écrire.	He begins *to write*.
Il refuse **de partir.**	He refuses *to leave*.
Il vient **pour étudier.**	He comes *to study*.

B. Using the -ing form instead of the infinitive after *sans* and *avant de*. Sometimes the infinitive is best translated as a present participle.

Il part **sans dire** au revoir.
He leaves *without saying* good-by.

Il étudie **avant de regarder** la télévision.
He studies *before watching* television.

C. Reducing three English words to two.   After **avant de** and **après**, both **avoir** and **être** mean *having*. Reduce three words to two—for example, *after having arrived* becomes *after arriving*.

Il va au cinéma **après avoir étudié.**
He goes to the movies *after studying (after having studied)*.

Elle commence à lire **après être entrée** dans la salle.
She begins to read *after entering (after having entered)* the room.

Ils sont sortis **avant d'avoir fini** leur travail.
They went out *before finishing (before having finished)* their work.

D. Translating *il faut* (must, it is necessary).   When **il faut** is followed by an infinitive, use *must* if possible; otherwise, use *it is necessary* or the passive construction ——*ing is necessary.*

Il faut étudier.	*You must* study. (Deduce who is involved.)
	It is necessary to study.
	Studying *is necessary*.

When a **que** clause follows **il faut,** use *must* if at all possible.

Il faut que vous finissiez l'expérience demain.
You *must* finish the experiment tomorrow.

When **il faut** is used in the negative (Sec. 33), you *cannot* use *it is not necessary.* **Il ne faut pas** means *must not.* It would be incorrect to use *It is not necessary to smoke* in the following case:

Il ne faut pas fumer.   *You must not* smoke.

32. Impersonal Verbs

Certain French verbs are impersonal and are used only in the infinitive and in the third person singular. In such cases the pronoun **il** does not refer to a person. Learn the following impersonal expressions.

| **il s'agit de** | it concerns, it is a matter of |
| **il paraît que** | it appears that |

il se peut que	it is possible that
il importe que	it is important that
il reste [+ noun]	[noun +] remain(s)

Note: **Il y a** is an impersonal expression meaning *there is, there are.*

Il y a des livres sur la table.
There are books on the table.

Il s'agit d'un roman d'André Gide.
It concerns a novel by André Gide.

Il reste trois expériences à faire.
Three experiments *remain* to be done.

Note that with **il reste** plus a noun, the noun is expressed first in the English equivalent.

il reste á voir = it remains to be seen

Exercises

Series B (Sections 29–32)

A. *Noun-adjectives.* Give English equivalents in natural-sounding English.

 1. un seul fait / un seul fait intéressant / ce seul fait bien intéressant
 2. une méthode / cette nouvelle méthode / les vraies méthodes expérimentales
 3. un concert / un petit concert / de petits concerts quotidiens
 4. une hypothèse / une célèbre hypothèse / la célèbre hypothèse newtonienne
 5. un mètre / un mètre carré / mille mètres carrés
 6. des piles / des piles nucléaires / des piles nucléaires mobiles
 7. les symphonies classiques / les magnifiques symphonies classiques / des symphonies magnifiques mais longues
 8. la musique moderne / la musique instrumentale / la musique instrumentale moderne
 9. des complications mécaniques / de nouvelles complications / de nouvelles complications mécaniques
 10. un caractère intelligible / un caractère mystérieux et sacré / un caractère intelligible mais mystérieux
 11. une occupation simple / des occupations plus simples / les occupations les plus simples
 12. un motif subtil / beaucoup de motifs malhonnêtes / plusieurs motifs subtils et malhonnêtes
 13. un goût exquis / un goût pur / un goût exquis et pur

---

2. **vrai, -e** *adj.* true, real 3. **quotidien, -ne** *adj.* daily 5. **carré, -e** *adj.* square 7. **mais** *conj.* but 10. **sacré** *adj.* sacred 11. **plus simples, les plus simples** (comparative and superlative forms) 12. **malhonnête** *adj.* dishonest 13. **goût** *m.* taste; **exquis, pur** (near-cognates)

14. le premier bâtiment / le bâtiment climatisé / le premier bâtiment climatisé
15. un système / un nouveau système / de nouveaux systèmes d'analyse
16. une découverte / une nouvelle découverte / une découverte entièrement nouvelle
17. du gaz carbonique / un peu de gaz carbonique / du gaz carbonique exhalé
18. la loi / les lois physiques et chimiques / les mêmes lois physiques et chimiques
19. une crise / une crise industrielle / des crises industrielles inattendues
20. une autre question / la même question / cette autre question importante

B. Give equivalents in good English.

Translation Aid: The preposition **avec** (*with*) when used with certain nouns corresponds to an adverb ending in *-ly*. Substitute the adverb for the *with* phrase in translation.

avec patience	patiently	(with patience)
avec bruit	noisily	(with noise)
avec soin	carefully	(with care)

21. les données observées / des données observées dans ce cas
22. une substance observée / une substance observée dans ce mélange
23. Il y a des forces accélérées. / Il y a des forces accélérées vers les centres.
24. Il s'agit de plusieurs substances résistantes. / Il s'agit de quelques substances résistantes aux hautes températures.
25. C'est une question relative. / C'est une question relative aux problèmes actuels.
26. Il s'agit d'une nation industrielle. / Il s'agit d'une nation hostile mais puissante.
27. Il s'agit de plusieurs méthodes difficiles mais utiles. / Il s'agit d'une autre méthode pour résoudre le problème.
28. Il reste un autre cas important. / Il reste d'autres cas à considérer.
29. Il s'agit de soixante échantillons étudiés en détail. / Il s'agit d'étudier ces échantillons avec soin.
30. Il importe d'examiner ces moteurs à pétrole. / Il est possible de compléter l'examen sans délai.
31. Il se peut que le bâton plongé dans l'eau soit brisé.
32. Le fait important est que la matière vivante est soumise partout aux mêmes lois physiques et chimiques.
33. Le professeur est là pour expliquer avec patience sa théorie des phénomènes économiques.

---

14. **climatisé, -e** *adj.* air-conditioned   16. **découverte** *f.* discovery; **entièrement** *adv.* entirely (The ending -ment is equivalent to *-ly*)   17. **exhalé** *pp.* exhaled   18. **loi** *f.* law   19. **crise** *f.* crisis (**une crise cardiaque** means *heart attack*);   26. **puissant, -e** *adj.* powerful   27. **résoudre** to solve   29. **soin** *m.* care   31. **soit** (from être*) is   32. **vivant, -e** *adj.* living; **soumise** (*pp.* of **soumettre***, *to subject*); **partout** *adv.* everywhere   33. **là** *adv.* there

34. Ces physiciens examinent les données pour pouvoir comprendre la théorie dont il s'agit.
35. Ce gaz a pour effet de modérer l'action de l'oxygène.
36. Il paraît que M. Brun déjeune avant de partir au bureau.
37. Il étudie ses problèmes financiers après être arrivé au bureau.
38. La mémoire est nécessaire pour toutes les opérations de la raison.
39. Les médecins sont partis sans trouver une solution satisfaisante.
40. Le prêtre commence à parler avec élégance.
41. Le calcul sert à étudier la variation des fonctions.
42. Il faut qu'ils arrivent à l'heure.

Test 4B, page 225

Readings

L'Oxygène

[43] L'oxygène est, de tous les corps, le plus répandu dans la nature. [44] Il existe non seulement dans l'air, dont il forme à peu près le cinquième en volume, mais il constitue les huit neuvièmes de la masse de l'eau, et il entre dans la constitution des végétaux† et des animaux; enfin la plupart des minéraux en contiennent.

L'Azote

[45] L'azote, gaz incolore, inodore et sans saveur, n'entretient ni la combustion ni la respiration. [46] Une bougie allumée placée dans un flacon ne contenant que de l'azote s'éteint. [47] Dans l'air ce gaz a pour effet de ralentir les combustions.

[48] L'azote entre dans la composition des végétaux et de la chair des animaux. [49] Il est indispensable à la vie des plantes. [50] La terre inculte en renferme toujours, mais en quantité insuffisante; le cultivateur doit lui en fournir sous forme d'engrais.

---

34. **pouvoir*** to be able; **comprendre*** to understand   36. **déjeuner** to have lunch; **partir*** to depart; **bureau** *m.* office   37. **étudier** to study   38. **toutes (tout, toute, tous)** *adj.* all   39. **sont partis** have departed, left   40. **prêtre** *m.* priest (A protestant minister is **un pasteur**)   41. **sert à** (from **servir***, *to serve*) serves to   44. **en** *pron.* (before a noun) in, (before an inflected verb) some, of it, etc. (Sec. 62), (before a present participle) while, by (Sec. 49); **contiennent** (from **contenir***, *to contain*)
45. **azote** *m.* nitrogen; **incolore** *adj.* (The prefix in- often signals an antonym; see Appendix A, 10C)
46. **bougie** *f.* candle; **allumer** to light; **flacon** *m.* flask; **ne contenant que** containing only; **s'éteint** goes out   47. **ralentir** to slow down   49. **vie** *f.* life   50. **inculte** *adj.* uncultivated; **renfermer** to contain

Un Mystère mathématique

[51] Un vieil Arabe est sur le point de mourir. Il appelle ses trois fils dans sa chambre pour leur dire comment il désire partager ses possessions. [52] Il dit à l'aîné que sa part sera la moitié, et au second fils que sa part sera un tiers. [53] Quant au cadet, sa part sera un neuvième de tous les biens de son père.

[54] Après un certain temps, le père meurt. [55] Les trois frères se réunissent pour partager les biens de leur père. [56] D'abord il semble ne pas y avoir de problème entre eux, mais bientôt, quand il s'agit de partager les chameaux laissés par leur père, les fils sont très perplexes. [57] Il y a dix-sept (17) chameaux: impossible de diviser dix-sept par deux, trois, ou neuf, sans couper en morceaux quelques-uns des animaux.

[58] Les fils ne désirent pas tuer de chameaux, et ils désirent obéir aux instructions de leur père. [59] Ils consultent donc un vieux derviche. [60] Il paraît que ce derviche est estimé de tout le monde à cause de sa sagesse.

[61] Le derviche est très sympathique et intelligent. [62] Il désire aider les trois fils à trouver une solution à leur problème assez complexe. [63] Le lendemain il arrive chez eux, et il demande à examiner les chameaux. [64] Il range les chameaux devant lui, et il attache son propre chameau à côté des autres.

[65] —Écoutez-moi, dit-il. Il y a maintenant dix-huit chameaux. [66] Que chacun prenne sa part!

[67] L'aîné en prend neuf (la moitié de 18), le second fils six (un tiers de 18), et le cadet deux (un neuvième de 18). [68] Les fils sont très contents. [69] Alors le derviche remonte sur son chameau et part, laissant les trois fils très intrigués.

---

51. **mourir*** to die; **fils** *m*. son; **leur** [to] them; **dire*** to tell; **partager** to divide up, to share   52. **aîné** *m*. eldest; **sera** (future of **être***, *to be*); **la moitié** half; **le tiers** *m*. one-third   53. **quant à** as for; **cadet** *m*. the youngest; **les biens** *m.pl*. property; **père** *m*. father   54. **meurt** (from **mourir***, *to die*)   55. **se réunir** to meet, to gather   56. **chameau** *m*. camel; **laisser** to leave   57. **couper** to cut; **morceau** *m*. piece   58. **tuer** to kill; **obéir** to obey   60. **de** by; **tout le monde** everybody; **sagesse** *f*. wisdom   63. **lendemain** *m*. next day; **chez eux** at their home   64. **ranger** to line up; **propre** (before a noun) own   65. **écoutez-moi** listen to me   66. **que chacun prenne** let each one take   69. **remonter** to remount, get back on; **part** (from **partir***, *to depart*); **laissant** (present participle of **laisser**, *to leave*) leaving

Essential Word Review I
Chapters 1-4

The following basic words, which have appeared in the footnotes, should be reviewed and learned. Other essential words, such as prepositions, common adjectives, and expressions of quantity, are listed within the "Structures" sections and are not included here. They too should be reviewed and learned.

To learn the words in this list, add them to the set of vocabulary cards that you have been making for the essential words in the grammar sections. On one side of an index card write the French word and on the other side its English equivalent. Then follow the instructions in the Introduction for studying the words.

The indented words in this list are related to those above them in some way. They may be synonyms, antonyms, verb forms, or even words that are commonly confused with the main entry. Whether or not they are indented, *all* words in this list should be added to your vocabulary.

Irregular verbs are marked with an asterisk (*).

Verbs

appeler* to call
avoir* to have
 a *pres.* has
comprendre* to understand
dire* to say, to tell
 parler to speak
être* to be
 sera *fut.* will be
 soit *subj.* be, will be
étudier to study
laisser to leave, to let
partir* to leave, to depart
 arriver to arrive
pouvoir* to be able, can
 savoir* to know, to know how to
rechercher to search for, to hunt for
rencontrer to meet, to encounter
reposer sur to be based on, to depend on
servir* à to serve as, to be used for
 sert à *pres.* serves to
tomber to fall
trouver to find
 chercher to look for
 se trouver to be located

Nouns

l'argent *m.*   money, silver
le bâtiment   building, ship
le corps   body, substance
l'eau *f.*   water
un état *m.*   state
une étoile *f.*   star
un être *m.*   (human) being, person
la faute   fault
la fois   time
  à la fois   at the same time
une histoire *f.*   story, history
le lendemain   the next day
la ligne   line
la moitié   half
le moyen   way
  au moyen de   by means of
le siècle   century
la vie   life

Adjectives

inattendu, -e   unexpected
lent, -e   slow
seul, -e   only, alone
suivant, -e   following
vrai, -e   true
  faux, fausse   false

5

Structures

33. Negative Forms of Verbs

When a verb is preceded by the negative fragment **ne** and followed by the completion **pas,** the verb is understood to be negative in sense.

$$\text{ne } [+ \text{ verb } +] \text{ pas}$$

Il **ne** désire **pas**...	He does *not* desire...
Il **ne** paraît **pas** que...	It does *not* appear that...
Il **ne** s'agit **pas** de...	It is *not* a matter of...
Ils **ne** sont **pas** arrivés.	They have *not* arrived.

The fragment **ne** is written **n'** before vowels and **h**'s:

Ils **n'**examinent **pas**...	They are *not* examining...
Il **n'a pas** examiné ce cas.	He has *not* examined this case.
Ils **n'**ont **pas** fait cela.	They have *not* done that.
Il **n'est pas** possible que...	It is *not* possible that...
Ils **n'**habitent **pas** Paris.	They do *not* live in Paris.

The phrase **pas encore** means *not yet.*

Il **ne** sait **pas encore**.	He doesn't know *yet*.

34. Alternative Negative Terms

Although **ne** invariably appears before a verb that has a negative sense, the second element of the negation (the part that normally follows the verb) may be some word other than **pas**. The word **pas** may be replaced by one of several alternative terms to modify the meaning, as follows.

Il **ne** désire **rien**.	He wants *nothing*.
	He doesn't want *anything*.
Il **ne** voit **personne**.	He sees *nobody*.
	He doesn't see *anybody*.

	rien		*nothing*
	plus		*no longer*
	personne		*not anybody, nobody*
ne [+ verb +]	jamais		*never*
	guère		*scarcely*
	ni . . . ni		*neither . . . nor*
	aucun, -e	[+ noun]	*no* [item mentioned]
	nul, -le		

Il **ne** paraît **plus** que. . .	It *no longer* appears that. . .
Ils n'examinent **jamais**. . .	They *never* examine. . .
Il **ne** s'agit **guère** de. . .	It is *scarcely* a matter of. . .
Ils n'aiment **ni** l'un **ni** l'autre.	They like *neither* one *nor* the other.
Il n'a **aucun** livre.	He has *no* book.
Il n'a **nulle** méthode.	He has *no* method.

Some of these alternative terms are sometimes used as subjects of a sentence; they then appear first, and **ne** still appears before the verb. (See Sec. 87A.)

Rien n'est arrivé.	*Nothing* has happened.
Aucun chevalier **ne** descend.	*No* knight comes down.
Personne ne me comprend.	*Nobody* understands me.

35. Negative Terms Before Infinitives

Both elements of a negative term are found together before infinitives.

Être ou **ne pas** être. . .	To be or *not* to be. . .
Il promet de **ne jamais** demander. . .	He promises *never* to ask. . .

36. The Construction *ne . . . que*

When **ne** precedes a verb, one expects **pas** or some other negative particle to follow the verb. However, if **que** follows the verb, leave the verb positive and translate **que** by *only*.

ne [+ verb +] **que**	*only*

Il **a** une méthode.
He has a method.

Il **n'a qu'**une méthode.
He has *only* one method.

Il **ne** s'agit **que** d'une expérience.
It concerns *only* one experiment.

Ils **n'**examinent **qu'**un seul échantillon.
They are examining *only* one sample.

It is possible for **que** to follow the verb at a distance. If **ne** precedes the verb and you do not find **pas** (**jamais, rien, guère,** etc.) immediately after the verb, scan the sentence to find the next **que** and use *only* at that point.

> Il **ne** trouve dans ce dictionnaire **que** des mots latins.
> He finds *only* Latin words in this dictionary.

Used with **faire** plus an infinitive, **ne...que** can express continuous action.

> Il **ne** fait **que** parler.   He talks *continuously*.
> Vous **ne** faites **que** vous plaindre.   You complain *constantly*.
>   All you do is complain.

When **que** is used in conjunction with the negative expression **ne...plus,** the sentence is negative and **que** means *except*.

> Il **ne** pense **plus** qu'à son travail.
> He *no longer* thinks about anything *except* his work.

37. The Verb *tenir** (to hold)

A. General. Irregular verbs cannot be recognized at all times by their stems (Sec. 20B), as there is often a dissimilarity between stems and infinitives. It is therefore expedient to learn the deviant forms as part of an irregular verb. Learn the following forms as part of **tenir**.

> *Regular:*   ten-
>
> *Irregular:*   tien-, tin-

Study the following examples.

> *Present:*
>
>   Il **tient** un livre.   He is holding a book.
>   Ils **tiennent** des livres.   They are holding some books.
>   Nous **tenons** un livre.   We are holding a book.
>
> *Imperative:*
>
>   **Tenons** un livre.   Let's hold a book.
>
> *Past Definite:*
>
>   Il **tint** un livre.   He held a book.
>   Ils **tinrent** des livres.   They held books.

In the future time, note the letter -r- (as in the French word **futuR**) before the ending.

> Il **tiendra** un livre.   He will hold a book.
> Nous **tiendrons** un livre.   We will hold a book.

Thus **tiendr-** can be called the future stem of **tenir**, and regardless of the ending it will be translated *will hold*.

B. Compounds of *tenir.* Having learned the two identifying stems for **tenir**, it will now be easy for you to recognize the following compounds of this verb.

Example:

retenir*	to *re*tain	nous retenons	we retain, remember
obtenir*	to *ob*tain	il obtient	he obtains
contenir*	to *con*tain	elle contient	it contains
maintenir*	to *main*tain	il maintiendra	it will maintain
			he will maintain
entretenir*	to support	il entretient	it supports

C. Idiomatic structure *tenir à.* The expression **tenir à** means *to be anxious to* [do something] or *to place a high value* [on something]. Consider these examples.

Il **tient** à examiner cet échantillon.	He *is anxious to* examine this sample.
Nous **tenons** à notre avis.	We *value* our opinion.
	We *cling to* our opinion.

Exercises

A. *Verbs.* Give English equivalents of the following verb forms and sentences.

1. ils mesurent / ils ne mesurent pas / ils ne mesurent jamais
2. ils sont / ils ne sont pas / ils ne sont guère / ils ne sont jamais
3. Elle étudie. / Elle n'étudie pas. / Elle n'étudie plus. / Elle **ne** fait qu'étudier.
4. il a / il n'a pas / Il n'a rien. / Il n'a que trois échantillons.
5. ils ont / ils n'ont pas / Ils n'ont rien. / Elles n'ont aucun programme.
6. Il étudie. / Il n'étudie guère. / Elle n'étudie jamais. / Elle n'étudie d'habitude que l'informatique.
7. il tient / il ne tient pas / Il ne tient rien. / Il ne tiendra guère.
8. ils obtiennent / ils n'obtiennent jamais / Ils n'obtiendront rien.
9. il entretient / Il n'entretient rien. / Il n'entretient qu'une seule hypothèse.
10. il prépare / Il ne prépare pas son examen. / Ils ne préparent rien.
11. Ils ne préparent aucune expérience. / Il ne prépare qu'un programme compilateur.
12. Il n'y a dans la classe que de bons étudiants. / Ils ne font que travailler†.
13. Ces trains ne transportent pas de marchandises. / Ils ne transportent que des voyageurs.

---

3. ne fait que does nothing but **6. d'habitude** *adv.* usually **10. préparer** to prepare (for) **12. travailler†** to work **13. marchandises** *f.pl.* merchandise (This is not the correct term with reference to railroads; select the term appropriate to the field. *Hint:* One does not speak of *merchandise trains*); **voyageur** *m.* traveler (Not only by sea, but by any means; again, select the correct word for a person traveling by train)

14. Ce train ne transporte entre Paris et Nice que des voyageurs. / Ces camions ne contiennent que des boîtes.

15. Cet événement n'arrive pas souvent. / Il n'arrive d'habitude qu'après les vacances.

16. L'avion supersonique n'arrive pas avant six heures. / Il n'arrive jamais en retard.

17. Les étudiants finissent leurs devoirs. / Ils ne finissent qu'une partie des devoirs.

18. Georges ne finit jamais. / Il ne finit jamais rien.

19. Il tient à étudier. / Paul tient à ne jamais étudier.

20. Nous tenons à gagner beaucoup d'argent. / Cet homme est pauvre: il n'a pas d'argent. / Il n'a ni argent ni maison.

21. Il y a une bonne méthode. / Il n'y a qu'une seule méthode efficace. / Il n'a aucune méthode.

22. Il reste une complication. / Il ne reste qu'une seule complication.

23. Il se peut que Robert arrive demain. / Il est impossible qu'il arrive à l'heure.

24. Le Louvre se trouve à Paris. / Il ne se trouve pas à Londres. / Jean-Paul tient à voir ce musée.

25. Ce professeur ne parle guère de ses expériences chimiques. / Il tient à ne pas discuter de ce sujet.

26. L'azote n'entretient ni la combustion ni la respiration.

27. La jeune princesse n'est point coupable d'un crime, mais aucun chevalier ne descend pour elle sur le terrain.

B. Recopy the following sentences. Underline all verbs twice and negatives (both elements) once. Enclose noun-adjective groups and prepositional phrases in parentheses, as below.

   Example:

   (En algèbre) il ne s'agit jamais (de l'étude) (de la variation) (des fonctions).

Now translate each sentence. Make a rough translation first, if necessary, then rewrite in polished English.

28. Il n'y a pas de substance radioactive dans cette matière.

29. Il n'y a rien d'important dans cet article.

30. Il s'agit d'une nouvelle théorie économique; il ne s'agit pas d'une bombe atomique.

31. Il ne reste qu'un cas simple mais intéressant.

32. Quelquefois la mer du Nord est complètement calme et unie; il n'y a donc pas de vagues.

---

15. **événement** *m.* event; **arriver** to happen (as well as *to arrive*); **vacances** *f.pl.* vacation; **après** *adv.* after   16. **avant** *adv.* before; **heures** o'clock, hours; **en retard** late   17. **devoirs** *m.pl.* (In the plural, especially in connection with schools, **devoirs** means *homework*)   20. **gagner** to earn (also *to win, to gain*); **pauvre** *adj.* poor; **maison** *f.* house   22. **il reste** (Impersonal verb form; see Sec. 32)   24. **musée** *m.* museum   25. **discuter de** to talk about, to discuss   27. **point** (slightly more emphatic synonym for **pas**); **coupable** *adj.* guilty; **chevalier** *m.* knight; **terrain** *m.* joustingground   32. **quelquefois** *adv.* sometimes; **mer** *f.* sea; **nord** *m.* north; **uni, -e** *adj.* smooth; **donc** (Used here for emphasis; omit it); **vague** *f.* wave

33. Nous n'avons constaté aucune différence de structure.
34. Son expérience ne comprend que deux parties.
35. Il n'y a que deux parties qu'il faut étudier au commencement.
36. On ne loue d'ordinaire que pour être loué.
37. La clémence des princes n'est souvent qu'une politique pour gagner l'affection des peuples.
38. L'amour de la justice n'est que la crainte de souffrir de l'injustice.
39. L'amour de la justice n'est, en la plupart des hommes, que la crainte de souffrir de l'injustice.
40. Il ne demande† que la faveur dont il a parlé.
41. L'homme ne s'occupe plus de l'essence impénétrable des choses.
42. Mais ce n'est qu'au dix-septième siècle que la révolution est accomplie et triomphe avec Kepler, Bacon et Descartes.
43. Pierre Fermat, qui était le plus puissant esprit mathématique de son temps, n'a rien publié.
44. Il admet que l'instinct puisse être un guide en cette matière, mais cela ne suffit pas.
45. On ne construit plus de bonnes salles de concert; on n'arrive à faire cela que par une étude très sérieuse de l'acoustique.
46. Haydn a écrit cent dix-huit symphonies; la collection complète, en copies très correctes, est à la bibliothèque de notre Conservatoire.
47. Beaucoup d'entre elles ne sont que de simples divertissements, écrits au jour le jour pour les petits concerts du prince Esterhazy.

Readings

La Gravitation

[48] Attraction ou pesanteur universelle.—De la première loi de Kepler on peut déduire l'existence d'une force dirigée vers le centre du soleil. [49] La loi du

---

33. **constater** to observe   34. **comprendre** to include (as well as the main meaning, *to understand*) 35. **commencement** *m*. beginning   36. **louer** to praise; **d'ordinaire** (synonym for **d'habitude**) 37. **clémence** *f*. (Near-cognate—unless you recognize words as being false friends, go ahead and guess at the meaning of words that are close to English); **politique**† *f*. tactic   38. **amour** *m*. love; **crainte** *f*. fear; **souffrir*** to suffer   40. **demander**† to ask for   41. **s'occuper de** to be occupied with, to be interested in; **chose** *f*. thing   42. **accompli** (past participle of **accomplir**, *to accomplish, to take place*); **triompher** (near-cognate)   43. **esprit** *m*. mind; **temps** *m*. time; **publier** (Guess)   44. **admet** (from **admettre***, *to contend* as well as *to admit*); **puisse être** can be; **suffit** (from **suffire***, *to suffice*)   45. **construit** (from **construire***, *to construct*); **arriver** to succeed (as well as *to arrive, to happen*); **cela** *pron*. that   46. **écrit** (past participle of **écrire***, *to write*) (The phrase **a écrit** can be reduced to one word: *wrote*); **bibliothèque** *f*. library; **notre** *adj*. our   47. **d'entre elles** among them; **divertissement** *m*. divertimento (This musical term is a cognate—it's in your English dictionary); **au jour le jour** day by day   48. **ou** or (Distinguish from **où**, *where, when*); **pesanteur universelle** *f*. gravity; **peut** (from **pouvoir***) can; **déduire*** to deduce; **dirigée** (past participle of **diriger**, *to direct*); **soleil** *m*. sun   49. **loi** *f*. law

mouvement elliptique, ou l'expression de la vitesse qui se déduit de cette loi, montre que l'intensité de cette force varie selon la distance au soleil. [50] L'intensité de la force qui s'appelle la pesanteur universelle varie en raison inverse du carré de la distance au soleil. [51] Enfin la troisième loi de Kepler montre qu'à égalité de distance au centre du soleil, l'intensité de la force motrice est proportionnelle à la masse de chaque planète et indépendante de la nature particulière de cette planète. [52] Tous les corps de la nature s'attirent mutuellement en raison directe des masses et en raison inverse du carré de la distance. [53] Mais les corps célestes agissent les uns sur les autres et sur le soleil lui-même, et de ces attractions diverses il résulte des perturbations. [54] L'étude de ces forces s'appelle la mécanique céleste, une partie importante de l'astronomie; c'est l'étude de la théorie des mouvements des astres.

Les Mathématiques

[55] Cette science a pour objet les propriétés de la grandeur en tant qu'elle est mesurable ou calculable. [56] Les mathématiques élémentaires, c'est la partie des mathématiques qui comprend l'arithmétique ou d'autres premières notions de cette science. [57] L'algèbre, la haute algèbre, et la géométrie sont classées parmi les mathématiques pures, c.-à-d. qui traitent de la grandeur d'une manière abstraite.

[58] La science des mathématiques appliquées comprend la mécanique et l'astronomie, qui considèrent les propriétés de la grandeur dans certains corps ou sujets.

[59] On appelle *quantité* ou *grandeur* tout ce qui est susceptible d'augmentation ou de diminution. Les longueurs, les superficies, les volumes des corps, etc., sont des quantités.

[60] L'arithmétique est la science des nombres, tandis que l'algèbre a pour but de généraliser et d'abréger la résolution des questions relatives aux quantités en général. [61] La géométrie est une science qui a pour but de mesurer l'étendue, dont les trois dimensions sont la longueur, la largeur, et la profondeur. [62] Enfin il y a le calcul infinitésimal (le calcul intégral et le calcul différentiel) qui sert à étudier la variation des fonctions.

L'Esprit pratique des Américains

[63] Il ne faut pas chercher aux États-Unis ce qui distingue l'homme des autres êtres de la création, ce qui est son extrait d'immortalité et l'ornement de ses jours.

---

49. **se déduit** is deduced; **montrer** to show; **selon** according to   50. **en raison de** in proportion to   51. **enfin** *adv.* finally; **motrice** *adj.* driving; **chaque** *adj.* each   52. **s'attirer** to be attracted   53. **agissent** (from **agir***, *to act*); **les uns sur les autres** on each other   54. **astre** *m.* star   55. **grandeur** *f.* size; **en tant que** insofar as   56. **premières notions** *f.pl.* basic ideas   56. **c.-à-d.** (abbrev. of **c'est-à-dire**, *that is to say*) i.e.; **traiter** to deal with   59. **tout ce qui** everything which; **superficie** *f.* area   60. **tandis que** *conj.* whereas; **abréger** to shorten   61. **étendue** *f.* size; **dont les trois dimensions** (Remember to translate the noun group first); **largeur** *f.* width; **profondeur** *f.* depth   62. **sert** (from **servir***, *to serve*)   63. **extrait** *m.* extract, essence

[64] Les lettres sont inconnues dans la nouvelle République. [65] L'Américain a remplacé les opérations intellectuelles par les opérations positives; ne lui imputez point à l'infériorité sa médiocrité dans les arts, car ce n'est pas de ce côté qu'il a porté son attention. [66] Jeté par différentes causes sur un sol désert, l'agriculture et le commerce ont été l'objet de ses soins. [67] Avant de penser, il faut vivre; avant de planter des arbres, il faut les abattre afin de labourer.

[68] Il n'y a dans le nouveau continent ni littérature classique, ni littérature romantique, ni littérature indienne: [69] classique, les Américains n'ont point de modèles; romantique, les Américains n'ont point de moyen-âge; indienne, les Américains méprisent les sauvages et ont horreur des bois comme d'une prison.

[70] Ce qu'on trouve en Amérique, c'est la littérature appliquée, servant aux divers usages de la société. C'est la littérature d'ouvriers, de négociants, de marins, de laboureurs. [71] Les Américains ne réussissent guère que dans la mécanique et dans les sciences, parce que les sciences ont un côté matériel. [72] Franklin et Fulton se sont emparés de la foudre et de la vapeur au profit des hommes. [73] Il appartenait à l'Amérique de doter le monde de la découverte par laquelle aucun continent ne pourra désormais échapper aux recherches du navigateur.

d'après René de Chateaubriand, *Mémoires d'outre-tombe*, Livre VIII

Test 5, page 227

---

64. **lettres** *f.pl.* literature; **inconnu, -e** *adj.* unknown   65. **remplacer** to replace; **imputer** to attribute (Note that the next phrase cannot be a prepositional phrase, so skip to the next independent noun group)   66. **jeté** (past participle of **jeter***, *to throw*); **sol** *m.* soil, land; **un sol désert** (Which word is the adjective in French? The word order tells you); **soin** *m.* care, attention   67. **vivre*** to live; **les abattre** fell them; **afin de** in order to; **labourer** to plow   69. **méprisent** (from **mépriser**, *to despise, to disdain*); **bois** *m.pl.* woods, forests   70. **servant** (present participle of **servir***); **divers** *adj.* various; **ouvrier** *m.* worker; **laboureur** *m.* farmer   71. **réussir** to succeed   72. **s'emparer de** to take possession of; **foudre** *f.* lightning   73. **appartenait** (imperfect of **appartenir***, *to belong*); **doter de** to endow with; **laquelle** which; **désormais** *adv.* henceforth; **échapper à** to escape from

6

Structures

38. Personal Pronouns Used as Subjects

Just as English verbs have first-, second-, and third-person forms with corresponding subject pronouns (*I, you, he,* etc.), French verbs have three persons in the singular and three in the plural for each tense, with corresponding personal pronouns.

A verb tense expresses the time of an action, an event, or a condition. French verbs have twelve commonly used tenses which fall roughly into three main time divisions: past, present, and future. You should learn the time significance of each tense when it is presented. In French, as in English, the present tense can express various kinds of present time.

- The actual present: the action is going on at this very moment.
  Il **examine** ce cas.   He *is examining* this case.

- The habitual present: the action occurs habitually.
  Il **examine** ce cas tous les jours.   He *examines* this case every day.

- An extension of the present: the action will occur in the future.
  Il **examine** ce cas demain.   He *will examine* (*examines*) this case tomorrow.

A. Subject pronouns.   Learn the following pronouns.

		singular		*plural*
first person	**je**	I	**nous**	we
second person	**tu**	you	**vous**	you
third person	**il**	he, it	**ils**	
	elle	she, it	**elles**	they
	on	one (Sec. 26)		

Although the third person has more than one subject form (**il, elle, ce, on, l'on,** etc.), there is only one verb form for the singular and one for the plural.

B. Meanings of subject pronouns.   Note the following special uses.

1. The pronoun **tu** is used only in speaking directly to one other person who is an intimate acquaintance—a member of the family, a close friend, a fellow "sufferer" such as another member of the military service to which the speaker belongs (but not one officer to another), or a fellow student—or to any small child or animal. Historically, **tu** was sometimes used to address another person who did not fall into any of the "familiar" categories but who was in a definitely lower social stratum (for example, in speaking to servants before the advent of democracy). It is an insult to use **tu** with people who should not be thus addressed.

2. The pronoun **vous** is used for *you* in all applications not mentioned above. It is called the "polite" form, as opposed to the intimate or "familiar" form **tu.** It is used in speaking to one or to several persons; it is always used in speaking to more than one person.

3. The pronouns **il** and **ils** refer to masculine nouns. The form **il** may refer to a person, in which case it is translated *he*, or to a masculine object like **le livre**, in which case **il** means *it*. The plural **ils** is always *they*.

4. The pronouns **elle** and **elles** refer to feminine nouns. In reference to a person **elle** means *she*; to a thing, *it*. The plural **elles** is always *they*.

5. The pronoun **on** is used for *one*, *they* (general), or *people* (general). It is used as the subject of a third-person singular verb form for an unspecified general subject (Sec. 26B).

On parle français en France.	*One* speaks French in France.
	They speak French in France.
	People speak French in France.

Better:

French is spoken in France.

The form **l'on** is sometimes seen, but there is no difference in translation.

39. Present Tense of Regular Verbs

The present tense of regular verbs may be recognized by the presence of the familiar *stem* which comes from the infinitive (Sec. 25). To this stem are added distinctive endings depending on the type of verb. The endings are presented in the following table.

	infinitives ending in			*remember*	
	-er	*-re*	*-ir*		
je	-e	-s	-is	e	(i)s
tu	-es	-s	-is	es	(i)s
il, elle, on	-e	(none)	-it	e	(i)t

	infinitives ending in			*remember*
	-er	*-re*	*-ir*	
nous	**-ons**	**-ons**	**-ISSons**	(ISS)ons
vous	**-ez**	**-ez**	**-ISSez**	(ISS)ez
ils, elles	**-ent**	**-ent**	**-ISSent**	(ISS)ent

Example: Present tense of regular **-er** verb **arriv/er** (*to arrive, to happen*)

j' **arrive**	I am arriving, arrive
tu **arrives**	you are arriving, arrive
il **arrive**	he is arriving, arrives; it is happening, happens
nous **arrivons**	we are arriving, arrive
vous **arrivez**	you are arriving, arrive
ils **arrivent**	they are arriving, arrive

Note that **je** becomes **j'** before vowels.

Example: Present tense of regular **-re** verb **vend/re** (*to sell*)

je **vends**	I am selling, sell
tu **vends**	you are selling, sell
il **vend**	he is selling, sells
nous **vendons**	we are selling, sell
vous **vendez**	you are selling, sell
ils **vendent**	they are selling, sell

Example: Present tense of regular **-ir** verb **fin/ir** (*to finish*)

je **finis**	I am finishing, finish
tu **finis**	you are finishing, finish
il **finit**	he is finishing, finishes
nous **finISSons**	we are finishing, finish
vous **finISSez**	you are finishing, finish
ils **finISSent**	they are finishing, finish

The temptation to translate a French verb consisting of one word by an English one-word verb should be resisted. Since the present tense normally indicates something actually in progress, the English equivalent is two words (the present progressive).

One-Word French Verb:	***Two-Word English Equivalent:***
Je **vais** au cinéma maintenant.	I *am going* to the movies now.

The single-word equivalent is used only for habitual action. Use it only if there is some indicator such as **toujours, tous les jours,** or **d'habitude.**

D'habitude je **vais** au cinéma le lundi.
Usually I *go* (not *am going*) to the movies on Mondays.

40. Future and Conditional Tenses of Regular Verbs

The future tense indicates an action that has not yet occurred but that is expected to happen; it is translated with the word *will* [do something].

The conditional tense is translated with the word *would* [do something].

A. Recognition. A verb may be recognized as being either future or conditional by the presence of the entire infinitive (up to and including the last -r) before the ending.

Compare

il arrive   il arrivera

In **il arrive** there is no **-r** before the ending, so no infinitive can be present. Thus the verb is not future or conditional, but present tense: *he is arriving, it is happening*, etc.

In **il arrivera** the presence of the **-r** near the end calls for a check. To see if the whole infinitive is present, we draw a slash after the **r** thus:

arriver/a

Since the verb before the line is the infinitive, we are dealing with a future or a conditional: either *will arrive* or *would arrive*—but which? To find out, examine the ending that follows the **-r**. There are two sets of endings, and it is the ending that determines the tense.

B. Ending Systems. The endings are presented in the following table.

	future (*will . . .*)		*conditional* (*would . . .*)	
je		-ai		-ais ⎫
tu		-as		-ais ⎬ (All have 3 letters)
il, elle, on		-a		-ait ⎭
nous	$R +$	-ons	$R +$	-ions ⎫
vous		-ez		-iez ⎬ (All include i)
ils, elles		-ont		-aient ⎭

If the FC (future-conditional) stem is followed by a "short" ending, the short translation *will* is used. Associate the short ending with the short tense name (future) and the short translation (*will*). If the FC stem is followed by a "long" ending, it is the tense with the long name (conditional) and the long equivalent (*would*).

nous **fini**ssons	*Present:*	we are finishing
nous **fini**rons	*Future:*	we will finish
nous **fini**rions	*Conditional:*	we would finish

ils **vend**ent	*Present:*	they are selling
ils **vend**ront	*Future:*	they will sell
ils **vend**raient	*Conditional:*	they would sell

Note: The portion **vendr** is the entire infinitive of **vendre** up to the **r**. This is typical of all -**re** verbs, in which the final -**e** of the infinitive must be absent from the future and conditional.

General Rule for Identification of Future and Conditional

1. If there is an **r** before the verb ending, check to see if the letters up to the **r** are the infinitive. **Note:** Infinitives ending in -**re** will have lost the final -**e** in the future and conditional stem.

2. If the FC (future-conditional) stem is present, notice whether the ending is short (future) or long (conditional).

3. If future, translate

   > *will* [do something]

   If conditional, translate

   > *would* [do something]

Exercises

A. *Verb structures.* Translate into English. In the first few items, verbs are given in the infinitive form, then in the present, future, and conditional. After the first few, they are in random order.

1. pour préparer / nous préparons / vous préparerez / elle préparerait
2. il faut donner / il donne / ils donneront / vous donneriez
3. sans étudier / j'étudie / vous étudierez / ils étudieraient
4. à chercher / tu cherches / ils chercheront / il chercherait
5. de trouver / vous trouvez / nous trouverons / il trouverait
6. pour expliquer / elle explique / il expliquera / nous expliquerions
7. sans dire* / il dit / il dira / ils diraient
8. pour réfléchir / il réfléchit / on réfléchira / nous réfléchirions
9. pour être* / il est / il sera / ils seraient
10. sans avoir* / il a / ils auront / elle aurait
11. pour arriver / il arrive / vous arriverez / ils arriveraient
12. il faut remarquer† / il remarquera / il ne remarquerait rien

---

1. **préparons** (Why can't this be future tense? Because -**ar** is not an infinitive ending, and **prépar-** is not a complete infinitive)   7. **dire*** to say (Do not confuse with **parler**, *to speak*)   9. **ser-** (special future and conditional stem of **être***)   10. **aur-** (special future and conditional stem of **avoir***) 12. **remarquer**† to notice

13. pour bâtir / on bâtirait / ils bâtissent
14. sans choisir / ils choisiront / nous choisissons
15. à tenir / il tient / il tiendra
16. pour obtenir / ils obtenaient / nous obtiendrons
17. tenir à / nous tenons à étudier / il tiendra à partir
18. sans être* / ils ne seront jamais / je ne serai plus
19. il faut avoir* / nous aurions / vous avez
20. il s'agit de / il ne s'agit pas de / il s'agira de
21. se composer de / il se compose de / elle se composerait de
22. de ralentir / ils ralentissent / il ralentira
23. pour découvrir* / il découvrira / il découvre
24. porter / il portera / portons ⸻ *earns a living*
25. de gagner / Il gagnera sa vie. / Ils gagneraient le match.
26. sans admettre* / ils admettront / ils admettent
27. il est possible / il sera possible / il serait possible
28. vous préparez / vous finissez / ils observent
29. ils bâtissent / je finis / il ne finira jamais = *he will never finish*
30. mettre* / je mets / nous admettrons

B. *Verbs.* Give English equivalents.

31. il a préparé / préparons / il faut préparer
32. nous donnons / nous avons donné / il aura donné
33. vous étudierez / il faut étudier / ils ont étudié
34. il construit* / ils construisent / il construira
35. contenir* / il contient / il ne contiendra que
36. produire* / cela se produit / on produira
37. pour comprendre* / il comprendra / ils ont compris
38. descendre / je descends / nous descendrions
39. ne pas demander† / il aura demandé / il demandera
40. ne pas finir / il finit / ils finissent

C. Translate the following sentences, rewriting or changing word order whenever necessary to achieve good English style.

41. Les trois frères se réuniront pour partager les biens de leur père.
42. Il sera impossible de diviser dix-sept chameaux par deux.
43. Les trois fils trouveront une solution. Il reste dix-sept chameaux.
44. Quand le derviche arrivera, il attachera son propre chameau à côté des autres.
45. Alors il y aura dix-huit chameaux qui seront rangés devant lui.
46. Quand les trois fils auront pris leurs chameaux, le derviche partira.
47. Lorsque le son rencontre un obstacle, il sera réfléchi et il produira un écho.

---

17. **tenir*** à to be eager to   22. **ralentir** to slow down (related to **lent, -e** *adj. slow*)   24. **portons** (When there is no subject, the verb is a command; see Sec. 80)   39. **demander†** to ask for (not *to demand*)

48. Horatio Nelson, le célèbre amiral anglais, a dit que la flotte de Napoléon à Aboukir serait détruite.
49. Ces cas se diviseront en deux groupes très différents.
50. Nous examinerons un échantillon de l'air atmosphérique; il est probable que nous trouverons dans cet échantillon un mélange de plusieurs gaz.
51. Le nouveau train dont la locomotive sera électrique portera des voyageurs mais pas de marchandises.
52. Il paraît que la plupart des substances minérales se présenteront sous des formes cristallines.
53. On préparera des plans pour une nouvelle construction à la Cité universitaire à Paris.
54. Ce sont les architectes qui prépareront les tracés du nouveau bâtiment.
55. Les données dont il examinera la valeur seront préparées par des physiciens† aux États-Unis.
56. La nouvelle maison de cet ingénieur se trouvera à Houston (Texas).

D. *Missing link.* Translate the following sentences.

   Translation Aid: In French it is common to withhold an expected direct object, interposing prepositional phrases. In English it is best to skip the prepositional phrases and go directly to the direct object, and thereafter recoup the skipped phrases.

   > Louis XVI **signe** avec les États-Unis **un traité de commerce.**
   > Louis XVI **signs a trade agreement** with the United States.

   In addition to verbs that obviously require a direct object (**observer, dire, préparer, diviser,** etc.), the following French verbs call for a direct object: **attendre** (*to wait for, to await*), **chercher** (*to look for, to get*), **demander** (*to ask for*), **écouter** (*to listen to*), **regarder**† (*to look at*).

57. Il observe sous le microscope électronique l'échantillon choisi.
58. Ils écoutent dans cette salle de théâtre magnifique une symphonie classique interprétée par l'Orchestre de Paris.
59. Ces protons décrivent sous l'action du champ magnétique vertical des cercles dans un plan horizontal.
60. Ses concepts constituent en une nouvelle théorie des phénomènes linguistiques.
61. Notre intelligence tient dans l'ordre des choses intelligibles le même rang que notre corps dans l'étendue de la nature. ——Pascal, *Pensées*, 72
62. Cette expérience aura pour but de découvrir la composition chimique de cette substance.

---

53. **Cité universitaire** residential campus of the University of Paris   54. **tracé** *m.* plan, tracing
55. **États-Unis** *m.pl.* United States   57. **choisi** (past participle of **choisir**, *to choose*)   59. **décrivent** (from **décrire***, *to describe*); **champ** *m.* field; **cercle** *m.* circle   60. **constituent** constitute, (here) combine, encompass   61. **tient** (from **tenir***, *to hold*); **rang** *m.* rank; **étendue** *f.* expanse; **Pensées** Thoughts, Reflections   62. **découvrir*** to discover

63. Nous ne ferons pas de parallèle entre les fusées engins soviétiques et les fusées engins américains sol-air.
64. Les premières applications des piles atomiques mobiles intéresseront certainement la propulsion des sous-marins.
65. Le sous-marin nucléaire dont la construction est commencée utilisera des neutrons lents et probablement de l'hélium pour le refroidissement de la pile.
66. L'installation de cette machine comprendra trois parties.
67. Si le soleil n'existait plus, qu'est-ce qui arriverait? Les planètes périraient, les animaux périraient, et voilà la terre solitaire et muette.
68. La perfection de l'humanité ne sera pas l'extinction, mais l'harmonie des nationalités.—Renan, *L'Avenir de la science.*
69. A l'avenir, un seul pouvoir gouvernera réellement le monde: ce sera la science, ce sera l'esprit.—Renan, *Lettre à Berthelot.*
70. Rostopshine sortira le dernier de Moscou, comme un capitaine de vaisseau quitte le dernier son bord dans un naufrage.

Readings

Le Calcul des probabilités

[71] La *probabilité* d'un événement est le rapport qui existe entre le nombre des cas favorables à cet événement et le nombre total de cas possibles. [72] La probabilité est donc représentée par une fraction toujours moindre que l'unité. [73] L'unité est le symbole de la certitude.

[74] Un événement doit être considéré comme probable lorsque sa probabilité est plus grande que ½; car les chances favorables sont plus nombreuses que les chances défavorables.

[75] La somme des probabilités de tous les événements possibles est toujours égale à l'unité. [76] Ainsi, quand on a une urne qui contient b boules blanches, n boules noires et r boules rouges, la probabilité d'extraire une boule blanche est exprimée par la fraction

$$\frac{b}{b + n + r},$$

---

63. **ferons** (from **faire***, *to make*) (The root **fer-** is a special future and conditional stem to be learned for this verb); **fusée engin** *f.* rocket missile; **sol-air** ground-to-air 64. **intéresser** to concern 65. **refroidissement** *m.* cooling (related to **froid,** *cold*) 67. **qu'est-ce que** what (Only the first word of this group appears in the translation); **périr** to perish; **muet, -te** *adj.* mute 68. **avenir** *m.* future 69. **à l'avenir** in the future; **seul, -e** *adj.* single; **gouverner** to govern; **réellement** *adv.* actually; **monde** *m.* world 70. **sortira le dernier** will be the last to leave; **vaisseau** *m.* ship; **quitter** to leave; **bord** *m.* ship; **naufrage** *m.* shipwreck 71. **événement** *m.* event; **rapport** *m.* relationship; **entre** *prep.* between; **nombre** *m.* number 72. **donc** therefore; **toujours** *adv.* always; **moindre que** less than 74. **doit** (from **devoir***, *to be able to*) must; **car** for; **nombreux, nombreuse** *adj.* numerous 75. **somme** *f.* sum 76. **ainsi** thus; **boule** *f.* ball; **blanc, blanche** *adj.* white; **extraire*** to draw, to extract; **exprimer** to express; **b, n, r** (These letters represent the French names of the colors. In English you might want to change the letters accordingly)

la probabilité d'extraire une boule noire est exprimée par $\dfrac{n}{b+n+r}$,

et la probabilité d'en tirer une boule de couleur rouge est $\dfrac{r}{b+n+r}$;

enfin la somme de ces trois fractions est égale à l'unité. [77] Cette évaluation suppose les cas également possibles.

[78] Si les cas ne sont pas également possibles, il faut déterminer d'abord leurs possibilités respectives; et la probabilité est alors la somme des possibilités de chaque cas favorable.

[79] Par exemple, au jeu bien connu de pile ou face, la probabilité d'amener pile au premier coup est évidemment ½; tandis que si l'on cherche la probabilité d'amener pile au moins une fois en deux coups, on peut ne compter que trois cas différents, à savoir: [80] pile au premier coup, ce qui dispense d'en jouer un second; face au premier coup et pile au second coup; enfin face au premier et au second coup:

[81] La probabilité d'amener pile au premier coup est toujours ½, mais celle des deux autres cas est ¼, en sorte que la probabilité cherchée est ½ + ¼ ou ¾. [82] On parvient au même résultat en considérant que les lettres A et B ne peuvent donner lieu qu'aux quatre arrangements également possibles—AA AB BA BB—et que trois de ces arrangements sont favorables à l'événement dont on cherche la probabilité.

[83] Si les événements sont indépendants les uns des autres, la probabilité de l'existence de leur ensemble est le produit de leurs probabilités particulières†. [84] On exprime cela d'ordinaire en disant que la probabilité composée est le produit des probabilités simples.

[85] Supposons par exemple que l'on ait assemblé dans un paquet les 13 cartes d'une même couleur qui se trouvent dans un jeu complet de 52 cartes, et qu'on demande la probabilité que les deux premières cartes du paquet soient un as et un deux. [86] La probabilité que l'as soit la première dans le paquet de 13 cartes est $^1/_{13}$; cette carte ôtée, il en reste 12, et la probabilité que le deux soit la première du nouveau paquet est $^1/_{12}$. [87] Ainsi la probabilité du concours de ces deux événements sera

---

76. **tirer** to draw   78. **si** if; **il faut** it is necessary; **d'abord** first of all; **alors** then   79. **jeu** *m.* game; **pile ou face** tails or heads (English order?); **amener*** (here) to get; **premier** first; **coup** *m.* toss; **évidemment**† obviously; **l'on** (same as **on**; used for euphony); **compter** to count; **à savoir** namely   80. **ce qui** which; **dispenser de** to obviate   81. **toujours** *adv.* still (more usual than *always*); **celle** that; **en sorte que** *conj.* so that, in such a way that   82. **parvient** (from **parvenir***, *to arrive*); **en considérant que** by considering that; **peuvent** (from **pouvoir***, *to be able to*) can; **donner lieu** allow, give rise to; **qu'aux** (Remember the **ne ... que** construction)   83. **les uns des autres** from one another; **ensemble** *m.* totality; **produit** *m.* product; **particulier**†, **particulière** *adj.* individual   84. **disant** saying; **composé, -e** compound   85. **ait** (from **avoir***, *to have*); **couleur** *f.* (here) suit (of playing cards); **jeu** *m.* deck (of playing cards); **deux premières** (English word order?); **soient** (from **être***, *to be*); **as** *m.* ace   86. **ôtée** (past participle of **ôter**, *to remove*)   87. **concours** *m.* coexistence

$$\frac{1}{13} \times \frac{1}{12} \text{ ou } \frac{1}{156}.$$

[88] Quand deux événements dépendent l'un de l'autre, la probabilité de l'événement composé est encore le produit de la probabilité du premier événement par la probabilité que, cet événement étant arrivé, l'autre arrivera. [89] Ainsi soient trois urnes A, B, C, dont deux ne renferment que des boules blanches, et dont une ne renferme que des boules noires. [90] On demande la probabilité d'extraire à la fois des urnes B et C des boules blanches. [91] La probabilité d'extraire de C une boule blanche est ⅔; et si cette boule est réellement extraite, la probabilité d'extraire une boule blanche de B serait ½. [92] La probabilité d'extraire à la fois des boules blanches des urnes B et C est donc

$$\frac{2}{3} \times \frac{1}{2} \text{ ou } \frac{1}{3}.$$

Critique des idées de Rousseau sur l'éducation des enfants

[93] Il paraît d'abord illogique de louer l'ancienne méthode, qui fait de l'étude des langues la base de l'éducation, et de considérer l'école de Pestalozzi comme une des meilleures institutions de notre siècle. [94] Je crois cependant que ces deux manières de voir peuvent se concilier. De toutes les études, celle qui donne chez Pestalozzi les résultats les plus brillants, ce sont les mathématiques. [95] Mais il me paraît que sa méthode pourrait s'appliquer à plusieurs autres parties de l'instruction, et qu'elle y ferait faire des progrès sûrs et rapides.

[96] Rousseau a senti que les enfants†, avant l'âge de douze à treize ans, n'ont point l'intelligence nécessaire pour les études qu'on exige d'eux, ou plutôt pour la méthode d'enseignement à laquelle on les soumet. [97] Ils répètent sans comprendre; ils travaillent sans s'instruire. Tout ce que Rousseau a dit contre cette éducation routinière est parfaitement vrai; mais, comme il arrive souvent, ce qu'il propose comme remède est encore plus mauvais que le mal.

---

88. **étant arrivé** having occurred 89. **soient** (from **être***) given (math); **renfermer** to contain 90. **extraire** (A direct object is required. The missing link information should be put to use here; see Appendix A, 3) 91. **extraite** drawn 93. **louer** to praise; **ancien, -ne** *adj.* (before noun) old (in the sense of *former*); **qui** that, which; **école** *f.* school; **Pestalozzi, Jean-Henri** Pédagogue suisse (1746–1827) qui s'intéressa surtout à l'instruction des enfants pauvres; **meilleures** *adj.* best; **notre** our ⟨94⟩ **crois** (from **croire***, *to believe, to think*); **cependant** however; **de voir** of viewing (the subject); **se concilier** to be reconciled; **celle qui** that which; **chez** in the case of ⟨95⟩ **pourrait** (**pourr-** is the future and conditional stem of **pouvoir**) could, might; **ferait faire des progrès** (See Sec. 55); **sûr, -e** *adj.* sure, certain ⟨96⟩ **Rousseau, Jean-Jacques** Philosophe et écrivain, né à Genève de parents français, 1712–1778. Ses goûts pour la nature et la solitude ont contribué au romantisme du siècle suivant; ses théories sur l'éducation se trouvent en partie dans son roman «*Emile*»); **senti** (past participle of **sentir**, *to feel*); **enfant**† *m. or f.* child; **exiger** to require; **eux** *pron.* them; **plutôt** rather; **enseignement** *m.* instruction; **soumet** (present of **soumettre***, *to subject*) ⟨97⟩ **répètent** (from **répéter**, *to repeat*); **s'instruire*** to learn; **tout ce que** everything that, all that; **routinier, -e** *adj.* routine; **ce qu'** (same as **ce que**) that (often *what*); **mal** *m.* evil (Contrast **le remède** with **le mal** in the translation)

[98] Un enfant qui, d'après le système de Rousseau, n'a rien appris jusqu'à l'âge de douze ans, aura perdu six années précieuses de sa vie; [99] ses organes intellectuels n'acquerront jamais la flexibilité que l'exercice, dès la première enfance, pouvait seul leur donner.

[100] Rousseau dit avec raison que les enfants ne comprennent pas ce qu'ils apprennent et il en conclut qu'ils ne doivent rien apprendre. [101] Pestalozzi a profondément étudié ce qui fait que les enfants ne comprennent pas, et sa méthode simplifie et gradue les idées de telle sorte qu'elles sont mises à la portée des enfants, et que l'esprit de cet âge arrive sans se fatiguer aux résultats les plus compliqués. [102] En passant avec exactitude par tous les degrés du raisonnement, Pestalozzi met l'enfant en état de découvrir lui-même ce qu'on veut lui enseigner.

[103] La méthode de Pestalozzi est exacte; il n'y a pas d'à peu près dans sa méthode. On comprend bien, ou l'on ne comprend pas: car toutes les propositions se touchent de si près, que le second raisonnement est toujours la conséquence immédiate du premier. [104] Rousseau a dit que l'on fatiguait la tête des enfants par les études que l'on exigeait d'eux; [105] Pestalozzi les conduit toujours par une route facile et positive. [106] Il ne leur en coûte pas plus de s'initier dans les sciences les plus abstraites que dans les occupations les plus simples. [107] Chaque pas dans ces sciences est aussi aisé (par rapport à l'antécédent) que la conséquence la plus naturelle tirée des circonstances les plus ordinaires. [108] Ce qui fatigue les enfants, c'est de leur faire sauter les intermédiaires, de les faire avancer sans qu'ils sachent ce qu'ils croient avoir appris. [109] Il y a dans leur tête alors une sorte de confusion qui leur rend tout examen redoutable, et leur inspire un invincible dégoût pour le travail. [110] Il n'existe pas de trace de ces inconvénients chez Pestalozzi: les enfants s'amusent de leurs études.

[111] La méthode de Pestalozzi, comme tout ce qui est vraiment bon, n'est pas une découverte entièrement nouvelle, mais une application éclairée et persévérante de vérités déjà connues. [112] La patience, l'observation, et l'étude philosophique des procédés de l'esprit humain, lui ont fait connaître ce qu'il y a

---

98. appris (past participle of apprendre*, to learn); jusqu'à until; perdu (past participle of perdre, to lose); année f. (same as an m.) year   99. acquerront (acquerr- is the future and conditional stem of acquérir*, to acquire); dès starting with…, from…on; pouvait (from pouvoir*, to be able to) could; seul alone; leur to them   100. apprennent (present of apprendre*, to learn); en conclut concludes from that; doivent (present of devoir*) must   101. ce qui fait que the reason (literally, what causes the fact that); gradue (present of graduer, to grade, to graduate); mises à la portée de put within the grasp of   102. en passant by going; met (present of mettre*, to put); en état de in a position to; veut (present of vouloir*, to want); lui [to] him   103. pas d'à peu près nothing approximate, no half measures; de si près so closely   104. tête f. (here) mind (also head)   105. conduit (present of conduire*, to lead)   106. en (Do not translate); coûte (present of coûter, to cost); les plus abstraites, les plus simples (superlatives; see Sec. 50B)   107. pas m. step; aussi aisé just as easy   108. leur faire sauter to have them skip (causative faire*; see Sec. 55); les faire avancer to oblige them to advance   109. rend (present of rendre, to render); redoutable frightening; leur inspire inspires them with; dégoût distaste   111. déjà already; connu (past participle of connaître*, to know)   112. lui ont fait connaître have revealed to him

d'élémentaire dans les pensées, et de successif dans leur développement; [113] et il a poussé plus loin qu'un autre la théorie et la pratique de la gradation dans l'enseignement. [114] On a appliqué avec succès sa méthode à la grammaire, à la géographie, à la musique; mais il serait fort à désirer que les professeurs distingués qui ont adopté ses principes, les fissent servir à tous les genres de connaissances....

d'après Madame de Staël, *De l'Allemagne*, Première partie, Chapitre XIX

Test 6, page 229

---

112. **de successif** (Do not translate **de**)   113. **poussé** (past participle of **pousser**, *to push*); **un autre** any other person   114. **les fissent servir** make use of them (causative **faire***; literally, *cause them to serve*)

7

Structures

41. Special Future and Conditional Stems

The general rule you learned in Chapter 6 for recognizing future and conditional forms of French verbs applies to both regular and irregular verbs. However, whereas the r characteristic of all future-conditional stems is part of the infinitive of regular verbs, in irregular verbs it is part of a special future and conditional stem that must be learned for each verb, as presented in the chart below.

infinitive	future-conditional stem	meaning
être*	ser-	will be, would be (sometimes, with a past participle, *will have*)
avoir*	aur-	will have, would have
faire*	fer-	will make, would make
aller*	ir-	will go, would go
tenir*	tiendr-	will hold, would hold
venir*	viendr-	will come, would come
pouvoir*	pourr-	will be able, would be able
vouloir*	voudr-	will want, would like
valoir*	[il] vaudr-	[it] will, would be worth
falloir	[il] faudr-	[it] will, would be necessary

Examples:

nous **serons** contents	*Future:*	we will be happy
nous **serions** contents	*Conditional:*	we would be happy
il **sera** arrivé	*Future:*	he will have arrived it will have happened
il **serait** arrivé	*Conditional:*	he would have arrived it would have happened
vous **obtiendriez**	*Conditional:*	you would obtain
ils **pourront**	*Future:*	they will be able
il **faudra** partir	*Future:*	it will be necessary to depart
elle **irait**	*Conditional:*	she, it would go

42. Past Tenses: Identifying Tenses by Elimination

The diagram below illustrates the three areas of time—present, past, and future—with time marching in the direction of the arrow.

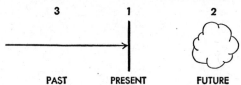

You already know how to recognize present, future, and conditional tenses. You can deduce past tenses by following a process of elimination. These steps will help you when you encounter an unknown verb form.

1. Check to see if it is *present* (you should recognize it as such at once).
2. If not, then check for the *future.*
   (a) Is there an **r** before the ending?
   (b) Is the stem an infinitive or a special irregular future stem?
3. If tests one and two fail, call it a past tense.

Remember the order of tense elimination, and follow it.

$$
\begin{array}{ccc}
1 & 2 & 3 \\
\text{Present} \longrightarrow & \text{Future} \longrightarrow & \text{Past}
\end{array}
$$

Problem 1:   Translate **il représenta**.
1. Present tense? No. This verb ends in **-a**, and the table of endings (Sec. 39) shows no such present tense ending for the subject **il**, or for any other subject. Present tense is eliminated. Go on to the second step.
2. Future or conditional? No. There is no **r** before the ending, so this possibility is eliminated.
3. Steps 1 and 2 have failed to furnish a translation. As a result, this must be a past tense. Translate accordingly: *he represented* or *it represented.*

Problem 2:   Translate **ils entrèrent** (from **entrer**).
1. Present tense? No. (Present is **ils entrent.**) Eliminated.
2. Future tense? It is possible because of the **r**. Examine more closely. The accent is not a part of the infinitive, so **entrèr** is not an FC stem. After the **r** you find **ent**. This is neither a future nor a conditional ending. (See the table in Sec. 40B.) Eliminated.
3. Translate as past tense: **they entered.**

Problem 3:   Translate **vous aurez examiné**.
The past participle is always translated the same way (here, **examined**). It is necessary only to inspect the auxiliary verb **aurez**. It is not the present tense (which would be **vous avez**); proceed to the future-conditional system. The test for this succeeds (**r** before the ending, and special future-conditional stem **aur-**). The short ending is future. Translate as: you **will have examined.**

43. Translation of the Imperfect Tense

The imperfect tense is a past tense that has the same endings as the conditional (Sec. 40B). The imperfect has different meanings depending on the context. To obtain the correct meaning in context, the best policy is to follow the order suggested below. (Replace forms of *do* by the actual verb.)

translation		*example:* **il parlait**
1) **was [do]ing**	(action in progress in the past)	he *was* speak*ing*
2) **used to [do]**	(habitual action in the past)	he *used to* speak
3) **[did]**	(background information)	he *spoke*

A. Identification of the imperfect.   Suppose that a verb tested by the elimination method proves to be a past tense. The usual procedure is to give a one-word equivalent in English: **observa**, *observed*. However, if you notice that in addition to being in the past tense, the verb has the same ending as a form of the conditional (**-ais, -ais, -ait, -ions, -iez, -aient**), you know that you have a verb in the imperfect tense. You then try the translations in the order given.

For example, to translate **il arrivait** (past, with conditional ending **-ait**), start with *he was arriving* (choice 1). If that meaning is unsatisfactory, try *he used to arrive* (choice 2). If that fails, use *he arrived* (choice 3).

The context will help you decide which translation to use. Consider the following examples.

(Every day) **il arrivait** (at eight o'clock.)

(The President was scheduled to address Congress on Monday.) **Il arrivait** (at the capital when we turned on the television set.)

In the first example, the translation *he used to arrive* gives precisely the idea of habitual action conveyed in the French phrase. You could use *arrived* (choice 3), but the nuance would be lacking. In the second example, *was arriving* indicates action in progress when something else (turning on the TV) occurred.

Do **not** use choices 1 and 2 when translating the imperfect tense of commonly used verbs such as **avoir, être, comprendre, vouloir,** and **pouvoir**.

infinitive	*imperfect*	*meaning*
avoir*	il **avait**	he had (not "*he was having*")
être*	il **était**	he was (not "*he was being*")
comprendre*	il **comprenait**	he understood (not "*he was understanding*")
vouloir*	il **voulait**	he wanted (not "*he was wanting*")
pouvoir*	il **pouvait**	he could

The incorrect translation of such forms is likely to convey a totally misleading meaning, one not intended by the French writer. In most instances, the correct English equivalent will come naturally to the native speaker of English.

B. Sample analysis.   Let us analyze the form **il examinait.** It is not present (**il examine**), and it is not future (no **r**, no infinitive); it is therefore past: *he examined.* Three translations are possible, as the ending is **-ait**, as for the conditional tense.

il **examinait**	1) he was examining (action in progress) 2) he used to examine (habitual action) 3) he examined (simple past)

The context of the reading will indicate the best selection. For instance, if the context were

Il examinait ce livre quand M. Dupont est entré.
He _____ this book when Mr. Dupont came in.

it is clear that (1) would be best. (The examination of the book was already in progress when Dupont entered.)
     Compare these verb forms.

Imperfect:	il **examin**ait	he was examining, used to examine, examined
Conditional:	il **examin**erait	he would examine
Present:	il **examin**e	he is examining, he examines
Past:	il **examin**a	he examined
Future:	il **examin**era	he will examine

44. The Verb *avoir** (to have)

Learn the following forms for identification of the verb **avoir** (*to have*).

Present Tense:

j'**ai**	I have	nous **avons**	we have
tu **as**	you have	vous **avez**	you have
il **a**	he, it has	ils **ont**	they have

Future and Conditional: Stem **aur-**

Imperfect:

j' **avais**	I had	nous **avions**	we had
tu **avais**	you had	vous **aviez**	you had
il **avait**	he had	ils **avaient**	they had

Past Definite:

j' **eus**	I had	nous **eûmes**	we had
tu **eus**	you had	vous **eûtes**	you had
il **eut**	he had	ils **eurent**	they had

Past Participle: eu, *had*

Il a eu   he has had, he had

Present Participle: ayant, *having* [Do not confuse with avant, *before* (in time).]

> *remember*
> stems   aur- (future and conditional)   eu- (past definite)
> as parts of avoir

You will find the complete conjugation of avoir in Appendix C, pages 190–193. Following are some idioms using avoir.

avoir besoin de	to need
avoir lieu	to take place
avoir beau [+ infinitive]	to [do something] in vain
avoir l'air [+ adjective]	to appear

Examples:

Il **a besoin** d'une machine à écrire.
He *needs* a typewriter.

Le concert **aura lieu** demain.
The concert *will take place* tomorrow.

Il **a beau** étudier: il ne comprend pas.
He studies *in vain*: he does not understand.

Ils **ont l'air** intelligent.
They *appear* intelligent.

Exercises

A. *Verbs*. Give English equivalents of the following verb structures.

1. a) arriver / pour arriver / il arrive / il arrivera
   b) il arriverait / ils arrivèrent / il arriva / il arrivait
   c) sans arriver / nous arrivions / nous arrivons / nous arriverons
   d) Cet événement n'arrive pas souvent. / Plusieurs voitures arrivèrent.
2. a) être* / il est / elle était / il sera / il serait
   b) il a été / nous étions / nous serons / nous serions
   c) il aura été / il aurait été / il était / il fut
   d) ils furent / ils ont été / ils étaient / il faut être

---

2. (b) été (past participle of être) been

3. a) donner / il donne / il donnait / il donnera
    b) ils donnèrent / ils ont donné / ils donneraient / ils donnent
    c) nous donnons / nous ne donnons pas / nous avons donné / nous ne donnerons rien
4. a) il y a / il y aura / il y avait / il y aurait
    b) il n'y a pas / il n'y aurait pas / il n'y avait pas / il n'y a rien d'intéressant
5. a) finir / il a fini / ils finissent / ils finirent
    b) ils finiront / ils finissaient / ils ont fini / ils finiraient
    c) je finirai / je finissais / j'aurai fini / je finirais
6. a) avoir / sans avoir / pour avoir / il a / il a eu
    b) il avait / il aura / ils auront / ils n'auraient pas
    c) j'eus / j'ai eu / j'avais / j'avais observé / je n'aurais pas fini
7. a) trouver / il a trouvé / il avait trouvé / il aura trouvé
    b) se trouver / il se trouve à Paris / il se trouvait à Paris
    c) Ils se trouveront devant un château. / Le livre se trouve sur la table.
8. a) prendre* / sans prendre / je prends / je pris
    b) il prendra / il prendrait / il aura pris / il avait pris
    c) ils prirent / ils prendront / ils prendraient / ils auraient pris
9. a) tenir / il tient / il tenait / il tiendra / il tiendrait
    b) il a tenu / il avait tenu / il aura tenu / il tint
    c) il maintient / il contient / il avait contenu / il aura retenu
10. a) il faut commencer / il faudra prendre / il faudrait observer
    b) il comprend / il comprenait / il voudrait partir
    c) ils pourront compléter / ils feront l'expérience / je viendrai voir le physicien
11. a) il découvre / ils découvriront / ils ont découvert / ils découvrirent
    b) j'ai demandé† / je demandai / j'avais demandé / je demanderai
    c) nous étudions / nous étudiions / nous étudierons / nous aurons étudié

B. Translate into good English.

12. Les garçons rêvaient à l'usage qu'ils feraient de l'argent qu'ils avaient trouvé.
13. Jacques achèterait une belle voiture de sport; il ferait un voyage en Suisse et en Italie.
14. S'il avait gagné assez d'argent, il aurait acheté une maison près du centre.
15. Au XVIIᵉ siècle la France était au niveau, sinon à la tête, du mouvement scientifique.
16. Descartes perfectionna la géométrie des courbes, ce qui lui permit de résoudre des problèmes qu'on croyait insolubles.

---

8. (a) **prendre*** to take (Look up the present tense forms, Appendix C, Irregular Verb Table 21); (b) **pris** (after a form of **avoir**, past participle of **prendre**, *to take*) 12. **rêver à** to dream about 13. **achèterait** (achèter- is the future and conditional stem of **acheter***, *to buy*); **voyage** *m.* trip; **Suisse** *f.* Switzerland 14. **s'il** if he; **gagner** to earn; **près de** near 15. **XVIIᵉ** (Centuries are designated by roman numerals); **au niveau de** abreast of 16. **courbe** *f.* curve; **lui permit** allowed him; **qu'** that; **croyait** (from **croire***, *to believe*; see Appendix C, Irregular Verb Table 5)

17. Pour Descartes comme pour Newton, le problème de l'univers physique était un problème de mécanique, et Descartes enseignera le premier, sinon la solution, du moins la vraie nature du problème.
18. Si nous n'avions pas d'orgueil, nous ne nous plaindrions pas de celui des autres.—La Rochefoucauld, *Maxime 34.*
19. Il est plus facile de connaître l'homme en général que de connaître un homme en particulier.
20. Il était une fois un roi qui était superstitieux mais qui ne voulait pas l'avouer.
21. L'astrologue prétendait† savoir ce qui arriverait dans l'avenir.
22. Nous prendrons dans cet ouvrage le terme «informatique» dans un sens limité et bien défini.
23. Si cette théorie de la radioactivité était générale, il faudrait admettre que tous les corps émettent de la radiation.
24. La dernière chose qu'on trouve en écrivant un ouvrage, est de savoir ce qu'il faut mettre la première.—Pascal.
25. Si tous les hommes savaient ce qu'ils disent les uns des autres, il n'y aurait pas quatre amis dans le monde.—Pascal, *Pensée 101.*
26. D'ordinaire mes lettres ne sont pas si longues. Le peu de temps que j'ai eu en a été cause. Je n'ai fait cette lettre si longue que parce que je n'ai pas eu le loisir de la faire plus courte.—Pascal, *Lettres provinciales*, XVI.

Readings

Le Promeneur solitaire: Rousseau chez lui

[27] De toutes les habitations où j'ai demeuré, aucune ne m'a rendu si véritablement heureux que l'Ile de Saint-Pierre au milieu du lac de Bienne. [28] Cette petite île, qu'on appelle à Neuchâtel «l'île de la Motte», est bien peu connue, même en Suisse. [29] Aucun voyageur, que je sache, n'en fait mention. Cependant elle est très agréable, et singulièrement située pour le bonheur d'un homme qui aime à se circonscrire.

---

17. **enseignera** (from **enseigner**, *to teach*); **du moins** at least; **vrai, -e** *adj.* true   18. **si** if; **orgueil** *m.* pride; **plaindre*** to complain; **celui** *pron.* that   19. **connaître*** to know; **l'homme** *m.* man (Omit the article); **que** than   20. **il était une fois** (Children's stories often begin with this phrase; **fois** means time); **roi** *m.* king; **voulait** (from **vouloir***, *to want*; see Irregular Verb Table Index, Appendix C); **l'** *pron.* it; **avouer** to admit   21. **astrologue** *m.* astrologer; **prétendre†** to claim; **avenir** *m.* future   22. **ouvrage** *m.* book; **sens** *m.* sense   24. **chose** *f.* thing; **en écrivant** in writing; **la première** first   25. **disent** (from **dire***, *to say*; see Irregular Verb Tables); **monde** *m.* world   26. **temps** *m.* time; **en** of it; **que parce que** (The first que is part of the ne...que construction; see Sec. 36); **parce que** because; **loisir** *m.* free time, leisure; **la** it   27. **où** where; **demeurer** to live; **rendu** (past participle of **rendre**, *to make, to render*); **heureux, heureuse** *adj.* happy; **que** as; **au milieu de** in the middle of; **lac** *m.* lake   28. **on appelle** is called (Note the missing link after **appelle**; skip the prepositional phrase); **connu, -e** (past participle of **connaître***)   29. **que je sache** as far as I know; **bonheur** *m.* happiness; **se circonscrire*** to have privacy

[30] Les rives du lac de Bienne sont plus sauvages et romantiques que celles du lac de Genève, parce que les rochers et les bois y bordent l'eau de plus près; [31] mais elles ne sont pas moins riantes. [32] S'il y a moins de culture de champs et de vignes, moins de villes et de maisons, il y a aussi plus de verdure naturelle, plus de prairies, d'asiles ombragés de bocages, des contrastes plus fréquents et des accidents plus rapprochés. [33] Comme il n'y a pas sur ces heureux bords de grandes routes commodes pour les voitures, le pays est peu fréquenté par les voyageurs; [34] mais il est intéressant pour les contemplatifs solitaires qui aiment à s'enivrer à loisir des charmes de la nature, et à se recueillir dans un silence que ne trouble aucun autre bruit que le cri des aigles, le ramage entrecoupé de quelques oiseaux, et le roulement des torrents qui tombent de la montagne. [35] Ce beau bassin, d'une forme presque ronde, enferme dans son milieu deux petites îles, l'une habitée et cultivée; l'autre plus petite, déserte et en friche.

[36] d'après Jean-Jacques Rousseau, *Les Rêveries d'un promeneur solitaire, Cinquième promenade*

Le Système solaire

[37] La terre que nous habitons fait partie d'un système de corps dits planètes qui tournent autour d'une étoile que nous appelons le soleil. [38] Le soleil possède au moins neuf planètes; il occupe à peu près le centre du système. [39] Il y a d'ailleurs de nombreuses comètes et des satellites de planètes qui font partie du système solaire.

[40] La terre est la troisième des planètes dans l'ordre des distances qui les séparent du soleil. [41] C'est un globe à peu près sphérique, dont le circuit est de 40.000 kilomètres et le diamètre moyen de 12.732 kilomètres. [42] Elle tourne sur elle-même en 23 heures 56 minutes 4 secondes, et autour du soleil dans l'espace de 365 jours ¼, ou une année. [43] Le diamètre autour duquel la révolution diurne s'opère s'appelle l'axe, dont les extrémités sont les pôles. [44] La terre est légèrement aplatie aux pôles.

[45] La révolution annuelle s'effectue suivant une courbe plane; c'est en effet une ellipse que décrit la terre en tournant autour du soleil. [46] L'axe de la terre

---

30. **celles** those; **rocher** *m.* rock; **y** there; **bordent** (from **border**, *to border*)   31. **riant, -e** *adj.* pleasant, agreeable   32. **culture** *f.* cultivation; **vigne** *f.* vineyard; **asile** *m.* retreat, shelter; **ombragé de** shaded by; **bocage** *m.* grove; **accidents** *m.pl.* hills (irregularities of the terrain); **rapproché** *adj.* close together   33. **comme** since; **il n'y a pas** (Missing link follows this; skip the prepositional phrase); **bord** *m.* shore; **grande route** *f.* highway; **commode** *adj.* convenient   34. **s'enivrer (de)** to delight in, become intoxicated by; **se recueillir** to collect one's thoughts; **ne trouble aucun bruit** (Place the noun before the verb); **bruit** *m.* noise; **aigle** *m.* eagle; **ramage** *m.* song, warbling; **entrecoupé** *adj.* intermittent; **oiseau** *m.* bird; **roulement** *m.* rumbling   35. **presque** *adv.* almost; **enfermer** to enfold, enclose; **habité**†, **-e** *adj.* inhabited; **en friche** uncultivated, fallow   37. **fait partie de** is part of; **dit, -e** *adj.* called; **autour** around; **étoile** *f.* star   39. **d'ailleurs** furthermore (Place it first in the sentence)   41. **circuit** *m.* circumference; **moyen, -ne** *adj.* average, mean; **kilomètres** (To convert to miles, multiply by .62137)   42. **sur elle-même** on itself, on its own axis   43. **duquel** which   44. **légèrement** *adv.* slightly; **aplatir** to flatten   45. **ellipse que** (Translate the next noun after **que**, then return to the verb: **que la terre décrit**)

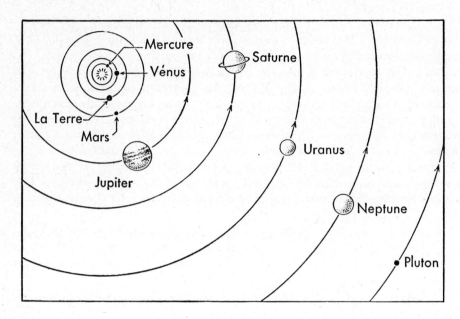

Les Planètes du soleil

est incliné (d'une façon variable) d'environ 23° 27′ 37″ à celui de l'écliptique. [47] La distance moyenne du soleil à la terre est d'environ 150 millions de kilomètres.

[48] Outre les planètes il y a des satellites qui tournent autour d'une planète principale. [49] Ainsi la terre est accompagnée, dans son mouvement de translation†, par la lune, qui tourne autour de la terre et sur elle-même. [50] La lune est 50 fois plus petite que la terre, dont elle est éloignée de 384.000 kilomètres. [51] Jupiter, la plus grande planète du soleil, a douze satellites; Saturne en a dix-sept, et de plus trois anneaux; Uranus possède quatre satellites.

[52] Des comètes innombrables se meuvent aussi autour du soleil. [53] Elles diffèrent essentiellement des planètes en ce qu'elles traversent l'espace dans tous les sens, suivant des orbites très allongées, et qu'elles sont accompagnées d'une traînée de lumière qu'on nomme la queue ou chevelure. [54] Il y a des comètes qui disparaissent et reviennent périodiquement, comme la célèbre comète dit de Halley qui reparaît tous les soixante-seize ans.

---

46. **d'environ** by about 48. **outre** in addition to 49. **ainsi** thus; **dans son mouvement de translation**† *f.* following its orbit 50. **éloigné, -e** *adj.* separated 51. **de plus** in addition; **anneau** *m.* ring 52. **se meuvent** (from **se mouvoir**, *to move*) 53. **sens** *m.* direction; **traînée** *f.* wake (like that of a ship); **queue** *f.* tail; **chevelure** *f.* coma (literally, *hair*) 54. **disparaissent** (from **disparaître***, *to disappear*); **reviennent** (from **revenir***, *to return, to come back*); **dit** called; **reparaît** (from **reparaître**, *to reappear*)

Un Esprit vif

[55] Il y avait une fois un roi qui était superstitieux, mais qui ne voulait pas l'avouer. [56] Il apprit qu'un certain homme dans son royaume prétendait† qu'il pouvait lire l'avenir dans les étoiles et prédire ce qui allait arriver.

[57] Le roi se croyait très habile et il se fâcha contre cet astrologue qui faisait ce que lui, le roi, ne pouvait faire. [58] Il le fit venir au palais royal, ayant résolu de le mettre à mort et, en même temps, de montrer à ses courtisans† que ses prétentions† étaient fausses.

[59] Suivant les ordres de leur maître deux soldats se tenaient prêts à jeter l'astrologue par la fenêtre, quand le roi leur donnerait le signal. [60] Se retournant† vers le pauvre homme qui venait d'entrer dans la grande salle du palais, le monarque lui dit:

[61] «Vous prétendez savoir ce qui va arriver dans l'avenir. [62] Eh bien, pouvez-vous prédire quand vous mourrez vous-même?»

[63] L'astrologue soupçonna ce que le roi avait l'intention de faire, et, après avoir réfléchi quelques instants, il répondit:

[64] «Sire, je ne puis pas prédire le jour de ma mort, mais je sais très bien que je mourrai exactement trois jours avant Votre Majesté.»

[65] Les deux soldats avaient beau attendre le signal. [66] Le roi se ravisa bien vite et, au lieu de tuer l'astrologue, il le pria de rester† au palais, de se soigner et de ne courir aucun danger. [67] Il fallait prendre le plus grand soin d'une vie si précieuse.

Test 7, page 231

---

56. **apprit** (from **apprendre,** *to learn, to find out*); **royaume** *m.* kingdom, realm; **prédire*** (compound of **dire***) to predict; **allait** (from **aller,** *to go*) 57. **habile** *adj.* talented; **se fâcher** to become angry; **ne pouvait faire** could not do (The **pas** of the negation is omitted with this verb sometimes; see COPS, Sec. 87) 58. **le fit venir*** summoned him (idiom, Sec. 55); **ayant** (present participle of **avoir*,** *to have*; the ending -ant on a verb indicates the English -ing ending); **résolu** (past participle of **résoudre,** *to resolve*); **mettre* à mort** to put to death; **courtisan**† *m.* courtier; **prétention**† *f.* claim; **fausse** *adj.* false 59. **suivant** (present participle of **suivre,** *to follow*); **maître** *m.* master; **soldat** *m.* soldier; **se tenir prêt** to hold oneself ready, to be prepared; **jeter*** to throw; **fenêtre** *f.* window 60. **se retourner**† to turn around; **venait d'entrer dans** had just entered (idiom, Sec. 69) 62. **eh bien** well (no meaning conveyed); **mourrez** (mourr- is the future and conditional stem of **mourir*,** *to die*) 63. **soupçonna** (from **soupçonner,** *to suspect*) 65. **avoir beau** [+ *inf.*] to [do something] in vain (idiom); **attendre** to wait for 66. **se raviser** to change one's mind; **au lieu de** instead of; **prier** to ask; **rester**† to remain; **se soigner** to take care of oneself; **courir*** to run 67. **il fallait** (from **il faut**)

8

Structures

45. Object Pronouns

A. General. A pronoun is a word that replaces a noun. It is usually used to eliminate unnecessary repetition of a noun already mentioned. Note the following English sentences, the second of which uses the pronoun *it* for this purpose.

> There is the new house. Mr. Ducrot is selling *the new house.*
> There is the new house. Mr. Ducrot is selling *it.*

B. Position of French pronouns. As you can observe in the second example above, the English pronoun is positioned exactly where the noun would have been. This is not true of French, where we find the object pronoun *before* the verb.

> Voilà la nouvelle maison. M. Ducrot vend **la nouvelle maison.**
> Voilà la nouvelle maison. M. Ducrot **la** vend.

In translating, therefore, read the verb first, then the pronoun:

> Nous **les** observons.　　We observe *them.*
> 　　2　　1　　　　　　1　　2

46. Direct and Indirect Object Pronouns

A. General. All object pronouns in French precede the verb (except in affirmative commands). The most widely used forms are the third-person forms shown on the chart below.

　　Indirect object pronouns mean *to* a person or persons. Direct object pronouns can refer to persons or things, and answer the question "what?" after the verb. For example, *Ducrot is selling...* [what?]. If the answer is *the house* or *it*, that answer is the direct object.

		indirect objects (to a person)	
le (l')*	it, him	lui	to him, to her
la (l')*	it, her		
les	them	leur	to them

The first column group is labeled *direct objects*.

---

*Both le and la become l' before a verb beginning with a vowel.

Il lit **le rapport.**	Il **le** lit.
	He is reading *it.*
Il ferme **la porte.**	Il **la** ferme.
	He is closing *it.*
Il ouvre **la porte.**	Il **l'**ouvre.
	He is opening *it.*
Il parle **au professeur.**	Il **lui** parle.
	He is talking *to him.*
Il écrit **à ses amis.**	Il **leur** écrit.
	He writes *to them.*

The other forms of the object pronouns are as follows. (Note that for these persons the forms are the same for both the direct and indirect object pronouns.)

singular		*plural*	
me	me, to me	**nous**	us, to us
te	you, to you (*familiar*)	**vous**	you, to you
vous	you, to you (*formal*)		

Direct Object:	Il vous voit.	He sees *you.*
Indirect Object:	Il vous parle.	He is talking *to you.*

B. The two *leur* forms.　How can you tell whether **leur** means *their* (belonging to them) or *to them*? When **leur** (or **leurs**) appears before a *noun*, it means *their*, and in translation it is left in its original position.

When **leur** appears in front of a *verb*, it means *to them*, and there is no **leurs** form. In translation, read the verb first and then translate **leur** as *to them*.

Il **leur** parle.	He speaks *to them.*
Il admire **leur** travail.	He admires *their* work.

47. Two Object Pronouns with a Single Verb

Sometimes there are two object pronouns before the verb. One is a direct object and the other an indirect object. As before, read the subject, skip the pronouns and go to the verb, then return to read the two object pronouns.

Jean **les lui** a donnés.
  1   2
	John gave *them to him* (*to her*).
	  1 2

Il **me l'**a racontée.
  1   2
	He told *it to me*.
	  1 2

Je **vous les** offrirai.
  1   2
	I will give *them to you*.
	  1 2

48. Compound Tenses and the Verb *être** (to be)

Compound tenses are formed with two components: the auxiliary verb (usually **avoir,** but with certain verbs **être**) plus the past participle of the main verb.

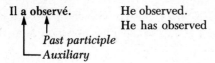

Il **a observé.**   He observed.
                          He has observed

Past participle
Auxiliary

A. The verb *être.**   Learn the present tense of **être.**

Present Tense:

je suis	I am	nous **sommes**	we are
tu **es**	you are	vous **êtes**	you are
il **est**	he is	ils **sont**	they are

When the present is used with a past participle of one of the verbs in the "house of être" (Sec. B below), the rough translations all contain a form of *have*; but you should use a one-word verb if possible whenever the auxiliary is in the present tense.

Il **est** arrivé.	He *arrived*.	(Better than *He has arrived.*)
Elle **est partie.**	She *left*.	(Better than *She has left.*)

Future and Conditional: Stem ser- [+ endings in Sec. 40B]

il sera	he will be	il serait	he would be

Notice that with verbs using **être** as an auxiliary, a form of *have* is used.

Il **sera arrivé** avant le directeur.
He *will have arrived* before the director.

Imperfect: Stem ét- [+ same endings as for the conditional tense]

j'étais	I was	nous étions	we were
tu étais	you were	vous étiez	you were
il était	he was	ils étaient	they were

Past Definite: Stem f- [+ -us type endings (Sec. 66C)]

il fut	he, it was	ils furent	they were

Past Participle: été, *been* (Used with auxiliary **avoir**)

il a été	he was
il avait été	he had been
il aura été	he will have been
il aurait été	he would have been

Present Participle: étant, *being*

étant fatigué	being tired	étant arrivé	having arrived

> *remember*
> Stems **ét-** (imperfect) **f(u)-** (past definite) **ser-** (future and conditional)
> **été** (past participle; auxiliary **avoir**)
> as parts of **être***

B. Verbs using the auxiliary *être* ("house of *être*").   The following verbs form their compound tenses with the auxiliary **être**. Notice that most of them are arranged in pairs by meaning for easier memorization.

aller,	venir	to go,	to come
entrer,	sortir	to enter,	to go out
arriver,	partir	to arrive,	to depart
monter,	descendre	to go up,	to descend
naître,	mourir	to be born,	to die
	rester	to remain	
	tomber	to fall	
	retourner	to come back	

The auxiliary **être** is always interpreted to represent a form of *to have* with the past participles of these verbs.

Il est entré.	He *came in.* (He *has entered.*)
Elle est partie.	She *has departed.*

Compounds of these verbs also use the auxiliary **être**: these include **revenir***, *to come back again;* **devenir***, *to become;* **rentrer**, *to go home.*

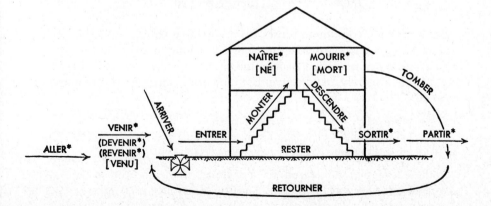

Il est revenu.	He came back.
Elle est devenue riche.	She became rich.

With verbs in the **être** group, the past participle always agrees in gender and number (like an adjective) with the subject of the sentence.

All reflexive verbs (Sec. 85) use the auxiliary **être**.

Il s'est levé.	He *got up.*
Il s'est couché.	He *went to bed.*

C. Compound past tense (passé composé).   For all other verbs the compound past tense is formed by using the present tense of the auxiliary **avoir** plus the past participle. Although literal translation is possible, usually you should convert to a one-word verb when the auxiliary is in the present tense.

Il **a compris.**	He *understood.* (Better than *He has understood.*)
Nous **avons trouvé**...	We *found*... (Better than *We have found*...)
Vous **êtes devenu**...	You *became*... (Better than *You have become*...)

D. Other compound tenses.   The auxiliary may be in any of the simple tenses. The resulting verbs can be translated literally. (The names of the tenses are given for information, but they are not essential.)

auxiliary verb tense	*example*	*meaning*	*name of tense*
Present	il **a pris**	he took	Passé composé
	il **est arrivé**	he arrived	
Imperfect	il **avait pris**	he had taken	Pluperfect
	il **était arrivé**	he had arrived	
Future	il **aura pris**	he will have taken	Future perfect
	il **sera arrivé**	he will have arrived	
Conditional	il **aurait pris**	he would have taken	Past conditional
	il **serait arrivé**	he would have arrived	
Present subjunctive	qu'il **ait pris**	that he took	Past subjunctive
	qu'il **soit arrivé**	that he arrived	

E. Distinguishing compound tenses from adjective structures.   When être is used before a past participle that does not belong to a verb in the "house of *être*" or a reflexive verb, no compound tense is involved. In such cases the past participle is merely an adjective. Use the normal meaning of être in this case (*to be*).

La porte **est** ouverte.	The door *is* open.
La leçon **est** finie.	The lesson *is* finished.
La leçon **sera** finie.	The lesson *will be* finished.

In these examples, neither **ouvrir*** nor **finir** is in the group of verbs using the auxiliary *être*; therefore a compound tense has not been formed. Use the appropriate tense of *to be* plus the past participle used as an adjective.

Exercises

A. *Object pronouns.* Translate into good English.

1. Nous examinons ce cas. Nous le trouvons compliqué.
2. Le journal décrit l'accident. Il le décrit en détail.
3. Le professeur explique sa théorie aux étudiants. Il la leur explique avec patience.
4. Le derviche donnera les chameaux aux trois fils. Il les leur donnera selon la formule de leur père.
5. Le ministre nous présentera son projet demain. Il nous le présentera à deux heures.
6. Les étudiants rendent leurs devoirs au professeur. Ils les lui rendent avant de quitter la salle.
7. Si je vois Marie, je lui dirai la nouvelle. Si je rencontre Pierre, je la lui dirai.
8. Quand j'aurai fini le rapport, je vous le donnerai tout de suite.
9. Je ne vous le donnerai pas avant de le vérifier.
10. Si Jean savait la réponse, il me la dirait.
11. C'est au début de 1975 que l'avion supersonique Concorde a été mis en service entre Paris et New York.
12. Un témoin du désastre de la flotte française à Aboukir nous l'a décrit.
13. Cette machine est-elle nécessaire? Oui, elle l'est.
14. Le roi regardait l'astrologue. Il ne le trouvait pas sympathique† mais il ne le lui dit pas.
15. L'oxygène est essentiel à la respiration des membres de l'équipage: il faut leur en fournir à bord du sous-marin.

B. *The verb être and the "house of être."* Translate.

16. Le directeur est arrivé devant l'immeuble. Il est monté au troisième étage; ensuite il est entré dans son bureau.
17. Le programmeur d'IBM est arrivé à l'aéroport vers dix heures du matin.
18. Il a pris un taxi pour aller à l'hôtel. Il est descendu du taxi devant l'hôtel Lutétia.
19. Les ingénieurs sont restés trois jours à Paris. Ils sont déjà partis.
20. L'étudiante est revenue à la bibliothèque où elle est restée pendant une heure.
21. La cathédrale de Notre-Dame de Paris fut achevée en 1245. On l'avait commencée en 1163.

---

5. **demain** tomorrow   6. **rendent** (from **rendre**, *to give*); **quitter** [+ noun] to leave [somewhere]   7. **si** if; **nouvelle** *f.* piece of news; **rencontrer** to meet, to encounter; **dirai** (from **dire***, *to say, to tell*)   8. **j'aurai fini** (The future is required in French, but not in English); **tout de suite** (synonym for **immédiatement**)   10. **savait** (from **savoir***, *to know*)   12. **témoin** *m.* witness; **flotte** *f.* fleet; **Aboukir** city in lower Egypt   13. **elle l'est** (The **l'** represents the preceding idea)   14. **sympathique**† *adj.* likeable   15. **équipage** *m.* crew (of a ship)   16. **immeuble** *m.* building; **étage** *m.* floor; **ensuite** *adv.* then   17. **vers** about, around; **du matin** A.M. (**matin** means *morning*)   20. **pendant** for, during

22. Cet événement étant arrivé, l'autre arrivera.
23. Napoléon est né en Corse mais il est mort à Sainte-Hélène en 1821.
24. La porte est fermée: on l'a fermée avant minuit.
25. Si le général avait eu le temps, il serait resté plus longtemps.
26. Le mécanicien s'est levé à six heures du matin; il s'est habillé. Ensuite il a quitté sa maison et il est allé en voiture à son travail.

Readings

Sous-marins atomiques

[27] Les premières applications des piles nucléaires mobiles intéresseront certainement la propulsion des navires, et tout d'abord celle des sous-marins.

[28] Le principal avantage escompté est un rayon† d'action pratiquement illimité sans ravitaillement en combustible et sans consommation d'oxygène.

[29] Un sous-marin pourrait naviguer pendant très longtemps en plongée, sans jamais faire surface, à la seule condition de fournir à son équipage l'oxygène nécessaire à sa respiration et de fixer l'excès de gaz carbonique exhalé, problèmes résolus depuis longtemps.

[30] L'eau qui entoure la coque d'un sous-marin assure une protection naturelle très efficace contre les rayonnements. [31] Seule la face de séparation entre la pile nucléaire et ses accessoires, d'une part, et le reste du bâtiment, d'autre part, devra recevoir un blindage convenable. [32] Au mouillage, le bâtiment devra disposer d'abris et de bassins spécialement aménagés.

[33] Le renouvellement du combustible partiellement brûlé sera facilité du fait qu'on pourra immerger les cylindres destinés à la purification soit dans des caissons dans les rades, soit en mer en certains points bien repérés où les services de récupération viendront les chercher.

[34] Deux prototypes d'installations motrices pour sous-marins sont à l'étude aux États-Unis, l'un par la General Electric au Knolls Laboratory, l'autre par la Société Westinghouse, en collaboration avec le Laboratoire d'Argonne au centre

---

24. **fermer** to close; **minuit** midnight   26. **mécanicien** *m*. mechanic; **s'est levé** (from **se lever**, *to get up*); **s'est habillé** (from **s'habiller**, *to get dressed*); **ensuite** *adv*. next, then; **travail** *m*. work   27. **navire** *m*. ship; **tout d'abord** first of all   28. **escompté** *adj*. anticipated; **rayon**† *m*. range, radius; **ravitaillement** *m*. replenishment; **combustible** *m*. fuel (So what is **ravitaillement en combustible**?)   29. **sans jamais** without ever; **depuis longtemps** a long time ago   30. **entourer** to surround; **coque** *f*. hull, shell; **rayonnement** *m*. radiation   31. **face de séparation** bulkhead, partition; **pile** *f*. reactor, pile; **d'une part...d'autre part** on the one hand...on the other hand); **devra** (from **devoir***) will have to; **blindage** *m*. shielding; **convenable** *adj*. appropriate   32. **mouillage** *m*. mooring; **disposer de** [X] to have [X] available; **abri** *m*. shelter; **aménager** to arrange   33. **brûlé** (past participle of **brûler**, *to burn*); **du fait** by the fact; **soit...soit** either...or; **destiné** à intended for; **caisson** *m*. receptacle; **rade** *f*. port; **en mer** at sea; **repéré** (past participle of **repérer**, *to mark*); **récupération** *f*. salvage; **chercher** to get, to seek   34. **à l'étude** under study

d'Arco dans l'Idaho. [35] Le premier doit utiliser une pile à neutrons intermédiaires avec refroidissement par un métal fondu.

[36] Le second, dont la construction est commencée, utilisera des neutrons lents et probablement de l'hélium pour le refroidissement de la pile. [37] On évalue les frais d'établissement de ce prototype à 26 millions de dollars.

La Mer

[38] La surface du globe se compose de grandes masses de terres appelées continents, et de grands bassins d'eau nommés mers. [39] A vrai dire il n'y a qu'une seule mer qui s'étend d'un pôle à l'autre, en couvrant à peu près les trois quarts de la surface de la terre. [40] Pour plus de commodité† on a divisé cette mer en plusieurs sections auxquelles on a donné des noms différents. [41] On distingue les mers extérieures, qui entourent les continents et les îles, des mers intérieures ou méditerranées, qui sont comprises entre les continents, mais qui pourtant communiquent avec la mer extérieure par une portion d'eau resserrée entre deux terres, et qui, suivant les pays, prend les noms de détroit, pas (e.g. le Pas de Calais), canal†, manche, ou bras.

[42] La mer pénètre dans certaines terres et y forme des enfoncements qu'on nomme golfes ou baies, lorsqu'ils ont une certaine dimension; s'ils sont d'une étendue assez peu considérable pour offrir un abri aux vaisseaux, ils prennent le nom de port, havre, anse ou rade.

[43] L'eau de la mer contient du sel commun (chlorure de sodium), du sulfate de soude, du chlorure de calcium et du chorure de magnésium.

[44] La couleur de la mer varie beaucoup; elle est vert-bouteille dans l'Atlantique qui baigne les côtes de France, de Hollande, et d'Allemagne; bleue dans la Méditerranée et dans les hautes latitudes, surtout quand elle est calme. [45] Dans le golfe de Guinée la mer est blanche; vermeille dans le golfe de Californie, et noire aux attérages des Maldives. [46] La mer Noire mérite bien son nom sur une partie des côtes de la Russie méridionale.

[47] Quand la mer est phosphorescente, sa surface tout entière paraît être en feu. [48] Ce phénomène, causé par la présence de divers† protozoaires et noctiluques, se montre communément dans les mers des pays chauds, où on le voit dans toute sa beauté; cependant on l'observe aussi dans les hautes latitudes.

---

35. **doit** (from **devoir***) is to, must; **refroidissement** *m.* cooling; **fondu** *adj.* molten, melted   37. **frais** *m.pl.* costs   39. **à vrai dire** in fact, to tell the truth; **les trois quarts** three-quarters   40. **commodité**† *f.* convenience; **auxquelles** to which   41. **compris** (past participle of **comprendre***, *to include*); **resserré** (past participle of **resserrer**, *to constrict*); **suivant** depending on; **détroit** *m.* narrows; **pas** *m.* strait; **Pas de Calais** Straits of Dover; **canal**† *m.* channel; **manche** *f.* channel (**la Manche** is *the English Channel*); **bras** *m.* arm   42. **y** in them; **enfoncement** *m.* bay; **lorsque** when; **étendue** *f.* size; **assez peu considérable** (see note, Sec. 22); **havre** *m.* harbor; **anse** *f.* bay   43. **sel** *m.* salt; **chlorure** *m.* chloride; **soude** *f.* soda   44. **couleur** *f.* color; **vert-bouteille** bottle-green; **baigne** (from **baigner**, *to bathe, to wash*); **côte** *f.* coast; **Allemagne** *f.* Germany   45. **vermeille** bright red, vermillion; **attérage** *m.* land approaches   46. **méridional, -e** *adj.* southern   47. **tout entière** entire (Here, **tout** is an adverb); **en feu** on fire   48. **divers**† various; **protozoaire** *m.* protozoan; **noctiluques** *f.pl.* phosphorescent organisms, noctiluca; **se montrer** to appear, to show itself; **chaud, -e** *adj.* warm

[49] La mer est sillonnée de toutes parts par des courants. [50] Dans l'Atlantique, le plus considérable est le gulf-stream, qui, partant du golfe du Mexique, s'avance jusqu'au cap Nord et au Spitzberg où il porte des fruits et les bois de l'Amérique tropicale. [51] Il se ramifie en diverses branches dont l'une, plus considérable que toutes les autres, redescend le long de la côte occidentale de l'Afrique.

[52] Quelquefois la mer est complètement calme. [53] Quand le vent souffle, la longueur et la hauteur de ses vagues varient suivant la force du vent, la proximité et la forme des continents. [54] Les vagues les plus hautes que l'on ait observées ne paraissent pas avoir dépassé vingt mètres. [55] Cependant une vague géante dont la hauteur dépassa trente-quatre mètres a été observée en 1933.

L'Étranger

[56] J'ai bien travaillé toute la semaine, Raymond est venu et m'a dit qu'il avait envoyé la lettre. [57] Je suis allé au cinéma deux fois avec Emmanuel qui ne comprend pas toujours ce qui se passe sur l'écran. [58] Il faut alors lui donner des explications. Hier, c'était samedi et Marie est venue. [59] Nous avons pris un autobus et nous sommes allés à quelques kilomètres d'Alger, sur une plage resserrée entre des roches et bordée de roseaux du côté de la terre.

[60] Ce matin, Marie est restée et je lui ai dit que nous déjeunerions ensemble. Je suis descendu pour acheter de la viande.

[61] Devant la porte, nous avons parlé avec Raymond, puis nous avons décidé de prendre l'autobus. La plage n'était pas loin, mais nous irions plus vite ainsi. [62] Raymond pensait que son ami serait content de nous voir arriver tôt. [63] Nous allions partir quand Raymond m'a fait signe de regarder en face. J'ai vu un groupe d'Arabes adossés à la devanture du bureau de tabac. [64] Ils nous regardaient en silence. Nous sommes allés vers l'arrêt d'autobus qui était un peu plus loin et Raymond m'a annoncé que les Arabes ne nous suivaient pas. [65] Je me suis retourné. Ils étaient toujours à la même place et ils regardaient avec la même indifférence l'endroit que nous venions de quitter.

d'après Albert Camus, *L'Étranger*

Test 8, page 233

---

49. sillonné (past participle of **sillonner**, *to furrow*)   50. **partant** (present participle of **partir***, *to start, to leave*); **cap**† *m.* cape; **Spitzberg** Spitzbergen   51. **se ramifier** to branch out; **redescendre** (a compound of **descendre**; translate the re- as *again* at the appropriate place in the English equivalent); **le long de** along; **occidental, -e** *adj.* western   53. **souffler** to blow; **hauteur** *f.* height   54. **dépasser** to exceed   55. **géant, -e** *adj.* giant; **trente-quatre** (See Numbers, Appendix D)   56. **semaine** *f.* week; **envoyé** (past participle of **envoyer***, *to send*)   57. **toujours** *adv.* always, still; **se passer** (synonym for **arriver**, *to happen*); **écran** *m.* screen   58. **hier** yesterday; **samedi** Saturday   59. **plage** *f.* beach; **entre** *prep.* between; **roche** *f.* rock; **bordée de** bordered with; **roseau** *m.* reed; **du côté de** on the side toward   60. **déjeuner** to have lunch; **viande** *f.* meat   61. **puis** then; **vite** *adv.* quickly   62. **tôt** early   63. **a fait signe** gestured (literally, *made a signal*); **en face** opposite; **adossé** leaning up against; **devanture** *f.* storefront; **bureau de tabac** *m.* tobacco shop   64. **arrêt** *m.* stop; **suivaient** (imperfect of **suivre***, *to follow*)   65. **se retourner** to turn around; **endroit** *m.* place, location; **venions de** had just (See Sec. 69)

Essential Word Review II

Chapters 5–8

This list includes essential words found in the notes, plus indented related words to be learned.

Verbs

acheter* to buy
  vendre to sell
arriver to arrive, to happen
  partir* to depart, to leave
arriver à to succeed in
chercher to look for, to get
  trouver to find
comprendre* to understand, to include
connaître* to be acquainted with
croire* to believe
  penser (à) to think (about)
découvrir* to discover
décrire* to describe
demander to ask (for)
devoir* must, ought to
   doit *pres.*
exiger to require
faire* partie de to be a part of
gagner to gain, to win, to earn
  perdre to lose
intéresser to interest, to concern
montrer to show
se passer to happen
  arriver to happen, to arrive
prendre* to take
   donner, offrir to give
quitter [+ noun] to leave [+ noun]
rendre to give, to render
rester to remain
sortir* (de) to go out (of), to leave
  entrer (dans [+ place]) to go in, to enter
tenir à to be eager to
travailler to work
traverser to cross
voir* to see
  regarder to look at

Nouns

la chose   thing
un endroit   place, location
un étage   floor
le matin   morning
le sens   direction
le temps   time
la terre   earth

Adjectives

chaque   each
convenable   appropriate
dernier, dernière   last
 premier, première   first
divers, -e   various
même (*before a noun*)   same
moyen, moyenne   average
notre   our

Adverbs

d'abord   first, first of all
 enfin   finally
déjà   already
 pas encore   not yet
demain   tomorrow
 aujourd'hui / hier   today / yesterday
ensuite, alors, puis   next, then
légèrement   slightly
où   where, when (time)
 ou *conj.*   or
 ou...ou   either...or
plutôt   rather
presque   almost
quelquefois, parfois   sometimes
réellement, en réalité   actually, in fact
tard   late
tôt   early
toujours   always, still

Other structural words and phrases

afin de   in order to
après   after
 avant   before (in time)

au moins / tout au moins   at least
aussi…que   just as…as
cela   that
ce qui, ce que   what
chez   at the home of, at the place of
business of, in the case of
comme   like, as, since
d'une part…d'autre part   on the one
hand…on the other hand
en effet   in fact
en réalité   actually, really
entre   between
il fallait   it was necessary
il reste   it remains
jusqu'à [+ noun]   as far as
jusqu'à ce que [+ clause]   until
pendant   during
pourtant   however
près de   near
loin de   far from
qu'est-ce qui   what
selon   according to
si   if, so [+ adjective or adverb]
soit…soit   either…or
vers   toward

9

Structures

49. Present Participles

French verb forms ending in **-ant** may be translated by an English equivalent ending in **-ing**.

contenant	containing
arrivant	arriving

This form is called the present participle. If it is preceded by **en**, translate **en** with the word *by* (if method is meant) or *while* (if the action is intended to be simultaneous with another action).

en finissant	by, while finishing
en considérant	by, while considering
en parlant	by, while speaking

The present participle of regular verbs is easily identified, but some irregular verbs have less recognizable forms that should be learned.

infinitive	present participle	meaning
être	étant	being, having
avoir	ayant	having
faire	faisant	doing, making
savoir	sachant	knowing
dire	disant	saying

50. Adjective Comparisons

A. Comparative form. The comparative of adjectives is expressed by placing **plus** (*more*) or **moins** (*less*) before the adjective.

un problème simple	a simple problem
un problème **plus** simple	a simple*r* problem
un problème **moins** simple	a *less* simple problem

When the adjective is one that normally precedes the noun (see the list in Sec. 15), the comparative forms also precede the noun.

une petite maison	a small house
une **plus** petite maison	a small*er* house

The adjective **bon, bonne** (*good*) has an irregular comparative form: **meilleur** (*m.*), **meilleure** (*f.*).

un bon livre	a good book
un **meilleur** livre	a *better* book
une **meilleure** idée	a *better* idea

B. Superlative form.   The superlative of adjectives is expressed by **le plus, la plus, les plus** (*most*) or **le moins, la moins, les moins** (*least*). The superlative form of the adjective usually follows the noun.

le problème **le plus** simple	the simple*st* problem
l'expérience **la plus** précise	the *most* precise experiment
l'article **le moins** précis	the *least* precise article

When a preceding adjective is used, the only difference between comparative and superlative is that the latter uses **le, la,** or **les.**

une plus grande maison	a big*ger* house
la plus grande maison	the big*gest* house

C. Comparisons with nouns and adjectives.   To compare quantities, French uses these constructions.

plus de...que	*more* [+ noun +] *than*
autant de...que	*as much* [+ noun +] *as* or *as many* [+ noun +] *as*
moins de...que	*fewer* [+ noun +] *than*

Jean a examiné **plus de** livres **que** Georges.
John examined *more* books *than* George.

Valérie a examiné **autant de** livres **que** vous.
Valerie examined *as many* books *as* you.

Pierre a examiné **moins de** livres **que** nous.
Pierre examined *fewer* books *than* we.

To compare a quality, French uses the following constructions.

plus...que	*more* [+ adjective +] *than*
aussi...que	*as* [+ adjective +] *as*
moins...que	*less* [+ adjective +] *than*

Paul est **plus** généreux **que** Louis.
Paul is *more* generous *than* Louis.

Marie est **aussi** généreuse **que** Marc.
Marie is (just) *as* generous *as* Mark.

Alain est **moins** généreux qu'Anne.
Alan is *less* generous *than* Anne.

D. Comparison of numbers.   When a number follows **plus** or **moins**, French uses **de** instead of **que** to mean *than*.

Il a plus **de** trois mille échantillons.   He has more *than* 3000 specimens.

51. The Pronoun *celui* (the one)

A. General.   Learn the following translations, which will always fit the context of passages being translated.

	singular		plural	
masculine	**celui**	the one	**ceux**	those (the ones)
feminine	**celle**		**celles**	

Note the sign of the plural: **-x, -s.**

reference

Nous étudions les satellites de Jupiter et **ceux** de Saturne.
We are studying the satellites of Jupiter and *those* of Saturn.

Note: **celui** replaces a noun already mentioned, to avoid an awkward repetition of the noun. In the above example, the use of **ceux** avoided repetition of **les satellites;** the form **ceux** (masculine plural) was selected because it represented a masculine plural noun (**les satellites**).

B. Special case.   When two nouns have previously been mentioned, the suffixes **-ci** (*the latter*) and **-là** (*the former*) are often appended to the appropriate form of **celui** for reference purposes.

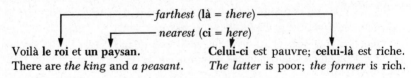

Voilà **le roi** et **un paysan**.   **Celui-ci** est pauvre; **celui-là** est riche.
There are *the king* and *a peasant*.   *The latter* is poor; *the former* is rich.

52. The Verb *prendre** (to take)

Learn the forms of **prendre**; the same basic forms are used in several compounds of this verb, such as **apprendre** (*to learn*), **comprendre** (*to understand*), **entreprendre** (*to undertake*), **se méprendre** (*to be mistaken*), **reprendre** (*to take back, to continue*), and **surprendre** (*to surprise*).

Present Tense:

je **prends**	I am taking, take	nous **prenons**	we are taking, take
tu **prends**	you are taking, take	vous **prenez**	you are taking, take
il **prend**	he, it is taking, takes	ils **prennent**	they are taking, take

Future and Conditional: Stem **prendr-** (Regular in formation)

Past Definite: Stem **pr-** [+ is type endings (Sec. 66C)]

je **pris**	I took	nous **prîmes**	we took
tu **pris**	you took	vous **prîtes**	you took
il **prit**	he took	ils **prirent**	they took

Past Participle: **pris**, *taken* (Used with auxiliary **avoir**)

Present Participle: **prenant**, *taking*

53. The Verb *faire** (to make, to do)

Present Tense:

je **fais**	I am doing, do	nous **faisons**	we are doing, do
tu **fais**	you are doing, do	vous **faites**	you are doing, do
il **fait**	he is doing, does	ils **font**	they are doing, do

Future and Conditional: Stem **fer-**

Past Definite: Stem **f-** [+ is type endings (Sec. 66)]

je **fis**	I did, made	nous **fîmes**	we did, made
tu **fis**	you did, made	vous **fîtes**	you did, made
il **fit**	he did, made	ils **firent**	they did, made

Past Participle: **fait**, *done, made* (Used with auxiliary **avoir**)

Present Participle: **faisant**, *doing, making*

Special Cases:

Il fait beau (mauvais).	The weather is fine (bad).
faire partie de...	to be part of..., to be a member of...
faire semblant de...	to pretend to...
faire son possible	to do one's best
faire remarquer que...	to point out that...
se faire	to occur, to happen

Examples:

Ce monsieur **fera partie de** la société.
This gentleman *will be a member of* the organization.

Cet animal **a fait semblant de** dormir.
This animal *pretended to* sleep.

Cela *se fait* avec lenteur.
That *happens* slowly.

Special Use: **faire***[+ infinitive] (See Sec. 55)

Exercises

A. *Present participles.* Give English equivalents of the following phrases.

1. en parlant français
2. en suivant les côtes
3. en abandonnant le projet
4. en obtenant des données
5. en résistant à la pression
6. en l'abandonnant
7. en faisant son possible
8. en disant ces mots
9. en fournissant de l'oxygène
10. étant difficile à faire
11. la voiture étant arrivée
12. l'événement étant arrivé
13. en considérant ce cas
14. en voyant le livre
15. sachant les faits
16. en les prenant
17. ayant fini l'expérience
18. ayant trouvé la solution
19. étant parti pour Londres
20. en faisant semblant de comprendre

B. Translate. In sentences containing **en** plus a past participle, be sure to differentiate **en** meaning *by* (expressing method) and **en** meaning *while* (expressing simultaneity).

21. François a réussi à l'examen en étudiant le français.
22. Pierre regardait la télévision en prenant du café.
23. Ayant développé un nouvel appareil, ce scientifique a contribué au progrès de notre étude.

---

8. **mot** *m.* word   9. **fournir** to furnish, to provide   15. **sachant** (present participle of **savoir***, *to know*)   19. **Londres** London   21. **réussir** to succeed, to pass (an exam); **le français** French (language)   22. **regarder** to watch   23. **appareil** *m.* apparatus

24. Suivant les ordres de leur maître, les deux soldats se tenaient prêts à jeter l'astrologue par la fenêtre.
25. Etant née à Paris de parents suisses, Madame de Staël était une des femmes les plus importantes de son temps.
26. On obtient ainsi des monolithes n'exerçant qu'une pression verticale.
27. La psychologie expérimentale considère la conduite du sujet comme une fonction des variables qui caractérisent l'*organisme* (ce mot étant pris au sens le plus large† et pouvant être remplacé par «personnalité»).

C. *Comparisons and celui.* Translate the following sentences.

28. Mais à ce moment-là je rencontrai des obstacles aussi grands que ceux que je voulais éviter.
29. J'ai trouvé une méthode aussi simple qu'utile pour faire toutes sortes d'opérations mathématiques.
30. Le gaz carbonique est beaucoup moins actif que l'oxygène.
31. Les vagues de la mer Méditerranée sont souvent aussi hautes que celles de l'Atlantique.
32. La comète de Halley est la plus célèbre de toutes les comètes.
33. Il y a aujourd'hui une puissance qui s'élève au-dessus des lois: c'est celle de l'ambition politique.
34. Les victoires du comte de Grasse contribuèrent à celles de Washington et de La Fayette.
35. L'autorité du gouvernement vient du consentement de ceux qui se sont soumis à cette autorité.
36. Toutes les fictions de l'incendie de Troie n'égaleront jamais la réalité de celui de Moscou, selon Bonaparte.
37. La base de l'enveloppe extérieure du soleil s'appelle la chromosphère: le passage de celle-ci à la photosphère s'effectue par une mince† zone intermédiaire, dite *couche renversante*.
38. Après avoir comparé les résultats du test d'un sujet avec ceux d'autres sujets, le conseiller d'orientation prend une décision.
39. Un triangle isocèle est celui qui a deux côtés égaux.
40. La France reste membre de l'alliance politique, mais ne fait plus partie de l'organisation militaire.

---

26. **exercer** to exert; **pression** *f.* pressure   27. **conduite** *f.* conduct, behavior; **sens** *m.* sense, meaning; **large†** *adj.* wide; **pouvant** (present participle of **pouvoir**, *to be able*); **remplacer** to replace   28. **rencontrer** to meet, to encounter; **voulais** (from **vouloir***, *to want*); **éviter** to avoid   33. **aujourd'hui** today; **puissance** *f.* power; **s'élever** to rise; **au-dessus de** above; **loi** *f.* law   34. **comte** *m.* Count (title); **de Grasse** (François-Joseph-Paul) (marin français qui se distingua pendant la guerre de l'indépendance américaine)   35. **consentement** *m.* consent; **se soumettre*** to subject oneself   36. **incendie** *m.* burning; **Troie** Troy; **égaler** to equal; **Moscou** Moscow   37. **s'effectuer** to be effected, to be accomplished; **mince†** *adj.* thin; **couche** *f.* layer; **renversant, -e** *adj.* reversing   38. **résultat** *m.* result; **conseiller d'orientation** *m.* guidance counsellor

Readings

En Suisse

[41] Il faut attribuer au caractère germanique une grande partie des vertus de la Suisse allemande. [42] Néanmoins il y a plus d'esprit public en Suisse qu'en Allemagne, plus de patriotisme, plus d'énergie, plus d'accord dans les opinions et les sentiments; [43] mais aussi la petitesse des États et la pauvreté du pays n'y excitent en aucune manière le génie; [44] on y trouve bien moins de savants et de penseurs que dans le nord de l'Allemagne, où le relâchement même des liens politiques donne l'essor à toutes les nobles rêveries, à tous les systèmes hardis qui ne sont point soumis à la nature des choses. [45] Les Suisses ne sont pas une nation poétique, et l'on s'étonne, avec raison, que l'admirable aspect de leur contrée n'ait pas enflammé davantage leur imagination. [46] Toutefois un peuple religieux et libre est toujours susceptible d'un genre d'enthousiasme, et les occupations matérielles de la vie ne sauraient l'étouffer entièrement. [47] On serait convaincu de cela par la fête des bergers, qui a été célébrée l'année dernière au milieu des lacs, en mémoire du fondateur de Berne.

[48] Cette ville de Berne mérite plus que jamais le respect et l'intérêt des voyageurs. Ses établissements de charité sont peut-être les mieux soignés de l'Europe: l'hôpital est l'édifice le plus beau, le seul magnifique de la ville. [49] Tout, dans la ville et le canton de Berne, porte l'empreinte d'un ordre sérieux et calme, d'un gouvernement digne et paternel. [50] Un air de probité se fait sentir dans chaque objet que l'on aperçoit; on se croit en famille au milieu de deux cent mille hommes, que l'on appelle nobles, bourgeois ou paysans, mais qui sont tous également dévoués à la patrie.

d'après Madame de Staël, *De l'Allemagne*, Volume 1, Chapitre 20

L'Encyclopédie: L'Autorité politique

[51] Aucun homme n'a reçu de la nature le droit de commander aux autres. [52] La liberté est un présent du ciel, et chaque individu a le droit d'en jouir

---

42. **néanmoins** nevertheless; **Allemagne** *f.* Germany; **accord** *m.* agreement, harmony   43. **petitesse** *f.* smallness; **état** *m.* state; **pauvreté** *f.* poverty; **génie** *m.* genius   44. **savant** *m.* scientist; **penseur** *m.* thinker; **nord** *m.* north; **relâchement** *m.* relaxation; **même** very; **lien** *m.* bond, connection; **donner l'essor** to give rise to; **hardi, -e** *adj.* bold; **ne...point** (more emphatic than **ne...pas**)   45. **s'étonner** to be astonished; **avec raison** rightly; **ait** (from **avoir**) has; **davantage** *adv.* more   46. **toutefois** in any case; **genre** *m.* kind; **ne sauraient** could not (See Sec. 87 on **ne** used alone); **étouffer** to stifle, to suppress   47. **convaincu** (past participle of **convaincre***, to convince); **fête** *f.* festival; **berger** *m.* shepherd   48. **soigné** (past participle of **soigner**, *to care for*)   49. **empreinte** *m.* imprint; **digne** *adj.* worthy   50. **se fait sentir** makes itself felt; **chaque** *adj.* each, every; **aperçoit** (from **apercevoir***, *to see, to perceive*); **au milieu de** in the midst of; **bourgeois** middle-class; **paysan** farmer, rural folk; **dévoué** (past participle of **dévouer**, *to devote*); **patrie** *f.* native land (**Dévoué à la patrie** can be translated by a single adjective in English, beginning with *pat-*)   51. **reçu** (past participle of **recevoir***, *to receive*)   52. **ciel** *m.* heaven; **droit** *m.* right; **en jouir** to enjoy it

aussitôt qu'il jouit de la raison. [53] Si la nature a établi quelque autorité, c'est la puissance paternelle. Mais la puissance paternelle a ses bornes; et dans l'état de nature elle finirait aussitôt que les enfants seraient en état de se conduire. [54] Toute autre autorité vient d'une autre origine que la nature. [55] Si l'on examine bien, on la fera toujours remonter à l'une de ces deux sources: ou la force et la violence de celui qui s'en est emparé; ou le consentement de ceux qui se sont soumis par un contrat fait ou supposé entre eux et la personne à qui ils ont cédé l'autorité.

[56] La puissance acquise par la violence n'est qu'une usurpation. Elle ne dure qu'autant que la force de celui qui commande l'emporte sur celle de ceux qui obéissent, [57] de sorte que si ces derniers deviennent à leur tour les plus forts, et qu'ils secouent le joug, ils le font avec justice. [58] La même loi qui a fait l'autorité la défait alors: c'est la loi du plus fort....

d'après Denis Diderot, *L'Encyclopédie*

Les Dauphins

[59] Le cerveau des dauphins est presque égal au nôtre. S'ils n'ont pas un langage au sens strict (ce qui n'est pas démontré), ils peuvent certainement communiquer entre eux. Ils vivent assez longtemps (20 à 30 ans au moins, autant qu'un homme préhistorique) pour acquérir expérience et savoir.

[60] C'est grâce à leur système d'écholocation qu'ils peuvent repérer et saisir leurs proies. L'appareil acoustique est en effet particulièrement développé chez les dauphins. Leur vie s'équilibre grâce à une constante exploration acoustique réalisée par l'écholocation. Ils sont sans cesse à l'écoute, aux aguets dans la mer. [61] C'est évidemment chez eux le sens qui domine. Aussi constate-t-on un grand développement du nerf auditif, le huitième, qui est le plus gros des nerfs crâniens. Dans le cortex, le centre auditif est exceptionnellement large. L'oreille est modifiée pour percevoir dans l'eau.

[62] Des expériences ont montré que les dauphins percevaient des fréquences de 150 kilohertz: 150 000 vibrations par seconde. La limite de l'audition humaine est de 14 à 16 kilohertz, ce qui correspond à un coup de sifflet strident. Celle des

---

52. **aussitôt que** as soon as   53. **borne** *f.* limit; **se conduire*** to conduct one's own affairs   55. **la fera...remonter** trace it back; **ou...ou** either...or; **s'en est emparé de** has seized it; **se sont soumis** have submitted; **eux** *pron.* them (See Sec. 79)   56. **autant que** *conj.* as long as; **l'emporter sur** to prevail over   57. **de sorte que** so that; **derniers** latter; **et qu'** and that (Here **qu'** is used instead of repeating the whole conjunction **de sorte que**); **secouer le joug** to shake off the yoke; **avec justice** (Use an adverb ending in *-ly*)   58. **défait** (present of **défaire***, *to destroy, to undo*)   59. **cerveau** *m.* brain; **dauphin** *m.* dolphin; **savoir** *m.* knowledge   60. **écholocation** *f.* (cognate); **repérer** to locate; **proie** *f.* prey; **s'équilibrer** to keep in balance, (here) to sustain; **à l'écoute** listening; **aux aguets** on the alert   61. **nerf** *m.* nerve; **crânien** *adj.* cranial; **percevoir** to hear sounds (literally, *to perceive*)   62. **coup de sifflet** *m.* blast of a whistle

singes est de 33 kilohertz, des chats de 50, des souris de 90. Seules les chauves-souris dépassent les dauphins en percevant des fréquences de 175 kilohertz.

[63] Le sens social des dauphins et leur attachement l'un pour l'autre ont donné à penser qu'ils étaient enclins à s'entraider. Nous avons été bien souvent témoins de scènes qui attestent la solidarité dont les mammifères marins sont capables. [64] A bord de la *Calypso* nous avons à plusieurs reprises constaté en pleine mer que, lorsque dans un banc un dauphin était blessé, deux ou trois de ses compagnons s'approchaient de lui pour le soutenir et l'aider. [65] Tout le groupe stoppait à faible distance et semblait attendre ce qui allait se passer. Si au bout d'un certain temps, les deux ou trois «parents†» ou «amis» du blessé ne réussissaient pas à lui faire reprendre la route, le banc tout entier se remettait en marche. [66] Ceux qui étaient intervenus les premiers auprès du blessé étaient bien obligés de l'abandonner sous peine de mort, car un dauphin ne peut pas vivre seul dans la mer, loin des siens.

d'après Jacques-Yves Cousteau et Philippe Diolé, *Les Dauphins et la liberté*

Test 9, page 235

---

62. **singe** *m.* monkey; **souris** *f.* mouse; **chauve-souris** *f.* bat   63. **entraider** to help each other; **mammifère** *m.* mammal   64. **à plusieurs reprises** several times, on several occasions; **en pleine mer** on the open sea, at sea; **banc** *m.* school (of fish); **soutenir** to sustain   65. **à faible distance** a short distance away; **reprendre la route** to resume the journey   66. **auprès de** *prep.* at the side of; **sous peine de mort** (here) or risk death

10

Structures

54. Inverted Word Order

A. Usage. In French, as in English, the usual order of words in a statement is the subject first, and the verb second.

Nous examinons ces données.   We are examining these data.
  1   2   1   2

In certain types of French sentences, however, an inverted word order is used—the order of the subject and the verb is reversed. This occurs mainly in questions; after certain adverbs including **peut-être** (*perhaps*), **aussi** (*therefore*), and **toujours** (*still*); and with explanatory verbs such as **dit-il** (*he said*) and **s'exclama-t-elle** (*she exclaimed*) used in direct quotations.

Observe the following examples.

Questions:
Parlez-vous français?
Do you speak French?

After Certain Adverbs:
Peut-être **viendra-t-il.**
Perhaps *he will come.*

Aussi **reste-t-elle** à la maison.
Therefore *she is remaining* at home.

Toujours **est-il** possible de trouver une solution.
It is still possible to find a solution.

Explanatory Verbs in Quotations:
—Bonjour, **dit-il.** Je suis arrivé.
"Hello," *he said.* "I have arrived."

Note that in translation you should use the correct sentence patterns of English. Thus, in questions, you may need to use *do*, as in the first example. In the next three examples, note the position of the adverbs at the beginning of the sentences. When these adverbs are positioned after the subject or verb, the word order is normal, and **aussi** and **toujours** take on their more common meaning of *also* or *too* and *always*.

Il viendra **peut-être**.   Elle **aussi** reste à la maison.
Perhaps he will come.   She is remaining at home *too*.
He may come.

Il est **toujours** possible de trouver une solution.
It is *always* possible to find a solution.

B. Punctuation of direct quotations.   The example pertaining to explanatory verbs in quotations shows the difference between French and English punctuation of a direct quotation. Note the French use of a dash before the words spoken. In English only the actual words spoken are enclosed in quotation marks; the explanatory verbs (*he said*) are not included.

C. Inversion after *que* or *qu'*.   When a clause introduced by **que** is immediately followed by a verb, skip the verb and go to the next independent noun group (one that is not part of a prepositional phrase). Then return to read the verb and the rest of the sentence.

> *remember*
> 1. Read **que** or **qu'** as *that*. (This does not apply to **qui**.)
> 2. Read the next noun group.
> 3. Return to the verb, then the remainder of the sentence.

Consider the following sentence.

Voilà les données qu'a examinées ce physicien.
　　　　　　　　1　　　3　　　　　　　2

Read normally up to **qu'** (*that*), skip to **ce physicien**, then return to the verb. The result is

There are the data *that this physicist* examined.
　　　　　　　1　　　　2　　　　　3

The examples below illustrate the procedure.

C'est sur ce principe qu'est basée l'analyse thermique.
　　　　　　　　　　que　　verb　　next noun
　　　　　　　　　　1　　　3　　　　2

It is on this principle *that thermal analysis* is based.
　　　　　　　　　　1　　　2　　　　　3

Voici un cas que n'explique aucun trouble organique.
　　　　　　que　　verb　　　　subject
　　　　　　1　　　3　　　　　2

Here is a case *that no organic trouble explains.*
　　　　　1　　　　2　　　　　3

If the noun already comes directly after **que**, read using the French word order.

C'est sur cette hypothèse **que** l'analyse est basée.
It is upon this hypothesis *that* the analysis is based.

55. Causative *faire*

A. General. The verb **faire** plus an infinitive means *to cause* [something] *to be done*.

When a form of **faire** is followed by an infinitive, use the following procedure.

1. Read **faire** as a form of *to cause*, using the appropriate tense.
2. Skip the infinitive.
3. Read the next noun structure (not a prepositional phrase).
4. Return to read the infinitive as *to be* plus the past participle of that verb.

This results in a rough translation that can be converted into more acceptable English using a form of *to have* [something done].

Le professeur **fera bâtir** une maison.
1   3   2

Rough Translation: The teacher *will cause* a house *to be built*.
                          1   2   3

Finished Translation: The teacher *will have* a house *built*.

Le roi **a fait venir** l'astrologue au palais royal.
The king *caused* the astrologer *to come* to the royal palace.
The king *had* the astrologer *come* to the royal palace.

The verb **faire** may be in the present, past, or future. Note the use of the past (**a fait**) in the last example.

B. Object pronouns with the causative *faire* construction. Direct and indirect object pronouns may replace nouns in the **faire** construction.

Le professeur fait avancer **les étudiants**.
The teacher has *the students* advance.

Le professeur **les** fait avancer.
The teacher has *them* advance.

La patience fait connaître la solution **aux physiciens**.
Patience makes the solution known *to the physicists*.

La patience **leur** fait connaître la solution.
Patience makes the solution known *to them*.

C. Fixed combinations.   Certain combinations of **faire** and an infinitive are so common that you may immediately substitute a single verb for them.

faire remarquer	to point out
faire voir	to show
faire savoir	to inform
faire arriver	to deliver
faire intervenir	to involve
faire semblant de	to pretend
faire venir	to summon

For example,

Il **fera voir** l'appareil aux professeurs.
He *will show* the apparatus to the teachers.
(Omit the step *He will cause the apparatus to be seen....*)

Il **le leur** fera voir.
He will show *it* to *them*.

56. The Verb *mettre** (to put)

The compounds of **mettre*** follow the same patterns as **mettre***: **admettre*** (*to admit*), **commettre*** (*to commit*), **émettre*** (*to emit*), **omettre*** (*to omit*), **permettre*** (*to permit*), **promettre*** (*to promise*), **soumettre*** (*to submit*), **transmettre*** (*to transmit*).

Present Tense:

je **mets**	I am putting	nous **mettons**	we are putting
tu **mets**	you are putting	vous **mettez**	you are putting
il **met**	he is putting	ils **mettent**	they are putting

Future and Conditional: Stem **mettr-** (Regular)

Past Definite: Stem **m-** [+ **is** type endings; see chart on page 117, Sec. 66C)

je **mis**	I put	nous **mîmes**	we put
tu **mis**	you put	vous **mîtes**	you put
il **mit**	he put	ils **mirent**	they put

Past Participle: **mis**, *put*

j'ai **mis**	I put
j'avais **mis**	I had put

Present Participle: **mettant**, *putting* (Regular)

Idiomatic Uses:

mettre au point	to perfect (same as **perfectionner**)
se mettre à [+ infinitive]	to begin (same as **commencer à**)

For example,

> Ils ont **mis au point** leur modèle d'informatique.
> They *perfected* their data-processing model.
>
> Il **se mit** à travailler.
> He *began* to work.

57. The Verb *savoir** (to know, to know how to)

When **savoir** is followed by a noun, it means *to know* a fact. When followed by an infinitive, it means *to know how to* and is often expressed in English by *can*.

Fact:
Il **sait** la date.   He *knows* the date.

Infinitive:
Il **sait** danser.   He *can* dance.

Do not confuse **savoir** with **connaître**, *to know* in the sense of *to be acquainted with*.

Present Tense:

je **sais**	I know	nous **savons**	we know
tu **sais**	you know	vous **savez**	you know
il **sait**	he knows	ils **savent**	they know

Future and Conditional: Stem **saur-**

Past Definite: Stem **s-** [+ **us** type endings]

je **sus**	I knew	nous **sûmes**	we knew
tu **sus**	you knew	vous **sûtes**	you knew
il **sut**	he knew	ils **surent**	they knew

Present Participle: **sachant**, *knowing*

Special Use in the Passé Composé: **su**, *found out* [+ noun], *managed to* [+ infinitive]

> Il **a su** la vérité.   He *found out* the truth.
> Il **a su** finir le travail.   He *managed* to finish the work.

58. The Verb *voir** (to see)

The compound verbs **revoir*** (*to see again*) and **prévoir*** (*to foresee, to predict*) have the same patterns as **voir***, except for the future and conditional of **prévoir**. The future-conditional stem of **prévoir** is **prévoir-**.

Like many irregular verbs, **voir*** has two stems in the present tense: **voi-** and **voy-**. The shaded L-shaped area below encloses forms that have an irregular stem in common. The **nous** and **vous** forms always have the same stem, usually (but not here) the same as the infinitive stem. (You will find this to be a consistent pattern when the present has two stems.)

Present Tense: Stem **voi-**

je **vois**	I see	nous **voyons**	we see
tu **vois**	you see	vous **voyez**	you see
il **voit**	he sees	ils **voient**	they see

Future and Conditional: Stem **verr-**

je **verrai**   I will see

Past Definite: Stem **v-** [+ **is** type endings]

je **vis**	I saw	nous **vîmes**	we saw
tu **vis**	you saw	vous **vîtes**	you saw
il **vit**	he saw	ils **virent**	they saw

Past Participle: vu (Similar to **savoir**, with past participle su)

Present Participle: **voyant**, *seeing*

59. The Verb *pouvoir** (to be able, can)

Present Tense: Stem **peu-**

je **peux** (puis)	I can	nous **pouvons**	we can
tu **peux**	you can	vous **pouvez**	you can
il **peut**	he can	ils **peuvent**	they can

Future and Conditional: Stem **pourr-**

Future:	il **pourra**	he, it will be able
Conditional:	il **pourrait**	he, it would be able
		he, it could

Past Definite: Stem **p-** [+ **us** type endings]

je **pus**	I was able, could	nous **pûmes**	we were able, could
tu **pus**	you were able, could	vous **pûtes**	you were able, could
il **put**	he was able, could	ils **purent**	they were able, could

Past Participle: **pu**, *been able*

il a **pu**   he was able, he succeeded in

Present Participle: **pouvant**, *being able*

	remember		
Stems	**peu-** (present)	**pourr-** (future)	**p(u)-** (past definite)
	as parts of **pouvoir***		

Exercises

A. *Causative **faire**.* Make a rough translation if necessary, then state in good English.

 1. L'ingénieur fait voir le cyclotron aux physiciens.
 2. Il le fait voir aux physiciens. (**le** replaces **le cyclotron**)
 3. Il leur fait voir le cyclotron. (**leur** replaces **aux physiciens**)
 4. Il le leur fait voir.
 5. Le professeur fera lire ce livre par les étudiants.
 6. Le professeur leur fera lire cette poésie.
 7. L'institutrice faisait chanter les élèves.
 8. Elle leur a fait chanter des chansons.
 9. Le vendeur nous a fait savoir les prix des marchandises.
10. On fait étudier les sciences naturelles à tous les étudiants.
11. Le directeur a fait bâtir une maison magnifique dans la banlieue.
12. J'ai fait réparer ce bâtiment par un charpentier.
13. Il ne faut pas faire travailler trop les enfants.
14. Le but est de faire produire du tabac à ces fermiers.
15. Le professeur a fait connaître les faits aux ministres†.
16. Beaumarchais se chargea de faire arriver des munitions en Amérique.
17. Descartes fit faire un pas† énorme à l'algèbre en inventant la notation des puissances par exposants numériques.

B. *Review of **dont**.* Enclose the **dont** phrase in parentheses and ascertain the meaning of the main clause outside the parentheses first. Then translate the complete sentence into natural-sounding English.

18. La planète dont le satellite est la lune s'appelle la Terre.
19. Les êtres vivants sont susceptibles de variations dont nous avons vu les évidences.
20. Le trapèze est une forme géometrique quatrilatère dont deux des côtés sont inégaux et parallèles.
21. Les gaz principaux dont l'atmosphère est composée sont l'oxygène et l'azote.
22. La théorie dont nous avons examiné la structure ne paraît guère solide.

C. *Inverted word order.* Translate.

23. C'est sur ce principe qu'est basée l'analyse thermique.
24. Il est intéressant de comparer ces résultats avec ceux que fournissent les méthodes classiques.

---

7. **institutrice** *f.* teacher (grade school)   8. **chanter** to sing; **chanson** *f.* song   9. **prix** *m.* price (also *prize*)   11. **bâtir** to build; **banlieue** *f.* suburbs   12. **réparer** to repair; **charpentier** *m.* carpenter   14. **produire*** to produce   15. **ministre**† *m.* cabinet minister, secretary of a department   16. **se charger de** to take responsibility for   17. **pas**† *m.* stride (also *pace, pass*); **exposant** *m.* exponent   19. **vu** (past participle of **voir**, *to see*); **évidences** (Note that some nouns used in the plural in French are singular in English, such as **les renseignements**, *information*; **les cheveux**, *hair*; **les connaissances**, *knowledge*; **des conseils**, *advice*; **les affaires**†, *business*)   22. **paraît** (present of **paraître***, *to appear*)

25. C'est au moyen-âge qu'ont été construites les cathédrales de Paris, de Rouen et de Chartres.

26. L'impression magique que produit la musique d'orchestre est renforcée par la grandeur de la salle.

27. Peut-être les philosophes aspirent-ils à devenir des législateurs.

28. Le gérant est malade, aussi ne vient-il pas au bureau aujourd'hui.

29. Ainsi la machine est beaucoup plus chère que ne l'était son devancier.

30. —Peut-être cela vous semble-t-il un peu étrange, dit-il.

31. —Il y a quelque chose, dit-il, qui m'inquiète un peu.

32. Voilà le médecin que nous avons rencontré à l'hôpital.

33. Voilà le médecin que cherchent les parents de la victime.

34. Voilà le médecin qui cherche les parents de la victime.

35. Les impressions qu'a rapportées Alexis de Tocqueville représentent une étude juste et révélatrice de la jeune République américaine.

36. La machine qu'a inventée Pascal au XVIIe siècle a facilité le calcul arithmétique.

D. Translate the following sentences.

37. Pour bien savoir les choses, il en faut savoir le détail, et comme il est presque infini, nos connaissances sont toujours superficielles et imparfaites. —La Rochefoucauld, *Maximes*, 106

38. On ne donne rien si libéralement que ses conseils. —*Maximes*, 110

39. Alors Micromégas prononça ces paroles: «Je vois plus que jamais qu'il ne faut juger de rien sur sa grandeur apparente.» —Voltaire

40. La plupart des lois semblent arbitraires: elles dépendent des intérêts, des passions, et des opinions de ceux qui les ont inventées, et de la nature du climat où les hommes se sont assemblés en société. —Voltaire, *Traité de la métaphysique*, Chapitre IX

41. Cela nous ferait voir les lois physiques qui ont opéré pendant cette expérience.

42. Les échantillons seront retirés du four dans une heure; ils sont alors transmis aux autres appareils de mesure.

43. La première mise en évidence directe des moments magnétiques nucléaires est la célèbre expérience de Rabi, que nous allons brièvement décrire.

44. Supposons qu'il y ait deux gaz auxquels il faut ajouter un troisième.

---

26. **produit** (present of **produire*** *to produce*; see Appendix C, Irregular Verbs); **grandeur** *f.* largeness; **salle** *f.* (concert) hall (usually this word is the general term for any room) 28. **gérant** *m.* manager; **vient** (present of **venir***, to come) 29. **ne** (Here, **ne** is used without a negative particle such as **pas, jamais.** This is often the case in literary usage after a comparison. No negation is implied. See Sec. 36); **l'** (The pronoun **l'** refers to the idea of expensive); **devancier** *m.* predecessor 31. **quelque chose** something; **inquiéter** to worry, to bother 32. **rencontrer** to meet; 33. **chercher** to look for 37. **en** *pron.* of them 40. **des intérêts...de la nature** (All the **de** forms revert to the verb **dépendre de,** *to depend on*; all therefore mean *on*) 42. **retirer** to withdraw; **four** *m.* oven; **dans une heure** in an hour; **transmettre*** to transfer 43. **mise en évidence** *f.* demonstration; **brièvement** *adv.* briefly; **décrire*** to describe 44. **supposer** to assume; **auxquels** to which; **ajouter** to add

45. Cela constitue une sorte de film cinématographique qui nous ferait voir la généalogie de chaque espèce.
46. On ne saurait déterminer précisément la provenance de la grande majorité des animaux.
47. Après avoir pris naissance dans le golfe du Mexique, le Gulf-Stream traverse l'Atlantique nord.
48. On voit que les résultats obtenus par les chercheurs de Yale nous permettront de modifier notre procédé.

Readings

Le Nouveau monde:
Impressions d'un Français

[49] Il n'y a pas de peuple sur la terre qui ait fait des progrès aussi rapides que les Américains dans le commerce et l'industrie. Ils forment aujourd'hui la seconde nation maritime du monde; et, bien que leurs manufactures† aient à lutter contre les obstacles naturels presque insurmontables, elles ne laissent pas de prendre chaque jour de nouveaux développements. [50] Mais ce qui me frappe le plus aux États-Unis, ce n'est pas la grandeur extraordinaire de quelques entreprises industrielles, c'est la multitude innombrable des petites entreprises.

[51] Presque tous les agriculteurs des États-Unis ont joint quelque commerce à l'agriculture; la plupart ont fait de l'agriculture un commerce.

[52] Il est rare qu'un cultivateur américain se fixe pour toujours sur le sol qu'il occupe. Dans les nouvelles provinces de l'Ouest principalement, on défriche un champ pour le revendre et non pour le récolter; [53] on bâtit une ferme dans la prévision que, puisque l'état du pays changera bientôt par suite de l'accroissement de ses habitants, on pourra en obtenir un bon prix.

[54] Tous les ans un essaim d'habitants du Nord descend vers le Midi et vient s'établir dans les contrées où croissent le coton et la canne à sucre. [55] Ces hommes cultivent la terre dans le but de lui faire produire en peu d'années de quoi les enrichir, et ils entrevoient déjà le moment où ils pourront retourner dans

---

45. **espèce** *f.* species 46. **provenance** *f.* origin 47. **prendre* naissance** to originate 48. **chercheur** *m.* researcher; **procédé** *m.* procedure 49. **peuple** *m.* nation, people; **ait** (same as **a**); **manufacture**† *f.* factory; **lutter** to struggle; **ne pas laisser de** not to fail to 50. **ce n'est pas** (Omit the redundant *ce* in translation); **innombrable** *adj.* innumerable, countless 51. **joint** (past participle of **joindre***, *to join*) 52. **se fixer** to settle down; **province** *f.* (here) territory; **défricher** to clear (land); **revendre** to resell (The prefix **re-** means *again*, as in English; place the word *again* at the end of the clause); **récolter** to harvest 53. **prévision** *f.* anticipation; **accroissement** *m.* increase; **en** for it 54. **tous les ans** every year; **essaim** *m.* swarm; **Midi** *m.* South; **où** (As with *que*, go to the next independent noun group, then return to the verb); **croissent** (present of **croître***, *to grow*); **sucre** *m.* sugar 55. **de quoi** what is necessary, enough; **entrevoir*** to see, to sense

leur patrie jouir de l'aisance ainsi acquise. [56] Les Américains transportent donc dans l'agriculture l'esprit du négoce, et leurs passions† industrielles se montrent là, comme ailleurs.

[57] Les Américains font d'immenses progrès en industrie, parce qu'ils s'occupent tous à la fois d'industrie; et pour cette même cause ils sont sujets à des crises industrielles très inattendues et très formidables.

[58] Comme ils font tous du commerce, le commerce est soumis chez eux à des influences tellement nombreuses et si compliquées, qu'il est impossible de prévoir à l'avance les embarras† qui peuvent naître. [59] Comme chacun d'eux se mêle plus ou moins d'industrie, au moindre choc que les affaires† y éprouvent, toutes les fortunes particulières† trébuchent en même temps, et l'État chancelle.

[60] Je crois que le retour des crises industrielles est une maladie endémique chez les nations démocratiques de nos jours. [61] On peut la rendre moins dangereuse, mais non la guérir, parce qu'elle ne tient pas à un accident, mais au tempérament même de ces peuples.

d'après Alexis de Tocqueville, Professions industrielles, *De la Démocratie en Amérique*

Superficies des figures planes

[62] La hauteur d'un triangle représente la perpendiculaire abaissée d'un de ses sommets sur le côté opposé pris pour base. [63] Le pied de la hauteur peut tomber à l'intérieur ou à l'extérieur du triangle. [64] La surface d'un triangle est égale au produit de la base par la moitié de la hauteur.

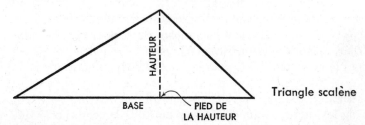

[65] Un triangle isocèle est celui qui a deux côtés égaux; un triangle équilatéral a les trois côtés égaux; un triangle scalène est celui dont les trois côtés sont

---

55. **jouir de** to enjoy; **aisance** *f.* ease, comfort   56. **donc** therefore (Place it first in the sentence, so as not to disrupt the main thought); **transportent** (This verb should be followed by a direct object. This is the missing link problem; see Appendix A, 3. Find the next independent noun after this verb, then return to the skipped prepositional phrase); **négoce** *m.* business; **passion**† *f.* enthusiasm; **se montrer** to show itself; **ailleurs** elsewhere   57. **s'occuper de** to be busy with; **tous** all (of them); **inattendu** (The opposite of **attendu,** *expected*)   58. **chez eux** in their country; **embarras**† *m.* difficulty; **naître*** to arise   59. **se mêler de** to be involved in, with; **au moindre** at the slightest; **affaires**† *f.pl.* business; **éprouver** to experience; **particulier**†, **particulière** *adj.* private; **trébucher** to totter, to be in danger; **chanceller** to be unstable, to totter   60. **retour** *m.* return   61. **guérir** to cure; **ne tient pas à** does not depend upon; **même** itself (see Appendix A, 3)   62. **hauteur** *f.* (see diagram); **abaisser** to drop, to lower   64. **surface** *f.* (a cognate, but another term is used in geometry) **la moitié** half

inégaux. [66] Un triangle rectangle est un triangle qui a un angle droit (c.-à-d. de 90 degrés).

[67] La hauteur d'un parallélogramme est la perpendiculaire qui mesure la distance entre deux côtés parallèles. [68] L'aire d'un parallélogramme quelconque est égale au produit de la base par la hauteur.

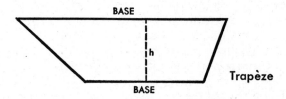

Trapèze

[69] Un trapèze est un quadrilatère dont deux des côtés sont inégaux et parallèles. [70] Les deux côtés parallèles forment les bases; la distance entre eux est la hauteur. [71] L'aire d'un trapèze s'obtient en multipliant la somme des bases par la moitié de la hauteur. [72] On peut aussi exprimer cela par la formule

$$\text{Aire du trapèze} = \frac{h}{2}\,(b + b')$$

[73] Un polygone régulier est celui dont tous les angles et tous les côtés sont égaux entre eux. [74] Tout polygone régulier peut être inscrit dans un cercle. Ce cercle peut être considéré comme un polygone régulier d'une infinité de côtés.

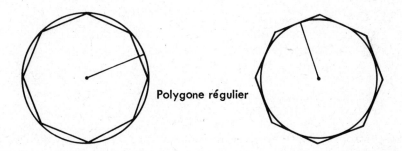

Polygone régulier

[75] Or un polygone régulier a pour mesure la moitié du produit de son périmètre par le rayon† du cercle inscrit:

$$\text{Aire du polygone} = \frac{1}{2}\,anr$$

lorsque a est le côté, n le nombre des côtés, et r le rayon du cercle inscrit.

---

68. **quelconque** any, ordinary   72. **exprimer** to express   74. **inscrit** (past participle of **inscrire***, *to inscribe*)   75. **or** now; **rayon**† *m.* radius

Qui va à la chasse perd sa place
(Proverbe)

[76] Un voyageur qui avait passé toute la journée† sous la pluie arriva un soir à une auberge dans une petite ville†. [77] Il espérait se sécher en attendant† son dîner, mais quand il entra dans la salle à manger il y vit sept autres voyageurs qui s'étaient déjà installés autour de la cheminée.

[78] Appelant l'aubergiste il lui dit: «Portez vite une douzaine d'huîtres à mon cheval.

—Comment, monsieur! A votre cheval!?

—Peut-être que cela vous semble un peu étrange, mais faites quand même ce que je vous dis.»

[79] L'aubergiste alla dans la cuisine chercher des huîtres. Après les avoir ouvertes il sortit à l'écurie, suivi de tous les voyageurs, qui avaient grande envie de voir manger des huîtres à un cheval.

[80] Quelques minutes plus tard ils rentrèrent tous.

[81] «Monsieur, dit l'aubergiste, votre cheval ne désire pas d'huîtres.

[82] —N'importe, répondit le voyageur, mettez-les sur la table. Je les mangerai moi-même.»

[83] Pendant l'absence des autres, il avait pris une bonne place près du feu.

Test 10, page 237

---

76. **pluie** *f.* rain; **auberge** *f.* inn;   77. **espérer*** to hope; **se sécher** to dry oneself; **attendre**† to wait for (The preposition *for* is included in the meaning of this verb); **salle à manger** *f.* dining room; **autour** around; **cheminée** *f.* fireplace   78. **aubergiste** *m.* innkeeper; **vite** *adv.* quickly; **une douzaine de** a dozen; **huîtres** *f.pl.* oysters; **cheval** *m.* horse; **quand même** even so, all the same   79. **écurie** *f.* stable; **suivi de** (past participle of **suivre***, *to follow*); **avoir*** **envie de** to want to; **voir manger** (Translate **voir**, then the next noun structure, **des huîtres**, then **manger**)   80. **rentrer** to come back in   82. **n'importe** it doesn't matter; **moi-même** myself   83. **pendant** during; **feu** *m.* fire

11

Structures

60. Supplemental Auxiliary Verbs

In addition to the auxiliary verbs **avoir** and **être**, which are used with past participles to form the compound tenses of verbs (Sec. 48), certain other helping verbs are commonly used as auxiliaries. These are referred to here as supplemental auxiliary verbs.

A. Usage. Unlike **être** and **avoir**, the supplemental auxiliary verbs are followed by an infinitive. You have learned the verb **pouvoir** (*to be able to, can*). Here is an example of **pouvoir** used as an auxiliary verb.

> Nous **pouvons** accepter les résultats de cette expérience.
> We *can* accept the results of this experiment.
> We *are able to* accept the results of this experiment.

B. Translation. The translation of an auxiliary verb followed by an infinitive presents no special difficulty. The proper tense of the auxiliary verb must be determined, of course. The infinitive that follows it can usually be expressed in English by an infinitive, as shown in the example above.

C. List of supplemental auxiliary verbs. Learn the following verbs, which are often used as auxiliaries.

savoir*	*to be able*	
pouvoir*	*to be able*	
vouloir*	[+ infinitive] *to want*	[to do something]
devoir*	*to be obliged*	
aller*	*to be going*	
laisser	*to allow* [something to be done]	

The verb **savoir*** (Sec. 57) means *to be able, to know how* (intellectual or learned ability). Use a form of *can* in the final translation, if possible.

Il **sait** taper à la machine.
He *can* type.

Il **saura** compléter le rapport.
He *will be able to* finish the report.

Nous ne **saurions** pas soutenir votre prétention.
We *would not be able to* support your claim.
We *could not* support your claim.

The verb **pouvoir*** (Sec. 59) means *to be able* (physical ability or permission). Use a form of *can* in the final translation, if possible.

Il ne **peut** pas partir demain.
He *can't* leave tomorrow.

Nous **pouvons** désintégrer plusieurs millions d'atomes.
We *can* disintegrate several million atoms.

The verb **vouloir*** (Sec. 63) means *to want*.

Einstein **voulait** prouver que l'espace et le temps sont identiques.
Einstein *wanted* to prove that time and space are identical.

The verb **devoir*** (Sec. 64) means *have to, must, to be required to*.

Le bâtiment **doit** recevoir un blindage qui convient.
The ship *must* be provided with appropriate shielding.

Le gérant **a dû** partir hier.
The manager *had to* leave yesterday.

Il **devra** revenir la semaine prochaine.
He *will have to* come back next week.

The verb **aller** (Sec. 65) means *to be going* [to do something]. When followed by an infinitive, the verb **aller** in the present tense or the imperfect indicates imminent action.

Nous **allons** fermer la porte.
We *are going to* close the door.

Il **allait** lire le rapport, mais le temps lui manquait.
He *was going to* read the report, but he lacked time.

The verb **laisser** means *to allow* [something to be done]. As with the causative **faire**, for better comprehension of a sentence using **laisser** plus an infinitive, first read the subject and the verb **laisser**, then the next noun or pronoun, then return to the dependent infinitive.

Le soldat **a laissé** passer le fermier.
The soldier *allowed* the farmer to pass.

Ce procédé **laisse** subsister des protons.
This procedure *allows* protons to remain.

Note that when **laisser** is not followed by an infinitive, it means *to leave*.

> Il **a laissé** de côté l'hypothèse de Maxwell.
> He *left* Maxwell's hypothesis aside.

61. The Pronoun *lequel* (which)

The word **lequel** has four basic forms.

	singular	plural	
masculine	**lequel**	**lesquels**	which
feminine	**laquelle**	**lesquelles**	

The contractions listed in Section 19 apply to this word, the first half of which is simply the definite article **le**.

With à: auquel

auquel, à laquelle, auxquels, auxquelles   to which

With de:

duquel, de laquelle, desquels, desquelles   of which, from which

All forms using **de** are replaceable with **dont** (Sec. 28).

62. The Pronoun *en* (some, of it, of them, from them)

The word **en** is used to replace a prepositional phrase beginning with **de** that does *not* refer to a person. It is always found before the verb (except in positive commands).

> Il a beaucoup **de livres**. Il **en** a beaucoup.
> He has many *books*. He has many [*of them*].

> Avez-vous **de l'argent**? **En** avez-vous?
> Have you *some money*? Have you *some*?
>   Do you have *any*?

> Nous avons examiné **des cas intéressants**. Nous **en** avons examiné.
> We have examined *some interesting cases*. We have examined *some*.

> Elles arrivent **de Paris** aujourd'hui. Elles **en** arrivent aujourd'hui.
> They are arriving *from Paris* today. They are arriving *from there* today.

> Prenez **du sucre**. Prenez-**en**.
> Take *some sugar*. Take *some*.

63. The Verb *vouloir** (to want)

The verb **vouloir** is used with a noun or as an auxiliary. The present tense, **je veux**, shows insistence and expresses a strong will or desire. The conditional, **je voudrais** (*I would like*), expresses a desire or request in a softer, more polite manner.

Present Tense: Stem veu-

je **veux**	I want		nous **voulons**	we want
tu **veux**	you want		vous **voulez**	you want
il **veut**	he wants		ils **veulent**	they want

Future and Conditional: Stem voudr-

Je **voudrais**   I would like

Past Definite: Stem voul- [+ us type endings]

je **voulus**	I wanted	nous **voulûmes**	we wanted
tu **voulus**	you wanted	vous **voulûtes**	you wanted
il **voulut**	he wanted	ils **voulurent**	they wanted

Past Participle: voulu, *wanted*

j'avais **voulu**   I had wanted

Present Participle: voulant, *wanting* (Regular)

remember

Stems   **veu-** (present)   **voudr-** (future and conditional)
as parts of **vouloir***

64. The Verb *devoir** (ought to, must, have to, should)

See Verb Table No. 8, page 195.

Present Tense: Stem doi-

je **dois**	I must		nous **devons**	we must
tu **dois**	you must		vous **devez**	you must
il **doit**	he must		ils **doivent**	they must

Future and Conditional: Stem devr-

Note the special meanings of the various tenses. The present implies a strong obligation, one that will be fulfilled.

Il **doit** examiner des données.
He *must* examine these data.

The future implies a future obligation, one that will be carried out.

Il **devra** finir ce travail.
He *will have to* finish this work.

The passé composé and past definite indicate a past obligation, now completed.

Il **a dû** partir hier.
Il **dut** partir hier.   He *had to* leave yesterday.

These forms also indicate probability that something happened in the past.

Il **a dû** partir hier.   He *must have* left yesterday.

The conditional means *should, ought to* (but probably will not).

Je **devrais** aller chez moi.
I *should* go home.

The imperfect means *was supposed to* (but probably didn't).

Il **devait** me voir à midi.
He *was supposed to* see me at noon.

remember

Stems   **doi-** (present)   **devr-** (future and conditional)
d(u)- (past definite)
as parts of **devoir***

65. The Verb *aller** (to go)

Present Tense: Stems **va-, vo-**

je **vais**	I am going	nous **allons**	we are going
tu **vas**	you are going	vous **allez**	you are going
il **va**	he is going	ils **vont**	they are going

Future and Conditional: Stem **ir-**

Past Definite: Stem **all-** [+ **ai** type endings], *went*

j' **allais**	I went	nous **allâmes**	we went
tu **allas**	you went	vous **allâtes**	you went
il **alla**	he went	ils **allèrent**	they went

Past Participle: **allé,** *gone* (Used with auxiliary **être**)

il est **allé**	he went, he has gone
il était **allé**	he had gone
il sera **allé**	he will have gone
il serait **allé**	he would have gone

Present Participle: **allant,** *going*

remember

Stems   **va-, vo-** (present)   **ir-** (future and conditional)
as parts of the verb **aller***

The verb **aller** most commonly refers to destination.

J'allais en ville quand j'ai vu Paul.
I *was going* downtown when I saw Paul.

Nous **sommes allés** à Nice par le train.
We *went* to Nice by train.

When used in the present and followed by an infinitive, **aller** expresses the immediate future.

Immediate Future:

Je vais étudier.   *I'm going to* study (right now).

The future (**j'étudierai**) describes an action that will occur later, but not necessarily soon.

Future Tense:

J'étudierai.   I will study.

Exercises

A. *Verbs.* Give the English equivalent of the following verb forms and structures.

   1. il sait / il saura / sachant les faits / il sait danser
   2. il peut / il se peut que / nous pourrons / il aura pu
   3. je voudrais / il a voulu / il voulait / il ne veut pas
   4. je dois / je devrais / il a dû / il devait / il dut
   5. il va / il allait / il est allé / nous irons
   6. Il saura résoudre ce problème. / Il sut la réponse.
   7. il pouvait comprendre / il pourra faire le travail
   8. Elle voulait aller en ville. / Elle voudrait visiter le musée.
   9. Je dois faire finir le travail par l'ouvrier. / Il a dû partir hier.
  10. en mettant / en prenant / en allant / en cherchant
  11. il voit / il a vu / il verra / en voyant
  12. il tient / en tenant / il a tenu / elle avait obtenu

B. *Supplemental auxiliaries, idioms, and false friends.* Translate the following sentences.

  13. Il sait danser. / Il saura finir le travail. / Il savait la réponse.
  14. Il peut rester. / Il se peut qu'il arrive. / Il pourra voyager.
  15. Il veut partir. / Il voudrait partir. / Nous voulions voir ce film.
  16. Il doit étudier. / Il devait étudier. / Il devrait étudier.
  17. Il va décrire l'appareil. / Il allait sortir. / Je vais me reposer.
  18. Il laisse passer le médecin. / Il a laissé tomber le dictionnaire. / Nous laisserons de côté cette théorie.
  19. J'ai dû étudier hier soir. / Je devais rentrer, mais je suis resté.
  20. Le bâtiment devra disposer de bassins spécialement aménagés.
  21. On pourra immerger les cylindres en mer.

---

8. **musée** *m.* museum   17. **se reposer** to rest   19. **hier soir** yesterday evening

22. Il doit faire venir l'astrologue. / Il pourra obtenir un bon prix.
23. Il sait la date. / Il connaît la France. / Il voudrait connaître l'Allemagne.
24. Il a voulu partir. / Il voulait prendre la moitié de l'argent.
25. Il tient deux livres à la main. / Il tient à résoudre ce problème. / Il a obtenu diverses réponses.
26. Vous prenez du sucre? / Il a appris une langue étrangère†. / Est-ce que vous comprenez?
27. Il fera ouvrir cette porte. / Ils ont fait bâtir une usine en Espagne.
28. Il a mis ses livres sur le bureau. / Il transmettra les renseignements.
29. Il a trouvé la solution en étudiant les données. / Sachant les faits, il a pu les expliquer clairement.
30. Les personnes faibles ne peuvent pas être sincères.

C. *Pronouns **en** and **lequel**.* Translate the following sentences. Be sure to use the correct meaning of the pronoun **en** (*for it, of them, from that, some*). The pronoun **lequel, -le** always means *which.*

31. L'oxygène: la plupart des minéraux en contiennent.
32. On a pris deux cartes. Il en reste onze.
33. Le diamètre autour duquel la révolution diurne s'opère s'appelle l'*axe*
34. Rousseau croit que les enfants ne comprennent pas ce qu'ils apprennent. Il en conclut qu'ils ne doivent rien apprendre.
35. On a divisé cette mer en plusieurs sections auxquelles on a donné des noms différents.
36. On bâtit une ferme dans la prévision qu'on pourra en obtenir un bon prix.
37. L'électricité est une découverte par laquelle la civilisation a été transformée.

Readings

Thorium et uranium 233

[38] Découvert en 1829 par Berzélius, le thorium est probablement une matière première de grand avenir pour l'industrie atomique, car il permet de fabriquer un isotope fissible d'uranium, l'uranium 233.

[39] Le thorium existe en quantités importantes† dans la nature. [40] Il est trois fois plus abondant que l'uranium dans l'écorce terrestre, et il présente sur l'uranium l'avantage d'avoir été concentré par l'érosion naturelle en gisements facilement exploitables et bien distribués géographiquement.

---

23. **connaît** (present of **connaître***, *to be acquainted with*) 26. **langue** *f.* language; **étranger, étrangère†** *adj.* foreign 27. **usine** *f.* factory, plant 38. **matière première** *f.* raw material 39. **important, -e†** *adj.* large 40. **écorce terrestre** *f.* Earth's crust; **gisement** *m.* stratum, layer; **exploitable** *adj.* workable

[41] Les principaux minerais de thorium sont la thorite (silicate de thorium et d'uranium) et la thorianite (oxydes de thorium et d'uranium), que l'on trouve dans l'île de Sri Lanka, dans le Texas, en Norvège et à Madagascar.

[42] L'extraction du minerai s'effectue par des méthodes primitives, la main-d'œuvre indigène le chargeant dans des paniers et le transportant ainsi à l'usine de traitement, qui opère par séparation magnétique, après tamisage et enrichissement.

[43] Les monazites sont les seules sources de terres rares actuellement exploitées. [44] Certaines ont des applications industrielles, comme le cérium, le lanthane, le néodyme et le praséodyme. D'autres, comme le samarium, l'europium, le terbium et l'erbium, ne servent qu'à des recherches de laboratoire. [45] Les terres rares sont utilisées dans la fabrication des noyaux d'électrodes en charbon pour arcs électriques. [46] Leurs oxydes peuvent servir au polissage des verres d'optique. [47] Avec le lanthane, on fabrique certains verres spéciaux et des filtres pour la photographie aérienne.

[48] Le thorium naturel se compose de 7 isotopes, dont le plus abondant est le thorium 232. [49] Ce dernier, en absorbant un neutron, donne du thorium 233, radioactif, qui, par émission β, avec une période de 23 minutes, se transforme en protactinium 233. [50] Une deuxième émission β, avec une période de 27 jours, donne l'isotope fissible 233 de l'uranium. [51] Ces opérations peuvent s'effectuer à l'échelle industrielle dans les piles avec irradiation du thorium, sous forme de carbonate ou de tétrafluorure, par des neutrons.

[52] L'uranium 233 peut être extrait par des solvants organiques, après une période d'attente de 4 à 6 mois, nécessaire pour que la presque totalité du protactinium ait eu le temps de se désintégrer (ce délai correspond à cinq à six fois la période de désintégration du protactinium); on assure ainsi la disparition des produits de fission les plus gênants, dont la période est courte.

[53] Néanmoins, toutes les opérations de traitement doivent être conduites à distance et avec de grandes précautions, l'intégralité de ces produits étant fortement radioactive.

Sociologie

[54] Dans l'ancien conflit qui mit longtemps en opposition la société et l'individu, aucun moyen terme ne semblait possible. D'une part, la contrainte sociale, le déterminisme rigoureux: l'individu, une marionnette sociale; de l'autre, la liberté d'action, l'originalité de l'invention, la contingence des lois: l'individu, un créateur social. [55] En introduisant la notion d'attitude en

---

41. **minerai** *m.* ore   42. **main-d'œuvre** *f.* labor, manpower; **indigène** *adj.* native, indigenous; **panier** *m.* basket; **tamisage** *m.* sifting, screening; **enrichissement** *m.* enrichment   43. **monazite** (cognate); **terre rare** *f.* rare earth (oxides of metals)   44. **lanthane** *m.* lanthanum; **néodyme** *m.* neodymium; **praséodyme** *m.* praseodymium   45. **noyau** *m.* nucleus, core; **charbon** *m.* carbon   46. **verre** *m.* glass   49. **période** *f.* half-life   51. **échelle** *f.* scale   52. **attente** *f.* waiting (cf. **attendre**); **mois** *m.* month; **pour que** *conj.* so that; **disparition** *f.* disappearance; **gênant, -e** *adj.* troublesome   53. **intégralité** *f.* entire collection   54. **mit** (Missing link: Go to **la société et l'individu** next)

sociologie, les auteurs contemporains entendent dissoudre ce prétendu conflit, trouver un compromis aux deux solutions extrêmes. Malheureusement, faute d'une définition rigoureuse, la notion d'attitude, en dépit de tous les espoirs qu'elle est en droit de susciter, soulève en définitive plus de problèmes qu'elle n'en résout.

[56] L'attitude est définie, en bref, comme une disposition positive ou négative, à agir ou ne pas agir, prise à l'égard d'un stimulus. La nature de ce stimulus est aussi peu déterminée que la disposition ou la prédisposition qu'il influence: il peut être organique, psychique ou culturel. [57] Dans de telles conditions la notion d'attitude englobe tout le domaine de la psychologie et de la sociologie, lesquelles disciplines pourraient être définies, en dernière analyse, comme l'étude scientifique des attitudes. [58] Cette schématisation voulue du problème vise à faire ressortir les insuffisances de la solution, plutôt des solutions proposées. En réalité des distinctions très subtiles sont parfois introduites. Toujours est-il qu'une trop grande extension est donnée à cette notion pour que l'on puisse s'en servir efficacement.

[59] En effet†, du point de vue sociologique, l'attitude définie comme une disposition à l'action est loin de donner tout ce qu'on est en droit d'attendre† d'une notion-clé, car il y a lieu, nous semble-t-il, de différencier ce qui est inné et individuel (domaine de la caractérologie), de ce qui est de provenance sociale. [60] Et dans ce dernier cas on pourrait distinguer, par ordre de généralité décroissante et d'importance croissante, les attitudes imposées (préjugés, clichés, tout ce qui relève de la conscience collective), les attitudes personnelles (comportement de l'individu quand il pense son action au lieu de réagir passivement) et les attitudes créatrices (initiatives prises par le réformateur en vue de réaliser l'idéal nouveau encore à l'état latent mais déjà pressenti par lui). [61] Or†, c'est précisément par la considération des attitudes créatrices du réformateur qu'il devient possible d'expliquer ce que la synthèse élaborée par lui doit, d'un côté, au milieu social qui l'a suscitée, de l'autre, à son génie personnel qui a su entrevoir, avant les autres, les tendances de la génération ascendante.

Test 11, page 239

---

55. **entendent** (from **entendre**, to understand) intend; **dissoudre*** to resolve; **prétendu** *adj.* ostensible; **faute de** for lack of; **en dépit de** in spite of; **espoir** *m.* hope, aspiration; **être en droit de** to have a right to; **susciter** to arouse; **soulever*** to raise; **résout** (from **résoudre***, *to resolve, to solve*)   56. **défini** (past participle of **définir**, *to define*); **en bref** in short; **agir** to act; **à l'égard de** with reference to; **aussi...que** (See Sec. 50C, Comparison)   57. **englober** to encompass   58. **viser** to aim; **faire ressortir** to reveal; **parfois** sometimes; **puisse** (from **pouvoir***) can; **se servir*** **de** to make use of (The word **en** represents **de cette nation**)   59. **en effet†** in fact; **attendre†** to expect (as well as *to wait for*); **clé** *f.* key; **il y a lieu** there is reason; **inné, -e** *adj.* innate; **provenance** *f.* origin   60. **décroissante** *adj.* decreasing; **relève** (from **relever***, *to arise*); **comportement** *m.* behavior; **pressenti** (past participle of **pressentir**, *to anticipate*)   61. **or†** now; **doit** (from **devoir***, *to owe*)

12

Structures

66. Past Definite Tense (Passé simple)

A. Identification. In following the rule for tense identification by elimination (Sec. 42), our procedure has been to check (1) for the present tense and (2) for the future or conditional, and then, if both of these tests fail, to call the verb under examination a past tense. It is to this last step that we now turn our attention in more detail.

A verb that is identified under the above rule as a past tense will probably be either the imperfect (Sec. 43) or the past definite. If the ending is **-ais, -ait, -ions, -iez,** or **-aient** (same as the ending for the conditional), we know that the verb is imperfect. Otherwise a simple verb is to be considered past definite.

B. Translation. The past definite tense is "just plain past." No fine-tuning is needed (as it is in the imperfect). The English equivalent simply expresses actions and events that occurred and were completed in the past.

infinitive	past definite form	meaning
examiner	il examina	he examined
remarquer	ils remarquèrent	they noticed
vendre	nous vendîmes	we sold
finir	vous finîtes	you finished
aller	il alla	he went
avoir	il eut	he had

C. Ending system of the past definite tense. There are three ending systems for the past definite:

- The "**ai**" system is used for all regular **-er** verbs and for one irregular verb (**aller***).

- The "**is**" system is used for all regular **-ir** and **-re** verbs and for certain important irregular verbs. The latter are shown below the double line in the table; the boldface letters represent the special stem for the verb, to which the regular endings are added.

› The "**us**" system applies only to irregular verbs (excluding those indicated in the other columns).

subject	ending system		
	ai (-er[1])	**is** (-ir and -re[2])	**us** (some irregular verbs[3])
je	-ai	-is	-us
tu	-as	-is	-us
il	-a	-it	-ut
nous	-âmes	-îmes	-ûmes
vous	-âtes	-îtes	-ûtes
ils	-èrent	-irent	-urent
	stems to which above endings are added for certain irregular verbs		
	all- (aller)	**d-** (dire) **f-** (faire) **m-** (mettre) **pr-** (prendre) **v-** (voir)	**d-** (devoir) **f-** (être) **e-** (avoir) **p-** (pouvoir) **voul-** (vouloir)

---

[1]All regular -er verbs and the irregular verb **aller** use the "**ai**" system of endings.
[2]All regular -ir and -re verbs use the "**is**" system of endings. In addition, certain irregular verbs use it. The special stems to which the endings are added are shown below the double line.
[3]Only irregular verbs use the "**us**" system of endings; the main exceptions are those indicated above which use the "**is**" system and **aller** (the only irregular verb to use the "**ai**" system).

Example: travailler (regular -er verb)

je **travaillai**	I worked		nous **travaillâmes**	we worked
tu **travaillas**	you worked		vous **travaillâtes**	you worked
il **travailla**	he worked		ils **travaillèrent**	they worked

Example: dire* (irregular verb, "**is**" system). Special stem **d-**

je **dis**	I said	nous **dîmes**	we said
tu **dis**	you said	vous **dîtes**	you said
il **dit**	he said	ils **dirent**	they said

Example: être* (irregular verb, "**us**" system). Special stem **f-**

je **fus**	I was	nous **fûmes**	we were
tu **fus**	you were	vous **fûtes**	you were
il **fut**	he was	ils **furent**	they were

D. Comparison of past definite and imperfect.   Whereas the imperfect has three distinctive meanings in English, the past definite has only one.

> *Past Definite:*   il examina   he examined
>
> *Imperfect:*   il examinait   he was examining
>   he used to examine
>   he examined

The context determines which translation of the imperfect to use, and the best choice is usually one of the first two. No choice has to be made with the past definite.

67. Expressions of Time

A. Certain adverbs expressing time are very useful in identifying verb tenses. Here are some commonly used adverbs of time that you should learn.

alors	then	aujourd'hui	today
bientôt	soon	demain	tomorrow
d'abord	at first, first of all	hier	yesterday
ensuite	next, then	le lendemain	the next day
longtemps	for a long time	désormais	henceforth
maintenant	now	quelquefois, parfois	sometimes
souvent	often	toujours	always, still
déjà	already	dès...	from...on
enfin	finally, at last		
puis	then, after, moreover		

depuis
il y a } *see notes 4|10*

B. In the construction

jusqu' à = until

> depuis [+ time]

when the word **depuis** is followed by a quantity of time, translate it with the equivalent *for*. Change the verb from present tense to the wording *have been* [*do*]*ing.*

> Nous étudions depuis trois heures et demie.
> We *have been studying for* three and a half hours.

If the verb tense is imperfect, change the verb to *had been* [*do*]*ing*.

> Nous étudiions depuis dix minutes quand elle est entrée.
> We *had been studying for* ten minutes when she came in.

If **depuis** is followed by a clock time (as opposed to a quantity of time), translate it with *since*.

> Nous sommes ici depuis midi.
> We have been here *since* noon.

C. The construction

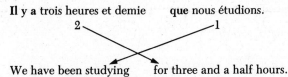

is identical in meaning with the **depuis** construction. However, **depuis** usually appears at the end of a sentence, whereas **il y a** [+ time +] **que** appears at the beginning and requires rearrangement of the English. Start at the word **que:**

Il y a trois heures et demie   que nous étudions.
　　　2　　　　　　　　　　　　　　　　　1

We have been studying   for three and a half hours.
　　　1　　　　　　　　　　　　　2

This structure is used only with quantities of time, not with clock time. Used in the imperfect, **il y avait** means *had been* [doing something] for the time indicated:

Il y **avait** une heure **que** Jean attendait.
John *had been* waiting *for* an hour.

D. The lack of **que** following the structure

il y a [+ time]

makes it quite different in meaning. It simply means [time +] *ago.*

Nous avons vu le professeur **il y a** dix minutes.
We saw the teacher ten minutes *ago.*

68. The Verb *venir** (to come)

There is a close resemblance between **venir** and **tenir** (Sec. 37). Compounds of **venir** follow the same construction system as **venir: convenir*** (*to suit, to agree*), **devenir*** (*to become*), **parvenir*** (*to attain*), **prévenir*** (*to inform, to warn*), **provenir*** de (*to come from*), **revenir*** (*to return*), **se souvenir*** de (*to remember*).

Present Tense: Stem **vien-**

je **viens**	I am coming	nous **venons**	we are coming
tu **viens**	you are coming	vous **venez**	you are coming
il **vient**	he is coming	ils **viennent**	they are coming

Future and Conditional: Stem **viendr-**

Imperfect: From the present ven~~ons~~

je **venais**   I was coming, used to come

Past Definite: Stem **vin-**, *came*

je **vins**	I came	nous **vînmes**	we came
tu **vins**	you came	vous **vîntes**	you came
il **vint**	he came	ils **vinrent**	they came

Past Participle: **venu**, *come* (Used with auxiliary **être**)

il est **venu**	he came
il était **devenu**	he had become

Present Participle: **venant**, *coming*

> *remember*
> Stems   **vien-** (present)   **viendr-** (future conditional)
> **vin-** (past definite)   **venu** (past participle)
> as parts of **venir***

69. Immediate Past

The structure **venir de** plus an infinitive expresses the idea of having just done something. Note its use in the present and the imperfect.

Present:	il vient de ...	he has just ...
Imperfect:	il venait de ...	he had just ...

Examples:

Nous **venons** d'examiner ce cas.
We *have just* examined this case.

Nous **venions** d'examiner ce cas.
We *had just* examined this case.

Exercises

A. *Verbs.* Translate.

1. il obtient / ils maintiendront / il retint / il mit au point
2. il a tenu / il aura obtenu / ils tinrent / il met
3. il a pris / il prit / il comprend / nous prenions
4. nous avons entrepris / il n'apprend rien / il prit
5. il fit bâtir une maison / il verra / en voyant / il fut
6. j'aurai vu / il voulut / il vit / il connaît / il eut
7. nous avons reconnu / il a dû partir / il a du travail
8. il devrait partir / il est parti / il fait partie de la société

9. pour mettre / on a mis / il sut / il saura / ils furent
10. il fait voir / il fera remarquer / il voulut / ils faisaient
11. il fait attention / il convient / il peut être / peut-être vient-il
12. cela me convient / en trouvant / ils vinrent / il vient de partir
13. je crois / il crut/ elle est devenue / elle devenait / elle sut
14. il faut revenir / pour comprendre / il y a une année / il permit
15. je me souviens de cela / je me souvenais de cela / il naquit à Paris
16. on a découvert / il découvrit / pour prévenir / il y a dix minutes
17. il réfléchissait / il écrivait / il écrivit / il a écrit
18. en travaillant / pour voyager / sachant / nous venions d'arriver

B. Translate into natural-sounding English.

19. Nous examinons ces données depuis deux mois.
20. Il y a une semaine que la classe étudie ce roman.
21. Il y avait huit jours que Duranger employait cet appareil.
22. La classe a discuté ce conte il y a une semaine.
23. Voilà un fait que nous savons depuis longtemps.
24. J'ai fini ce travail il y a vingt minutes.
25. Nous voyageons en Europe depuis trois semaines.
26. Nous étions à Avignon il y a quinze jours.
27. Il y a quinze jours qu'ils attendent les résultats.
28. Ils viennent d'apprendre la nouvelle.
29. Je viens d'acheter une voiture neuve.
30. Rimbaud venait de quitter Londres quand il est arrivé à Bruxelles.
31. Descartes découvrit la loi de la réfraction.
32. Il crut, avec Galilée, au mouvement de la terre autour du soleil.
33. Pascal créa le calcul des probabilités pour aider son ami, le chevalier de Méré, à réussir aux jeux de hasard.
34. Pierre Fermat fut peut-être le plus puissant esprit† mathématique de son siècle.
35. Un Français appelé Denis Patin mit au point le bateau à vapeur.
36. Il n'aime plus cette personne qu'il aimait il y a dix ans.
37. Il y a trois ans qu'il étudie la médecine.
38. Un jour la belle Cunégonde rencontra le jeune Candide en revenant au château, et elle rougit.
39. Elle laissa tomber son mouchoir, et Candide le ramassa.

---

15. **naqu-** (past definite stem of **naître***) 20. **roman** *m.* novel (literary genre) 22. **discuter** to discuss; **conte** *m.* short story 28. **nouvelle** *f.* news 29. **neuf, neuve** *adj.* new, brand–new 30. **Bruxelles** Brussels (Belgium) 33. **le chevalier de Méré** (Do not translate titles and names); **jeux** *m.pl.* games 34. **puissant, -e** *adj.* powerful 36. **personne** *f.* person (Although the noun is feminine, it applies to either a man or a woman) 37. **médecine** *f.* medicine (field and profession) (Do not confuse with **le médecin**, *doctor*, or with **le médicament**, *medicine, drug*) 38. **rougir** to blush 39. **mouchoir** *m.* handkerchief; **ramasser** to pick up

Readings

La Guerre d'Amérique (1775–1783)

[40] La guerre de Sept ans, si favorable, politiquement, à l'Angleterre, avait ruiné ses finances en portant sa dette à la somme de deux milliards et demi, qui exigeaient un intérêt annuel de 99 millions de francs. [41] La métropole pensa à se décharger sur ses colonies d'une partie de ce pesant fardeau. [42] Elle mit un impôt sur le papier timbré, plus tard sur le verre, le papier et le thé. [43] Des émeutes la forcèrent à supprimer ces taxes: on ne garda que la dernière. [44] Mais les habitants de Boston, invoquant le grand principe de la constitution anglaise selon lequel nul n'est tenu de se soumettre aux impôts qui n'ont pas été votés par ses représentants, jetèrent à la mer une cargaison de thé venue de Londres, plutôt que de payer le droit, et la guerre éclata (1775). [45] L'insurrection gagna toutes les provinces; l'année suivante, leurs députés, réunis en congrès général à Philadelphie, publièrent la déclaration d'indépendance où se remarquaient les principes suivants, qui semblaient sortir du sein de la philosophie française: [46] «Tous les hommes ont été créés égaux; ils ont été doués, par le Créateur, de certains droits inaliénables; pour s'assurer la jouissance de ces droits, les hommes ont établi parmi eux des gouvernements dont la juste autorité émane du consentement des gouvernés; [47] toutes les fois qu'une forme de gouvernement quelconque devient destructive des fins pour lesquelles elle a été établie, le peuple a le droit de la changer et de l'abolir.»

[48] La France accueillit avec enthousiasme une révolution où elle se reconnaissait. [49] Les trois députés américains, Arthur Lee, Silas Deane, et surtout le vieux Franklin, si célèbre déjà comme physicien, furent, pendant leur séjour à Paris, l'objet d'une ovation perpétuelle. [50] Le marquis de la Fayette, à peine âgé de vingt ans, fréta lui-même un vaisseau qu'il chargea d'armes.

[51] Le gouvernement redoutait cependant une rupture avec l'Angleterre. Turgot avait demandé qu'on restât neutre, croyant que l'Angleterre gagnerait plus à reconnaître l'indépendance de ses colonies qu'à les tenir frémissantes sous le

---

40. **guerre** *f*. war; **Angleterre** *f*. England; **dette** *f*. debt; **milliard** *m*. billion; **exiger*** to require   41. **métropole** *f*. mother country; **se décharger sur X de Y** to unload Y on X; **pesant, -e** *adj*. heavy; **fardeau** *m*. burden, load   42. **impôt** *m*. tax; **papier timbré** *m*. stamped papers, legal documents; **plus tard** later; **thé** *m*. tea   43. **émeute** *f*. riot; **supprimer** to cancel, to suppress; **garder** to keep, to retain   44. **habitant** *m*. resident, inhabitant; **nul n'est tenu** nobody is required; **jeter** to throw; **cargaison** *f*. cargo; **droit** *m*. tax, duty   45. **où** (should be followed by the next noun, then the intervening verb); **sein** *m*. heart (figurative)   46. **doué de** (from **douer**, *to endow*) endowed with; **droit** *m*. right; **jouissance** *f*. enjoyment; **parmi eux** among themselves   47. **quelconque** any…whatsoever; **fin** *f*. (same as **le but**)   48. **accueillir** to welcome   49. **séjour** *m*. stay, visit; **ovation** *f*. acclaim   50. **à peine** scarcely; **fréter** to charter; **vaisseau** *m*. ship, vessel; **charger** to load (See note 41)   51. **redouter** to fear; **Turgot, Robert-Jacques** (économiste français et plus tard contrôleur des Finances sous Louis XVI); **frémissant, -e** *adj*. trembling

joug. [52] De Vergennes se contenta d'envoyer d'abord des secours indirects en armes, argent et munitions, que Beaumarchais se chargea de faire arriver.

[53] Louis XVI n'aimait pas la guerre; il ne voulait point surtout passer pour l'agresseur. Pourtant il signa avec les États-Unis un traité de commerce, corroboré d'une alliance offensive et défensive, si l'Angleterre déclarait la guerre à la France. [54] L'ambassadeur anglais fut aussitôt rappelé.

[55] L'année 1781 fut pour la France la plus heureuse de cette guerre. Le comte de Grasse remporta une série de brillants succès. [56] Ses victoires contribuèrent à celles que Washington, Rochambeau et La Fayette remportèrent sur le continent américain. [57] Le 11 octobre 1781, ils forcèrent le général Cornwallis à capituler dans York-Town, avec 7000 hommes, 6 vaisseaux de guerre et 50 bâtiments marchands. [58] Ce fait d'armes fut décisif pour l'indépendance américaine. [59] Les Anglais, qui occupaient encore New-York, Savannah, Charlestown, ne firent plus que s'y défendre.

Les Sciences au dix-septième siècle

[60] Dans les sciences, la France était au niveau du mouvement scientifique, mais non à la tête. [61] Car, si elle avait Descartes et Pascal, à d'autres pays appartenaient Kepler, Galilée, Newton et Leibnitz.

[62] L'antiquité et le moyen âge avaient pu cultiver avec succès les sciences de raisonnement; mais l'étude du monde physique était frappée de stérilité, tant que les vraies méthodes d'expérimentation n'étaient pas trouvées. [63] Et elles ne pouvaient l'être qu'après qu'on eut acquis la confiance que l'univers est gouverné par des lois immuables, et non par les volontés arbitraires de puissances capricieuses. [64] L'alchimie, la magie, l'astrologie, toutes ces folies du moyen âge devinrent des sciences, du moment que l'homme s'efforça de saisir les lois qui les produisent. [65] Ce temps commence avec Copernic, au seizième siècle; mais ce n'est qu'au dix-septième que la révolution est accomplie et triomphe avec Kepler, Bacon et Descartes.

[66] Descartes fit faire un pas immense à l'algèbre en inventant la notation des puissances par exposants numériques, et à la géométrie des courbes, ce qui lui

---

51. **joug** *m.* yoke   52. **Vergennes, Charles, comte de** (ministre des affaires étrangères sous Louis XVI, après avoir été ambassadeur à Constantinople et à Stockholm; un des plus habiles diplomates du roi); **d'abord** (Since this usually interrupts a main thought, place it first in the sentence); **secours** *m.* aid; **se charger de** to take responsibility for; **faire arriver** (See Sec. 55)   53. **pourtant** however; **traité de commerce** *m.* trade agreement, treaty   54. **aussitôt** *adv.* (same as **immédiatement, tout de suite**); **rappelé** (past participle of **rappeler**, *to recall*)   55. **Grasse, François Joseph Paul, comte de** (marin français qui s'illustra pendant la guerre d'Amérique); **remporter** to win   57. **bâtiment** *m.* ship (as well as *building*); **marchand, -e** *adj.* merchant   58. **fait d'armes** *m.* military action   62. **frapper** to strike; **tant que** as long as   63. **l'être** (The l' refers to **trouvées** in the preceding sentence); **acquis** (past participle of **acquérir***, *to acquire*); **volonté** *f.* will   64. **s'efforcer de** to strive to; **saisir** to grasp, to seize, to understand   65. **Copernic** Copernicus   66. **pas** *m.* step (forward); **exposant** *m.* exponent

permit de résoudre des problèmes qu'on croyait insolubles. [67] Il découvrit la loi de réfraction; il crut, avec Galilée, au mouvement de la terre autour du soleil, et son chimérique *système des tourbillons* (suivant lequel le soleil et les étoiles fixes sont le centre d'autant de tourbillons de matière subtile, qui font circuler les planètes autour d'eux), a été le germe de la célèbre *hypothèse newtonienne de l'attraction.* [68] Pour Descartes comme pour Newton, le problème de l'univers physique est un problème de mécanique et Descartes enseignera le premier, sinon la solution, du moins la vraie nature du problème.

[69] Pascal, à douze ans, lisait les *Éléments* d'Euclide; à seize ans, il composa son traité *Des sections coniques.* Un peu plus tard il créa le calcul des probabilités, démontra la pesanteur de l'air par la fameuse expérience du Puy-de-Dôme, imagina le haquet et peut-être la presse hydraulique. Il a certainement inventé la machine à calculer.

[70] Pierre Fermat (1601–1665), conseiller au parlement† de Toulouse, n'a rien publié, mais fut peut-être le plus puissant esprit mathématique de son temps. [71] Il partagea avec Descartes la gloire d'avoir appliqué l'algèbre à la géométrie, et imagina la méthode *de maximis et de minimis*, en même temps que Pascal créa le calcul des probabilités.

[72] L'abbé Mariotte (1620–1665) reconnut que le volume d'un gaz, à une température constante, varie en raison inverse de la pression qu'il supporte.

[73] Denis Patin, né à Blois en 1647, créa ou perfectionna plusieurs machines et pensa le premier à employer la vapeur condensée comme force motrice. [74] En Allemagne, sur la Fulda il fit des expériences avec un *bateau à vapeur* qui remontait le courant. [75] De stupides mariniers brisèrent la machine du grand physicien, qui mourut à Londres dans la misère†.

[76] Trois étrangers† que Colbert invita en France justifièrent par leurs travaux les faveurs du roi. [77] Le Danois Rœmer détermina la vitesse des rayons solaires; le Hollandais Huygens découvrit l'anneau et un des satellites de Saturne; l'Italien Dominique Cassini en vit quatre autres. [78] On doit encore à Huygens l'invention des horloges à pendule, et à Cassini les premières opérations qui devaient servir à mesurer la terre; [79] il les exécuta avec l'abbé Picard, professeur d'astronomie au Collège de France, et tous deux commencèrent en 1669 la

---

67. **chimérique** *adj.* fanciful; **tourbillon** *m.* eddy, whirlpool; **d'autant de** of so many; **subtil, -e** *adj.* rarefied, thin   68. **enseigner** to teach; **le premier à** [+ infinitive] the first to [do something]; **sinon** if not   69. **lisait** (from **lire***, *to read*); **pesanteur** *m.* weight; **Puy-de-Dôme** (a mountain near Clermont-Ferrand in central France, where Pascal carried out his experiment: a mercury column was carried from the base to the summit, 4806 feet, and the change in the level of the mercury in the column demonstrated the effect of atmospheric pressure); **haquet** *m.* dray (two-wheeled cart for heavy loads)   70. **conseiller**† *m.* legal official; **parlement**† *m.* court of law; **publier** to publish, to print   71. **maximus et minimus** maximum and minimum (refers to functions used in calculus)   73. **le premier** (See note 68); **la Fulda** (name of a river); **force motrice** *f.* motive power   74. **remonter le courant** to go upstream   75. **marinier** *m.* sailor; **briser** to break, to destroy; **misère**† *f.* poverty   76. **étranger**† *m.* foreigner; **Colbert, Jean-Baptiste** (contrôleur général des finances sous Louis XIV)   77. **Danois** *m.* Dane   78. **horloge** *f.* clock   79. **tous deux** both of them

méridienne qui fut prolongée plus tard jusqu'au Roussillon. [80] C'est d'après la mesure du degré donnée par Picard, que Newton put enfin calculer la force qui retient la lune dans son orbite.

Test 12, page 241

Essential Word Review III

Chapters 9–12

Verbs

agir   to act
attendre† [+ noun]   to wait for [+ noun]
avoir envie de [+ infinitive]   to feel like [doing something]
éviter   to avoid
pouvoir   to be able, can
  puisse *pres. subj.*   can, is able to
recevoir   to receive
  reçu *pp.*   received
regarder   to look at
réussir (à)   to succeed (in); to pass (an exam)
se servir de   to make use of
venir   to come
  venir de [+ infinitive]   to have just [done something]

Nouns

le champ   field
un état   state
un événement   event
le genre   kind, genre (literary)
la journée†   day
la loi   law
la mise en évidence   demonstration
le mois   month
la moitié   half
le mot   word
le pays   country (nation)
  la campagne   country (countryside)
la personne   person (either sex)
le procédé   procedure
la provenance   origin
le résultat   result
le retour   return
  être de retour   to be back
le sens   sense, meaning
la voiture   car, vehicle

Adjectives

étranger, étrangère†   foreign
important, -e†   big, important
large†   wide

neuf, neuve (brand-)new
quelconque ordinary, any
tous all

Adverbs

ailleurs elsewhere
 d'ailleurs moreover, anyway
aussitôt immediately
 immédiatement, tout de suite immediately
autour around (physical location)
 au sujet de about (a topic)
 vers about (a time, number)
bientôt soon
davantage more
dedans inside
 dehors outside
désormais henceforth
longtemps a long time
souvent often
 rarement rarely
vite quickly

Other structural words and phrases

au-dessus de above
 au-dessous de below
aussitôt que as soon as
donc therefore
pour que so that
quelconque any, ordinary
quelque chose something

13

Structures

70. Relative Pronouns

A. General.   The term *relative pronoun* is used to designate certain words that link two simple sentences together by pointing out the bond, or relationship, between them. As a simple example, take the two sentences below:

Haydn a composé cent quatre symphonies.
Haydn était autrichien.

The repetition of the name Haydn characterizes poor—or at least juvenile —style. These two sentences can be related in two ways, depending on which sentence is considered the more important. If we take the first as the main thought (main clause), we may insert the second by replacing Haydn with **qui** (*who*).

> Haydn,   a composé cent quatre symphonies.
>   **qui** était autrichien,

Or, inverting the situation to make the second the main clause,

>   **qui** a composé cent quatre symphonies,
> Haydn,   était autrichien.

In each case the word **qui** was the link used to relate the clauses: hence the name *relative pronoun*.

B. Translations.   The reader needs to be aware of the following meanings for **qui**, **que** (**qu'**), and **lequel**.

qui	who, whom	⎱
que	that	⎰ = that
lequel	which	

The form **qu'** represents **que**, never **qui**.

C. Details of Relative Pronouns

Qui: If the antecedent is a person, use *who;* if a thing, use *which* or *that.* The verb immediately follows.

> Il y avait une fois un roi **qui** était superstitieux.
> Once upon a time there was a king *who* was superstitious.

> C'est une maison **qui** est très coûteuse.
> It's a house *that* is very costly.

Que or qu':   Since **que** or **qu'** must be followed by a noun or pronoun in English, if necessary skip the verb and translate the next independent noun structure first, then return to the verb.

> Voilà le livre **que** cherche **la dame.**
> There is the book *that the lady* is looking for.

> Voilà la machine **qu'**inventa **Pascal** au XVIIe siècle.
> There is the machine *that Pascal* invented in the 17th century.

> Voilà le médecin **que nous** cherchions.
> There is the doctor *whom we* were looking for.

Ce qui and ce que: These forms (pronounced /ski/ and /skə/) are used when there is no expressed antecedent. They refer only to things, never to people. Their equivalent in English is usually *what.*

> Je sais **ce que** vous désirez acheter.
> I know *what* you want to buy.

> Je sais **ce qui** se passe dans la rue.
> I know *what* is going on in the street.

Lequel and qui as Objects of a Preposition: As the object of a preposition **qui** always refers to a person and is translated by *whom;* **lequel** is translated by *which.*

> L'ingénieur **avec qui** j'ai parlé est suisse.
> The engineer *with whom* I spoke is Swiss.

> Le stylo **avec lequel** j'ai écrit était mauvais.
> The pen I wrote with (*with which* I wrote) was bad.

1. Gender as It Affects Meaning

Although knowledge of the gender of nouns is not prerequisite to reading French, it is obviously useful in the development of reading skill and comprehension. Some nouns have different meanings depending on their gender. Learn the following pairs of nouns with the articles that distinguish their meanings.

Masculine		*Feminine*	
un aide	assistant	**une aide**	aid, assistance
le critique	critic (*person*)	**la critique**	criticism (*analysis*)
le livre	book	**la livre**	pound (*weight*)

	Masculine		*Feminine*
le manche	handle	**la manche**	sleeve
		La Manche	English Channel
le mémoire	~~N~~ memoir, memorandum	**la mémoire**	memory
le mode	manner, mood	**la mode**	fashion
le moule	model, mould	**la moule**	mussel
le page	page boy	**la page**	page (of a book)
le parti	party (*political*)	**la partie**	part, game
le pendule	pendulum	**la pendule**	clock
le poêle	stove	**la poêle**	frying pan
le poste	post, position (*employment*)	**la poste**	post office
le somme	nap, sleep	**la somme**	sum (*math*)
le tour	turn (to do something)	**la tour**	tower
le voile	veil	**la voile**	sail (of a ship)

In a sentence such as **Nous examinions le pendule**, it is important to know whether the object under scrutiny was the *pendulum* (masculine) or the *clock* (feminine). Obviously, the context may have made it clear which to expect.

72. The Adjective *tout* (all)

A. General.   Like most other adjectives, **tout** has four forms that correspond with the forms of the nouns it modifies. The adjective **tout** normally precedes the noun.

	masculine	*feminine*	*meaning*
singular	tout	toute	each, every
	tout le*	toute la*	the whole
plural	tous les*	toutes les*	all (of) the

---

*If **le, la,** or **les** appears, *the* is part of the translation.

tout livre	every book, each book	**toute la maison**	the whole house
tout le livre	the whole book	**tous les livres**	all the books
toute maison	every house, each house	**toutes les maisons**	all the houses

B. Idioms using tout.   Learn the following fixed expressions.

tous deux	both	**tout autre**	quite otherwise
tout à coup	suddenly	**tout de suite**	immediately
tout d'un coup	at one go	**tout à l'heure**	right away, just
tout à fait	completely		now, a moment
tout le monde	everybody		ago
tout [évident]	quite [evident]	**pas du tout**	not at all
		tout au plus (moins)	at most (least)

73. The Verb *ouvrir** (to open)

Verbs following the same pattern as **ouvrir*** include **couvrir*** (*to cover*), **découvrir*** (*to discover, to reveal*), **offrir*** (*to offer, to give*), and **souffrir*** (*to suffer*).

Present Tense:

j' **ouvre**	I am opening	nous **ouvrons**	we are opening
tu **ouvres**	you are opening	vous **ouvrez**	you are opening
il **ouvre**	he is opening	ils **ouvrent**	they are opening

Note: Although **ouvrir** ends in **-ir**, it does *not* follow the ending system for **-ir** verbs. Instead it uses endings of **-er** verbs. The past participle is also irregularly formed.

Future and Conditional: Stem **ouvrir-** (regular formation)

Imperfect:

il **ouvrait**   he was opening, used to open

Past Definite: Stem **ouvr-** [+ **-is** type endings]

Present Participle: **ouvrant**, *opening*

Past Participle: **ouvert**, *opened* (Used with auxiliary **avoir**)

couvrir	**couvert**	covered
découvrir	**découvert**	discovered
offrir	**offert**	offered, given
souffrir	**souffert**	suffered

Exercises

A. *Relative pronouns.* Translate into natural-sounding English.

1. La personne qui regarde cette statue est un touriste allemand.
2. La personne que regardent les touristes est leur guide.
3. Un triangle isocèle est celui qui a deux côtés égaux.
4. C'est un silence que ne trouble aucun bruit.
5. Il n'y a pas de peuple qui fasse des progrès aussi rapides que les Américains.
6. Ce qui me frappe c'est la grandeur des entreprises industrielles.
7. Un voyageur qui avait passé la journée sous la pluie arriva à une auberge vers minuit.
8. Voici les minerais que l'on trouve dans l'île de Sri Lanka.

---

5. **fasse** (present subjunctive of **faire**, with same meaning as present indicative; see Appendix C, Irregular Stem Index)

9. L'oxygène est un gaz qui forme la partie active de l'atmosphère.
10. La probabilité que cherchent les statisticiens n'est pas facile à calculer.
11. Cette petite île qu'on appelle l'île de la Motte à Neuchâtel est peu connue des Français.
12. L'astrologue faisait ce que le roi ne pouvait faire.
13. L'autobus qu'ont pris mes amis arrivera à Nice ce soir.
14. Ce qu'on trouve en Amérique, c'est une littérature appliquée.
15. C'est une ellipse que décrit la terre en tournant autour du soleil.
16. Les passants regardaient l'endroit que nous venions de quitter.

B. *The adjective **tout** and verbs like **ouvrir**.* Translate into natural-sounding English.

17. Toutes les expériences physiques exigent des appareils coûteux. [costly]
18. Tout problème financier doit être résolu tout de suite.
19. On a ouvert toutes les portes du théâtre; elles sont toujours ouvertes.
20. J'ai lu tous les livres qu'on m'a offerts.
21. J'admire énormément tous les romans policiers qu'a écrits Agatha Christie.
22. Le jeune homme a offert toutes ces fleurs à sa petite amie.
23. Le continent qu'a découvert Christophe Colomb était l'Amérique.
24. Tout le monde sait que c'est le professeur Einstein qui découvrit la formule $E = mc^2$.
25. Tous les chats sont gris, la nuit. [at night]

Readings

La Linguistique générative

[26] Dans son ouvrage *Structures syntaxiques*, Noam Chomsky introduit les premières transformations dans la description syntaxique. [27] Ses concepts de compétence et de performance, de structure de surface et de structure profonde constituent en une théorie d'ensemble nouvelle des phénomènes linguistiques. Un nouveau mouvement est né: celui de la *linguistique générative*. [28] La rapide diffusion du mouvement de la linguistique générative en Europe peut s'expliquer non seulement par une tendance très générale d'ouverture de l'Europe aux conceptions américaines, mais également par certains aspects de la théorie générative elle-même. [29] Par exemple, elle renoue avec certaines traditions anciennes de la grammaire, en même temps qu'elle

---

16. **passant** *m.* passer-by; **venions de** (idiom; see Sec. 69)   19. **porte**† *f.* door; **toujours** *adv.* (Use a meaning other than *always*)   22. **fleur** *f.* flower; **petite amie** *f.* girlfriend   25. **chat** *m.* cat; **gris, -e** *adj.* gray; **la nuit** at night   26. **syntaxique** *adj.* syntactic   29. **renouer** to tie in; **lié** (past participle of **lier**, *to connect*)

redécouvre sous des formes nouvelles des concepts liés au développement de la linguistique structurale européenne.

[30] La linguistique générative a permis d'incontestables progrès dans la compréhension des phénomènes syntaxiques: [31] elle a réinterprété et approfondi en phonologies les découvertes du structuralisme: elle a donné enfin une impulsion nouvelle à la psycholinguistique et à la linguistique appliquée. [32] Cependant, malgré les nombreuses recherches entreprises en sémantique, c'est dans ce domaine, ou plutôt dans celui des relations entre grammaire et sémantique, qu'apparaissent les difficultés les plus prononcées de la théorie générative.

[33] C'est vers la résolution de ces problèmes que s'oriente actuellement la linguistique, problèmes qui sont eux-mêmes la source de perspectives théoriques (sémantique générative).

Candide ou l'optimisme

Comment Candide fut élevé dans un beau château, et comment il fut chassé de là

[34] Il y avait en Westphalie, dans le château de M. le baron de Thunder-ten-tronckh, un jeune garçon à qui la nature avait donné les mœurs les plus douces. [35] Il avait le jugement assez droit avec l'esprit le plus simple†: c'est, je crois, pour cette raison qu'on le nommait Candide.

[36] Monsieur le baron était un des plus puissants seigneurs de la Westphalie, car son château avait une porte et des fenêtres. [37] Sa grande salle même était ornée d'une tapisserie. [38] Tous les chiens de ses basses-cours composaient une meute dans le besoin; ses palefreniers étaient ses piqueurs; le vicaire du village était son grand aumônier. [39] Ils l'appelaient tous Monseigneur, et ils riaient quand il faisait des contes.

[40] Madame la baronne, qui pesait environ trois cent cinquante livres, s'attirait par là une très grande considération, et faisait les honneurs de la maison avec une dignité qui la rendait encore plus respectable. [41] Sa fille Cunégonde, âgée de dix-sept ans, était haute en couleur, fraîche, grasse, appétissante. [42] Le fils du baron paraissait en tout digne de son père. [43] Le précepteur Pangloss était l'oracle de la maison, et le petit Candide écoutait ses leçons avec toute la bonne foi de son âge et de son caractère.

---

31. **approfondi** (past participle of **approfondir**, *to extend*) (Note that **profond** means *deep*, and **approfondir** is literally *to make deeper*) 34. **mœurs** *f.pl.* manners; **doux, douce** *adj.* gentle 35. **simple†** *adj.* uncomplicated, straightforward; **nommer** to name 37. **grande salle** *f.* great hall; **orner** to decorate; **tapisserie** *f.* tapestry, rug 38. **chien** *m.* dog; **basse-cour** *f.* farmyard; **meute** *f.* pack (hunting pack); **besoin** *m.* need; **palefrenier** *m.* stable boy; **piqueur** *m.* huntsman; **aumônier** *m.* chaplain 39. **Monseigneur** Milord; **rire*** to laugh; **faire des contes** to tell stories 40. **s'attirer** to attract to oneself, to win; **par là** because of that, for that reason 41. **fille** *f.* daughter; **frais, fraîche** *adj.* fresh (complexion); **gras, -se** *adj.* plump; **appétissant, -e** *adj.* tempting 42. **digne** *adj.* worthy 43. **écouter** to listen to; **foi** *f.* faith

[44] Pangloss enseignait la métaphysico-théologico-cosmolo-nigologie. [45] Il prouvait admirablement qu'il n'y a point d'effet sans cause, et que, dans ce meilleur des mondes possibles, le château de monseigneur le baron était le plus beau des châteaux et madame la meilleure des baronnes possibles.

[46] «Il est démontré, disait-il, que les choses† ne peuvent être autrement: car, tout étant fait pour une fin, tout est nécessairement pour la meilleure fin. Remarquez bien que les nez ont été faits pour porter des lunettes; aussi avons-nous des lunettes. [47] Les jambes sont visiblement instituées pour être chaussées, et nous avons des chausses. [48] Les pierres ont été formées pour être taillées et pour en faire des châteaux; aussi monseigneur a un très beau château; le plus grand baron de la province doit être le mieux logé; et, les cochons étant faits pour être mangés, nous mangeons du porc toute l'année: [49] par conséquent, ceux qui ont avancé que tout est bien ont dit une sottise; il fallait dire que tout est au mieux.»

d'après Voltaire, *Candide ou l'optimisme*, Chapitre I

Candide ou l'optimisme (suite)

[50] Candide écoutait attentivement, et croyait innocemment: car il trouvait Mlle Cunégonde extrêmement belle, quoiqu'il ne prît jamais la hardiesse de le lui dire. [51] Il concluait qu'après le bonheur d'être né baron de Thunder-ten-tronckh, le second degré de bonheur était d'être Mlle Cunégonde; le troisième, de la voir tous les jours; et le quatrième, d'entendre maître Pangloss, le plus grand philosophe de la province, et par conséquent de toute la terre.

[52] Un jour, Cunégonde, en se promenant auprès du château, dans le petit bois qu'on appelait parc, vit entre des broussailles le docteur Pangloss qui donnait une leçon de physique expérimentale à la femme de chambre de sa mère, petite brune très jolie et très docile. [53] Comme Mlle Cunégonde avait beaucoup de disposition pour les sciences, elle observa sans souffler les expériences réitérées dont elle fut témoin; elle vit clairement la raison suffisante du docteur, les effets et les causes, et s'en retourna tout agitée, toute pensive, toute remplie du désir d'être savante, songeant qu'elle pourrait bien être la raison suffisante du jeune Candide, qui pouvait aussi être la sienne.

[54] Elle rencontra Candide en revenant au château, et rougit; Candide rougit aussi; elle lui dit bonjour d'une voix entrecoupée, et Candide lui parla sans

---

44. **Pangloss** (The names are symbolic: **pan**, *universal;* **gloss**, *words.* **Pangloss** represents a theory of systematic optimism which Voltaire ridicules in this story); **nigologie** (from **nigaud**, *stupid*) stupidity   46. **démontrer** to demonstrate; **chose**† *f.* thing; **fin** *f.* purpose, end; **lunettes** *f.pl.* glasses; **aussi** [+ inversion] therefore (Sec. 81)   47. **jambe** *f.* leg; **chaussé** (past participle of **chausser**, to shoe) **chausse** *f.* shoe   48. **pierre** *f.* stone; **tailler** to cut, to trim; **cochon** *m.* pig; **manger** to eat   49. **sottise** *f.* foolish thing; **au mieux** at its best   50. **Mlle** (abbrev. of **mademoiselle**) Miss; **quoique** *conj.* although; **hardiesse** *f.* boldness   51. **bonheur** *m.* happiness   52. **broussailles** *f.pl.* brushwood; **brune** *f.* brunette   53. **souffler** to breathe; **raison suffisante** *f.* (a technical term used by Leibnitz, which Voltaire is satirizing); **songer** to think, to reflect; **bien** *adv.* certainly; **la sienne** *poss. pron.* hers   54. **rougir** (same as **devenir rouge**); **entrecoupé** (past participle of **entrecouper**, *to break*)

savoir ce qu'il disait. [55] Le lendemain, après le dîner, comme on sortait de table, Cunégonde et Candide se trouvèrent derrière un paravent; Cunégonde laissa tomber son mouchoir, Candide le ramassa; [56] elle lui prit innocemment la main, le jeune homme baisa innocemment la main de la jeune demoiselle avec une vivacité, une sensibilité, une grâce toute particulière; leurs bouches se rencontrèrent, leurs yeux s'enflammèrent†, leurs genoux tremblèrent, leurs mains s'égarèrent. [57] M. le baron de Thunder-ten-tronckh passa auprès du paravent, et, voyant cette cause et cet effet, chassa Candide du château à grands coups de pied dans le derrière; [58] Cunégonde s'évanouit; elle fut souffletée par madame la baronne dès qu'elle fut revenue à elle-même; et tout fut consterné dans le plus beau et le plus agréable des châteaux possibles.

d'après Voltaire, *Candide ou l'optimisme*, Chapitre I

Test 13, page 243

---

55. **paravent** *m.* screen   56. **baiser** to kiss; **s'enflammer**† to light up; **genou** *m.* knee; **s'égarer** to wander   58. **s'évanouir** to faint

14

Structures

74. Adjectives with Variable Meanings According to Position

There are a few adjectives whose meaning depends on their position in relation to the noun modified. The five most important are listed below.

	before the noun	after the noun (or as predicate adjective)
ancien, -ne	former	ancient, old
propre	own	clean, neat
seul, -e	only, single	alone
même	same	very, itself, himself, herself
grand, -e (person)	great	tall

Examples:

also:
certain — "not that young anymore"
une personne d'un certain âge
une personne d'un âge certain
   implies old

mon **ancien** professeur	my *former* professor
l'histoire **ancienne**	*ancient* history
L'église est **ancienne**.	The church is *old*.
ma **propre** chambre	my *own* room
ma chambre **propre**	my *clean* room
La chambre est **propre**.	The room is *clean*.
la **même** histoire	the *same* story
l'histoire **même**	the story *itself*, the *very* story

P. 185
App. A #9

When **même** is the first word in a sentence or clause, it means *even*.

Même le roi ne pouvait prédire l'avenir.
Even the king could not predict the future.

136

75. Possessive Adjectives

The following chart shows the forms of the possessive adjectives.

	before a noun that is		
masculine singular	*feminine singular*	*plural*	*meaning*
mon	ma	mes	my
ton	ta	tes	your (familiar)
son	sa	ses	his, her, its*
	notre	nos	our
	votre	vos	your
	leur	leurs	their

---

*Meaning based on the antecedent (earlier mentioned) noun.

Unlike the possessive adjective in English, the French possessive adjective agrees in gender and number with the thing possessed, rather than with the possessor. As a result, **son** can mean *his, her,* or *its,* and so can **sa** and **ses**.

Albert a **son** livre.	Albert has *his* book.
Marie a **son** livre.	Marie has *her* book.

In the two examples above, the possessive adjective **son** is used regardless of whether the owner is male or female, because the object possessed, **livre,** is masculine singular.

Whereas in French the possessive adjective is generally repeated before each noun, in English it is used only with the first noun. You should follow English usage in translation.

Robert va en ville avec **son** père, **sa** mère et **son** frère.
Robert is going downtown with *his* father, mother, and brother.

76. The Adverb and Pronoun y (there)

The word **y** replaces a prepositional phrase. Its most common meaning is *there,* replacing a prepositional phrase designating a *location,* or one beginning with **à** not referring to a person.

```
┌──────── replacing ────────┐
                            ▼
```
Nous **y** allons.	Nous allons **à Paris.**
We are going *there.*	We are going *to Paris.*

When used with other verbal constructions that require the preposition **à** (**au, aux**) after the verb, **y** retains the meaning of the phrase it replaces.

Nous pensons à ce problème.   Nous *y* pensons.
We are thinking *about* this problem.   We are thinking *about it*.

Il y a (*there is, there are*) is a fixed expression formed with **y** and the third person of **avoir.** It is also used in other tenses.

Il y avait des étudiants dans le café.   *There were* some students in the café.
Il y aura une fête.   *There will be* a party.
Il y aurait plusieurs possibilités.   *There would be* several possibilities.

Il y a is used to refer to something that is not in view or that the speaker does not wish to point at. The word **voilà** is used for *there is* when the object can be pointed out.

Il y a une librairie en ville.
There is a bookstore downtown.

Voilà une librairie.
There (pointing) *is* a bookstore.

77. Conjunctions

Below are listed some important conjunctions that you should become familiar with.

A. Two-part conjunctions, separated in the sentence

et ... et   both ... and
ou ... ou   }
soit ... soit }   either ... or

Examples:

Il a lu **et** les romans **et** les contes de Voltaire.
He has read *both* the novels *and* the short stories of Voltaire.

B. One-word conjunctions

et	and	**quand**	when
mais	but	**quoique**	although
ou	or	**néanmoins**	nevertheless
si	if	**pourtant** }	however
que	that	**cependant** }	
comme	as		

C. Conjunctions incorporating *que*

parce que	because
alors que } **tandis que** }	whereas
afin que } **pour que** }	in order that, so that
jusqu'à ce que	until
à moins que ... (ne)	unless

also p. 155
App. A → more Conjunctions

de sorte que
de façon que   } so that
de manière que   )

puisque = since, therefore
as

Examples:

Nous resterons **à moins que** vous **ne** vouliez partir.
We will stay *unless* you want to leave. (ineffective **ne**)

78. Use of the Irregular Stem Index

The Irregular Stem Index on pages 200–203 will help you find meanings of verb forms not usually listed in dictionaries.

This Index consists of two parts: the Alphabetical Listing and the Ending Table. To identify a verb form, look for it first in the Alphabetical Listing. If you do not find the verb spelled out in full, drop the last letter and start again. Continue dropping end letters and checking until you find a listing—in some cases you may end up with just one letter.

For example, to identify **ils purent**, you look for **purent**, then (since you do not find it) **puren-**, **pure-**, **pur-**, **pu-**, and finally **p-**. (Although you do find **pu** in the listing, the absence of the hyphen indicates that **pu** is a complete word, and not a part of **purent**.) You find the following information after **p-**:

p- (pouvoir 20) *PDu* was able, could
1   2   3   4

1. The word **pouvoir** is the infinitive of the form **purent**.
2. The number 20 is the number of the verb table (p. 197) where tenses are displayed with their essential forms.
3. *PDu* is the Tense Indicator—in this case, past definite. The italic *u* means that the next letter is *u*, as is in fact the case for **purent**.
4. When there is only one tense indicator, the meaning is given, ready for use. (You may, however, verify the form by consulting the Ending Table. Look along the *PDu* line to see if the remainder of the verb (-**urent**) appears there. If so, you have the complete verb: **p-** from the Alphabetical Listing and the rest from the Ending Table.)

Sometimes you must make simple English agreement from the meaning given. Here, for example, *was able* should be changed to *were able* for the subject *they*.

If you find a form in the Alphabetical Listing that is followed by two or more italic Tense Indicators, you must check each tense on the ending table to see which one you are dealing with.

Suppose you were looking for **il saurait**. You would (after dropping -**t**, then -**it**, then -**ait**) find the following entry in the Alphabetical Listing:

saur- (savoir 24) *F* will know *C* would know, would be able

Go to the ending table, and on line *F* look for the completion of the verb form (**-ait**). If it is not there, you know that the tense is not future, and that the meaning *will know* is not the correct one. You then look on line *C* in the ending table, and there you will indeed find the completion of the verb (**-ait**). This tells you to use the meaning that follows *C* in the Alphabetical Listing—that is, *he would know*, or *he would be able*.

Exercises

A. *Adjectives.* Give English equivalents.

1. le même roman / la même personne / la théorie même
2. le même personnage / même le président / le directeur même
3. une statue ancienne / un ancien élève / l'histoire ancienne
4. mon ancien professeur / une culture ancienne / un ancien combattant
5. leurs propres livres / ma propre chambre / une salle propre
6. leur propre ordinateur / nos propres idées / notre programme même
7. votre décision seule / vos seules décisions / sa propre évaluation
8. l'université: son ordinateur / sa bibliothèque / ses étudiants
9. Mme Leblanc: son ordinateur / sa bibliothèque / ses étudiants
10. M. Dupont: son ordinateur / sa bibliothèque / ses programmes
11. Paul: sa propre voiture / Marie: son avion à réaction
12. La France: ses grands auteurs / Victor Hugo: sa poésie célèbre
13. Voilà Robert, son père, sa mère et ses frères.

B. *Conjunctions and the adverb y.* Translate into natural-sounding English.

14. Napoléon était un grand homme, mais il n'était pas un homme grand.
15. Les chimistes s'occupent des éléments, tandis que les psychologues ne s'occupent que des phénomènes mentaux.
16. Le triangle isocèle est construit de sorte que deux des côtés sont égaux.
17. La psychologie emploie et l'observation directe et la méthode clinique.
18. Ce train transporte et des passagers et des marchandises.
19. Je crois cependant que ces deux formes de gouvernement peuvent se concilier.
20. Nous irons au cinéma à moins que vous ne soyez trop fatigué. / Nous y arriverons vers sept heures du soir.

---

4. **ancien combattant** (one word in English) 11. **avion à réaction** *m.* jet aircraft 18. **marchandises** (in railroad terminology, not *merchandise*) 19. **se concilier** to be reconciled 20. **ne** (Ne is often used without **pas** or an alternative negative particle after certain conjunctions: **à moins que, de peur que, avant que, sans que, de crainte que**. It should be ignored in translation. See Sec. 87); **soyez** (from **être**) (See Appendix C, Irregular Stem Index); **du soir** P.M. (literally, *in the evening*)

21. La flotte française fut détruite à Aboukir. L'amiral anglais Nelson y a surpris les Français.
22. La jeune femme arriva devant la boutique. Elle y entra parce qu'elle voulait acheter quelque chose pour son enfant†.
23. L'ingénieur a pris un taxi pour aller à son hôtel. Il y est descendu quelques minutes plus tard.
24. On immergera les cylindres soit en mer soit dans les rades.

C. *General review.* Translate into good English.

25. Fermat était le plus puissant esprit mathématique du 17e siècle.
26. Einstein énonça le premier la théorie de la relativité.
27. Guy Patin pensa le premier à employer la vapeur comme force motrice.
28. La théorie de la relativité a été exposée par Einstein il y a plus de soixante-dix ans.
29. La nature de l'attitude est aussi peu déterminée que les conditions qui l'ont formée.
30. L' uranium est beaucoup moins abondant que le thorium.
31. Il y a des sociétés internationales qui ont fait construire des gratte-ciel au centre de Paris.
32. Il n'y a pas de peuple qui ait fait des progrès aussi rapides que les Américains.

D. *Irregular stem index.* Find the meanings of the following verb forms. (Are any of them to be found in the dictionary?)

33. ils crurent   34. nous mîmes   35. il naquit   36. il tint
37. qu'il voie   38. ils suivirent   39. ils purent   40. il a dû

Readings

Une Entrevue entre le Pape et l'Empereur

[In this tale by Alfred de Vigny, Renard tells under what circumstances he witnessed an interview in which Napoleon tried unsuccessfully to domineer the Pope. At the time (1804) Renard was a page to the Emperor. As he happened to be in the room at the château of Fontainebleau when Napoléon suddenly returned, he hid behind some curtains.]

[41] Le hasard†, notre maître à tous, fit apparaître au grand jour l'âme de Napoléon.—Un jour, ce fut peut-être le seul de sa vie, il rencontra plus fort que

---

21. **flotte** *f.* fleet; **détruite** (past participle of **détruire***, *to destroy*); **Aboukir** (ville en Egypte, près d'Alexandrie)   22. **enfant**† *m.* or *f.* child (*Infant* is **un bébé**)   26. **énoncer** to state   28. **soixante-dix** (See Numbers, Appendix D)   31. **société** *f.* corporation; **gratte-ciel** *m.* (*invariable*) skyscraper   41. **hasard**† *m.* chance; **au grand jour** in broad daylight; **plus fort** (same as **une personne plus forte**)

lui et recula un instant devant un ascendant plus grand que le sien.—J'en fus témoin. Voici ce qui arriva:

[42] Nous étions à Fontainebleau. Le Pape venait d'arriver. L'Empereur l'avait attendu† impatiemment pour le sacre, et l'avait reçu en voiture. Il revenait au château. J'avais laissé plusieurs officiers dans la chambre qui précédait celle de l'Empereur, et j'étais resté seul dans la sienne. [43] Je regardais des lettres lorsque le bruit des tambours qui battaient *aux champs* m'apprit l'arrivée subite de l'Empereur. J'eus à peine le temps de me jeter dans une alcôve fermée par des rideaux.

[44] L'Empereur était fort agité. Il marchait seul dans la chambre comme quelqu'un qui attendait avec impatience quelque chose. Il s'avança vers la fenêtre et se mit à y tambouriner une marche avec les ongles. Une voiture roula dans la cour. Il cessa de battre, frappa des pieds comme impatienté par la vue de quelque chose qui se faisait avec lenteur, puis il alla brusquement à la porte et l'ouvrit au Pape.

[45] Pie VII entra seul. Bonaparte se hâta de refermer la porte derrière lui, avec une promptitude de geôlier. Je sentis une grande terreur, je l'avoue, en me voyant en tiers avec de telles gens. Cependant je restai sans voix et sans mouvement, regardant et écoutant de toute la puissance de mon esprit.

[46] Le Pape était d'une taille élevée; il avait un visage allongé, jaune, souffrant, mais pleine d'une noblesse sainte et d'une bonté sans bornes. Il entra lentement, avec la démarche calme et prudente d'une femme âgée. Il vint s'asseoir, les yeux baissés, sur un des grands fauteuils romains dorés et chargés d'aigles, et attendit ce que lui allait dire l'autre Italien.

[47] Napoléon ne cessa pas de marcher dans la chambre quand le Pape fut entré; il se mit à rôder autour du fauteuil comme un chasseur prudent. Il se mit alors à parler, en marchant circulairement et jetant des regards perçants dans les glaces de l'appartement où se réfléchissait la figure grave du Saint-Père, et le regardant en profil quand il passait près de lui, mais jamais en face, de peur de sembler trop inquiet de l'impression de ses paroles:

[48] «Il y a quelque chose,» dit-il, «qui me reste sur le cœur, Saint-Père, c'est que vous consentez au sacre de la même manière que l'autre fois au concordat, comme si vous y étiez forcé. Vous avez un air de martyr devant moi, vous êtes là

---

41. **reculer** to fall back, to recoil; **ascendant** *m.* influence, presence; **le sien** *poss. pron.* his; **témoin** *m.* witness   42. **venait de** (Recall the special construction, Sec. 69); **attendu**† (past participle of **attendre**, *to wait for*. To attend is **assister** à); **sacre** *m.* coronation; **la sienne** *poss. pron.* his   43. **tambour** *m.* drum; **aux champs** (Official salute, ruffles and flourishes); **subit, -e** *adj.* sudden; **eus** (See Appendix C, Irregular Stem Index); **se jeter** to rush; **rideau** *m.* curtain   44. **fort** (same as **très**); **se mit à** (from **se mettre à**, Sec. 56); **tambouriner** to drum, to tap; **ongle** *m.* fingernail; **cour** *f.* courtyard; **frapper des pieds** to stamp; **se faisait** (Sec. 53); **lenteur** *f.* slowness (In English, **avec lenteur** is one word ending in *-ly*)   45. **Pie VII** Pope Pius VII (pope from 1800 to 1823, held captive at Fontainebleau until 1814); **se hâter de** to hasten to; **geôlier** *m.* jailer; **avouer** to admit, to confess; **en tiers** as a third party; **gens** *f.pl.* people   46. **taille** *f.* stature; **borne** *f.* limit; **fauteuil** *m.* armchair; **doré** *adj.* gilded, golden; **chargé d'aigles** decorated with imperial eagles; **Italien** (Both the Pope and Napoléon were of Italian extraction)   47. **rôder** to prowl; **chasseur** *m.* hunter; **jetant** (from **jeter**, *to cast, to throw*); **perçant** (from **percer**, *to pierce*); **glace** *f.* mirror; **où** (Missing link; see Appendix A, 3); **inquiet, inquiète** *adj.* worried   48. **qui me reste sur le cœur** that hurts me, that weighs on my heart; **concordat** (agreement between Napoléon and the Pope in 1801); **y** into it

comme résigné, comme offrant au ciel vos douleurs. Mais, en vérité, ce n'est pas là votre situation, vous n'êtes pas prisonnier, par Dieu! vous êtes libre comme l'air.»

[49] Pie VII sourit avec tristesse et le regarda en face.

«Oui,» reprit Bonaparte avec plus de force, «vous êtes parfaitement libre; vous pouvez vous en retourner à Rome, la route vous est ouverte, personne ne vous retient.»

Le Pape soupira et leva sa main droite et ses yeux au ciel sans répondre; ensuite il laissa retomber très lentement son front† ridé et se mit à considérer la croix d'or suspendue à son cou.

[50] «Moi, je ne sais pas,» reprit Napoléon, «pourquoi vous auriez de la répugnance à siéger à Paris pour toujours. Je vous laisserais, ma foi, les Tuileries, si vous vouliez. Ne voyez-vous pas bien, Padre, que c'est là la vraie capitale du monde? Moi, je ferais tout ce que vous voudriez; je vous mettrais ensuite dans la main les vraies clefs du monde, et comme Notre-Seigneur a dit: «Je suis venu avec l'épée,» je garderais l'épée, moi; je vous la rapporterais seulement à bénir après chaque succès de nos armes.»

[51] Il s'inclina légèrement en disant ces dernières paroles.

Le Pape, qui jusque là n'avait cessé de demeurer sans mouvement, comme une statue égyptienne, releva lentement sa tête, sourit avec mélancolie, leva ses yeux en haut et dit, avec un soupir paisible, comme s'il eût confié sa pensée à son ange gardien invisible:

«*Commediante!*»

[52] Bonaparte sauta de sa chaise et bondit comme un léopard blessé. Une vraie colère le prit. Il me semblait qu'il allait arriver quelque terrible et grande chose.

[53] La bombe éclata tout à coup.

«Comédien! Moi! Ah! je vous donnerai des comédies à vous faire tous pleurer comme des femmes et des enfants. Mon théâtre, c'est le monde; le rôle que j'y joue, c'est celui de maître et d'auteur; pour comédiens, j'ai vous tous, Pape, Rois, Peuples! [54] Comédien! Ah! Il faudrait être d'une autre taille que la vôtre pour m'oser applaudir ou siffler, signor Chiaramonti! Savez-vous bien que vous ne seriez qu'un pauvre curé, si je le voulais? Vous et votre tiare, la France vous rirait au nez, si ne je gardais mon air sérieux en vous saluant.»

[55] Il se tut. Je n'osais pas respirer. J'avançai la tête pour voir si le pauvre vieillard était mort d'effroi. Le même calme dans l'attitude, le même calme sur le

---

48. **douleur** *f.* grief   49. **soupirer** to sigh; **laissa retomber** (Next independent noun group precedes retomber in the translation); **front**† *m.* forehead; **croix** *f.* cross, crucifix; **cou** *m.* neck   50. **siéger** to have headquarters; **ma foi** indeed; **Tuileries** (A palace adjoining the Louvre, erected by Catherine de' Medici in 1564, destroyed by fire in 1874; only a park remains on the site); **clef** *f.* key; **épée** *f.* sword; **bénir** to bless   51. **s'incliner** to bow; **là** then; **soupir** *m.* sigh (See **soupirer**, note 49); **paisible** *adj.* peaceful; **eut** (from **avoir**, *to have*); **pensée** *f.* thought; **commediante** (in Italian) come-dian   52. **sauter** to jump; **bondir** to bound; **il allait arriver** (Impersonal il: place the real subject **chose** with modifiers before the verb)   53. **éclater** to explode   54. **la vôtre** *poss. pron.* yours; **siffler** to hiss; **curé** *m.* priest; **tiare** Pope's tiara; **rirait** (from **rire***, *to laugh*); **au nez** in your face   55. **se tut** (from se **taire***, *to fall silent*); **vieillard** *m.* old man; **effroi** *m.* fright

visage. Il leva une seconde fois les yeux au ciel et, après avoir encore jeté un profond soupir, il sourit avec amertume et dit:

«*Tragediante.*»

[56] Bonaparte, à ce moment-là, était au bout de la chambre, appuyé sur la cheminée de marbre aussi haute que lui. Il partit comme un trait, courant sur le vieillard; je crus qu'il allait le tuer. Mais il s'arrêta court, prit, sur la table, un vase de porcelaine de Sèvres, et le jetant sur le plancher, le broya sous ses pieds. [57] Puis, tout d'un coup, il s'assit et demeura dans un silence profond et une immobilité formidable. Il devint triste, sa voix fut sourde et mélancolique et, dès sa première parole, je compris que ce Protée, dompté par deux mots, se montrait lui-même.

[58] «C'est vrai! Tragédien ou Comédien.—Tout est rôle, tout est costume pour moi depuis longtemps et pour toujours. Quelle fatigue! Quelle petitesse! Poser! Toujours poser!...»

d'après Alfred de Vigny, *La Canne de Jonc*

Orientation et sélection professionnelles

[59] Comment utilise-t-on actuellement les résultats des tests en orientation et en sélection?

Lorsqu'un individu vient demander des conseils d'orientation à un spécialiste, celui-ci peut se servir de quelques tests appropriés à son cas. [60] Après avoir comparé les résultats de son sujet avec ceux d'autres sujets ayant servi pour la validation des tests, le conseiller d'orientation peut dire: «Vous êtes suffisamment intelligent pour réussir dans un des domaines qui vous intéressent, mais voici ce qui me paraît vous intéresser le plus. Ce domaine exige une très grande aptitude mécanique et vos résultats montrent que vous l'avez. [61] Il y a donc des chances que si vous vous appliquez, vous réussirez très bien.» Par ailleurs, il peut être obligé de dire: «Vos réponses à certaines questions de ce test (d'intelligence) ne permettent pas de croire que vous pourrez avoir le diplôme de médecin, mais les autres tests (aptitudes mécaniques) indiquent que vous êtes exceptionnellement doué pour la technique et que vous réussirez probablement très bien dans une industrie qui exige ces dons.»

[62] Le conseiller d'orientation ne dit pas à l'individu qu'il réussira ou ne réussira pas dans un certain domaine car il y a bien d'autres conditions qui

---

55. **amertume** *f.* bitterness; **tragediante** (in Italian) tragedian   56. **appuyé** (past participle of **appuyer**, *to lean*); **cheminée** *f.* mantel; **trait** *m.* arrow; **crus** (from **croire***); **plancher** *m.* floor; **broyer** to grind   57. **sourd, -e** *adj.* hollow, dull; **dès** from; **Protée** Proteus (In Greek mythology, a sea god, son of Poseidon—the Roman god Neptune—who would assume various shapes and forms when captured; what is the analogy with Napoléon?); **dompté** (past participle of **dompter**, *to subdue, to break*); **se montrer** to reveal oneself   58. **est ... depuis** (See Sec. 67B) (The verb is translated by a past tense, rather than the present); **petitesse** *f.* pettiness   59. **orientation** *f.* guidance   60. **exige** (from **exiger**, *to require*)   61. **par ailleurs** in other cases; **doué** (past participle of **douer**, *to endow*) gifted; **don** *m.* gift

contribuent au succès ou à l'échec dans chaque travail, en plus de celles que mesurent les tests.

[63] Le prognostic est plus facile lorsqu'il s'agit de sélection que d'orientation professionnelle. Le psychologue peut dire par exemple avec beaucoup de certitude que parmi les individus ayant donné de mauvais résultats aux tests d'aptitudes, il n'y aura pas plus de 20 pour 100 de réussite s'ils suivent la formation† de pilote et que 90 pour 100 environ seront pilotes lorsqu'il s'agira d'individus ayant très bien réussi à ces tests.

[64] Ce que doivent faire ceux qui se servent des tests de sélection, c'est de déterminer quel est le score critique (le score au-dessous duquel un individu ne peut pas être admis à exercer le métier donné), qui élimine le plus grand nombre d'échecs potentiels, tout en éliminant le moins possible d'individus qui paraissent pouvoir réussir.

Test 14, page 245

---

62. **échec** *m.* failure; **en plus de** in addition to 63. **réussite** *f.* success; **formation**† *f.* training 64. **métier** *m.* occupation, trade, profession

15

Structures

79. Disjunctive Pronouns

Disjunctive pronouns, also called emphatic or stress pronouns, are used:

1. after a preposition ~~object~~
2. alone, or isolated from the main sentence
3. as part of a compound subject

The word *disjunctive* (made up of *dis-*, meaning "not," and *juncture*, meaning "joined") indicates that this type of pronoun is separated from the verb rather than immediately before it like most other pronouns. Note the use of the disjunctive pronoun **moi** in the following examples. **Moi** corresponds to the subject pronoun **je**.

After a Preposition:

Alain a étudié ce cas avec **moi**.
Alain studied this case with *me*.

Alone:

Qui est là? **Moi**.
Who is there? *Me*.

Isolated, for Emphasis:

Je ne suis pas allé à Lyon, **moi**.
I didn't go to Lyon.

As Part of a Compound Subject:

Alain et **moi**, nous avons étudié ce cas.
Alain and *I* studied this case.

(In French the pronoun **nous** summarizes the compound subject. It is not translated.)

Disjunctive pronouns are also used

4. after c'est and ce sont (*it is*)
5. with -même

C'est **moi** qui parlerai au directeur.
It is *I* who will speak to the director.

C'est **lui** qui arrive.
He's arriving.

J'ai rangé les livres **moi-même**.
I put the books away *myself*.

Ils ont réparé la voiture **eux-mêmes**.
They repaired the car *themselves*.

Below is a chart of the disjunctive pronouns in French.

subject	disjunctive pronouns	meaning
je	**moi**	me
tu	**toi**	you
il	**lui**	him, it
elle	**elle**	her, it
on	**soi**	oneself
nous	**nous**	us
vous	**vous**	you
ils	**eux**	them
elles	**elles**	them

80. Imperatives

A. **Forms for *nous* and *vous*.**   The imperative is used to give orders and directions and to make requests and suggestions. For most verbs the **nous** and **vous** imperative forms are the same as the **nous** and **vous** forms of the present tense, minus the subject pronouns.

present	imperative	meaning
nous finissons	**Finissons!**	Let's finish!
vous finissez	**Finissez!**	Finish!
nous parlons	**Parlons!**	Let's talk!
vous parlez	**Parlez!**	Speak!

B. **Forms for *tu*.**   When addressing a close friend or relative, you use the familiar form of the imperative. This form corresponds to the **tu** form of the present tense for most verbs. Note that the final -s is dropped after -e or -a.

present	imperative	meaning
tu finis	**Finis** ta leçon!	Finish your lesson!
tu parles	**Parle** français!	Speak French!
tu vas	**Va** en ville!	Go downtown!

C. Special imperatives *avoir, être,* and *savoir.* The imperative forms of **avoir, être,** and **savoir** are as follows.

	nous	*vous*	*tu*
avoir	ayons	ayez	aie
être	soyons	soyez	sois
savoir	sachons	sachez	sache

For example,

Aie du courage!	Have courage! Be brave!
Soyez sage!	Be good!
Sachons le sujet à fond!	Let's know the subject thoroughly!

These forms are based on the subjunctive (Sec. 82).

81. The Adverb *aussi* and the Expression *aussi bien . . . que*

A. The adverb *aussi.* Usually the word **aussi** is equivalent to *also,* unless it appears at the beginning of a clause. In such a case it means *therefore.*

Nous avons étudié ce cas **aussi**.	We studied this case *also.*
Aussi avons-nous étudié ce cas.	*Therefore* we studied this case.

Note the inverted word order when **aussi** appears at the beginning of a clause or sentence (Sec. 54).

B. The expression *aussi bien . . . que.* The phrase **aussi bien ... que** conveys the meaning of *both ... and* or, in the location of **que,** *as well as.*

L'air atmosphérique contient **aussi bien** de l'azote **que** de l'oxygène.
Atmospheric air contains *both* nitrogen *and* oxygen.
Atmospheric air contains nitrogen *as well as* oxygen.

Ce poisson chasse **aussi bien** en eau profonde qu'en surface.
This fish hunts *both* in deep water *and* near the surface.
This fish hunts in deep water *as well as* near the surface.

Circumflex Accent (ˆ): A Cue to Past Tenses

The circumflex accent in the ending of a verb form (always over the vowel **a, i,** or **u**) indicates either the simple past (past definite, Sec. 66) or the imperfect subjunctive. The tense elimination system continues to work.

1. **â, î,** or **û** plus **-mes** or **-tes** is the past definite tense. Translate it as a simple past tense.

nous finîmes	we finished
vous allâtes	you went

2. â, î, or û plus -t only is the imperfect subjunctive. It may be translated as a simple past tense also. It is a literary form for formal writing, and sometimes expresses *would* or *might* [do something].

> Je doutais qu'il **vendît** sa maison.
> I doubted that he *sold* (or would sell) his house.

Exceptions: The following are present tense forms.

il paraît (paraître*)	it seems, he seems
il connaît (connaître*)	he knows, he is acquainted with
il plaît (plaire*)	it pleases, he pleases
il croît (croître*)	it grows
il croit (croire*)	he believes

Exercises

A. *Disjunctive pronouns.* Translate into good English.

1. Bonaparte s'appuyait sur une cheminée plus haute que lui.
2. —Tout est illusion pour moi depuis longtemps, dit-il.
3. —Moi, je ne sais pas ce qu'il faut faire, reprit le professeur.
4. Elle se hâta de refermer la porte derrière elle.
5. Les grands hommes sont forts, mais le hasard est plus fort qu'eux.
6. Les hommes ont établi parmi eux des gouvernements dont la juste autorité émane du consentement des gouvernés.
7. La Fayette, à peine âgé de vingt ans, fréta lui-même un vaisseau qu'il chargea d'armes.
8. Le voyageur, ayant appris que son cheval ne voulait pas d'huîtres, les a mangées lui-même.
9. Les bras de l'étoile de mer se régénèrent facilement; si l'un d'eux se trouve pris, l'animal se libère en l'abandonnant.
10. Le roi n'aimait pas l'astrologue qui faisait ce que lui, le roi, ne pouvait faire.
11. Voilà Madame Dupont: voici son opinion à elle.
12. Voilà Monsieur Leblanc: voici son opinion à lui.

B. *Imperatives.* Translate into good English.

13. Examinons les résultats de cette expérience physique.
14. Supposons qu'il y ait un événement dont on veut calculer la probabilité.
15. Faites confirmer ces renseignements, s'il vous plaît.
16. Mettez au point cet appareil avant de l'essayer.
17. Allons au cinéma. Prenons la voiture plutôt que le métro.

---

3. **reprit** (from **reprendre***, *to take up again, to resume*)   4. **se hâta de** (Recall the importance of the circumflex accent for meaning)   10. **ne pouvait** (Negation of **pouvoir** is complete with **ne** alone; see COPS, Sec. 87)   16. **essayer*** to try (same as **tâcher de, chercher à**)   17. **métro** *m.* subway (from **chemin de fer métropolitain,** *metropolitan railroad*)

18. Laisse de côté tes théories complexes.
19. Sachez que la plupart des plantes sont autotrophiques en matière de vitamines.
20. N'oubliez pas de rédiger le rapport avant demain.

C. *General review and aussi.* Translate into good English.

21. Les nez sont faits pour porter des lunettes; aussi avons-nous des lunettes.
22. Nos étudiants étudient aussi bien la physique que les mathématiques.
23. La géologie est une science qui a pour but l'étude aussi bien des minéraux que de la forme extérieure de notre globe.
24. La nature chimique des minéraux est leur caractère le plus facile à reconnaître: aussi leur classification est-elle actuellement basée sur cela.
25. En étudiant les vieilles choses, on comprend les nouvelles.
26. L'avenir commence à l'instant.
27. Si tous les hommes savaient ce qu'ils disent les uns des autres, il n'y aurait pas quatre amis dans le monde. —Pascal, *Pensées 101.*
28. Notre intelligence tient dans l'ordre des choses intelligibles le même rang que notre corps dans l'étendue de la nature. —Pascal, *Pensées 72.*
29. La puissance des mouches: elles gagnent des batailles, empêchent notre âme d'agir, mangent notre corps. —Pascal, *Pensées 367.*
30. Le premier arrivé est le premier servi.
31. Effrayer un oiseau n'est pas le moyen de le prendre.
32. Ne dis pas «va», mais vas-y toi-même.
33. Celui qui a un grand nez pense que tout le monde en parle.
34. Le temps perdu ne se retrouve jamais.
35. Vous regardiez la lune et vous êtes tombé dans un puits.

Readings

Une Critique de Thomas Wolfe

[36] Les héros de Wolfe sont tous atteints d'un complexe d'infériorité. C'est ce qui les rend craintifs et sauvages, les prédispose au rôle de victimes et rend leur solitude plus aiguë. [37] Cette idée de la solitude revient dans l'œuvre de Wolfe comme un leitmotif obsédant, et l'Amérique entière s'y trouve englobée: «. . . car

---

20. **rédiger** to write, to compose   25. **les nouvelles** (**Choses** is understood)   26. **à l'instant** (same as **immédiatement, tout de suite, en ce moment**)   28. **tient** (Missing link: must be followed by its remote direct object, the next independent noun group, not a prepositional phrase); **rang** *m.* rank   29. **mouche** *f.* housefly; **empêcher** to prevent; **agir** to act, to take action   31. **effrayer** to frighten; **oiseau** *m.* bird   33. **celui** *pron.* he (the one)   34. **perdre** to lose   35. **puits** *m.* well   36. **atteint** (past participle of **atteindre***, *to afflict, to attain*); **craintif, -ve** *adj.* timid, fearful; **aiguë** *adj.* acute   37. **leitmotif** *m.* recurring theme (in music); **obsédant** *adj.* obsessive, haunting; **englobé** (past participle of **englober,** *to include*)

nous sommes si perdus, si nus, si seuls en Amérique. [38] Des cieux immenses et cruels s'incurvent au-dessus de nous, et tous autant que nous sommes, nous allons, chassés éternellement, et nous n'avons plus de foyers.... [39] Car l'Amérique possède des milliers de lumières et de températures, et nous marchons dans les rues, nous marchons dans les rues de la vie, toujours seuls.»

[40] Parfois, l'horreur de l'isolement s'accompagne de claustrophobie. George Webber, dans sa chambre, connaît: «une solitude indicible. [41] Seul, il essaya de faire rentrer dans les limites de sa petite chambre toute la folie de la terre, et il frappait les murs de ses poings pour s'élancer de nouveau sauvagement dans les rues, ces rues terribles sans une pause, sans un tournant, sans une porte qu'il pût franchir.»

[42] Thomas Wolfe a eu le tort de croire qu'il pourrait faire tenir debout un monde créé à son échelle. Il n'a jamais songé qu'il infligeait à ses lecteurs une torture égale, quoique inverse, à la sienne. [43] La lecture d'un de ses romans nous laisse étourdis, assourdis et contusionnés, dans un état voisin de celui où se trouvent, quand ils survivent, les fous inoffensifs qui franchissent dans un tonneau les chutes du Niagara. [44] Riche de dons exceptionnels, Thomas Wolfe les a gâchés pour avoir fait fausse route. Il n'était pas né romancier. Il était né poète. [45] Non poète élégiaque et intime; son souffle trop puissant eût fait éclater les pipeaux. Son domaine était cette poésie dramatique qui, d'après Diderot, «veut quelque chose d'énorme, de barbare et de sauvage.»

Les Circuits logiques:
Méthodes de test non-déterministes

[46] Les progrès technologiques de ces dernières années ont permis la fabrication de circuits logiques intégrés à petite, moyenne et grande échelles. A l'heure actuelle, les circuits logiques ont remplacé les sous-ensembles à éléments discrets dans de nombreuses applications. [47] L'apparition de cette nouvelle technique, la micro-électronique, pose de nombreux problèmes. D'importants travaux ont été faits sur la synthèse et la simplification des circuits logiques. [48] Avec l'évolution rapide de la technologie qui permet d'obtenir des composants de plus en plus complexes, à des prix sans cesse décroissants, les problèmes de mini-

---

37. **nu, -e** *adj.* naked   38. **s'incurvent** (from **s'incurver**, *to bend, to curve*); **tous autant que nous sommes** (idiom) the whole lot of us; **foyer** *m.* home (Idea is related to Thomas Wolfe's novel *You Can't Go Home Again*)   40. **isolement** *m.* isolation; **indicible** *adj.* unspeakable   41. **faire rentrer** to gather (literally, *to cause to come in*) (Missing link is involved in the syntax here); **folie** *f.* madness; **frapper** to strike; **poing** *m.* fist; **s'élancer** to dash; **de nouveau** (same as **encore une fois**); **tournant** *m.* corner; **franchir** to enter   42. **tenir debout** to maintain; **échelle** *m.* scale; **songé** (past participle of **songer**, *to think, to dream*); **infliger** to inflict   43. **étourdi** *adj.* stunned; **assourdi** *adj.* deafened; **contusionné** *adj.* bruised, contused; **voisin de** akin to; **fou** *m.* madman; **franchissent** (from **franchir**, *to go over*); **tonneau** *m.* barrel   44. **gâcher** to waste, to squander; **romancier** *m.* (celui qui écrit des romans)   45. **souffle** *m.* breath (for playing **le pipeau**, *a shepherd's pipe*); **éclater** to explode   46. **sous-ensemble** *m.* assembly; **à** of, having; **discret, -e** *adj.* separate   48. **composant** *m.* component; **prix** *m.* price; **décroissant, -e** *adj.* decreasing; **minimisation** *f.* miniaturization

misation ont progressivement perdu de leur intérêt pratique. [49] Par contre, le test des circuits logiques, permettant de savoir si les composants utilisés ou les ensembles réalisés fonctionnent correctement, a pris une importance croissante. C'est au problème du test que nous allons nous intéresser.

[50] Les difficultés de production et de contrôle ainsi que la nouveauté des circuits complexes rendent les tests indispensables. Il est nécessaire d'effectuer des contrôles au cours des différentes phases de la vie d'un circuit intégré. [51] On a ainsi notamment des contrôles de production faits en fin de fabrication par le constructeur, des contrôles d'entrée faits par l'utilisateur à la réception des circuits, ou juste avant leur montage sur les cartes imprimées, des contrôles de maintenance destinés à détecter les défauts dûs à une dégradation qui n'apparaît qu'après une certaine période de fonctionnement.

[52] Les causes de défauts sont nombreuses et variées : erreurs de marquage, déréglages d'appareils de mesures instables, mauvaise programmation.... Une autre catégorie de défauts provient des imperfections existant dans l'emploi des méthodes chimiques et physiques d'élaboration des circuits. [53] La plupart de ces défauts sont détectés au niveau du contrôle de production. Certains entraîneront des dégradations qui n'apparaîtront qu'après une certaine période de stockage ou de fonctionnement. [54] C'est pourquoi l'utilisateur devra effectuer des tests d'entrée et de maintenance. Le problème du test des circuits logiques intégrés paraît d'autant plus important qu'il se pose aussi bien aux fabricants qu'aux utilisateurs de tels circuits.

Test 15, page 247

que j'apprenne
que tu apprennes
qu'elle apprenne
que nous apprenions
que vous appreniez
qu'elles apprennent

---

50. **ainsi que** as well as   51. **notamment** in particular; **entrée** *f.* installation; **montage** *m.* mounting, installation; **destiné** à intended for; **défaut** *m.* defect; **dégradation** *f.* deterioration   52. **déréglage** *m.* faulty adjustment, faulty reading   53. **entraîner** to cause   54. **effectuer** to carry out, to make; **tel,-le** *adj.* such

16

Structures

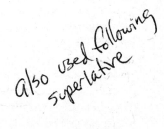

also used following superlative

82. Subjunctive Mood

So far the French verbs you have studied have been in the indicative mood, representing concrete fact or reality. This chapter introduces the subjunctive mood, used to express conditions and actions that are uncertain or that reflect a subjective attitude on the part of the speaker or writer.

The subjunctive is used often in French. It is generally found in subordinate **que** clauses when the verb in the main clause implies doubt, possibility, will, wish, or emotion.

A. The present subjunctive. The present subjunctive is translated by the present or future. Context and time indicators such as **aujourd'hui, demain,** and **la semaine prochaine** are clues to the correct tense of the English equivalent.

Je doute que Robert **vienne** demain.
I doubt that Robert *will come* tomorrow.

Je doute que Robert **vienne** maintenant.
I doubt that Robert *is coming* now.

Je veux que Robert **vienne** avec nous.
I want Robert *to come* with us.

B. Present subjunctive forms. The subjunctive is easy to recognize because the subjunctive endings are the same for all verbs, except **être** and **avoir.** The subjunctive of regular verbs is formed by adding these endings to the **ils** stem of the present tense:

-e	-ions
-es	-iez
-e	-ent

	from	
ils parlent	*ils finissent*	*ils rendent*
(-er verb)	*(-ir verb)*	*(-re verb)*
que je parle	que je finisse	que je rende
que tu parles	que tu finisses	que tu rendes
qu'il parle	qu'il finisse	qu'il rende

	from	
ils parlent *(-er verb)*	*ils finissent* *(-ir verb)*	*ils rendent* *(-re verb)*
que nous parl**ions** que vous parl**iez** qu'ils parl**ent**	que nous finiss**ions** que vous finiss**iez** qu'ils finiss**ent**	que nous rend**ions** que vous rend**iez** qu'ils rend**ent**

C. Irregular present subjunctives.   The verbs **avoir** and **être** have completely irregular present subjunctive forms.

avoir	**aie, aies, ait, ayons, ayez, aient**
être	**sois, sois, soit, soyons, soyez, soient**

have, will have
be, will be;
have, will have [+ past participle]

The following verbs have irregular present subjunctive stems, to which the regular endings are added.

faire	**fass-** [+ regular endings]
savoir	**sach-** [+ regular endings]
pouvoir	**puiss-** [+ regular endings]

do, make; will do, will make
know, will know; know how
be able, will be able; can

Some verbs have two stems in the present subjunctive, one used for **je, tu, il/elle,** and **ils/elles** forms (the L-area), and the other used for **nous** and **vous** forms.

infinitive	*present subjunctive*	
aller	que j'**aille** que tu **ailles**	que nous **allions** que vous **alliez**
tenir	que je **tienne** que tu **tiennes**	que nous **tenions** que vous **teniez**
prendre	que je **prenne** que tu **prennes**	que nous **prenions** que vous **preniez**
voir	que je **voie** que tu **voies**	que nous **voyions** que vous **voyiez**
vouloir	que je **veuille** que tu **veuilles**	que nous **voulions** que vous **vouliez**
devoir	que je **doive** que tu **doives**	que nous **devions** que vous **deviez**
venir	que je **vienne** que tu **viennes**	que nous **venions** que vous **veniez**

avoir

que j'aie
que tu aies
qu'elle ait
que nous ayons
que vous ayez
qu'elles aient

être

que j'sois
que tu sois
qu'elle soit
que nous soyons
que vous soyez
qu'elles soient

D. Past subjunctive. The past subjunctive is identical to the passé composé (Sec. 48C) in meaning. Here is the past subjunctive of **parler** (auxiliary **avoir**) and **entrer** (auxiliary **être**). Like the passé composé, this tense uses the auxiliary (in the present subjunctive rather than in the present indicative) plus the regular past participle of the main verb.

parler

que **j'aie** parlé	that I spoke, have spoken
que **tu aies** parlé	that you spoke, have spoken
qu'il **ait** parlé	that he spoke, has spoken
qu'elle **ait** parlé	that she spoke, has spoken
que **nous ayons** parlé	that we spoke, have spoken
que **vous ayez** parlé	that you spoke, have spoken
qu'ils **aient** parlé	that they spoke, have spoken
qu'elles **aient** parlé	that they spoke, have spoken

entrer

que **je sois** entré(e)	that I entered, have entered
que **tu sois** entré(e)	that you entered, have entered
qu'il **soit** entré	that he entered, has entered
qu'elle **soit** entrée	that she entered, has entered
que **nous soyons** entré(e)s	that we entered, have entered
que **vous soyez** entré(e)(s)	that you entered, have entered
qu'ils **soient** entrés	that they entered, have entered
qu'elles **soient** entrées	that they entered, have entered

Examples:
Je suis content que Robert **soit arrivé** hier.
I am glad that Robert *arrived* yesterday.

Nous doutons qu'il **ait fini** ses recherches.
We doubt that he *has finished* his research.

83. Possessive Pronouns

Possessive pronouns (*mine, yours, his, hers, its, ours, theirs*) take the place of a noun group that includes possession.

Noun Group		*Possessive Pronoun*	
votre petite maison	your little house	**la vôtre**	yours
mes recherches	my research	**les miennes**	mine
son roman historique	his historical novel	**le sien**	his

Possessive pronouns in French consist of two words: a form of the definite article (of the same number and gender as the noun represented) and a pronoun form.

		replacing a noun that is		
masculine singular	*feminine singular*	*masculine plural*	*feminine plural*	*meaning*
le mien	la mienne	les miens	les miennes	mine
le tien	la tienne	les tiens	les tiennes	yours (fam.)
le sien	la sienne	les siens	les siennes	his, her, its
le nôtre	la nôtre	les nôtres		ours
le vôtre	la vôtre	les vôtres		yours
le leur	la leur	les leurs		theirs

M. Brun a fini ses recherches et j'ai fini les miennes.
Mr. Brun has finished his research and I have finished *mine.*

Robert aime son appartement et Lucille aime **le sien.**
Robert likes his apartment and Lucille likes *hers.*

Votre voiture marche bien, mais **la mienne** est en panne.
Your car runs well, but *mine* is broken down.

The distinction among the columns is of little concern to a reader, since all forms on the same line have the same meaning. It is the writer who must select the correct form, depending on the gender and number of the noun group replaced. In the last example, **la mienne** (*mine*) was used because it replaces **ma voiture** (*my car*).

Notice that the *adjectives* **notre** and **votre** do not have a circumflex accent, whereas the two-word possessive pronouns do.

84. The Verbs *partir* and *se servir de*

A. The verb *partir* (to leave, to depart).   The present tense of **partir** is irregular. A short stem (the first three letters of the infinitive) is used for the singular forms of the verb and a regular stem for the plural forms. Note also the endings: -s, -s, -t, -ons, -ez, -ent.

Present Tense:

je **pars**	I am leaving	nous **partons**	we are leaving
tu **pars**	you are leaving	vous **partez**	you are leaving
il **part**	he is leaving	ils **partent**	they are leaving

Passé composé:

il est **parti**   he left, departed

The verbs **servir, sentir, mentir, dormir,** and **sortir** are similarly formed in the present tense. Note their forms in the passé composé.

infinitive	passé composé	meaning
servir	il a servi	he served
sentir	il a senti	he felt
mentir	il a menti	he lied
dormir	il a dormi	he slept
sortir	il est sorti	he went out

Sortir, like **partir,** uses the auxiliary **être** in compound tenses (Sec. 48B).

B. **The reflexive verb *se servir de* (to use).**   Here are the present tense forms of **se servir de.**

Present Tense:

je **me sers de** ce livre	I am using this book
tu **te sers de** ce livre	you are using this book
il **se sert de** ce livre	he is using this book

nous **nous servons de** ce livre	we are using this book
vous **vous servez de** ce livre	you are using this book
ils **se servent de** ce livre	they are using this book

Examples:

"One uses..."

On se sert d'un microscope électronique pour étudier ces particules.
An electronic microscope *is used* to study these particles.

Il se servira d'une machine à écrire pour préparer le rapport.
He *will use* a typewriter to prepare the report.

Je me suis servi de ce dictionnaire.
I *used* this dictionary.

Note that **servir à** means *to be used for.*

Un stylo **sert à** écrire.   A pen *is used* for writing.

Exercises

A. *Subjunctive.* Translate into natural-sounding English.

1. Je doute qu'il arrive demain.   *I doubt that he'll come tomorrow*
2. Il se peut qu'il vienne aujourd'hui.   *It is possible that he'll arrive today.*
3. Nous regrettons qu'elle soit partie.   *We regret that she has left*
4. Le professeur ne pense pas que Georges comprenne.
5. Pensez-vous que Marie soit déjà sortie?   *Do you think that Marie already left?*
6. Il faut que vous finissiez l'expérience la semaine prochaine.   *It is necessary that you finish the experiment next week.*
7. Il est bon que vous sachiez la vérité.
8. C'est la meilleure étudiante que je connaisse.   *best*

9. Croyez-vous que le directeur soit malade? *combustion engines*

10. Il faut que nous partions demain. *are too powerful*

11. Il est possible que ces <u>moteurs à réaction</u> soient trop puissants.

12. Il se peut qu'on obtienne un bon prix pour ce produit.

13. Ne montrez jamais les dents à moins que vous ne puissiez mordre.

14. Il n'y a pas de peuple qui ait fait des progrès aussi rapides que les Américains.

15. Une période de quatre à six mois est nécessaire pour que le protactinium ait le temps de se désintégrer.

16. Aucun voyageur, que je sache, ne fait mention de l'île de la Motte.

17. Supposons qu'on ait assemblé dans un paquet les treize cartes d'une même couleur qui se trouvent dans un jeu complet de 52 cartes.

18. Quelle est la probabilité que l'as soit tiré le premier?

19. Il n'est pas bon de faire avancer les élèves sans qu'ils sachent ce qu'ils croient avoir appris.

20. Il faut que les professeurs fassent servir les principes de Pestalozzi à tous les genres d'enseignement.

B. *Possessive pronouns and **servir**.* Translate into natural-sounding English.

21. Voilà votre voiture et la mienne.

22. Je me suis servi de notre ordinateur et du vôtre.

23. Notre laboratoire est moins grand que le leur.

24. Paul a fini son rapport mais Marie n'a pas achevé le sien.

25. L'empereur recula un instant devant un pouvoir plus grand que le sien.

26. Wolfe infligeait à ses lecteurs une torture égale à la sienne.

27. Les étudiants se servent d'un dictionnaire.

28. Un dictionnaire sert à définir des mots.

Readings

La Masse et l'énergie

[29] C'est en 1905 qu'un jeune physicien fort peu connu, Albert Einstein, posa les principes de base d'une théorie très révolutionnaire, celle qui prit le nom de relativité. Il s'agissait d'interpréter les fameuses expériences de Michelson, selon lesquelles la mesure de la vitesse de la lumière donnait toujours le même résultat et était parfaitement indépendante de l'état de mouvement de la terre au moment où on l'effectuait. Le mouvement relatif de la terre dans l'espace ne pouvait donc pas être mis en évidence par ces expériences.

[30] La théorie de la relativité a également une autre base: l'ensemble des lois

---

13. **à moins que ... ne** (Disregard the **ne** in translation. See Sec. 77)   16. **aucun ... ne** (This **ne** merely validates the meaning of **aucun** at the beginning of a sentence; Sec. 34)   29. **l'effectuait** (from **effectuer**, *to carry out, to perform*) (The **l'** refers to the preceding noun phrase **la mesure de la vitesse de la lumière**)   30. **l'ensemble des lois** all the laws

de l'électromagnétisme possède une certaine forme mathématique, cette forme est simple, elle a été trouvée à partir de l'expérience effectuée sur la terre. [31] Or, la terre n'est pas privilégiée; le caractère de simplicité de ces lois doit être le même sur un autre astre en mouvement relatif et uniforme par rapport à la terre. [32] Or, les relations de la mécanique classique ne permettent pas de conserver cette formulation quand on change ainsi le système de coordonnées. [33] Il a fallu envisager d'autres transformations, celles de Lorentz, pour permettre, en passant d'un système de référence à un autre en translation uniforme par rapport au premier (par exemple d'un astre à un autre en mouvement relatif uniforme), de conserver les lois de l'électromagnétisme. [34] Pour tenir compte de tout cela, Einstein a énoncé les deux principes suivants: 1e Les lois phénomènes physiques sont les mêmes dans tous les systèmes en translation uniforme les uns par rapport aux autres; 2e Pour tous ces systèmes, la vitesse de la lumière est la même dans toutes les directions.

[35] Ces principes ne semblent pas très révolutionnaires, mais leurs conséquences vont modifier considérablement les notions de temps et d'espace. Il est utile d'attirer l'attention sur certains aspects de ces principes. Lorsque nous sommes dans un train, si le mouvement est parfaitement uniforme, nous sommes incapables de nous apercevoir du mouvement du train par des expériences mécaniques faites à l'intérieur du wagon. [36] Dans le cas où il y a accélération, c'est fort différent: si le train freine brusquement, nous sommes projetés vers l'avant et nous nous apercevons du mouvement. [37] Le principe d'Einstein est, somme toute, une extension de cette notion mécanique à l'ensemble des phénomènes physiques, *y compris les phénomènes lumineux*. Nous ne pouvons pas, par des expériences faites sur la vitesse de la lumière, nous rendre compte de l'état de mouvement de notre wagon ou même de la terre sur laquelle nous nous trouvons.

[38] La relativité restreinte a beaucoup de conséquences, mais l'une des plus importantes est *l'identité de la masse et de l'énergie*. A partir des principes énoncés ci-dessus, il est possible de définir *une relation entre la masse d'un corps et son énergie,* ou plutôt entre les changements de masse d'un corps et l'énergie correspondante. La relation d'Einstein est $E = mc^2$. [39] Cela signifie qu'à toute énergie correspond une masse et réciproquement: ainsi, lorsque dans une réaction il y a *libération d'énergie,* cela veut dire qu'il y a nécessairement *perte d'une partie de la masse,* qui peut se calculer très facilement par la relation d'Einstein. L'exemple le plus extraordinaire est celui de la fission de l'uranium.

L'Entrée de Napoléon à Moscou

[40] La débâcle avait commencé à Moscou; les routes de Cazan étaient couvertes de fugitifs à pied, en voiture, isolés ou accompagnés de serviteurs. [41] A l'approche des longs convois de blessés† russes qui se présentaient aux portes,

---

31. **privilégié** (past participle of **privilégier**, *to privilege*) privileged, an exception   32. **coordonnées** *f.pl.* coordinates (math)   37. **wagon** *m.* railroad car   38. **relativité restreinte** *f.* special theory of relativity   41. **blessé**† *m.* wounded; **russe** *adj.* Russian

toute espérance s'évanouit. [42] Kutusoff avait flatté Rostopschine de défendre la ville avec quatre-vingt-onze mille hommes qui lui restaient. Rostopschine demeurait seul.

[43] La nuit descend: des émissaires vont frapper mystérieusement aux portes, annoncent qu'il faut partir et que la ville est condamnée. [44] Des matières inflammables sont introduites dans les édifices publics et dans les bazars, dans les boutiques et les maisons particulières†. Les pompes sont enlevées. [45] Alors Rostopschine ordonne d'ouvrir les prisons; les malfaiteurs relâchés reçoivent, avec leur grâce, les instructions pour procéder à l'incendie de la ville quand le moment sera venu. [46] Rostopschine sort le dernier de Moscou, comme un capitaine de vaisseau quitte le dernier son bord dans un naufrage.

[47] Napoléon, monté à cheval, avait rejoint son avant-garde. Moscou resplendissait à la lumière du jour, avec ses deux cent quatre-vingt-quinze églises, ses quinze cents châteaux, ses maisons ciselées, colorées en jaune, en vert, en rose. [48] Le Kremlin faisait partie de cette masse couverte de fer poli ou peinturé. Au milieu d'élégantes villas de briques et de marbre, la Moskowa coulait parmi des parcs ornés de bois de sapins. [49] Ce fut le 14 septembre (1812), à deux heures de l'après-midi, que Bonaparte aperçut sa nouvelle conquête.

[50] Une acclamation s'élève: «Moscou! Moscou!» s'écrient les soldats français. Les acclamations cessent; on descend muet vers la ville. Aucune députation ne sort des portes pour présenter les clefs dans un bassin d'argent. [51] Le mouvement de la vie était suspendu dans la grande cité. Quelques-uns de nos officiers pénètrent dans la ville; ils reviennent et disent à Napoléon: «Moscou est déserte!—Moscou est déserte? C'est invraisemblable! Qu'on m'amène les boyards.» [52] Point de boyards, il n'est resté que des pauvres qui se cachent. Rues abandonnées, fenêtres fermées: aucune fumée ne s'élève des foyers d'où s'en échapperont bientôt des torrents. Pas le plus léger bruit. Bonaparte hausse les épaules.

[53] Murat, s'étant avancé jusqu'au Kremlin, y est reçu par les hurlements des prisonniers devenus libres pour délivrer leur patrie. On est contraint d'enfoncer les portes à coups de canon.

[54] Napoléon fit une course le long de la Moskowa, ne rencontra personne. Il

---

41. **espérance** *f.* hope; **s'évanouir** to vanish   42. **Kutusoff, Michail** (prince et maréchal russe, vainqueur à la bataille de Smolensk; plus tard général en chef de l'armée russe); **flatter** to persuade (by flattery); **Rostopschine, Fedor** (homme politique russe, gouverneur de Moscou en 1812 lors de l'invasion des Français; c'est lui qui ordonna l'incendie de la ville)   43. **frapper** to knock   44. **boutique** *f.* shop; **particulier, particulière**† *adj.* private; **pompe** *f.* fire pump; **enlevé** (past participle of **enlever,** *to remove, to take away*)   45. **grâce** *f.* pardon   46. **bord** *m.* ship; **naufrage** *f.* shipwreck   47. **resplendir** to glitter; **église** *f.* church; **ciselé** (past participle of **ciseler,** *to sculpt*) sculptured, carved; **jaune** *adj.* yellow; **vert, -e** *adj.* green; **rose** *adj.* pink   48. **fer** *m.* iron; **peinturé** (past participle of **peindre,** *to paint*) painted; **marbre** *m.* marble; **Moskowa** Moskva River; **couler** to flow; **sapin** *m.* fir tree   50. **bassin** *m.* platter, tray   51. **invraisemblable** *adj.* unbelievable, incredible; **amener** to bring; **boyard** *m.* boyar (member of the Russian nobility)   52. **point de** (same as **pas de**); **pauvres** *m.pl.* poor people; **cacher** to hide; **fumée** *f.* smoke; **foyer** *m.* hearth, fireplace; **léger, légère** *adj.* slight, light; **bruit** *m.* noise; **hausser les épaules** to shrug one's shoulders   53. **hurlement** *m.* shout; **patrie** *f.* country; **enfoncer** to break down   54. **faire une course** to take a ride

revint à son logement, nomma le maréchal Mortier gouverneur de Moscou. La garde impériale et les troupes étaient en grande tenue pour paraître devant un peuple absent. [55] Bonaparte apprit bientôt avec certitude que la ville était menacée de quelque événement. A deux heures du matin on vient lui dire que le feu commence. [56] Le vainqueur quitte le faubourg de Dorogomilow et vient s'abriter au Kremlin: c'était la matinée du 15. Il éprouva un moment de joie en pénétrant dans le palais de Pierre le Grand.

[57] On contient d'abord l'incendie; mais la seconde nuit il éclate de toutes parts. Une bise violente pousse les étincelles et lance les flammèches sur le Kremlin: il renfermait un magasin à poudre; un parc d'artillerie avait été laissé sous les fenêtres mêmes de Bonaparte. [58] De quartier en quartier nos soldats sont chassés par les effluves du volcan.

[59] Le bruit se répand que le Kremlin est miné. Des serviteurs se trouvent mal, des militaires se résignent. La Tour de l'Arsenal, comme un haut cierge, brûle au milieu d'un sanctuaire embrasé. [60] Comment fuir? En cherchant de tous les côtés, on découvre une poterne qui donnait sur le Moskowa. Le vainqueur avec sa garde se dérobe† par ce guichet de salut. [61] Autour de lui dans la ville, des voûtes se fondent en mugissant, des clochers se penchent, se détachent et tombent. Des charpentes, des poutres, des toits craquant, pétillant, s'abîment dans un Phlégéthon dont ils font rejaillir la lame ardente et des millions de paillettes d'or. [62] Bonaparte ne s'échappe que sur les charbons refroidis d'un quartier déjà réduit en cendres.

[63] Du rivage de Sainte-Hélène, Napoléon revoyait brûler Moscou. «Jamais» dit-il, «en dépit de la poésie, toutes les fictions de l'incendie de Troie n'égaleront la réalité de celui de Moscou.»

d'après Chateaubriand, *Mémoires d'outre-tombe*, Livre XXI, Chapitre 4

Test 16, page 249

---

54. **en grande tenue** in full-dress uniform   56. **faubourg** *m.* suburb; **abriter** to take shelter, to take refuge (**un abri** is *shelter*)   57. **éclater** to break out; **de toutes parts** (same as **partout**); **bise** *f.* wind; **étincelle** *f.* spark; **flammèches** *f.* sparks   58. **quartier** *m.* section (of town), neighborhood; **effluve** *m.* effluvium (fumes); **volcan** *m.* volcano (used metaphorically here)   59. **bruit** *m.* rumor (What is the other meaning used in this passage?); **mal** *adv.* ill; **cierge** *m.* candle; **embrasé** (past participle of **embraser**, *to set on fire*) fiery   60. **fuir** to flee, to escape; **poterne** *m.* postern (back door); **se dérober**† to escape; **guichet de salut** *m.* safety hatch   61. **se fondre** to collapse; **mugir** to roar; **clocher** *m.* steeple, bell-tower; **se pencher** to lean, to bend; **charpente** *f.* wooden framing; **poutre** *f.* beam; **toit** *m.* roof; **pétiller** to crackle; **s'abîmer** plunge down; **Phlégéthon** (une des rivières des Enfers où coulaient des flammes au lieu d'eau); **rejaillir** to spurt; **ardent, -e** *adj.* fiery; **paillette** *f.* spark; **d'or** golden   63. **en dépit de** in spite of; **Troie** Troy (détruit par l'incendie vers 2300 avant J.-C.); **égaler** to equal

Essential Word Review IV

Chapters 13–16

Verbs

amener to bring, bring along (someone)
 apporter to bring (something)
atteindre to attain; to afflict
avouer to admit
cesser (de) [+ infinitive]   to stop, to cease [doing something]
écouter to listen (to)
 entendre to hear
effectuer to carry out, to execute (a plan)
effrayer to frighten
 faire peur à [+ noun]   to frighten [someone]
égaler to equal
empêcher to prevent
entraîner to cause
essayer to try
 chercher à to try to
frapper to strike
manger to eat
oser to dare
perdre to lose
 chercher to look for
 trouver to find
savoir to know
sembler to seem
 paraître to seem, to appear
soupirer to sigh
tâcher de to try to

Nouns

le besoin need
le bonheur happiness
la clé (clef) key
le défaut fault, defect, imperfection
une échelle scale
le fer iron
la fin end
la formation† training
les gens people
le métier trade, profession
le milieu environment
le prix price
la taille height, size

Adjective

tel, telle such

Adverbs

bien certainly
de nouveau again
en ce moment now

Other structural words and phrases

ainsi que as well as
destiné à intended for
en dépit de in spite of
quoique although

17

Structures

85. More About Reflexive Verbs

Reflexive verbs (**verbes pronominaux**) are frequently used in French. Reflexives are verbs whose action reflects back to the subject or doer. The pronoun **se** preceding the infinitive marks the verb as reflexive; for example: **se laver** (*to wash oneself*), **s'amuser** (*to enjoy oneself*), **se trouver** (*to be located*) (see Sec. 27).

Reflexive verbs use two pronouns, the subject pronoun and a reflexive pronoun of the same person.

singular	*plural*
je me	nous nous
tu te	vous vous
il/elle se	ils/elles se

A. The present and the passé composé. Here are the present and the passé composé of the reflexive verb **se dépêcher** (*to hurry*).

Present Tense:

je me **dépêche**	I am hurrying
tu te **dépêches**	you are hurrying
il se **dépêche**	he is hurrying
nous nous **dépêchons**	we are hurrying
vous vous **dépêchez**	you are hurrying
ils se **dépêchent**	they are hurrying

Passé composé:

je me suis **dépêché(e)**	I hurried
tu t'es **dépêché(e)**	you hurried
il s'est **dépêché**	he hurried
elle s'est **dépêchée**	she hurried
nous nous sommes **dépêché(e)s**	we hurried
vous vous êtes **dépêché(e)(s)**	you hurried
ils se sont **dépêchés**	they hurried
elles se sont **dépêchées**	they hurried

Note the use of the auxiliary **être** in the passé composé of the reflexive verb and the agreement of the past participle. For other tenses, see the summary on pages 190–192.

B. Reflexive pronouns as direct or indirect objects. The reflexive pronoun is often readily identified as a direct or indirect object of the verb, thus making the meaning simple to deduce.

Direct Object:

Nous nous habillons vers sept heures du matin.
We get dressed (dress ourselves) around 7 A.M.

Indirect Object:

Il se demande si Robert viendra.
He wonders (asks himself) whether Robert will come.

C. Idiomatic meanings. Some inherently pronominal verbs and expressions have idiomatic meanings that have nothing to do with their being reflexive. Here are some examples.

il s'agit de	it is a question of, it concerns
il se peut que	it may be that, perhaps
se douter de (or **que**)	to suspect that
se passer	to take place, happen
se passer de [+ noun]	to do without, dispense with
se plaindre de [+ noun]	to complain about
se souvenir de [+ noun]	to remember
s'enfuir	to run away, flee

Examples:

Elle **se doutait que** le patron ne l'aimait pas.
She *suspected that* the boss didn't like her.

Nous nous demandons ce qui **se passe** dans la rue.
We wonder what *is happening* in the street.

Je **me passe** d'auto.
I *get along without* a car.

Il **se plaint du** bruit que font les voisins.
He *complains about* the noise the neighbors make.

D. Reflexives expressing the passive. Some pronominal verbs used reflexively in the third person singular or plural in French are equivalent to the passive voice in English.

Le tabac **se vend** ici.	Tobacco *is sold* here.
Les journaux **se vendent** là-bas.	Newspapers *are sold* over there.
Cela ne **se dit** pas.	That *isn't said*.
Cela ne **se fait** pas.	That *isn't done*.
Cela **s'explique** facilement.	That *can* easily *be explained*.

E. Reciprocal meaning.   Some verbs that are not inherently pronominal are used reflexively to show reciprocal meaning (*to each other, at one another,* etc.). This occurs only in the plural form of the verbs.

> Ils **se sont** vus, mais ils ne **se sont** pas **parlé.**
> They *saw each other*, but they didn't *speak to each other.*

> Nous **nous sommes souri.**
> We *smiled at one another.*

> Vous **vous téléphonez** tous les jours?
> Do you *call each other* every day?

86. Interrogatives

A. Interrogative words.   Questions that ask for specific information are introduced by interrogative words such as those listed below. Note that, except after **qui,** inversion of subject and verb usually occurs.

qui	who, whom	pourquoi	why
que, qu'	what	comment	how
quand	when	combien de [+ noun]	how many
où	where	quel, quelle [+ noun]	which, what
d'où	from where		

Examples:

Qui a raison?	*Who* is right?
Que sais-je?	*What* do I know?
Qu'avez-vous pensé de ce livre?	*What* did you think about this book?
Quand partons-nous?	*When* are we leaving?
D'où vient ce télégramme?	*Where* is the telegram *from?*
Pourquoi vas-tu à Paris?	*Why* are you going to Paris?
Comment vont-ils se débrouiller?	*How* are they going to manage?
Combien de langues parle-t-elle?	*How many* languages does she speak?
Quelle voiture préférez-vous?	*Which* car do you prefer?

B. Questions with *est-ce que.*   The form **est-ce que** (**est-ce qu'** before a vowel), used before a statement to formulate a question, is most frequently encountered in dialogue. No translation of **est-ce que** is used in English.

> *Statement:*   Le directeur est arrivé.
> *Question:* Est-ce que le directeur est arrivé?

Sometimes question words precede **est-ce que.** Again **est-ce que** is ignored in the English equivalent of the sentence.

> **Pourquoi est-ce que** la secrétaire téléphone?
> Why is the secretary calling?

Qu'est-ce que vous faites?
What are you doing?

Combien de livres est-ce que vous voulez commander?
How many books do you want to order?

C. Questions formed by inversion. When a question is formed with a noun subject without **est-ce que,** you will find a subject pronoun in inverted location. Do not translate this redundant pronoun:

Pourquoi votre succès est-il assuré?
Why is your success assured?

Comment les professeurs ont-ils trouvé votre étude?
How did the professors like your research paper?

When **est-ce que** is used, there is no superfluous subject pronoun.

Pourquoi est-ce que l'ordinateur ne marche pas?
Why isn't the computer running?
Why is the computer down?

D. Affirmation with *n'est-ce pas*. When a question is asked with the intention of securing agreement, the expression **n'est-ce pas** is appended. The phrase **n'est-ce pas** is invariable in French, whereas its English counterpart takes on a variety of forms.

Vous comprenez, **n'est-ce pas?**	You understand, *don't you?*
Cet article est long, **n'est-ce pas?**	This is a long article, *isn't it?*
Vous pouvez venir dîner, **n'est-ce pas?**	You can come to dinner, *can't you?*

87. Use of *ne* without *pas*

The word **ne** is generally associated with negation. You know that negation normally requires two elements, the word **ne** before the verb and the word **pas** or some other negative word (**jamais, plus, rien,** etc.) after the verb (Sec. 34). In reading, however, you often encounter **ne** used in other specific ways that call for different interpretations.

A. The word *ne* with no negative value. When it appears in the following places, **ne** does not have negative value.

1. With remote **que.** If you are interpreting a sentence with **ne** that does not have **pas** or any other negative word directly after the verb, look further along for **que** and the meaning *only* (Sec. 36). The verb remains positive.

2. At the beginning of a sentence. When a sentence or clause begins with **ne** preceded by **rien, personne, aucun (aucune),** or **nul (nulle),** **ne** merely

serves to reinforce meaning; it has no negative bearing on the verb (Sec. 34).

Rien n'est impossible.	*Nothing* is impossible.
Personne n'a répondu.	*No one* answered.
Aucune réponse **n'**est nécessaire.	*No* answer is necessary.
Nulle date **n'**a été spécifiée.	*No* date was specified.

3. After certain conjunctions. The conjunctions **à moins que** ... **ne** (*unless*) and **de peur que** ... **ne** (*for fear that*) include a superfluous **ne** that should not be interpreted as negative.

Nous dînerons ici **à moins que** vous **ne** vouliez partir.
We'll have supper here *unless* you want to leave.

Note that if **pas** is added, the clause will obviously become negative.

Nous dînerons ici **à moins que** vous **ne** vouliez **pas** rester.
We'll have supper here *unless* you don't want to stay.

B. **Effective negation with *ne* alone: "COPS."**   In reading, you will find that **ne** often retains its negative value when used alone with certain verbs. These verbs (COPS) are **cesser** (*to cease*), **oser** (*to dare*), **pouvoir** (*to be able*), and **savoir** (*to know, to know how to*).

Les personnes faibles **ne peuvent** être des directeurs efficaces.
Weak people *cannot* be effective directors.

Je **ne saurais** donner tous les détails.
I *couldn't* (possibly) give all the details.

Françoise **n'a pas osé** sécher le cours.
Françoise *didn't dare* cut the class.

Madame Clôporte **ne cesse** de parler d'elle-même.
Mrs. Clôporte *doesn't stop* talking about herself.

The negation may, of course, be completed by **pas** or an alternative term if the writer desires.

88. Dictionary Techniques

A. **Determination of need.**   Do not reach for the dictionary as soon as you come to a word you don't know. At least finish the sentence, leaving a blank for the unknown word. It might be advisable even to read another sentence or two. Doing so will establish two important things: (1) the context and general subject under discussion and (2) the possibility that you can make a good educated guess as to the meaning.

B. **Choice of dictionary.**   Select a reasonably large desk or unabridged dictionary, so that there are plenty of examples under each word. You will also need an English dictionary, since many words you can't find in the French-English dictionary are already English cognates! (A pocket dictionary is likely to be nearly useless.)

C. Basic information needed.   There is much more to finding a word in the dictionary than simply consulting an alphabetical listing. You must know the following:

1. The exact spelling (including accent marks) of the word sought.
2. The part of speech involved (and gender if a noun).
3. The general category or topic involved.
4. The system used in your dictionary, usually explained in detail in the preliminary pages. It is well worth taking the time to examine the abbreviations, signs, and symbols adopted in the dictionary you are using.

D. Parts of speech.   If you know whether the word you are seeking is a noun, adjective, adverb, verb, or preposition, you will more easily find the correct head-word under which to search.

Our original analysis will be of help in doing this. By putting parentheses around noun groups, you can identify prepositions, articles, adjectives, and nouns:

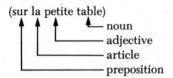

(sur la petite table)
— noun
— adjective
— article
— preposition

The adjective reveals the gender of the noun, as does the article. Outside the sets of parentheses are the verbs and adverbs:

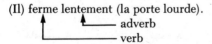

(Il) ferme lentement (la porte lourde).
— adverb
— verb

E. Reconstructing infinitives of verbs.   If you are seeking a verb, the infinitive form is what you need to find. Determine what the infinitive is by separating a known verb ending from the form. If the verb is **ils pêchaient**, you know that **-aient** is an ending, so you may assume that the stem is **pêch-**. The most likely ending is **-er**; other possibilities are **-ir** and **-re**. Thus you seek **pêcher** as a first choice, being careful about the accent mark.

You will find **pécher** (*vi*) (*vi* indicates an intransitive verb, one that cannot have a direct object), **pêcher** (*vt*) (*vt* indicates a transitive verb, one that can have a direct object), and **pêcher** (*nm*). The latter is eliminated, since you are seeking a verb. The accent is critical, since **pécher** means *to sin* whereas **pêcher** means *to fish*.

Use the Irregular Stem Index in this book when convenient.

F. Division of dictionary entries by topic or category. First scan the entry under the head-word to see what general categories or topics are clearly separated. They are usually numbered or otherwise labeled. Thus if you were looking for **le quai** and the general topic were railroad travel, you would find that for railway stations this word means *platform* whereas for freight ships it means *wharf*.

Next examine the examples in which the word is used, to see if there is a special meaning. Suppose, for example, you were trying to translate **Revenons à nos moutons.** You would probably have *Let's go back to our* _____. Looking up **mouton**, you would find that it means *sheep*; but the topic was not animal husbandry. A close search should reveal this as a special expression meaning *Let's get back to the subject*.

If the words you find do not make sense, you must take time to sift through the dictionary article for the meaning that fits the context and logical line of reasoning.

G. Paired words unraveled. When you have a noun group of two words, remember that the second word is usually the adjective. This is true even when both seem to be nouns. Translate the second word first.

une courbe **plane**	a *plane* curve
un costume **tailleur**	a *tailor-made* suit

Similarly, remember that a word directly after a verb is likely to be an adverb. Translate it first.

il parle **souvent**	he *often* speaks

Generally, in French word groups the most important word has the first position, and the modifiers follow. Look up the most important word first, then the modifiers (adjectives, adverbs).

Exercises

A. *Reflexives in context.* Translate into natural-sounding English.

1. Maintenant il s'agit de traduire des phrases en anglais.
2. Nous nous doutons que ce sera une tâche intéressante.
3. Nous ne doutons pas de la valeur et de l'importance des ordinateurs.
4. Je ne me souviens pas de toutes les conjonctions en français.
5. Savez-vous ce qui se passait dans la rue quand le directeur est revenu?
6. Il se peut qu'il y ait un examen la semaine prochaine.
7. Quand les étudiants entendront cela, ils s'enfuiront.

---

2. **tâche** *f.* task, job

8. Les livres techniques ne se vendent pas dans cette librairie.
9. Les scientifiques ne peuvent pas se passer de leurs ordinateurs.
10. Le chef d'état et le général se sont souvent parlé au sujet de l'économie.

B. *Interrogation.* Translate the following questions.

11. Quand est-ce que vous ferez vos devoirs de français?
12. Pourquoi a-t-on construit la Tour Eiffel?
13. Qu'est-ce que Lawrence et Livingston ont bâti en 1932?
14. Qui a inventé la première machine à calculer?
15. Quand Berzélius a-t-il découvert le thorium?
16. Quelle est la capitale de la France?
17. Quels romans de Thomas Wolfe avez-vous lus?
18. Est-ce que vous préférez les romans ou les pièces de théâtre?
19. Qu'est-ce qui a détruit la ville de Moscou en 1812?
20. Combien de soldats Rostopschine avait-il pour défendre la ville?
21. Évidemment les ordinateurs sont des appareils très compliqués, n'est-ce pas?
22. Vous savez taper à la machine, n'est-ce pas?
23. D'où cette machine vient-elle?
24. Où est-ce que nous allons passer les vacances cet été?

C. *The particle ne.* Translate into natural-sounding English.

25. Vous réussirez à moins que vous ne fassiez trop de fautes.
26. On n'a trouvé dans la ville que des prisonniers relâchés par le gouverneur russe.
27. Les soldats français s'enfuyaient du Kremlin de peur que l'incendie ne l'atteigne bientôt.
28. Aucune photographie de cette fusée ne se trouve dans cette encyclopédie.
29. Rien n'empêche ces messieurs de compléter l'expérience.
30. On ne peut résoudre ces problèmes mathématiques qu'en se servant d'un ordinateur.

D. *Reading a dictionary entry.* Following the procedure described in Section 88, use the dictionary extract below to determine the meaning of **mousse** in each sentence; translate the sentence.

MOUSSE[1] **1:** *nf* **(a)** (*Bot*) moss
    (b) (*écume*) [*bière, eau*] froth, foam; [*savon*] lather;
    [*champagne*] bubbles. **la ~ sur le verre de bière** the head
    on the beer
    (c) (*Culin.*) mousse. **~ au chocolat** chocolate mousse
    (d) (*caoutchouc*) **caoutchouc ~** *nm* foam rubber
2: mousse carbonique (fire-fighting) foam
MOUSSE[2] *nm* ship's boy, cabin boy
MOUSSE[3] *adj.* blunt (knife blade, point, etc.)

31. Les petits garçons se lançaient une balle en caoutchouc mousse.
32. Le capitaine ne remarqua pas le mousse qui se tenait devant la porte.
33. Mettant son bock sur la table, il regardait la mousse blanche pétiller et disparaître lentement.
34. La lame de mon couteau est mousse.
35. On s'est servi de mousse carbonique pour éteindre les flammes.
36. Pour s'orienter le soldat a examiné un arbre; la mousse sur le tronc de l'arbre lui offrait des renseignements.
37. Il s'est mis à se laver: l'eau formait avec le savon une mousse qui montait et gonflait.

E. *Using a dictionary.* In a dictionary find meanings for the following phrases. Decide which word is critical and look it up first. Translate the phrase.

38. La formation professionnelle des ingénieurs…
39. Il ouvre la porte avec une fausse clé.
40. C'est un tour de passe-passe.
41. J'ai d'autres chats à fouetter.
42. Il a une araignée au plafond.

Readings

L'Islam

[43] Ces quelques remarques épistémologiques se proposent simplement de rappeler la dialectique historique que nous avons cru discerner dans notre étude des événements qui sont intervenus en Arabie occidentale à la veille de l'Islam. [44] Ils ont été accompagnés de profonds bouleversements socio-politiques lesquels, à leur tour, ont provoqué un changement important dans l'idéologie à chaque nouvelle étape de l'évolution, pour aboutir finalement à la réforme coranique. [45] Mais celle-ci, du fait même qu'elle s'adressait à un vaste groupement ethnique composé de sociétés différemment évoluées, était souvent amenée soit à composer, soit à enregistrer un état de fait, à adopter un *modus vivendi*.

[46] L'infrastructure religieuse de la société arabe dont l'idéologie, depuis l'Islam, semble en équilibre, n'est donc pas aussi simple qu'on pourrait le croire. [47] Elle ne se comprend en définitive qu'à la lumière des formations historiques qui lui ont donné naissance. [48] Et c'est précisément le but que nous nous sommes proposé dans le présent travail en écrivant, en quelque sorte, une introduction à l'histoire du sacré chez les Arabes. Il est temps de faire le point sur notre acquis.

---

43. **veille** *f.* eve   44. **coranique** *adj.* pertaining to the Koran   48. **sacré** *m.* sacred things; **faire le point** to take stock, to assess

[49] Dans cet état protodémocratique qu'est la société nomade où l'anarchisme individuel constitue sans cesse une menace au pouvoir, la souveraineté, en dépit de son usurpation partielle par le chef, se trouve encore à l'état diffus. [50] Elle est en fait la chose du groupe tout entier, et le seigneur nomade qui n'a rien d'un despote, est considéré comme le dépositaire de la loi coutumière et l'organe qui en assure le bon fonctionnement. [51] Son autorité, souvent contestée, est en raison de la sagesse et de la circonspection dont il fait preuve dans l'administration des intérêts collectifs.

Le Passe-muraille

[52] Il y avait à Montmartre, au troisième étage du 75 *bis* de la rue d'Orchampt, un excellent homme nommé Dutilleul qui possédait le don singulier de passer à travers les murs sans en être incommodé. Il portait un binocle, une petite barbiche noire et il était employé de troisième classe au ministère de l'Enregistrement. En hiver, il se rendait à son bureau en autobus, et, à la belle saison, il faisait le trajet à pied, sous son chapeau melon.
[53] Dutilleul venait d'entrer dans sa quarante-troisième année lorsqu'il eut la révélation de son pouvoir. Un soir, une courte panne d'électricité l'ayant surpris dans le vestibule de son petit appartement de célibataire, il tâtonna un moment dans les ténèbres et, le courant revenu, se trouva sur le palier du troisième étage. [54] Comme sa porte d'entrée était fermée à clé de l'intérieur, l'incident lui donna à réfléchir et, malgré les remontrances de sa raison, il se décida à rentrer chez lui comme il en était sorti, en passant à travers la muraille. [55] Cette étrange faculté, qui semblait ne répondre à aucune de ses aspirations, ne laissa pas de le contrarier un peu et, le lendemain samedi, profitant de la semaine anglaise, il alla trouver un médecin du quartier pour lui exposer son cas. . . .
[56] Le premier cambriolage auquel se livra Dutilleul eut lieu dans un grand établissement de crédit de la rive droite. Ayant traversé une douzaine de murs et de cloisons, il pénétra dans divers coffres-forts, emplit ses poches de billets de banque et, avant de se retirer†, signa son larcin à la craie rouge, du pseudonyme de Garou-Garou, avec un fort joli paraphe qui fut reproduit le lendemain par tous les journaux. [57] Au bout d'une semaine, ce nom de Garou-Garou connut une extraordinaire célébrité. La sympathie du public allait sans réserve à ce prestigieux cambrioleur qui narguait si joliment la police. [58] Il se signalait chaque nuit par un nouvel exploit accompli soit au détriment d'une banque, soit à celui d'une bijouterie ou d'un riche particulier. [59] A Paris comme en province, il n'y avait point de femme un peu rêveuse qui n'eût le fervent désir d'appartenir

---

52. **Montmartre** (a section of Paris); **75** *bis* 75a; **ministère d'Enregistrement** Registration Department (legal); **la belle saison** end of spring, summer, and beginning of fall   53. **troisième étage** (In France the ground floor is called the **rez-de-chaussée**, and the floor above that is the **premier étage**. Hence you must add one to the number of floors to find the American equivalent)   55. **semaine anglaise** *f.* (Weekend with two consecutive days off, Saturday and Sunday)   57. **narguer** to scoff at, to thumb one's nose at

corps et âme au terrible Garou-Garou. [60] Cependant, Dutilleul devenu l'un des hommes les plus riches de Paris, était toujours ponctuel à son bureau†.

—d'après Marcel Aymé, *Le Passe-muraille*

Océanographie biologique

[61] L'océanographie biologique comporte l'étude de la vie des êtres marins, *dans leur milieu*, notamment leur reproduction, leur développement, leur croissance, les conditions du peuplement de la mer et du fond, leur répartition géographique, leurs migrations, les corrélations entre les cycles physiologiques et les cycles du milieu marin, l'évolution des groupements des populations d'animaux marins. [62] Mais il est évident que la vie des organismes présents dans la mer dépend de la quantité de substances nutritives qui s'y trouvent. Outre les sels nutritifs et l'oxygène dissous, les composés du carbone y jouent un rôle important qu'on apprécie par l'estimation de la quantité de matière organique produite par le plancton végétal (phytoplancton) dans les conditions où il se trouve, au point de vue de la température, de l'éclairement et de la turbulence du milieu. [63] L'évaluation, devenue précise, de cette productivité de la mer, de sa répartition géographique en fonction des éléments physiques du milieu, est une des grandes conquêtes de l'océanographie biologique moderne.

[64] L'étude de l'anatomie, de la systématique des espèces recueillies à la mer ressortit à la zoologie et à la biologie marines et non pas à l'océanographie biologique. Celle-ci est une étude écologique et comporte nécessairement une investigation simultanée portant sur les caractères physiques essentiels du milieu.

[65] Chaque spécialiste de ces disciplines voit le milieu sous un certain jour et la confrontation habituelle du point du vue de ces spécialistes est seule capable d'aboutir à la compréhension du *mécanisme* des phénomènes marins, condition d'une *prévision* de ces phénomènes en tous points, stade ultime de la connaissance d'un milieu. [66] L'océanographie est par excellence un travail d'équipe tant à la mer qu'au laboratoire. Carrefour des disciplines scientifiques, elle tire son unité de l'unité et de la continuité du milieu qu'elle étudie, et aussi des impératifs qu'impose à l'observation et à la mesure la mer elle-même.

Test 17, page 251

---

61. **comporter** to comprise; **croissance** *f.* growth; **peuplement** *m.* population; **fond** *m.* sea floor; **répartition** *f.* distribution   62. **outre** *prep.* in addition to; **dissous** (past participle of **dissoudre**, *to dissolve*); **éclairement** *m.* light(ing)   64. **recueillies** (past participle of **recueillir**, *to gather*); **ressortir à** to belong to   65. **aboutir à** resulting in   66. **équipe** *f.* team; **tant à ... que** as much in ... as; **carrefour** *m.* crossroads, junction

Supplementary Readings

Page d'écriture

Deux et deux quatre
quatre et quatre huit
huit et huit font seize...
Répétez! dit le maître
Deux et deux quatre
quatre et quatre huit
huit et huit font seize.
Mais voilà l'oiseau-lyre
qui passe dans le ciel
l'enfant le voit
l'enfant l'entend
l'enfant l'appelle:
Sauve-moi
joue avec moi
oiseau!
Alors l'oiseau descend
et joue avec l'enfant
Deux et deux quatre ...
Répétez! dit le maître
et l'enfant joue
l'oiseau joue avec lui ...
Quatre et quatre huit
huit et huit font seize
et seize et seize qu'est-ce qu'ils font?
Ils ne font rien seize et seize
et surtout pas trente-deux
de toute façon
et ils s'en vont.
Et l'enfant a caché l'oiseau
dans son pupitre
et tous les enfants
entendent sa chanson
et tous les enfants
entendent la musique
et huit et huit à leur tour s'en vont
et quatre et quatre et deux et deux
à leur tour fichent le camp
et un et un ne font ni une ni deux
un à un s'en vont également.
Et l'oiseau-lyre joue
et l'enfant chante

et le professeur crie:
Quand vous aurez fini de faire le pitre!
Mais tous les autres enfants
écoutent la musique
et les murs de la classe
s'écroulent tranquillement.
Et les vitres redeviennent sable
l'encre redevient eau
les pupitres redeviennent arbres
la craie redevient falaise
le porte-plume redevient oiseau.

——Jacques Prévert, *Paroles*

Spécialisation technique

Alphonse et Téléphone sont deux paysans qui habitent les bayous de la Louisiane. Ils travaillent pendant la journée à la charpente d'une maison neuve. Ils ont commencé par mettre quelques planches en place sur le mur de l'est, et maintenant Alphonse s'occupe d'une façon très assidue à enfoncer des clous à coups de marteau. Téléphone, au lieu de l'aider comme il faut, fait tout autrement. Il prend un clou dans la boîte qui se trouve par terre, il l'examine minutieusement, et puis il le rejette par terre. Il continue ainsi l'examen des clous, un à un, en les rejetant tous sur la terre. Enfin Alphonse s'impatiente, car c'est lui qui fait tout seul le travail destiné à tous les deux.

—Hé Téléphone! s'écrie-t-il, qu'est-ce que tu fais là, par exemple? Qu'est-ce qui t'empêche de m'aider un tout petit peu?

—Il s'agit de ces clous-ci, répond l'autre, d'un ton très sérieux. Ils sont tous défectueux; je ne puis pas les employer.

—Et pourquoi diable pas? réplique le premier, très impatienté.

—C'est que la tête se trouve à la fausse extrémité.

—Idiot! s'écrie Alphonse. Ces clous-là sont réservés pour l'autre côté de la maison!

Les Aptitudes musicales

Les tests d'aptitudes musicales, qui ne sont pas nombreux, sont présentés sur des disques. Le test du Talent Musical de Seashore, par exemple, sert à examiner la discrimination de la hauteur, de l'intensité, du rythme, du timbre, du temps et de la mémoire du son. Le sujet doit également différencier deux sons qui se suivent de près. On calcule les percentiles pour chaque test.

Il est compréhensible qu'un individu puisse avoir un score élevé aux tests de Seashore, mais être un mauvais pianiste ou violoniste n'ayant pas l'habileté des doigts requise. Mais même étant très habile une personne ne peut pas réussir dans le domaine musical si elle ne sait pas discriminer les hauteurs, l'intensité et les temps.

Les tests de Seashore et d'autres dans ce genre sont utilisés dans les écoles pour la sélection pour la carrière musicale. Un psychologue qui applique ces tests à un groupe d'élèves, tombe parfois sur quelqu'un qui, bien que n'ayant reçu aucune formation musicale, fait preuve d'un grand talent musical et qui peut être ainsi dirigé vers la carrière musicale, tandis que ceux qui se révèlent comme n'ayant aucun don, doivent être déconseillés au cas où ils voudraient poursuivre dans cette voie.

Généralités sur la perception du son

Le son, formé par la propagation de variations périodiques ou irrégulières de la pression atmosphérique, se caractérise par sa fréquence et par son intensité.

La fréquence d'un son—en cycles ou en hertz—correspond au nombre de vibrations par seconde émises par la source sonore.

L'oreille humaine ne perçoit que les ondes de la bande sonore dont les fréquences sont comprises entre 30 et 20.000 hertz: en deçà, il s'agit d'infrasons et au-delà, il s'agit d'ultrasons.

Aux fréquences faibles correspondent les sonorités graves et aux fréquences élevées correspondent les sonorités aiguës. Les bruits ne sont généralement pas formés de sons purs, mais de combinaisons de sons émis sur des fréquences différentes et apparaissant au même instant («spectre sonore»).

Le spectre couvre une bande de fréquences et donne ainsi la structure du bruit qui peut avoir en même temps des composantes graves, moyennes et aiguës. De plus, pour un même bruit, les niveaux d'intensité sonore varient d'une bande de fréquences à l'autre. Il est donc nécessaire d'expliquer brièvement en quoi consiste le niveau d'intensité sonore.

Schématiquement, *l'intensité* correspond à la quantité de bruit que nous percevons, alors que la fréquence correspond à sa qualité. Pour mesurer les niveaux d'intensité acoustique, on utilise une unité logarithmique—*le décibel* (db)—parce que l'échelle des variations de pression auxquelles l'oreille normale réagit est énorme: de 0,0002 microbar à 1.000 microbar. La sensation sonore varie, en effet, comme le logarithme de l'excitation physique exercée sur le tympan: le rapport entre le son le plus faible perçu et le son le plus fort qui provoque la douleur est de mille milliards.

Température et constitution du Soleil

Examinons, maintenant, les caractères intimes du foyer solaire. Au point de vue chimique, il est constitué des mêmes éléments que le globe terrestre, mais ils se trouvent là dans des conditions totalement différentes. En effet, la température du Soleil, d'après les plus sûres déterminations ayant pu être effectuées, est de 6 000° environ; du moins, s'agit-il de la température de la surface visible dont nous recevons le rayonnement, car elle croît de plus en plus vers le centre, où elle doit atteindre, d'après les calculs des astrophysiciens, plusieurs millions de degrés.

De notre point de vue donc, tout doit être volatilisé. Mais, d'autre part, en raison de la dimension et de la masse du Soleil, des pressions formidables entrent en jeu, qui atteignent, à l'intérieur, plusieurs milliards d'atmosphères. Aussi éprouve-t-on quelque mal à concevoir vraiment ce qu'il en est de substances soumises à de telles conditions. Les termes de solide, de liquide et de gaz concernent des propriétés relatives au domaine terrestre. Sans doute, pour définir correctement l'état de la matière solaire, de nouveaux mots seraient-ils à créer! Faute de mieux, et pour notre compréhension, il reste malgré tout suggestif de parler d'état gazeux car ce sont les lois connues de la physique relatives à l'état gazeux qui lui conviennent. Notons pourtant que sous l'effet des pressions considérables, ces éléments gazeux acquièrent une densité et des propriétés qui les rendent plutôt comparables à ce que nous désignons communément sous le nom de liquide, et peut-être de solide, dans l'intérieur du globe.

En fait, les couches superficielles du Soleil, décrites plus loin, sont seules accessibles à l'investigation directe. Ce qu'on peut supposer, quant à la constitution des régions profondes de la masse, découle de vues théoriques, et l'on admet généralement une température centrale extraordinairement élevée— 20 à 25 millions de degrés, peut-être—avec une densité fortement croissante, dépassant largement celle des métaux les plus lourds.

Photosphère, Chromosphère et Couronne sont les trois grandes divisions de l'ensemble observable du Soleil. Elles jouissent chacune de propriétés particulières, et nous les examinerons en détail successivement. Cependant, soulignons dès maintenant qu'elles ne sont pas indépendantes: les phénomènes qui s'y produisent se rattachent plus ou moins intimement les uns aux autres et procèdent tous de l'activité variable du fantastique foyer solaire.

Architecture ogivale: XIIIe siècle

Tous les éléments de l'art sont dans la nature; l'art lui-même n'est que dans la pensée de l'homme, comme tous les phénomènes que la chimie constate se trouvent dans la matière, tandis que la science chimique n'est que dans l'âme humaine. Suivant les temps, l'esprit dégage l'un ou l'autre de ces éléments. Ainsi, à l'inverse du paganisme qui mettait la beauté au-dessus de l'expression, le christianisme a mis l'expression au-dessus de la beauté. C'est le caractère de l'art au moyen âge, et le treizième siècle le porte à sa plus grande hauteur. Le triomphe de l'architecture ogivale est enfin assuré. L'arc se brise, s'effile et s'élance, afin de porter plus haut, plus près du ciel, la voûte du temple et la prière des peuples. C'est alors que sont élevées ces montagnes de pierre ciselée à jour—ces cathédrales de Paris, de Rouen, d'Amiens, de Chartres, de Reims, de Bourges, de Strasbourg et la Sainte-Chapelle de Saint Louis, à Paris—qui remplacent l'architecture romane, lourde encore et massive, par des temples où se montrent toutes les hardiesses de la pensée, toute l'élévation, toute la ferveur du sentiment religieux. Le nouveau style, né au nord de la Loire, passe la Manche, le Rhin, et les Alpes: et des colonies d'artistes français vont le porter à Cantorbéry, à Utrecht, à Milan, jusqu'en Suède. Une statuaire grossière, mais naïve, décore les portails, les galeries, les cloîtres; et la peinture sur verre a, pour produire de magiques effets dans les vitrages, des secrets que nous venons à peine de retrouver.

Avantages réels de la société américaine

Lorsque les ennemis de la démocratie prétendent qu'un seul fait mieux ce dont il se charge que le gouvernement de tous, il me semble qu'ils ont raison. Le gouvernement d'un seul, en supposant de part et d'autre égalité de lumières, met plus de suite dans ses entreprises que la multitude. Il montre plus de persévérance, plus d'idée d'ensemble, plus de perfection de détail, un discernement plus juste dans le choix des hommes. Ceux qui nient ces choses n'ont jamais vu de république démocratique, ou n'ont jugé que sur un petit nombre d'exemples.

La démocratie, lors même que les circonstances locales et les dispositions du peuple lui permettent de se maintenir, ne présente pas le coup d'œil de la régularité administrative et de l'ordre méthodique dans le gouvernement; cela est vrai. La liberté démocratique n'exécute pas chacune de ses entreprises avec la même perfection que le despotisme intelligent; souvent elle les abandonne avant d'en avoir retiré le fruit, ou en hasarde de dangereuses: mais à la longue elle produit plus que lui; elle fait moins bien chaque chose, mais elle fait plus de choses. Sous son empire, ce n'est pas surtout ce qu'exécute l'administration publique qui est grand, c'est ce qu'on exécute sans elle et en dehors d'elle. La démocratie ne donne pas au peuple le gouvernement le plus habile, mais elle fait ce que le gouvernement le plus habile est souvent impuissant à créer; elle répand dans tout le corps social une inquiète activité, une force surabondante, une énergie qui n'existent jamais sans elle, et qui, pour peu que les circonstances soient favorables, peuvent enfanter des merveilles. Là sont les vrais avantages.

——Alexis de Tocqueville, *De la démocratie en Amérique*

Langue et société

Les propriétés qui caractérisent l'excellence linguistique tiennent en deux mots, *distinction* et *correction*. Le travail qui s'accomplit dans le champ littéraire produit les apparences d'une langue originale en procédant à un ensemble de dérivations qui ont pour principe un *écart* par rapport aux usages les plus fréquents, c'est-à-dire "communs", "ordinaires", "vulgaires".

La langue légitime est une langue semi-artificielle qui doit être soutenue par un travail permanent de correction qui incombe à la fois à des institutions spécialement aménagées à cette fin et aux locuteurs singuliers. Par l'intermédiaire de ses grammairiens, qui fixent et codifient l'usage légitime, et de ses maîtres qui l'imposent et l'inculquent par d'innombrables actions de correction, le système scolaire tend, en cette matière comme ailleurs, à produire le besoin de ses propres services et de ses propres produits, travail et instruments de correction.

La langue légitime doit sa constance (relative) dans le temps (comme dans l'espace) au fait qu'elle est continûment protégée par un travail prolongé d'inculcation contre l'inclination à l'économie d'effort et de tension qui porte par exemple à la simplification analogique (*vous faisez* et *vous disez* pour *vous faites* et *vous dites*). Plus, l'expression correcte doit l'essentiel de ses propriétés sociales au fait qu'elle ne peut être produite que par des locuteurs possédant la maîtrise pratique de *règles* savantes, explicitement constituées par un travail pédagogique.

En effet, le paradoxe de toute pédagogie institutionnalisée réside dans le fait qu'elle vise à instituer comme schèmes fonctionnant à l'état pratique des règles que le travail de grammairiens dégage de la pratique des professionnels de l'expression écrite (du passé) par un travail d'explicitation et de codification rétrospectives. Le «bon usage» est le produit d'une compétence qui est une *grammaire incorporée*: le mot de grammaire étant pris sciemment (et non tacitement, comme chez les linguistes) dans son vrai sens de système de règles savantes, dégagées *ex post* du discours effectué et instituées en normes impératives du discours à effectuer.

Il s'ensuit qu'on ne peut rendre raison complètement des propriétés et des effets sociaux de la langue légitime qu'à condition de prendre en compte non seulement les conditions sociales de production de la langue littéraire et de sa grammaire mais aussi les conditions sociales d'imposition et d'inculcation de ce code savant comme principe de production et d'évaluation de la parole.

Contre la technocratie, jouer la connaissance

La connaissance fait peur. L'intelligence et le talent sont vénérés, mais pas la connaissance. C'est que celle-ci comporte le risque du changement; elle s'impose à l'homme sans tenir compte ni de ses désirs ni de l'image qu'il a de ses besoins; elle bouleverse le monde intellectuel et social en place.

Promesse de développement certes, elle est aussi et d'abord épreuve de réalité. D'où l'ambivalence que manifestent à son égard le simple citoyen aussi bien que le responsable. Nous savons tous que les gains à espérer d'une découverte et d'un progrès matériel seront payés d'un coût humain, culturel et social. Tout développement de la connaissance est un risque, car il mènera à un changement qui se fera, même si c'est avec nous et par nous, sans que nous puissions en contrôler le cours. Une société capable d'accepter ce risque se développera, une société qui de façon ou d'autre le refuse, déclinera.

Comme toutes les sociétés modernes, plus encore peut-être que d'autres sociétés, la société française cultive à cet égard la contradiction: la science lui semble bonne, mais à condition de rester désincarnée. La technologie en revanche, dangereuse et inhumaine, serait accessible aux pires manipulations. Pour nous protéger contre la connaissance, nous avons, nous Français, imaginé un personnage mythique qui nous est bien utile parce que nous pouvons le charger de tous les péchés, le «technocrate». D'où l'image d'un savant noble et pur, d'un technocrate arrogant et haïssable. Nos élites et nos gouvernants eux-mêmes sont partagés. Certes, ils savent que la science non seulement rapporte, mais commande l'avenir; ils sont donc prêts à investir. Mais la crainte d'être mis en question subsiste: on veut des résultats tangibles et sans risques; on investit dans les programmes et non dans les hommes; on s'efforce de diriger la science, au lieu de constituer et de soutenir des communautés scientifiques ouvertes. D'où une politique ambitieuse et étroite, faite de brefs instants d'enthousiasme secouant arbitrairement la routine et de longues périodes d'assoupissement, et une pratique à courte vue soumise aux pressions des groupes d'intérêt, qu'a fini par constituer l'*establishment* scientifique.

Pourtant, aucune réforme de la société ne réussira qui ne s'appuie sur cette valeur fondamentale que représente la connaissance, laquelle ne doit pas être vécue comme une valeur de vérité mais comme une valeur de développement, c'est-à-dire d'utilité: à l'interrogation métaphysique, la science répond par une possibilité d'action; jamais elle ne tiendra lieu de vérité révélée, pas plus sous sa forme marxiste abâtardie que sous ses formes positivistes plus rigoureuses.

Toute stratégie de changement doit donc accorder une priorité à la connaissance, par conséquent œuvrer pour que les communautés scientifiques et technologiques soient vigoureuses et ouvertes, pour que les relations soient plus rapides et vivantes entre la connaissance fondamentale, la connaissance appliquée et l'utilisation finale. Il est du devoir de tout gouvernement de lutter pour rendre les citoyens conscients de ces enjeux. Son rôle n'est pas tant de faire les bons choix de développement que de rendre la société capable d'accepter de prendre des risques et d'effectuer elle-même ces choix. Pour cela, il est nécessaire de prendre au sérieux tant les problèmes des communautés scientifiques et techniques, porteuses de connaissances nouvelles, que les craintes des Français devant les risques de changement inhérents à ces connaissances. Les deux sont liés, et les solutions pas nécessairement contradictoires. Les craintes du public en effet sont compréhensibles mais se trompent de direction. La technocratie ne naît pas des progrès de la connaissance, mais bien plutôt de ses blocages ou de ses mauvaises orientations. Ouvrir le monde de la connaissance, tel est précisément le moyen de rendre le développement scientifique plus efficace et de diminuer les risques d'accaparement technocratique.

Les Radars

Le radar contient un émetteur et un récepteur placés *côte à côte*. On fait fonctionner l'émetteur pendant un temps très court, pendant lequel le récepteur est rendu insensible, puis on rend sensible le récepteur et on attend. S'il se trouve dans le voisinage un objet important capable de réfléchir les ondes, comme un navire ou un avion, l'onde réfléchie est alors reçue par le récepteur. Le temps écoulé permet d'apprécier la distance du radar à l'objet réfléchissant. L'utilisation d'une antenne directive (que l'on peut orienter à volonté) permet de rechercher le maximum d'intensité d'un écho et de déterminer ainsi la direction de cet objet.

On peut se représenter le fonctionnement du radar par une analogie sonore. Supposons qu'une personne munie d'un porte-voix pousse des cris en tournant sur elle-même de manière à envoyer ses cris successivement dans toutes les directions.

Elle pourra ainsi déceler les arbres, les maisons, les falaises qui lui renverront un écho sonore lorsque le porte-voix passera dans leur direction. C'est d'ailleurs à peu près ce que font pour se diriger les chauves-souris, en émettant, dans l'air, des ondes élastiques analogues aux ondes sonores, mais de fréquence supérieure (ondes ultra-sonores).

Le radar est donc un appareil qui permet de déceler l'existence d'objets réfléchissants et de connaître leur position par l'observation des réflexions qu'ils produisent sur les ondes électromagnétiques. Son nom provient de l'abréviation des mots *RAdio Detection And Ranging.*

La plupart des radars ont un indicateur de lecture constitué essentiellement par un tube oscilloscopique donnant une sorte de carte sur laquelle les objets réfléchissants s'inscrivent en points lumineux. On sait que sur un tube oscilloscopique il n'y a à chaque instant qu'un point plus ou moins lumineux et que ce point peut se déplacer très vite en laissant une luminosité rémanente, qui donne l'impression d'une image fixe. Dans l'indicateur de radar, le point lumineux (ou spot) se trouve normalement au centre du tube. Le récepteur du radar, quand il reçoit une onde réfléchie, agit sur le spot et le rend nettement lumineux. Il s'ensuit que chaque objet réfléchissant donnera une image brillante à une distance du centre proportionnelle à sa distance au radar.

La Statistique

L'un des objectifs du statisticien est de résumer le plus possible un ensemble d'observations se rapportant à un phénomène. Il atteint déjà cet objectif quand au lieu d'envisager une population—c'est-à-dire l'ensemble des observations qui pourraient être faites—il n'examine qu'un échantillon. Il atteint encore cet objectif quand il se propose de synthétiser par *quelques nombres* les n données d'un échantillon. Le meilleur échantillon est celui qui constitue l'image la plus représentative de la population, de même que *les meilleures caractéristiques* adoptées seront celles qui renseigneront le plus fidèlement et le plus totalement sur l'échantillon. En soi, c'est une gageure de fixer de telles qualités, car il est utopique de croire que l'information apportée par 100 observations puisse être condensée sans perdre sa valeur. Néanmoins, selon le but que l'on se fixe dans une étude, il reste possible de fournir de ces observations une connaissance satisfaisante, quitte à respecter certaines conditions. Grosso modo, les meilleures caractéristiques seront celles qui d'une part seront *objectives* et présenteront une signification assez concrète, et qui d'autre part *dépendront de toutes les observations* et demeureront *peu sensibles aux variations* de l'échantillonnage. Ajoutons encore qu'elles doivent être relativement *faciles à calculer.*

Appendices

Appendix A
Hints on Simplifying Translation

1. Transitional Words

In French sentences transitional words like **d'abord, d'ailleurs,** and **donc** occur in various positions in which they may interrupt the main thought. In translation place such words at the beginning of the sentence.

L'ordre des opérations est **donc** le suivant.
Therefore the order of operations is the following.

2. Parenthetical Information

Phrases set off by commas or parentheses may be skipped during the initial reading of the French in order not to lose the main thought. In the second reading, however, reinstate these phrases.

La physique est essentiellement, **comme l'astronomie,** une science de mesures précises.

First try: Physics is essentially a science of precise measurements.
Final: Physics, *like astronomy*, is essentially a science of precise measurements.

Note that in English translation, the word order is improved by placing *like astronomy* close to the subject.

3. Missing Link (ML)

In English sentences the direct object is usually positioned immediately after the verb.

I looked down and *saw a coin* lying on the sidewalk.

verb   direct object

In French the direct object is frequently delayed.

I looked down and *saw*, lying on the sidewalk, gleaming in the

           ↑
    verb   *direct object*
                                        ↓

sunlight and partially hidden by a stone, *a coin.*

When you come to a verb that seems to demand a direct object, skip the following phrases until you come to the first independent noun group (one that is not a prepositional phrase); translate it, then return to the portions skipped.

Les protons **décrivent,** (sous l'action du champ magnétique,) **des cercles** dans un plan horizontal.
The protons *describe circles* in a horizontal plane under the influence of the magnetic field.

4. The Conjunction *que* with a Remote Noun Subject

Remember to find the next independent noun phrase when a clause begins with **que** or **qu'** followed by a verb. (Review Sec. 54C.)

Voilà le lion **qu'a tué M. Dubois.**
There is the lion *that Mr. Dubois* killed.

If you fail to place a noun after **que,** the meaning will be altered.

5. The Constructions *ce qui* and *ce que*

Both **ce qui** and **ce que** mean *what* most of the time.

6. The Preposition *avec* plus a Noun

The construction **avec** [+ noun] can sometimes be replaced by an adverb ending in *-ly*.

avec patience	patient*ly*
avec bruit	noisi*ly*
avec enthousiasme	enthusiastical*ly*

7. Idioms of High Frequency

Familiar idioms can be of help.

venir de	(Sec. 69)	to have just
tenir à	(Sec. 37C)	to be eager to
se mettre à	(Sec. 56)	to begin to

avoir besoin de		to need
il y a		there is, are
il y a [time]	(Sec. 67D)	[time] ago
il y a [time] que	(Sec. 67C)	for [time]

8. Tricky Pairs

Be alert to word pairs that are related, and make distinctions between words that closely resemble each other but have distinctive meanings.

ou / où	or / where, when
peut être / peut-être	can be / perhaps
a / à	has / to
sur / sûr	on / sure
soit ... soit	either ... or
ou ... ou	either ... or
d'une part ... d'autre part	on the one hand ... on the other hand
de ... à	from ... to

9. The Various Meanings of *même*

Be aware of variations in the meaning of **même**.   reflexive
At the beginning of a sentence or clause, it means *even*.

> **Même** le roi ...   *Even* the king ...

Directly before a noun, it means *same*.

> Le **même** professeur ...   The *same* teacher ...

Directly after a noun, it means *very, itself, himself,* or *herself*.

> La théorie **même** est ridicule.   The theory *itself* is ridiculous.

Hyphenated to a disjunctive pronoun, it means *-self*.

> Il l'a fait **lui-même**.   He did it *himself*.

10. Prefixes and Suffixes

A. Two suffixes revealing meaning

-ment	-ly	**parfaitement**	perfectly
-ant	-ing	**en arrivant**	upon arriving

B. Two noun endings revealing gender are

-tion	feminine	la nation
-ment	masculine	le compartiment

C. Five prefixes that create antonyms or negatives

dé-	décroissance	decrease
	(croissance)	(growth)
	défavorable	*un*favorable
dés-	désagréable	*dis*agreeable
	désobéir	to *dis*obey
in-	incolore	color*less*
	incommode	*in*convenient
	inattendu	*un*expected
	inhabité	*un*inhabited
mal-	malheureux	*un*happy, *un*fortunate
	malfaiteur *m*.	lawbreaker
	malhonnête	dishonest
mé-	mécontent	*dis*contented
	se méfier	to *mis*trust
	(se fier)	(to trust)

D. The prefix *re-* meaning *again, back, to repeat*

re-	recommencer	to begin again
	refaire	to redo
	relire	to read again, to reread
	revenir	to come back, to return

The prefix **re-** becomes **r-** before a verb that begins with a vowel.

ramener	to bring back
rappeler	to call back, to remind
rouvrir	to reopen

Appendix B
Regular Verbs

	-er *verbs* (parler)	**-ir** *verbs* (finir)	**-re** *verbs* (vendre)
Infinitive	parler	finir	vendre
Present Participle	parlant	finissant	vendant
Past Participle	parlé	fini	vendu

Indicative mood

Present:

je parle	je finis	je vends
tu parles	tu finis	tu vends
il parle	il finit	il vend
nous parlons	nous finissons	nous vendons
vous parlez	vous finissez	vous vendez
ils parlent	ils finissent	ils vendent

Imperfect:

je parlais	je finissais	je vendais
tu parlais	tu finissais	tu vendais
il parlait	il finissait	il vendait
nous parlions	nous finissions	nous vendions
vous parliez	vous finissiez	vous vendiez
ils parlaient	ils finissaient	ils vendaient

Past Definite (Passé simple):

je parlai	je finis	je vendis
tu parlas	tu finis	tu vendis
il parla	il finit	il vendit
nous parlâmes	nous finîmes	nous vendîmes
vous parlâtes	vous finîtes	vous vendîtes
ils parlèrent	ils finirent	ils vendirent

Future:

je parlerai	je finirai	je vendrai
tu parleras	tu finiras	tu vendras
il parlera	il finira	il vendra
nous parlerons	nous finirons	nous vendrons
vous parlerez	vous finirez	vous vendrez
ils parleront	ils finiront	ils vendront

Conditional:

je parlerais	je finirais	je vendrais
tu parlerais	tu finirais	tu vendrais
il parlerait	il finirait	il vendrait

nous parlerions	nous finirions	nous vendrions
vous parleriez	vous finiriez	vous vendriez
ils parleraient	ils finiraient	ils vendraient

Imperative mood

parle	finis	vends
parlons	finissons	vendons
parlez	finissez	vendez

Compound Tenses

Passé Composé:

j' ai parlé	j' ai fini	j' ai vendu
tu as parlé	tu as fini	tu as vendu
il a parlé	il a fini	il a vendu
nous avons parlé	nous avons fini	nous avons vendu
vous avez parlé	vous avez fini	vous avez vendu
ils ont parlé	ils ont fini	ils ont vendu

Pluperfect:

j' avais parlé	j' avais fini	j' avais vendu
tu avais parlé	tu avais fini	tu avais vendu
il avait parlé	il avait fini	il avait vendu
nous avions parlé	nous avions fini	nous avions vendu
vous aviez parlé	vous aviez fini	vous aviez vendu
ils avaient parlé	ils avaient fini	ils avaient vendu

Past Perfect:

j' eus parlé	j' eus fini	j' eus vendu
tu eus parlé	tu eus fini	tu eus vendu
il eut parlé	il eut fini	il eut vendu
nous eûmes parlé	nous eûmes fini	nous eûmes vendu
vous eûtes parlé	vous eûtes fini	vous eûtes vendu
ils eurent parlé	ils eurent fini	ils eurent vendu

Future Perfect:

j' aurai parlé	j' aurai fini	j' aurai vendu
tu auras parlé	tu auras fini	tu auras vendu
il aura parlé	il aura fini	il aura vendu
nous aurons parlé	nous aurons fini	nous aurons vendu
vous aurez parlé	vous aurez fini	vous aurez vendu
ils auront parlé	ils auront fini	ils auront vendu

Conditional Perfect:

j' aurais parlé	j' aurais fini	j' aurais vendu
tu aurais parlé	tu aurais fini	tu aurais vendu
il aurait parlé	il aurait fini	il aurait vendu
nous aurions parlé	nous aurions fini	nous aurions vendu
vous auriez parlé	vous auriez fini	vous auriez vendu
ils auraient parlé	ils auraient fini	ils auraient vendu

Subjunctive mood

Present:

que je	parle	que je	finisse	que je	vende
que tu	parles	que tu	finisses	que tu	vendes
qu'il	parle	qu'il	finisse	qu'il	vende
que nous	parlions	que nous	finissions	que nous	vendions
que vous	parliez	que vous	finissiez	que vous	vendiez
qu'ils	parlent	qu'ils	finissent	qu'ils	vendent

Past:

que j'	aie parlé	que j'	aie fini	que j'	aie vendu
que tu	aies parlé	que tu	aies fini	que tu	aies vendu
qu'il	ait parlé	qu'il	ait fini	qu'il	ait vendu
que nous	ayons parlé	que nous	ayons fini	que nous	ayons vendu
que vous	ayez parlé	que vous	ayez fini	que vous	ayez vendu
qu'ils	aient parlé	qu'ils	aient fini	qu'ils	aient vendu

Reflexive verb: *se laver* (summary in *il* form)

Present:	il se lave	he is washing [himself]*
Imperfect:	il se lavait	he was washing
Past Definite:	il se lava	he washed
Future:	il se lavera	he will wash
Conditional:	il se laverait	he would wash
Present Subjunctive:	qu'il se lave	he is washing, will wash
Passé Composé:	il s'est lavé	he washed
Pluperfect:	il s'était lavé	he had washed
Past Perfect:	il se fut lavé	he had washed
Future Perfect:	il se sera lavé	he will have washed
Conditional Perfect:	il se serait lavé	he would have washed
Past Subjunctive:	qu'il se soit lavé	he has washed

---

*Himself is understood throughout.

Verb using the auxiliary *être: entrer* (summary in *il* form)

Present:	il entre	he is entering
Imperfect:	il entrait	he was entering
Past Definite:	il entra	he entered
Future:	il entrera	he will enter
Conditional:	il entrerait	he would enter
Present Subjunctive:	qu'il entre	he is entering, will enter
Passé Composé:	il est entré	he entered
Pluperfect:	il était entré	he had entered
Past Perfect:	il fut entré	he had entered
Future Perfect:	il sera entré	he will have entered
Conditional Perfect:	il serait entré	he would have entered
Past Subjunctive:	qu'il soit entré	he has entered

Appendix C
Irregular Verbs

Irregular verbs often have two stems: an irregular one in the L-shaped area outlined below and a second one (which often conforms to the infinitive stem spelling) for the **nous-** and **vous-** forms. Forms 1, 2, and 3 frequently have the endings -s, -s and -t, while forms 3, 4, and 5 have standard endings. This common pattern is illustrated below:

1	-s	4	-ons	}	*infinitive stem*
2	-s	5	-ez		
3	-t	6	*-ent		*irregular stem*

---

*An additional consonant is often inserted here, as shown by the doubled **n** in **venir**.

Example: venir (*to come*)

je	viens	nous venons	}	*infinitive stem* **ven-**
tu	viens	nous venez		
il	vient	ils viennent		*irregular stem* **vien-**

In the present subjunctive, some verbs have a single stem in all six forms, whereas others have two stems. In the latter case, the L-area pattern pertains, with the **nous-** and **vous-** forms sharing a stem that often is the regular infinitive stem (Sec. 82).

Auxiliary Verbs: *être* and *avoir*

Infinitive	être	avoir
Present Participle	étant	ayant
Past Participle	été	eu

Indicative mood

Present:

je suis	I am	j' ai	I have
tu es		tu as	
il est		il a	
nous sommes		nous avons	
vous êtes		vous avez	
ils sont		ils ont	

Imperfect:

j'	étais	I was, used to be	j'	avais	I had, used to have

j'   étais   I was, used to be
tu   étais
il   était
nous   étions
vous   étiez
ils   étaient

j'   avais   I had, used to have
tu   avais
il   avait
nous   avions
vous   aviez
ils   avaient

Past Definite (Passé simple):

je   fus   I was
tu   fus
il   fut
nous   fûmes
vous   fûtes
ils   furent

j'   eus   I had
tu   eus
il   eut
nous   eûmes
vous   eûtes
ils   eurent

Future:

je   serai   I will be
tu   seras
il   sera
nous   serons
vous   serez
ils   seront

j'   aurai   I will have
tu   auras
il   aura
nous   aurons
vous   aurez
ils   auront

Conditional:

je   serais   I would be
tu   serais
il   serait
nous   serions
vous   seriez
ils   seraient

j'   aurais   I would have
tu   aurais
il   aurait
nous   aurions
vous   auriez
ils   auraient

Passé Composé:

j'   ai été   I was, have been
tu   as été
il   a été
nous   avons été
vous   avez été
ils   ont été

j'   ai eu   I had, have had
tu   as eu
il   a eu
nous   avons eu
vous   avez eu
ils   ont eu

Pluperfect:

j'   avais été   I had been
tu   avais été
il   avait été
nous   avions été
vous   aviez été
ils   avaient été

j'   avais eu   I had had
tu   avais eu
il   avait eu
nous   avions eu
vous   aviez eu
ils   avaient eu

Past Perfect:

j'	eus été	I had been	j'	eus eu	I had had
tu	eus été		tu	eus eu	
il	eut été		il	eut eu	
nous	eûmes été		nous	eûmes eu	
vous	eûtes été		vous	eûtes eu	
ils	eurent été		ils	eurent eu	

Imperative mood

sois	be		aie	have
soyons	let us be		ayons	let us have
soyez	be		ayez	have

Subjunctive mood

Present:

que je sois	that I be		que j' aie	that I have
que tu sois			que tu aies	
qu'il soit			qu'il ait	
que nous soyons			que nous ayons	
que vous soyez			que vous ayez	
qu'ils soient			qu'ils aient	

Imperfect (rarely encountered):

que je fusse	that I were		que j' eusse	that I had
que tu fusses			que tu eusses	
qu'il fût			qu'il eût	
que nous fussions			que nous eussions	
que vous fussiez			que vous eussiez	
qu'ils fussent			qu'ils eussent	

Past:

que j' aie été	that I was		que j' aie eu	that I had
que tu aies été			que tu aies eu	
qu'il ait été			qu'il ait eu	
que nous ayons été			que nous ayons eu	
que vous ayez été			que vous ayez eu	
qu'ils aient été			qu'ils aient eu	

Pluperfect (rarely encountered):

que j' eusse été	that I had been		que j' eusse eu	that I had had
que tu eusses été			que tu eusses eu	
qu'il eût été			qu'il eût eu	
que nous eussions été			que nous eussions eu	
que vous eussiez été			que vous eussiez eu	
qu'ils eussent été			qu'ils eussent eu	

Table of Irregular Verbs

The key recognition forms are given in the order used in the recognition rule (Sec. 42). The following symbols are used.

Pres   Present tense. Given in full. (The first form is used with **je**, the second with **tu**, etc.) Note the letters of the **nous** form that are italicized. These italicized letters form the stem to which imperfect endings are added (Sec. 43).

FC   Future and conditional stem. Note the characteristic **r-** ending. (See Sec. 40 and 41.)

PD   Past definite stem and the **je** ending. This form identifies the pattern the verb follows (Sec. 66).

PP   Past participle, used in compound tenses (Sec. 48). The auxiliary verb is given in parentheses, followed by a basic example in one of the compound tenses.

PresP   Present participle (English *-ing* form) (Sec. 49). Note that in most cases this form consists of the imperfect stem to which **-ant** has been added.

Subj   Present subjunctive stem(s). For one-stem verbs, only one form is shown. For two-stem verbs, both the L-area and **nous**-area stems are shown.

Index to table of irregular verbs   Numbers refer to verb numbers in the Table of Irregular Verbs.

1. **aller**, *to go* (Sec. 65)
   Pres   vais, vas, va; *all*ons, allez, vont
      F   **ir**-ai (-as, -a; -ons, -ez, -ont)
      C   **ir**-ais (-ais, -ait, -ions, -iez, -aient)
    PD   **all**-ai (-as, -a; -âmes, -âtes, -èrent)
    PP   **allé** (être) elle est allée
   PresP   **allant**
   Subj   { qu'il **aill**-e
          { que nous **all**-ions

2. **connaître**, *to know*
   Pres   **connais, connais, connaît**; *connaiss*ons, **connaissez, connaissent**
    FC   **connaîtr**-
    PD   **conn**-us
    PP   **connu** (avoir) il avait connu
   PresP   **connaissant**
   Subj   qu'il **connaiss**-e
   and **apparaître**, *to appear;* **disparaître**, *to disappear;* **paraître**, *to appear;*
   reconnaître, *to recognize.*

3. **construire**, *to construct*
   Pres   **construis, construis, construit**; *construis*ons, **construisez,**
          construisent
    FC   **construir**-
    PD   **construis**-is
    PP   **construit** (avoir) il a construit
   PresP   **construisant**
   Subj   qu'il **construis**-e
   and **reconstruire**, *to reconstruct.*

4. **courir**, *to run*
   Pres   **cours, cours, court**; *cour*ons, **courez, courent**
    FC   **courr**-
    PD   **cour**-us
    PP   **couru** (avoir) il a couru
   PresP   **courant**
   Subj   qu'il **cour**-e
   and **parcourir**, *to travel through.*

5. **croire**, *to believe*
   Pres   **crois, crois, croit**; *croy*ons, **croyez, croient**
    FC   **croir**-
    PD   **cr**-us
    PP   **cru** (avoir) il a cru
   PresP   **croyant**
   Subj   { qu'il **croi**-e
          { que nous **croy**-ions

6. **décrire,** *to describe*
   Pres **décris, décris, décrit;** *décriv*ons, **décrivez, décrivent**
   FC **décrir-**
   PD **décriv-is**
   PP **décrit** (avoir) il a décrit
   PresP **décrivant**
   Subj qu'il **décriv-e**
   and **écrire,** *to write.*

7. **déduire,** *to deduce*
   Pres **déduis, déduis, déduit;** *déduis*ons, **déduisez, déduisent**
   FC **déduir-**
   PD **déduis-is**
   PP **déduit** (avoir) il a déduit
   PresP **déduisant**
   Subj qu'il **déduis-e**

8. **devoir,** *ought, must, to owe* (Sec. 64)
   Pres **dois, dois, doit;** *dev*ons, **devez, doivent**
   FC **devr-**
   PD **d-us**
   PP **dû** (avoir) il a dû
   PresP **devant**
   Subj ⎰ qu'il **doiv-e**
        ⎱ que nous **dev-ions**

9. **dire,** *to say, to tell*
   Pres **dis, dis, dit;** *dis*ons, **dites, disent**
   FC **dir-**
   PD **d-is**
   PP **dit** (avoir) il a dit
   PresP **disant**
   Subj qu'il **dis-e**
   and **contredire,** *to contradict;* **prédire,** *to predict.*

10. **envoyer,** *to send*
    Pres **envoie, envoies, envoie;** *envoy*ons, **envoyez, envoient**
    FC **enverr-**
    PD **envoy-ai**
    PP **envoyé** (avoir) il a envoyé
    PresP **envoyant**
    Subj ⎰ qu'il **envoi-e**
         ⎱ que nous **envoy-ions**

11. **éteindre,** *to extinguish*
    Pres **éteins, éteins, éteint;** *éteign*ons, **éteignez, éteignent**
    FC **éteindr-**
    PD **éteign-is**

PP   **éteint** (avoir) ils avaient éteint
PresP   **éteignant**
Subj   qu'il **éteign-e**

12. **faire,** *to make, to do* (Sec. 53)
    Pres   **fais, fais, fait;** *fais*ons, **faites, font**
    FC   **fer-**
    PD   **f-is**
    PP   **fait** (avoir) nous avons fait
    PresP   **faisant**
    Subj   qu'il **fass-e**

13. **falloir,** *to be necessary* (Sec. 31)
    Pres   il **faut** (only form)
    FC   il **faudr-**
    PD   il **fallut**
    PP   il a **fallu**
    Subj   qu'il **faille**

14. **mettre,** *to put* (Sec. 56)
    Pres   **mets, mets, met;** *met*ons, **mettez, mettent**
    FC   **mettr-**
    PD   **m-is**
    PP   **mis** (avoir) il aura mis
    PresP   **mettant**
    Subj   qu'il **mett-e**
and **admettre,** *to admit;* **commettre,** *to commit;* **permettre,** *to permit;* **remettre,** *to remit.*

15. **mourir,** *to die*
    Pres   **meurs, meurs, meurt;** *mour*ons, **mourez, meurent**
    FC   **mourr-**
    PD   il **mour-ut**
    PP   **mort** (être) il est mort
    PresP   **mourant**
    Subj   { qu'il **meur-e**
          { que nous **mour-ions**

16. **naître,** *to be born*
    Pres   **nais, nais, naît;** *nais*sons, **naissez, naissent**
    FC   **naîtr-**
    PD   **naqu-is**
    PP   **né** (être) elle est née
    PresP   **naissant**
    Subj   qu'il **naiss-e**
and **renaître,** *to be reborn.*

17. **ouvrir**, *to open* (Sec. 73)
    Pres   **ouvre, ouvres, ouvre;** *ouv*r**ons, ouvrez, ouvrent**
    FC   **ouvrir-**
    PD   **ouvr-**is
    PP   **ouvert** (avoir) nous avons ouvert
  PresP **ouvrant**
   Subj   qu'il **ouvr-**e
and **couvrir**, *to cover;* **découvrir**, *to discover;* **offrir**, *to offer;* **souffrir**, *to suffer.*

18. **paraître**, *to appear*
    Pres   **parais, parais, paraît;** *parais*s**ons, paraissez, paraissent**
    FC   **paraîtr-**
    PD   **par-**us
    PP   **paru** (avoir) il a paru
  PresP **paraissant**
   Subj   qu'il **paraiss-**e
and **apparaître**, *to appear;* **disparaître**, *to disappear;* **reparaître**, *to reappear.*

19. **partir**, *to depart* (Sec. 84)
    Pres   **pars, pars, part;** *part*o**ns, partez, partent**
    FC   **partir-**
    PD   **part-**is
    PP   **parti** (être) nous sommes partis
  PresP **partant**
   Subj   qu'il **part-**e
and **repartir**, *to depart again.*

20. **pouvoir**, *to be able* (Sec. 59)
    Pres   **puis (peux), peux, peut;** *pou*v**ons, pouvez, peuvent**
    FC   **pourr-**
    PD   **p-**us
    PP   **pu** (avoir) j'ai pu
  PresP **pouvant**
   Subj   qu'il **puiss-**e

21. **prendre**, *to take* (Sec. 52)
    Pres   **prends, prends, prend;** *pre*n**ons, prenez, prennent**
    FC   **prendr-**
    PD   **pr-**is
    PP   **pris** (avoir) il a pris
  PresP **prenant**
   Subj   { qu'il **prenn-**e
             { que nous **pren-**ions
and **apprendre**, *to learn;* **comprendre**, *to understand,* *to include;* **entreprendre**, *to undertake;* **reprendre**, *to take back;* **surprendre**, *to surprise.*

22. **produire**, *to produce*
   - Pres   produis, produis, produit; *produis*ons, produisez, produisent
   - FC   produir-
   - PD   produis-is
   - PP   produit (avoir) ils ont produit
   - PresP   produisant
   - Subj   qu'il **produis**-e

   and **conduire**, *to conduct;* **construire**, *to construct;* **déduire**, *to deduct;* **détruire**, *to destroy;* **introduire**, *to introduce;* **reproduire**, *to reproduce;* **traduire**, *to translate.*

23. **recevoir**, *to receive*
   - Pres   reçois, reçois, reçoit; *rece*vons, recevez, reçoivent
   - FC   recevr-
   - PD   reç-us
   - PP   reçu (avoir) vous avez reçu
   - PresP   recevant
   - Subj   { qu'il **reçoiv**-e
          { que nous **recev**-ions

   and **apercevoir**, *to perceive;* **concevoir**, *to conceive.*

24. **savoir**, *to know* (Sec. 57)
   - Pres   sais, sais, sait; *sa*vons, savez, savent
   - FC   saur-
   - PD   s-us
   - PP   su (avoir) il avait su
   - PresP   sachant
   - Subj   qu'il **sach**-e

25. **servir**, *to serve* (Sec. 84)
   - Pres   sers, sers, sert; *ser*vons, servez, servent
   - FC   servir-
   - PD   serv-is
   - PP   servi (avoir) cela a servi
   - PresP   servant
   - Subj   qu'il **serv**-e

26. **sortir**, *to go out* (Sec. 84)
   - Pres   sors, sors, sort; *sor*tons, sortez, sortent
   - FC   sortir-
   - PD   sort-is*
   - PP   sorti (être) elle est sortie
   - PresP   sortant
   - Subj   qu'il **sort**-e

27. **suivre**, *to follow*
   - Pres   suis, suis, suit; *sui*vons, suivez, suivent
   - FC   suivr-

PD   suiv-is
PP   suivi (avoir) il a suivi
PresP   suivant
Subj   qu'il suiv-e
and **poursuivre**, *to pursue.*

28. **tenir**, *to hold* (Sec. 37)
    Pres   **tiens, tiens, tient**; *te*n**ons, tenez, tiennent**
    FC   **tiendr-**
    PD   **tins, tins, tint**; **tînmes, tîntes, tinrent**
    PP   **tenu** (avoir) j'ai tenu
    PresP   **tenant**
    Subj   { qu'il **tienn-e**
           { que nous **ten-ions**
and **appartenir**, *to belong to;* **contenir**, *to contain;* **entretenir**, *to maintain;*
maintenir, *to maintain;* **obtenir**, *to obtain;* **retenir**, *to retain, to remember;*
soutenir, *to sustain.*

29. **valoir**, *to be worth*
    Pres   **vaux, vaux, vaut**; *va*l**ons, valez, valent**
    FC   **vaudr-**
    PD   **val-us**
    PP   **valu** (avoir) il aurait valu
    PresP   **valant**
    Subj   { qu'il **vaill-e**
           { que nous **val-ions**

30. **venir**, *to come* (Sec. 68)
    Pres   **viens, viens, vient**; *ve*n**ons, venez, viennent**
    FC   **viendr-**
    PD   **vins, vins, vint**; **vînmes, vîntes, vinrent**
    PP   **venu** (être) elles sont venues
    PresP   **venant**
    Subj   { qu'il **vienn-e**
           { que nous **ven-ions**
and **convenir**, *to agree, to be appropriate;* **intervenir**, *to intervene;* **prévenir**,
to warn; **parvenir**, *to attain;* **provenir de**, *to stem from;* **se souvenir de**, *to
remember;* **revenir**, *to come back.*

31. **voir**, *to see* (Sec. 58)
    Pres   **vois, vois, voit**; *vo*y**ons, voyez, voient**
    FC   **verr-**
    PD   **v-is**
    PP   **vu** (avoir) il a vu
    PresP   **voyant**
    Subj   { qu'il **voi-e**
           { que nous **voy-ions**
and **prévoir** (except in F., C.: **prévoir-**), *to foresee*

want (Sec. 63)

ux, veux, veut; *voul*ons, voulez, veulent

oudr-

oul-us

voulu (avoir) il a voulu

PresP **voulant**

Subj { qu'il **veuill**-e
{ que nous **voul**-ions

Special form: **veuillez** [+ *inf.*], *please*

Ending Table

(For detailed instructions, see pages 139–140.)

This table can be used to identify irregular verbs even if the infinitive is not known. Symbols indicate the tenses for which each stem is used.

		endings					
symbol	*tense*	*je (1)*	*tu (2)*	*il (3)*	*nous (4)*	*vous (5)*	*ils (6)*
Pres 1	Present	-s	-s	-t			
Pres 1x	Present	-x	-x	-t			
Pres 2	Present				-ons	-ez	
Pres 3	Present						-ent
Imperf	Imperfect	-ais	-ais	-ait	-ions	-iez	-aient
C	Conditional	-ais	-ais	-ait	-ions	-iez	-aient
F	Future	-ai	-as	-a	-ons	-ez	-ont
PDi	Past Definite	-is	-is	-it	-îmes	-îtes	-irent
PDu	Past Definite	-us	-us	-ut	-ûmes	-ûtes	-urent
Subj 1	Present Subj.	-e	-es	-e			-ent
Subj 2	Present Subj.				-ions	-iez	
PP	Past Participle						

Irregular Stem Index: Alphabetical Listing

Find as much of the verb as possible on this list. The italicized abbreviations are tense indicators, which enable you to find the remainder of the verb in the Ending Table above. The line of the ending table containing the rest of the verb will confirm the correct meaning.

See Sec. 78, page 139, for full details of the use of this material.

aill- (aller 1) *Subj 1* go(es), will go
aperçu (apercevoir 23) *PP* perceived, seen
ay- (avoir) *Pres 2; Subj* have
connai- (connaître 2) *Pres 1* know(s)
connaiss- (connaître 2) *Pres 2, 3; Subj 1, 2* know; *Imperf* knew
connaîtr- (connaître 2) *F* will know; *C* would know

connu (connaître 2) *PP* known
courr- (courir 4) *F* will run; *C* would run
couru (courir 4) *PP* run
cr- (croire 5) *PDu* believed
croi- (croire 5) *Pres 1, 3; Subj 1* believe(s)
croy- (croire 5) *Pres 2; Subj 2* believe; *Imperf* believed, used to believe
cru (croire 5) *PP* believed
d- (dire 9) *PDi* said
d- (devoir 8) *PDu* had to, must have
décriv- (décrire 6) *Pres 2; Subj 1, 2* describe(s); *Imperf* was describing
déduis- (déduire 7) *Pres 2; Subj 1, 2* deduce(s); *PDi* deduced
dev- (devoir 8) *Pres 2; Subj 2* must, owe; *Imperf* were to
devr- (devoir 8) *F* will have to; *C* would have to, ought to
dis- *Pres 2* (Except **vous dites**), *3* say; *Subj 1, 2* say, will say; *Imperf* said, was
  saying, used to say
dit (dire 9) *PP* said
doi- (devoir 8) *Pres 1* must, owe
doiv- (devoir 8) *Pres 3; Subj 1* must, owe
dû (devoir 8) *PP* had to
e- (avoir) **-us, -us, -ut, -ûmes, -ûtes, -urent** *PDu* had
écri- (écrire 6) *Pres 1* write(s)
écriv- (écrire 6) *Pres 2, 3; Subj 1, 2* write(s); *Imperf* wrote, was writing; *PDi*
  wrote
enverr- (envoyer 10) *F* will send; *C* would send
envoi- (envoyer 10) *Pres 1, 3* (regular **-er** endings) send; *Subj 1* send(s), are
  sending
envoy- (envoyer 10) *Pres 2; Subj 2* send; *Imperf* were sending, used to send
ét- (être) *Imperf* was, were, used to be
f- (être) **-us, -us, -ut, -ûmes, -ûtes, -urent** *PDu* was (were)
f- (faire 12) **-is, -is, -it, -îmes, -îtes, -irent** *PDi* did, made, caused
fai- (faire 12) *Pres 1* do, make
fais- (faire 12) *Pres 2* (Except **vous faites**) make, are making, do, are doing;
  Imperf used to make, used to do, were making, were doing
fall- (falloir 13) **il fallut** *PD* it was necessary
fass- (faire 12) *Subj 1, 2* make, do, cause [something] to be done
faudr- (falloir 13) **il faudra** *F* it will be necessary; **il faudrait** *C* it would be
  necessary
fer- (faire 12) *F* will do, will make; *C* would do, would make
ir- (aller 1) *F* will go; *C* would go
m- (mettre 14) *PDi* put
met- (mettre 14) *Pres 1* (Except **il met**) put(s)
mett- (mettre 14) *Pres 2, 3; Subj 1, 2* put, are putting; *Imperf* were putting, used
  to put
meur- (mourir) *Pres 1, 3; Subj 1* to be dying, dies
mis (mettre 14) *PP* put
mour- (mourir) *Pres 2; Subj 2* are dying; *Imperf* was dying; *PDu* died

mourr- (mourir) *F* will die; *C* would die

nai- (naître 16) *Pres 1* (Except **il naît**) spring(s) from, is born

naiss- (naître 16) *Pres 2, 3; Subj 1, 2* spring(s) from, is born; *Imperf* was being born, was originating

naîtr- (naître 16) *F* will be born; *C* would be born

naqu- (naître 16) *PDi* was born

né (naître 16) *PP* born

offert (offrir 17) *PP* offered

ouvert (ouvrir 17) *PP* opened

p- (pouvoir 20) *PDu* was able, could

par- (paraître 18) *PDu* appeared

parai- (paraître 18) *Pres 1* (Except **il paraît**) appear(s)

paraiss- (paraître 18) *Pres 2, 3; Subj 1, 2* appear(s); *Imperf* were appearing, used to appear, appeared

peu- (pouvoir 20) *Pres 1x* can

peuv- (pouvoir 20) *Pres 3* can

pourr- (pouvoir 20) *F* will be able; *C* would be able, could

pouv- (pouvoir 20) *Pres 2* can; *Imperf* used to be able, could

pr- (prendre 21) *PDi* took

pren- (prendre 21) *Pres 2; Subj 2* take, are taking; *Imperf* were taking, used to take, took

prenn- (prendre 21) *Pres 3; Subj 1* take(s), are taking

pris (prendre 21) *PP* taken

produi- (produire 22) *Pres 1* produce(s)

produis- (produire 22) *Pres 2, 3; Subj 1, 2* produce(s); *Imperf* were producing, used to produce, produced

pu (pouvoir 20) *PP* been able

pui- (pouvoir 20) *Pres 1* can (1st and 2nd persons only)

puiss- (pouvoir 20) *Subj 1, 2* can, may be able, will be able

reç- (recevoir 23) *PDu* received

recev- (recevoir 23) *Pres 2; Subj 2* receive, are receiving; *Imperf* were receiving, used to receive, received

recevr- (recevoir 23) *F* will receive; *C* would receive

reçoi- (recevoir 23) *Pres 1* receive(s)

reçoiv- (recevoir 23) *Pres 3; Subj 1* receive

s- (savoir 24) *PDu* knew

sach- (savoir 24) *Subj 1, 2* know(s), may know

sai- (savoir 24) *Pres 1* know(s); can [do something] (before infinitive)

saur- (savoir 24) *F* will know, will be able; *C* would know, would be able

sav- (savoir 24) *Pres 2, 3* know(s), can; *Imperf* used to know, knew, could [do something]

ser- (servir 25) *Pres 1* serve(s)

ser- (être) *F* will be; *C* would be

soi- (être) *Pres 1; Subj* am, are, is, will be

sor- (sortir 26) *Pres 1* leave(s), go(es) out, take(s) out (with direct object)

sort- (sortir 26) *Pres 2, 3* leave(s), go(es) out; *Imperf* was going out, used to go out; *PDi; Subj 1, 2* go out, leave

soy- (être) *Pres 2; Subj* are, will be

sui- (suivre 27) *Pres 1* follow(s)

suiv- (suivre 27) *Pres 2, 3; Subj 1, 2* follow(s); *Imperf* were following, used to follow, followed; *PDi* followed

t- (tenir 28) **-ins, -ins, -int, -înmes, -întes, -inrent** *PD* held

ten- (tenir 28) *Pres 2; Subj 2* hold, are holding; *Imperf* were holding, used to hold, held

tenu (tenir 28) *PP* held

tien- (tenir 28) *Pres 1* hold(s)

tiendr- (tenir 28) *F* will hold; *C* would hold

tienn- (tenir 28) *Pres 3; Subj 1* hold

v- (voir 31) *PDi* saw

vaill- (valoir 29) *Subj 1* is (are) worth

val- (valoir 29) *Pres 2, 3; Subj 2* are worth; *Imperf* were worth; *PDu* were worth

vau- (valoir 29) *Pres 1x* is worth

vécu (vivre) *PP* lived

ven- (venir 30) *Pres 2; Subj 2* come, are coming; *Imperf* were coming, used to come, came

venu (venir 30) *PP* (with auxiliary être) come

verr- (voir 31) *F* will see; *C* would see

veu- (vouloir 32) *Pres 1x* want(s)

veul- (vouloir 32) *Pres 3* want

veuill- (vouloir 32) *Subj 1* want(s), wish(es)

vien- (venir 30) *Pres 1* come(s), (followed by **de** [+ infinitive]) have just

viendr- (venir 30) *F* will come; *C* would come

vienn- (venir 30) *Pres 3; Subj 1* come, are coming

v- (venir 30) **-ins, -ins, -int, -înmes, -întes, -inrent** *PD* came

voi- (voir 31) *Pres 1, 3; Subj 1* see(s)

voudr- (vouloir 32) *F* will want to; *C* would like to

voul- (vouloir 32) *Pres 2* want; *Imperf* wanted; *PDu* wanted; *Subj 2* want

voy- (voir 31) *Pres 2; Subj 2* see; *Imperf* saw

vu (voir 31) *PP* seen

Verb Endings Summary

	-er (-é)	-ir (-i)	-re (-u)	some irregular
		verb type (past participle ending)		
Present Indicative	-e	-is	-s	-s (x)
	-es	-is	-s	-s (x)
	-e	-it	-[1]	-t
	-ons	-*iss*ons	-ons	-ons
	-ez	-*iss*ez	-ez	-ez[2]
	-ent	-*iss*ent	-ent	-ent[3]
Imperfect (stem from **-ons** form of present)			-ais	
			-ais	
			-ait	
Conditional (stem: infinitive up to the **-r** + endings)			-ions	
			-iez	
			-aient	
Future (stem: same as conditional above)			-ai	
			-as	
			-a	
			-ons	
			-ez	
			-*ont*	
Past Definite (*Passé simple*)	-ai[4]	-is[5]	-us[6]	
	-as	-is	-us	
	-a	-it	-ut	
	-âmes	-îmes	-ûmes	
	-âtes	-îtes	-ûtes	
	-èrent	-irent	-urent	
Present Subjunctive			-e	
			-es	
			-e	
			-ions	
			-iez	
			-ent	

---

[1]If stem does not end in **-d** or **-t**, add the ending **-t**.
[2]Except for **être, faire,** and **dire,** which take the ending **-es**.
[3]Except for **avoir, aller, être,** and **faire,** which take the ending **-ont**.
[4]The only irregular verb using these PD endings is **aller**.
[5]Irregular verbs using these PD endings include **dire, voir, mettre, écrire, faire, prendre, partir,** and **ouvrir**.
[6]Irregular verbs using these PD endings include **avoir, être, pouvoir, lire,** and **savoir**.

Appendix D
Numbers

Cardinal Numbers

1	un, une	15	quinze	70	soixante-dix
2	deux	16	seize	71	soixante et onze
3	trois	17	dix-sept	75	soixante-quinze
4	quatre	18	dix-huit	80	quatre-vingts
5	cinq	19	dix-neuf	81	quatre-vingt-un
6	six	20	vingt	90	quatre-vingt-dix
7	sept	21	vingt et un	91	quatre-vingt-onze
8	huit	22	vingt-deux	100	cent
9	neuf	30	trente	101	cent un
10	dix	31	trente et un	200	deux cents
11	onze	32	trente-deux	201	deux cent un
12	douze	40	quarante	1000	mille
13	treize	50	cinquante	1990	(date) dix-neuf
14	quatorze	60	soixante		cent quatre-vingt-dix

Cardinal Numbers in Alphabetical Order

billion† (10^{12})	trillion	huit	8	quatre-vingt-un	81
cent	100	mille	1000	quinze	15
cent un	101	mille un	1001	seize	16
cinq	5	un milliard (10^9)	billion	sept	7
cinquante	50	un million (10^6)	million	six	6
deux	2	neuf	9	soixante	60
deux cents	200	onze	11	soixante-dix	70
deux cent un	201	quarante	40	treize	13
dix	10	quatorze	14	trente	30
dix-huit	18	quatre	4	trois	3
dix-neuf	19	quatre-vingt-dix	90	un, une	1
dix-sept	17	quatre-vingt-onze	91	vingt	20
douze	12	quatre-vingts	80	vingt et un	21

Notes

1. **-aine** added to a number indicates an approximate number.
   une dizaine   about ten
   une vingtaine   about twenty, a score

2. In French the comma is used for a decimal.
   3,1416   pi (π)

3. In numbers 1,000 and above, a period is used to set off thousands.
   15.000   fifteen thousand

Appendix E
Suggested Dictionaries

General Dictionaries

Apollo French-English Dictionary. Paris: Librairie Larousse.
Collins Robert French-English, English-French Dictionary. London: Collins.
Harrap's New Collegiate French and English Dictionary. Lincolnwood, IL: National Textbook.
Saturne French-English Dictionary. Paris: Librairie Larousse.

Technical French-English Dictionaries

Automobile	*Elsevier's* Dictionary of Automobile Engineering*, by K. Kondo.
Banking	*Elsevier's Banking Dictionary*, 2nd ed., by J. Ricci.
Building	*Elsevier's Dictionary of Building Tools and Materials*, by L. Y. Chaballe and J. P. Vandenberghe.
Chemistry	*Elsevier's Dictionary of Chemistry Including Terms from Biochemistry*, by A. F. Dorian.
Chromatography	*Dictionary of Chromatography*, by Hans-Peter Angelé. Heidelberg: Dr. Alfred Huthig Verlag.
Computers	*Elsevier's Dictionary of Computers, Automatic Control and Data Processing*, 2nd ed., by W. E. Clason.
Data Processing	*Four-Language Technical Dictionary of Data Processing, Computers and Office Machines*, by Erich Bürger. Oxford: Pergamon Press.
Electronics	*Dictionnaire de l'électrotechnique, des télécommunications et de l'électronique*. Paris: Dunod.
Engineering	*Comprehensive Dictionary of Engineering and Technology*, by Richard Ernst, two volumes. Cambridge: Cambridge University Press.
Measurement	*Elsevier's Dictionary of Measurement and Control*, by W. E. Clason.
Medical	*Elsevier's Medical Dictionary in Five Languages*, 2nd rev. ed., by A. Sliosberg.
Nautical	*Elsevier's Nautical Dictionary*, 2nd ed. Compiled by J. P. Vandenberghe and L. Y. Chaballe.
Nuclear Science	*Elsevier's Dictionary of Nuclear Science and Technology*, 2nd rev. ed., by W. E. Clason.
Television and Video	*Elsevier's Dictionary of Television and Video Recording*, by W. Clason.

---

*The Elsevier dictionaries are technical dictionaries that are published in different languages, including English, French, Spanish, Italian, Dutch, German, and in some cases Swedish and Russian. Listed here are some of the more recent titles of the seventies and eighties, with French editions published by Dunod, Paris.

Appendix F
False Friends

Words marked with an asterisk (*) have the obvious meaning plus the additional meaning indicated.

actuel, -le *adj.*   current, present-day
actuellement *adv.*   currently
affaires *f.pl.*   business
agréer   to accept
amateur *m.*   fan, enthusiast
apparition *f.*   appearance
application *f.*   diligence, zeal, careful attention
appointements *m.pl.*   salary
arrêt *m.*   stop; decree, decision, judicial order (legal)
assister à   to attend, be present at
attendre   to wait for
axe *m.*   axis
billion *m.*   trillion (a million million, 10^{12})
blesser   to wound
brutal, -e *adj.*   violent
bureau *m.*   office; desk
but *m.*   goal, purpose, aim
cabinet *m.*   small office, study
cap *m.*   cape (*geographic*)
car *m.*   interurban bus
car *conj.*   for, because
caractère* *m.*   (moral) character
cargo *m.*   freighter (ship)
causer*   to chat, to converse
cave *f.*   basement, cellar
chair *f.*   flesh
chambre* *f.*   bedroom
chance *f.*   good luck
  chances *f.pl.*   odds
charge *f.*   burden, load
chose *f.*   thing
circulation* *f.*   traffic
coin *m.*   corner
collège *m.*   (private) high school
comédien *m.*   actor
commode *adj.*   convenient, easy
commode *f.*   chest of drawers
commodité *f.*   convenience
conférence* *f.*   lecture

confus, -e *adj.*   embarrassed
correction* *f.*   correctness
courrier *m.*   mail, letters
court, -e *adj.*   short
crayon *m.*   pencil
crier   to shout
davantage *adv.*   more
déception *f.*   disappointment
défendre*   to forbid, to prohibit
délivrer   to liberate
demander   to ask (for), to request
dérober   to escape; to steal, to rob
distrait, -e *adj.*   absentminded; inattentive
divers, -e *adj.*   various, several, different
doubler   to pass (a car)
douter: se douter de   to suspect
drap *m.*   sheet
dresser   to raise, to set up
  —une liste   to draw up a list
économie*: **faire des économies**   to save, to economize
éditer   to publish
éditeur *m.*   publisher
effet: en effet   in fact
embarras *m.*   difficulty, trouble
ensemble *m.*   set (*math.*)
errer   to wander
étiquette* *f.*   label, tag
étranger *m.*   foreigner; stranger
étranger, étrangère *adj.*   foreign, strange, unfamiliar
éventuel, -le   possible
éventuellement *adv.*   possibly, theoretically
évidemment *adv.*   obviously
expérience* *f.*   experiment
expérimenté, -e *adj.*   experienced
exposition *f.*   exhibit, exhibition, display
figure *f.*   face (of a person)

fixer   to establish, to attach
football *m.*   soccer
force* *f.*   strength, power
formation* *f.*   training
front *m.*   forehead
garder* to keep, to retain
grappe *f.*   bunch
hasard *m.*   chance
histoire* *f.*   tale, story
hôte* *m.*   guest
hôtel particulier *m.*   private house
ignorer   to be unaware of, not to know
important, -e* *adj.*   big, large
inconvénient *m.*   disadvantage
inférieur, -e* *adj.*   lower
inhabité, -e *adj.*   uninhabited
journée *f.*   day
large *adj.*   wide
lecture *f.*   reading
librairie *f.*   bookstore
licence* *f.*   master's degree (approx.)
location *f.*   rental
machin *m.*   gadget, gizmo
magasin *m.* (= **boutique**)   store, shop
manufacture *f.* (= **fabrique,**
   usine) factory
ministre *m.*   statesman
misérable *adj.*   poor; worthless
misère* *f.*   poverty
monnaie *f.*   change, currency
monument* *m.*   public building
net, -te *adj.*   clear, distinct; neat, clean
notoriété *f.*   fame, good reputation
occasion* *f.*   opportunity, chance
   d'occasion   used
office *f.*   pantry
office *m.*   public function; church service
or *m.*   gold
or *conj.*   now
papier* *m.*   paper (material—*not* a
   newspaper)
parent* *m.*   relative
particulier, particulière *adj.*   private,
   special
partie *f.*   part
pas *m.*   pass (mountain, water); step
passer (un examen)   to take (an exam)
peine *f.*   difficulty, trouble
personnage* *m.*   character (play, novel)
peuple *m.*   nation

photographe *m.*   photographer
phrase *f.*   sentence (grammar)
physicien *m.*   physicist
pièce *f.*   room; play; document; coin
placard *m.*   closet
plat, -e *adj.*   flat
poser*   to place, to put; to ask (a question)
prétendre   to claim
prévenir   to warn, to inform
prévention *f.*   prejudice
procès *m.*   trial, hearing
procureur *m.*   magistrate
proposition* *f.*   clause (grammar)
propre *adj.*   clean; own
quai* *m.*   train station platform
quart *m.*   one quarter
quitter   to leave
raisin *m.*   grape
ralentir   to slow down
rayon *m.*   ray, beam; shelf
réalisation *f.*   accomplishment
réclamer   to ask for, to demand
reconnaissance* *f.*   gratitude
regretter   to miss, to long for
relation *f.*   friend, acquaintance
remarquer   to notice
rente *f.*   yearly income
répétition* *f.*   rehearsal
rester   to stay, to remain
retirer   to remove
retourner   to go back
   se retourner   to turn round
réunion *f.*   meeting
revue* *f.*   magazine
roman *m.*   novel
rude *adj.*   crude, rough
sage *adj.*   well-behaved; prudent
sale *adj.*   dirty; nasty
saluer*   to greet
sauver: se sauver   to escape, to run
   away
science* *f.*   knowledge
   les sciences* humaines *f.pl.*   social
      studies
sensible *adj.*   sensitive; perceptible
sensibilité *f.*   sensitivity; feeling
sentence *m.*   aphorism, maxim
situation* *f.*   job, position; condition
sort *m.*   fate
souvenir *m.*   memory

spirituel, -le *adj.*   witty
store *m.*   window shade
succéder   to come after, to follow
supplier   to beg, to implore
supporter   to endure, to bear
sympathique* *adj.*   likeable, congenial
tour *f.*   tower
tour *m.*   turn; trick
traitement* *m.*   salary (professional)
translation *f.*   transfer
travailler   to work
tuteur *m.*   guardian

unique *adj.*   single
usé, -e *adj.*   worn, worn out, thread-
  bare
user   to wear down, to deteriorate
vacance *f.*   vacancy
  les vacances *f.pl.*   vacation
vague *f.*   wave (water)
versatile *adj.*   indecisive
vilain, -e *adj.*   mean
visiter   to visit (place—*not* people)
wagon *m.*   railway car; subway car

Name __BILL CONKLIN_____   Section _____ Date _____

A. *Vocabulary.* Write the English equivalent of each of the following items. Indicate its gender by circling *m.* or *f.* (*masculine* or *feminine*) and its number by circling *s.* or *pl.* (*singular* or *plural*). If the French noun is a false friend, place a dagger (†) after it.

		French	Gender	Number
1.	geology	la géologie	m. ~~f.~~	~~s.~~ pl.
2.	goal	le but	~~m.~~ f.	~~s.~~ pl.
3.	publishers	les éditeurs	~~m.~~ f.	s. ~~pl.~~
4.	series	la série	m. ~~f.~~	~~s.~~ pl.
5.	nations	les nations	m. ~~f.~~	s. ~~pl.~~
6.	machine	la machine	m. ~~f.~~	~~s.~~ pl.
7.	symbol	le symbole	~~m.~~ f.	~~s.~~ pl.
8.	difficulty	la difficulté	m. ~~f.~~	~~s.~~ pl.
9.	doctors	les médecins	~~m.~~ f.	s. ~~pl.~~
10.	theater	le théâtre	~~m.~~ f.	~~s.~~ pl.

B. *Noun-adjective groups.* Translate each noun-adjective group, using the correct English word order. Indicate the gender and number of each French noun by circling the appropriate symbols.

		French	Gender	Number
11.	the modern buildings	les édifices modernes	m. f.	s. ~~pl.~~
12.	the current theory	la théorie actuelle	m. ~~f.~~	~~s.~~ pl.
13.	the nuclear physicist	la physique nucléaire	m. ~~f.~~	~~s.~~ pl.
14.	the religious symbols	les symboles religieux	m. f.	s. ~~pl.~~
15.	the lyric poem	le poème lyrique	~~m.~~ f.	~~s.~~ pl.
16.	the scientific movement	le mouvement scientifique	~~m.~~ f.	~~s.~~ pl.
17.	the vertical surface	la surface verticale	m. ~~f.~~	s. ~~pl.~~
18.	(the) romantic literature	la littérature romantique	m. ~~f.~~	~~s.~~ pl.
19.	the pacific coast	la côte pacifique	m. ~~f.~~	~~s.~~ pl.
20.	(the) physical geography	la géographie physique	m. ~~f.~~	~~s.~~ pl.

© 1987 Houghton Mifflin Company. All rights reserved.

211

C. *Using context to determine meaning.* Translate the French words in **boldface** type. A context (meaning pattern) is given parenthetically in English to help you recall the appropriate meaning.

reading	21.	(Our professor assigned us a long chapter as our) **lecture** (for tomorrow).
publisher	22.	(Houghton Mifflin is the) **éditeur** (of this book).
the principal goal	23.	(The study of weather is) **le but principal** (of the science of meteorology).
simple experiment	24.	(Pascal's principle can be demonstrated by a) **expérience simple.**
wide	25.	(The Boulevard Saint-Michel is rather) **large.**
currently	26.	(We are studying) **actuellement** (French vocabulary).
convenience	27.	(For greater) **commodité** (let's take our Cadillac).
lecture	28.	(I have to get to the campus early; I have a) **conférence** (in politics).
disadvantages	29.	(This situation has many) **inconvénients.**
because	30.	(I have a very small car) **car** (I am not rich).

D. *Word order.* In item 26 above, the word **actuellement** has been placed in its French position, after the verb it modifies. Write out the complete sentence in English, using correct English word order.

We are currently studying French vocabulary.

© 1987 Houghton Mifflin Company. All rights reserved.

Name _BILL CONKLIN_ _____ Section _____ Date _____

A. *Vocabulary.* Translate the following items, indicating number and gender by circling the appropriate symbols.

			Gender	Number
1.	a condition	une condition	m. f.	s. pl.
2.	(some) facts	des faits	m. f.	s. pl.
3.	the level	le niveau	m. f.	s. pl.
4.	the sons	les fils	m. f.	s. pl.
5.	(some) buildings	des édifices	m. f.	s. pl.
6.	(the) tennis	le tennis	m. f.	s. pl.
7.	(some) physicists physiques [context]	des physiciens	(m. f.)	s. pl.
8.	the bookstore	la librairie	m. f.	s. pl.
9.	the choice	le choix	m. f.	s. pl.
10.	(some) experiments	des expériences	m. f.	s. pl.

B. *Prepositional phrases.* Underline the prepositions in each phrase, and enclose each prepositional phrase in parentheses. Then translate.

Example: (sous un poids énorme) under an enormous weight

11. (par l'action d'un courant électrique) by the action of an electrical current
12. (sous des influences externes) under (some) external influences
13. (sur un principe physique) on a physics principle
14. (à côté d'un hôpital important) beside a large hospital
15. (derrière des autobus) behind some buses
16. (dans des gaz dangereux) in some dangerous gases
17. (sous des poids cylindriques) under (some) cylindrical weights

C. *Meaning in context.* Translate the French words in **boldface** type, taking into account the given English context. Decide, as part of the problem, whether to include words like *the* and *some* in your final translation.

18. (There must be) **des moyens** (of solving this problem).   Some means

© 1987 Houghton Mifflin Company. All rights reserved.

19. **Les moyens** (can be found in our laboratory).   *The means*

20. (There are) **des raisons** (for our tremendous success).   *(some) reasons*

21. (Did Napoleon have) **des choix** (of strategy at Moscow)?   *(some) choices*

22. (The farmer keeps) **des animaux** (in the barn).   *{some animals*

23. (I very much enjoy drinking) **le café**.   *(the) coffee*

24. (In New Orleans' French quarter) **les cafés** (stay open all night).   *the café's*

25. (Oisette Murphée had) **des yeux** (of a beautiful blue).   *(some) eyes*

26. **Les yeux** (of Texas are upon you).   *The eyes*

D. *Plural nouns.* Circle the correct plural form of each of the following French nouns, and write in the space provided the letter(s) that makes the noun plural.

_____27. un animal   (a) les animals   (b) des animaux   (c) les animaux

_____28. un gaz   (a) des gaz   (b) les gaz   (c) des gazes

_____29. le fait   (a) des faits   (b) le faits   (c) les faits

_____30. un œil   (a) des œils   (b) les œix   (c) des yeux

_____31. une théorie   (a) les théories   (b) des théories   (c) unes théories

© 1987 Houghton Mifflin Company. All rights reserved.

Name_____ Section_____ Date_____

A. *Adjective identification and translation of noun-adjective groups.* For each item, first underline the adjective and enclose the noun-adjective group (with the article) in parentheses. Indicate gender and number in the space provided. Then translate. Finally, indicate that a noun-adjective group does not follow the general rule of position of adjectives by marking it with a check (√).

		Gender	**Number**
1. _____	une façade gothique	*m. f.*	*s. pl.*
2. _____	l'opinion publique	*m. f.*	*s. pl.*
3. _____	le rayonnement cosmique	*m. f.*	*s. pl.*
4. _____	des émulsions photographiques	*m. f.*	*s. pl.*
5. _____	la fameuse expérience	*m. f.*	*s. pl.*
6. _____	une série géométrique	*m. f.*	*s. pl.*
7. _____	des concepts fondamentaux	*m. f.*	*s. pl.*
8. _____	les faits précis	*m. f.*	*s. pl.*

B. *Prepositional phrases.* Each of the following items is composed of two or more prepositional phrases—that is, noun-adjective groups preceded by a preposition. (1) Underline each preposition; (2) enclose each prepositional phrase in parentheses; and (3) translate.

9. par un système simple de l'analyse chimique_____

_____

10. des torrents de métal liquéfié_____

_____

11. par l'intelligence nécessaire pour les expériences_____

_____

12. par un courant alternatif de haute fréquence_____

_____

13. dans une librairie en face de l'université_____

_____

14. avec des physiciens dans le laboratoire_____

_____

© 1987 Houghton Mifflin Company. All rights reserved.

C. *Noun-adjective groups and prepositional phrases.* Underline prepositions, and place parentheses around noun-adjective groups and around prepositional phrases. Then translate.

15. avec la forme et [and] la proximité des continents_____

_____

16. l'existence d'une force vers le centre_____

_____

17. sur une partie des côtes de la Russie méridionale_____

_____

18. de la théorie des mouvements des planètes_____

_____

19. le centre exact d'un système planétaire_____

_____

20. l'énorme talent d'un architecte célèbre_____

_____

21. le plan de la façade de la cathédrale de Saint-Pierre à Rome_____

_____

© 1987 Houghton Mifflin Company. All rights reserved.

Name ___BILL CONKLIN___ Section _____ Date _____

A. *Noun-adjective groups with modifiers in both preceding and following positions.*
Translate into good English.

1. plusieurs grands bâtiments ___several large buildings___

2. beaucoup de théories intéressantes ___many interesting theories___

3. assez de pression verticale ___enough vertical pressure___

4. trop de longues expériences ___too many long experiments___

5. la Symphonie fantastique de Berlioz ___Berlioz' Symphony Fantastique___

6. cinq mauvais résultats ___five bad results___

7. Einstein: sa théorie de la relativité ___Einstein: his theory of relativity___

B. *The forms des, du, de la, and de l'.* The translation of these words may be (a)
omitted, with the word *some* understood, or (b) translated *of the*. Which of the
possible meanings is correct in each of the sentences below? Translate words in
boldface type.

8. (The sides) **des maisons** (are made of stone). ___of the houses___

9. (There are) **des maisons** (on both sides of this street) ___(some) houses___

10. (The volume) **des gaz** (we studied is variable). ___of the gases___

11. (Our meter detected) **des gaz** (in this room). ___(some) gas___

12. (Please give me) **du café**. ___(of) ~~the~~ ^{some} coffee___

13. (We are speaking) **du but** (which we want to attain). ___of the goal___

14. (We are concerned) **du but** (which we want to attain). ___about the goal___

15. (We need) **du papier**. ___(of) ~~the~~ ^{some} paper___

16. (The surface) **du papier** (is smooth). ___of the paper___

17. (A measurement) **de l'énergie** (of this system is being made). ___of the
energy___

18. (Future production of electricity will require) **de l'énergie nucléaire**. _____
___nuclear energy___

© 1987 Houghton Mifflin Company. All rights reserved.

C. *Possessive adjectives.* Translate the words in **boldface** type, taking into account the antecedent of the possessive pronoun given before each phrase.

19. Einstein: **sa théorie** de la conservation de l'énergie _his theory of energy conservation_

20. Madame Curie: **sa théorie** de la radioactivité _her theory of radioactivity_

21. Einstein et Curie: **leurs théories scientifiques** _their scientific theories_

22. Mozart: **ses opéras comiques** _his comic operas_

23. Madame Curie: **ses contributions** à la science _her contributions to science_

24. Haydn: **sa symphonie** N° 94 (*la Surprise*) _his symphony #94 (the Surprise)_

25. uranium: **son poids atomique** _its atomic weight(s?)_

26. les architectes: **leur dessein complet** _their complete design_

27. l'université: **ses bâtiments magnifiques** _its magnificent buildings_

28. le professeur: **ses recherches** _his research_

© 1987 Houghton Mifflin Company. All rights reserved.

Name_____ Section_____ Date_____

A. *Noun-adjective groups including an adverb.* Translate into good English.

1. un globe à peu près sphérique_____

2. des orbites très allongées_____

3. des surfaces plus ou moins verticales_____

4. un animal peu féroce_____

5. une impression assez vague_____

6. une température légèrement réduite_____

7. une histoire beaucoup trop longue_____

8. une matière fortement radioactive_____

9. un auteur très intelligent_____

10. leur bibliothèque partiellement climatisée [*air-conditioned*]_____

_____

B. *Prepositional phrases used as attributes.* Enclose prepositional phrases in parentheses, and translate.

11. aux maisons en brique_____

12. des animaux à quatre pattes_____

13. un avion à réaction_____

14. cet homme aux cheveux blancs_____

15. la salle de lecture dans la bibliothèque_____

16. des planchers de béton armé_____

17. une montre en or_____

C. *Sentences.* Translate.

18. Plusieurs gaz composent l'air atmosphérique de la terre._____

_____

19. Des vibrations résultent de la compression de l'air._____

_____

© 1987 Houghton Mifflin Company. All rights reserved.

20. La théorie la plus importante est la théorie de la relativité d'Einstein.

_____

21. La géométrie est une des diverses branches des mathématiques pures. _____

_____

22. Le gouvernement des États-Unis d'Amérique a la forme démocratique. _____

_____

23. Le personnage central de la trilogie *U.S.A.* de Dos Passos est un Américain typique. _____

_____

_____

24. La machine à calculer inventée par Blaise Pascal facilite le travail mathématique. _____

_____

_____

25. Actuellement les architectes parisiens construisent des bâtiments très modernes. _____

_____

_____

© 1987 Houghton Mifflin Company. All rights reserved.

Name_____ Section_____ Date_____

A. *Subject pronouns.* Translate the words in **boldface** type, taking into account the antecedent of the subject pronoun given before each phrase.

1. la lumière: **elle parcourt l'air**_____

2. la classe: **elle finit la lecture**_____

3. le directeur: **il présente son projet**_____

4. les généraux: **ils présentent leur stratégie**_____

5. les nations: **elles forment l'O.N.U.** [*UN*]_____

6. l'événement: **il est arrivé**_____

7. la structure: **elle est examinée**_____

8. l'orchestre: **il exécute la musique**_____

B. *Reflexive verbs.* For each of the following sentences, (1) enclose noun-adjective groups and prepositional phrases in parentheses; (2) underline the complete reflexive verb form; and (3) translate the sentence.

9. Ces règles se déduisent des données. _____

_____

10. L'ambassadeur britannique se trouve à Paris. _____

_____

11. Ces phénomènes s'observent facilement. _____

_____

12. Les étudiants se dépêchent d'aller en classe. _____

_____

13. L'université se compose de plusieurs facultés. *The university is composed of several departments.*

14. Le chimiste s'occupe d'une nouvelle expérience. _____

_____

_____

15. Le son se produit dans l'air. _____

16. L'extraction de l'or s'effectue par des méthodes primitives. _____

_____

© 1987 Houghton Mifflin Company. All rights reserved.

17. La vie se transforme avec le développement de nouvelles technologies.

_____

_____

C. *Sentences containing* **dont** *phrases*. Enclose the **dont** phrase in parentheses, and translate the sentences into natural-sounding English.

18. La planète dont le satellite est la Lune s'appelle la Terre. The planet
whose satellite is the (Lunar) moon is named (the) Earth

19. Voilà le théâtre dont le professeur parle dans ses conférences. There is
the theater of which the professor spoke in his lectures.

20. Ces trois théories, dont la première est la plus utile, traitent de l'économie.
These three theories, of which the first is the most
useful, are concerned with the economy (with economics?)

21. Les animaux dont nous parlons sont distribués uniformément sur la surface
du globe. The animals of which we speak are
distributed uniformly over the surface of the earth.

_____

© 1987 Houghton Mifflin Company. All rights reserved.

Name_____ Section_____ Date_____

A. *Larger noun-adjective groups.* Underline the noun, and translate the phrase.

   1. une nouvelle théorie physique_____

        _____

   2. un autre gaz combustible_____

   3. la même surface brillante_____

        _____

   4. la littérature américaine actuelle_____

   5. une autre question difficile mais importante_____

        _____

   6. leur nouvelle expérience partiellement complétée_____

        _____

   7. d'autres jeunes officiers inexpérimentés_____

   8. son université célèbre et respectée_____

        _____

B. *Participle-prepositional phrase linkage.* Enclose noun-adjective groups and prepositional phrases in parentheses. If there is a linkage required between a participle and a following prepositional phrase, mark the link with an arrow. Translate.

   9. un grand bâtiment orienté au nord_____

        _____

  10. le disque solaire éclipsé par la lune_____

  11. la totalité des faits observés_____

  12. la totalité des faits observés par ces physiciens_____

        _____

© 1987 Houghton Mifflin Company. All rights reserved.

13. huit nouveaux échantillons examinés en détail par ces messieurs_____

_____

14. trois opérations compliquées par des difficultés mécaniques_____

_____

15. des cylindres destinés à la purification de l'eau_____

_____

16. plusieurs lois promulguées par le corps législatif_____

_____

17. quelques résultats intéressants obtenus par des spécialistes indépendants

_____

18. la limite fixée à un maximum de 100 ou 125 étudiants par année_____

_____

C. *Infinitives and impersonal verbs.* Underline impersonal verbs, and translate the sentences.

19. Il faut étudier pour avoir de bons résultats._____

_____

20. Il importe que Charles réalise son projet sans consulter les autres._____

_____

21. Il est difficile d'expliquer cette nouvelle méthode._____

_____

22. Il faut commencer maintenant._____

23. Après avoir observé ce fait, il doit préparer un nouveau plan._____

_____

24. Il est trop tard pour commencer à étudier après être arrivé à l'examen final.

_____

© 1987 Houghton Mifflin Company. All rights reserved.

Name_____ Section_____ Date_____

A. *Negation.* Underline both negative elements (**ne** and **pas,** for example) in each sentence, and translate.

1. Ces vaisseaux ne contiennent pas d'eau. _____

    _____

2. Aucun professeur n'observe suffisamment la vraie intelligence des étudiants.

    _____

3. Les fils de l'Arabe n'ont que dix-sept chameaux. _____

    _____

4. L'aîné des trois fils ne retient que huit animaux. _____

    _____

5. Les derviches ne refusent jamais leurs services à personne. _____

    _____

6. Rien d'extraordinaire n'arrive maintenant. _____

    _____

7. Les trois jeunes hommes ne semblent plus mécontents. _____

8. Il n'y a pas encore d'hélicoptère atomique. _____

    _____

9. Il ne reste que sept expériences biochimiques à faire. _____

    _____

10. Ce jeune homme n'est guère responsable de cet accident. _____

    _____

B. *The verb **tenir** and its compounds.* Underline the verb, place parentheses around structural groups, and translate.

11. Obtenons un échantillon de cette matière. _____

12. Nous tenons à visiter le Louvre à Paris. _____

    _____

© 1987 Houghton Mifflin Company. All rights reserved.

13. Le professeur tient à parler français en classe. _____
_____

14. Pendant la durée de l'expérience il faut maintenir une température constante. _____
_____
_____

15. L'azote n'entretient jamais la combustion. _____
_____

C. *Essential vocabulary.* Translate the underlined words.

16. Les satellites accompagnent une planète. Or, la Lune accompagne la Terre. La Lune est <u>donc</u> un satellite. _____

17. <u>D'après</u> la théorie de Bohr . . . . _____

18. <u>En outre,</u> Voltaire détestait Rousseau. _____

19. Les Américains sont souvent admirés <u>à cause de</u> leur esprit pratique. _____

20. <u>Avant</u> l'algèbre et la géométrie, il faut étudier les mathématiques élémentaires. _____

21. <u>Enfin</u> l'origine de la lune reste une énigme. _____

22. Cette figure géométrique <u>n'a que</u> trois côtés; c'est donc un triangle. _____

© 1987 Houghton Mifflin Company. All rights reserved.

Name _____ Section _____ Date _____

A. *Verb recognition.* Examine each of the following verb forms and indicate whether the tense is present, future, or conditional by circling the appropriate abbreviation provided. Then give the English equivalent. (In the case of the present tense, two translations are required.)

1. _____ nous étudions   *Pres* *F* *C*
2. _____ elle réfléchirait   *Pres* *F* *C*
3. _____ vous serez   *Pres* *F* *C*
4. _____ ils obtiendront   *Pres* *F* *C*
5. _____ j'arriverai   *Pres* *F* *C*
6. _____ tu arrives   *Pres* *F* *C*
7. _____ ils bâtissent   *Pres* *F* *C*
8. _____ nous bâtirons   *Pres* *F* *C*
9. _____ ils choisissent   *Pres* *F* *C*
10. _____ elles choisiraient   *Pres* *F* *C*
11. _____ ils vendent   *Pres* *F* *C*
12. _____ il maintiendra   *Pres* *F* *C*
13. _____ vous finiriez   *Pres* *F* *C*
14. _____ nous entrons   *Pres* *F* *C*
15. _____ nous entrerons   *Pres* *F* *C*

For the following verbs, analyze *only the auxiliary* (not the past participle) as present, future, or conditional. Then translate the whole verb form.

16. _____ nous avons navigué   *Pres* *F* *C*
17. _____ il aura parlé   *Pres* *F* *C*
18. _____ elle serait arrivée   *Pres* *F* *C*
19. _____ il aurait examiné   *Pres* *F* *C*
20. _____ vous auriez préparé   *Pres* *F* *C*
21. _____ il sera allé   *Pres* *F* *C*

© 1987 Houghton Mifflin Company. All rights reserved.

B. *Sentence analysis.* Underline all verbs, and enclose structural groups in parentheses. Translate.

22. Nous déterminerons les possibilités des différents cas. _____

_____

23. Je terminerai ici mon explication des moyens employés pour la circulation de l'air dans ce bâtiment. _____

_____

24. Aucun homme mortel ne trouvera la solution du problème de l'univers. _____

_____

25. Les deux soldats dans la grande salle du palais attendront le signal du roi.

_____

26. Il y a un procédé qui donnera des résultats satisfaisants. _____

27. Je désire examiner les données et le rapport à la fois. _____

_____

28. Le nouveau sous-marin utilisera une pile atomique à neutrons lents. _____

_____

29. Quand nous visiterons le Louvre, nous chercherons le tableau qui s'appelle *La Joconde.* _____

_____

© 1987 Houghton Mifflin Company. All rights reserved.

Name_____ Section_____ Date_____

A. *Imperfect tense.* Give translations in order of preference:

1. il examinait   (a)_____ (b)_____
    (c)_____

2. il donnait   (a)_____ (b)_____
    (c)_____

3. nous préparions   (a)_____ (b)_____
    (c)_____

4. vous finissiez   (a)_____ (b)_____
    (c)_____

5. ils se composaient de   (a)_____
    (b)_____

6. elle obtenait   (a)_____ (b)_____
    (c)_____

7. on remarquait   (a)_____ (b)_____

8. il était   (a)_____ (b)_____

9. il se trouvait   (a)_____ (b)_____

10. il arrivait   (a)_____ (b)_____
    (c)_____

    [second meaning]   (a)_____ (b)_____
    (c)_____

11. il se lavait   (a)_____ (b)_____

12. je tenais à   (a)_____ (b)_____

© 1987 Houghton Mifflin Company. All rights reserved.

B. *Tense elimination.* Analyze the following verb forms, using the three-step method of general identification of time. Indicate your answers as follows: if a step fails, mark the appropriate row with an X; if a step succeeds, circle the appropriate row. Then translate into English.

Note: If the verb form contains a past participle, underline it and analyze *only the auxiliary verb* according to the steps.

		(1)	(2)	(3)
13. _____	nous examinâmes	Pres	FC	Past
14. _____	ils étaient	Pres	FC	Past
15. _____	il aura	Pres	FC	Past
16. _____	vous admettrez	Pres	FC	Past
17. _____	on divisera	Pres	FC	Past
18. _____	elles observèrent	Pres	FC	Past
19. _____	Napoléon arriva	Pres	FC	Past
20. _____	il était	Pres	FC	Past
21. _____	il faudra partir	Pres	FC	Past
22. _____	nous voudrions	Pres	FC	Past
23. _____	ils préparent	Pres	FC	Past
24. _____	vous finîtes	Pres	FC	Past
25. _____	il a donné	Pres	FC	Past
26. _____	j'avais parlé	Pres	FC	Past
27. _____	j'ai parlé	Pres	FC	Past
28. _____	j'aurais parlé	Pres	FC	Past
29. _____	il aura obtenu	Pres	FC	Past
30. _____	il obtiendrait	Pres	FC	Past
31. _____	il avait obtenu	Pres	FC	Past
32. _____	il y aura	Pres	FC	Past

© 1987 Houghton Mifflin Company. All rights reserved.

Name_____ Section_____ Date_____

A. *Object pronoun.* Translate the following fragments containing object pronouns (shown in **boldface** type), taking into account the antecedent of the object pronoun given before each phrase.

1. la maison: nous l'avons bâtie_____

2. le professeur: je **lui** parle_____

3. la dame: je **lui** parle_____

4. les tableaux: vous **les** regardez_____

5. l'expérience: il l'a terminée_____

6. les officiers: elle **leur** parlait_____

7. la table: nous **la** désirons_____

8. la leçon: nous **la** détestons_____

9. le livre: ils **le** regardaient_____

10. le colonel: vous **le** trouverez_____

B. *Double object pronouns.* Underline the object pronouns in each sentence and translate the complete sentence. (Do not translate the antecedents given before the sentence.)

11. l'étudiant, le texte: Je le lui donne. _____

_____

12. la dame, le livre: Je le lui donne. _____

_____

13. les amis, les invitations: Nous les leur donnerons. _____

_____

14. les directeurs, la situation: Nous la leur expliquerons. _____

_____

15. la cliente, l'auto: Nous la lui montrâmes. _____

_____

16. le document: Nous vous le préparions. _____

_____

© 1987 Houghton Mifflin Company. All rights reserved.

233

17. les avantages: Vous nous les aviez signalés. _____

_____

18. les résultats: Ils me les rapporteront. _____

_____

19. la conclusion: Ne me la cachez pas! _____

_____

20. l'histoire, les étudiants: Racontez-la-leur. _____

_____

C. *Compound tenses.* Translate the following fragments.

21. Il est allé _____

22. Ils sont sortis _____

23. Elle sera partie _____

24. Il aura fini _____

25. Il a été observé _____

26. Il l'aurait ouverte _____

27. Il est tombé _____

28. Nous sommes restés ici _____

© 1987 Houghton Mifflin Company. All rights reserved.

Name_____ Section_____ Date_____

A. *Comparisons.* Each of the following sentences contains a comparison. Underline both terms of the comparison (the second term is always **que**). Then translate the sentence.

1. A l'équinoxe les nuits sont aussi longues que les jours. _____

2. La pyramide de Chéops est beaucoup plus grande que celle du pharaon Mykérinos, roi d'Égypte de la IVe dynastie. _____

   _____

3. L'eau contient plus d'atomes d'hydrogène que d'oxygène. _____

   _____

4. La terre est une planète qui est moins grande que Saturne. _____

   _____

5. Aujourd'hui il y a plus de locomotives diesel que de locomotives électriques.

   _____

6. Il y a autant de grands bâtiments à Houston qu'à Dallas. _____

   _____

B. *Present participles and infinitives.* Translate the underlined words, taking into account the context.

7. Dupré s'est coupé au doigt <u>en préparant</u> cet appareil.   _____

8. <u>Sachant les faits</u>, le général abandonna le terrain.   _____

9. <u>En disant bonjour</u>, il s'inclina profondément.   _____

10. Il a appris le français <u>en étudiant</u> ses leçons.   _____

11. Le nouvel élève entra <u>sans parler</u>.   _____

12. Le professeur parlait français <u>en regardant</u> le pauvre Charles.   _____

13. Les grands philosophes ont inspiré le peuple <u>en proclamant</u> les principes de la liberté.   _____

14. <u>Étant entré</u> dans l'appartement, il a fermé la porte.   _____

15. La vieille dame est tombée <u>en descendant</u> l'escalier.   _____

© 1987 Houghton Mifflin Company. All rights reserved.

C. *The pronoun celui.* Translate the underlined words.

16. cette constatation et celle de Bohr   _____

17. ce livre et celui de Mallarmé   _____

18. ces événements et ceux d'hier [*yesterday*]   _____

19. le livre de Bohr et celui d'Oppenheimer; nous   _____
    avons discuté celui-là

D. *The verbs faire and prendre.* Translate.

20. La Belgique fait partie de la Communauté économique européenne (Marché
    commun ou CEE). _____

    _____

    _____

21. Il faisait beau hier; le soleil brillait. _____

    _____

22. Napoléon fit tout son possible pour vaincre les Russes. _____

    _____

23. Comprenez-vous l'importance du travail de Cuvier et de Lavoisier? _____

    _____

24. Le roi fut bien surpris quand il apprit ce que l'astrologue avait à lui dire. ____

    _____

© 1987 Houghton Mifflin Company. All rights reserved.

Name_____ Section_____ Date_____

A. *Inverted word order.* Translate.

1. Voici la théorie qu'a présentée M. Darwin dans son livre *De l'origine des espèces.* _____

   _____

   _____

2. Ne comprenez-vous pas l'intention de Voltaire en écrivant *Candide?*_____

   _____

   _____

3. Le voyageur faisait semblant d'avoir un cheval extraordinaire._____

   _____

4. Peut-être pourrons-nous aller à Mars à l'avenir au moyen d'une fusée._____

   _____

   _____

5. Comment calcule-t-on la surface d'un triangle?_____

   _____

6. Commander des huîtres pour son cheval, comme l'a fait le voyageur, a semblé bien étrange à l'aubergiste._____

   _____

   _____

7. Les symphonies qu'ont composées Haydn et Mozart sont du style qu'on appelle aujourd'hui *classique.* _____

   _____

   _____

© 1987 Houghton Mifflin Company. All rights reserved.

B. *Causative faire.* Identify the causative **faire** construction by underlining the inflected form of **faire** and the infinitive that follows it. Translate the sentence.

   8. Pendant la réunion nous ferons voir le nouvel appareil aux physiciens.

   _____

   _____

   9. Dans *Micromégas* Voltaire fait remarquer qu'il est très difficile pour un historien de ne rapporter que les faits. _____

   _____

   10. J'ai besoin de cette machine; je la ferai transporter dans l'autre laboratoire cet après-midi. _____

   _____

   11. En entrant dans la classe le professeur dit bonjour aux élèves; puis il leur fait traduire des phrases françaises en anglais. _____

   _____

   12. Ce monsieur est malade; faites venir le médecin immédiatement! _____

   _____

C. *Sentences with mettre, savoir, pouvoir, and voir.* Translate.

   13. Jacques sait danser, mais il ne peut pas; il lui faut rester à la maison. _____

   _____

   14. D'après De Tocqueville, les Américains ne mirent pas longtemps à développer le commerce et l'industrie. _____

   _____

   15. Les voyageurs n'avaient jamais vu un cheval manger des huîtres. _____

   _____

   _____

© 1987 Houghton Mifflin Company. All rights reserved.

Name _____ Section _____ Date _____

A. *Meanings in context.* Write the appropriate English meaning of the underlined words as used in the following sentences.

1. Supposons qu'il y ait deux gaz <u>auxquels</u> il faut ajouter un troisième. _____

2. Voilà la méthode <u>dont</u> il a parlé. _____

3. Prenons un événement <u>dont</u> la probabilité est connue. _____

4. Examinons le centre <u>auquel</u> cette force est dirigée. _____

5. Voyons <u>en quoi</u> consiste l'enseignement médical. _____

6. Pour bien connaître les choses, il faut <u>en</u> savoir le détail. _____

7. L'animal se libère <u>en abandonnant</u> le bras qui est pris. _____

8. <u>En tout cas</u>, ces faits nous suffiront. _____

9. Le thorium est important pour l'industrie atomique parce qu'on <u>s'en sert</u> pour fabriquer l'uranium 233. _____

10. L'étude scientifique <u>dont</u> on parle ici soulève beaucoup de questions. _____

B. *Vocabulary.* Write a common English equivalent of each of these words.

11. souvent _____   16. ensuite _____

12. plusieurs _____   17. jusqu'à _____

13. presque _____   18. ainsi _____

14. cependant _____   19. surtout _____

15. bientôt _____   20. au lieu de _____

© 1987 Houghton Mifflin Company. All rights reserved.

C. *Supplemental auxiliary verbs.* Translate.

21. On doit assurer aux producteurs français un prix de l'énergie électrique comparable à celui à l'étranger. _____

_____

_____

22. Les examens psychotechniques ont pour objet de déterminer les aptitudes intellectuelles et techniques des recrues de l'armée; au moyen de ces tests on peut éliminer les personnes sans capacité. _____

_____

_____

_____

23. Nous allons maintenant déterminer l'élasticité de cette matière. _____

_____

24. Pendant longtemps les sociologues ont laissé subsister le débat entre la société et l'individu sans le résoudre. _____

_____

_____

25. Les personnes qui ne disent pas la vérité devraient avoir une bonne mémoire.

_____

_____

26. On peut déduire l'existence d'une force dirigée vers le soleil. _____

_____

27. Les auteurs contemporains veulent introduire des notions nouvelles. _____

_____

28. Georges sait très bien jouer du piano, mais il ne veut pas le faire. _____

_____

© 1987 Houghton Mifflin Company. All rights reserved.

Name_____ Section_____ Date_____

A. *Tense discernment.* Translate the following sentences, and identify the tense of the verbs in **boldface** type.

1. La Fayette n'**avait** que vingt ans lorsqu'il **combattit** pour la cause américaine. _____

   _____

   (Tense of **avait:** _____;   of **combattit:** _____)

2. Le professeur **parlait** au sujet de la littérature allemande quand cet élève **est entré.** _____

   (Tense of **parlait:** _____;   of **est entré:** _____)

3. L'Angleterre **imposa** des taxes que les colonistes **trouvaient** injustes. _____

   _____

   (Tense of **imposa:** _____;   of **trouvaient:** _____)

4. Quand j'**étais** assez jeune, j'**allais** à Paris avec ma famille. _____

   _____

   (Tense of **étais:** _____;   of **allais:** _____)

   Did the speaker make the trip once or several times? How can you tell?_____

   _____

5. Descartes et Pascal **furent** les plus grands hommes scientifiques français de leur temps. _____

   (Tense of **furent:** _____;   Infinitive of this verb: _____)

6. Louis Pasteur **mit** au point une technique pour la purification du lait. _____

   _____

   (Tense of **mit:** _____)

© 1987 Houghton Mifflin Company. All rights reserved.

B. *Expressions of time.* Underline the expressions of time, and translate the sentences.

7. L'Amérique déclara son indépendance il y a plus de deux siècles. _____

    _____

    _____

8. Il y a trois ans que mon frère étudie la médecine à l'université. _____

    _____

9. Nous étudions le français depuis douze semaines, à peu près. _____

    _____

10. Depuis quand êtes-vous dans la salle de classe? _____

    _____

11. Nous venons de lire quelques phrases en français. _____

    _____

12. Quand le chimiste est entré dans le laboratoire, un élève venait de détruire une partie du bâtiment en faisant une expérience défendue. _____

    _____

    _____

    _____

13. Il est rare qu'un Américain se fixe pour toujours sur le sol qu'il occupe.

    _____

14. Dès que la pression est suffisante, on introduit une petite quantité d'un gaz déterminé. _____

    _____

    _____

© 1987 Houghton Mifflin Company. All rights reserved.

Name_____ Section_____ Date_____

A. *Relative clauses*. Separate the **que** or **qui** clauses from the main clause by diagonals (/) as has already been done in the first example. Underline the main clause. Translate the sentences.

1. Candide,/que le baron chassa du paradis terrestre,/marcha longtemps sans savoir précisément où. _____

   _____

2. La machine qu'inventa Pascal au dix-septième siècle était une calculatrice mécanique._____

   _____

3. Napoléon, qui était de retour sur le continent depuis trois mois, fut vaincu par le général Wellington à Waterloo. _____

   _____

4. Voilà la tête du poisson que mangea Alphonse. _____

   _____

5. Voilà le lion qui mangea le professeur de français._____

   _____

6. Le monsieur que cherchent les touristes est leur guide._____

   _____

7. Albert Einstein, le célèbre physicien et mathématicien qui travaillait à Princeton, était venu d'Allemagne._____

   _____

© 1987 Houghton Mifflin Company. All rights reserved.

B. *The uses of tout.* Give English equivalents.

8. tous les jours_____
9. toujours_____
10. toutes les histoires_____
11. toute l'histoire_____
12. tous les bâtiments_____
13. tout le bâtiment_____

14. tout de suite_____
15. tous les poissons_____

16. tout à fait_____
17. Il est tout chaud._____
18. tous les végétaux_____
19. Je les aime tous._____
20. le livre tout entier_____
21. Tout chien [dog] est un lion chez lui._____

_____

_____

C. *Sentence drill.* Translate.

22. Thomas Edison a découvert une méthode pour enregistrer le son, ce qui rend possible le phonographe moderne._____

_____

_____

23. Ce qui rend les héros de Wolfe si sauvages, c'est leur complexe d'infériorité. _

_____

24. C'est Jacques Cartier qui, en 1534, a découvert le Canada._____

_____

25. Notre globe est recouvert de masses de terre et d'eau._____

_____

26. Tout ce qui est susceptible d'augmentation ou de diminution s'appelle quantité._____

_____

27. C'est à la solution du problème immédiat que nous allons nous intéresser._

_____

© 1987 Houghton Mifflin Company. All rights reserved.

Name _____ Section _____ Date _____

A. *Adjectives.* Translate.

1. Le Colisée de Rome est un monument ancien. _____

   _____

2. L'ancien maire de la ville est devenu ministre de l'Éducation. _____

   _____

3. Le général de Gaulle a écrit cette lettre de sa propre main. _____

   _____

4. Voilà la seule composition de Ravel que je n'aime pas. _____

   _____

5. Votre explication seule ne prouve pas le fait. _____

   _____

6. Nous avons obtenu les mêmes résultats que vous. _____

   _____

7. Nos mesures furent justes; c'est l'échantillon même qui n'était pas pur. _____

   _____

8. Un certain général français est célèbre pour les mots qu'il prononça pendant
   la première guerre mondiale: «Ils ne passeront pas.» _____

   _____

   _____

9. Votre nouvelle expérience nous fournira une preuve certaine. _____

   _____

© 1987 Houghton Mifflin Company. All rights reserved.

B. *Conjunctions and y.* Translate.

10. Quoiqu'il veuille visiter la Californie, il ne peut pas encore y aller. _____
_____

11. Ce procédé pourrait se faire et dans le laboratoire et dans la fabrique. _____
_____
_____

12. N'ayez pas peur: les soldats ne jetteront pas l'astrologue par la fenêtre avant que le roi ne leur donne le signal. _____
_____
_____

13. C'est une question difficile que vous me posez; j'y penserai pendant deux ou trois jours avant de vous donner ma réponse. _____
_____
_____

14. Allez-vous à Monte-Carlo pour devenir riche en appliquant les lois de probabilité qu'a créées Pascal? Oui, j'y vais. _____
_____
_____

15. Le jeune page se précipita dans l'alcôve de la chambre et y resta pendant toute la scène. _____
_____

16. Pensez-vous qu'un test d'aptitude puisse être considéré comme une preuve certaine de succès ou d'échec éventuels? _____
_____
_____

© 1987 Houghton Mifflin Company. All rights reserved.

Name _____ Section _____ Date _____

A. *Disjunctive pronouns.* Underline the disjunctive pronouns used in the following sentences; translate the entire sentence in each case. (If the disjunctive pronoun is used for emphasis, be sure that your translation conveys this fact.) Avoid redundancy.

1. Moi, je m'intéresse à la littérature. Henri ne s'intéresse qu'aux sciences, lui.

_____

_____

2. Alain et moi, nous sommes allés au cinéma hier soir pour voir un film italien.

_____

_____

3. C'est toi qui lis tout le temps, pas elle. _____

_____

4. Connaissez-vous Pierre et Marie? Eh bien, ce microscope est à lui. _____

_____

5. Quel rôle avez-vous joué vous-même dans cette affaire? _____

_____

B. *Imperatives.* Translate.

6. Supposons maintenant qu'il y ait trois électrodes. _____

_____

7. Mettez l'appareil photographique sur cette longue table-là. _____

_____

8. Soyez comme vous voudriez paraître. _____

_____

9. Les candidats au doctorat? Qu'ils viennent me voir à trois heures vingt cet après-midi. _____

_____

_____

10. Finissons cette expérience! Il ne nous reste que dix minutes. _____

_____

© 1987 Houghton Mifflin Company. All rights reserved.

C. *The adverb aussi and the expression aussi bien ... que.* Translate.

11. La littérature française a beaucoup contribué à la culture du monde, aussi faut-il la lire. _____

_____

_____

12. Nous devons à Louis Pasteur aussi bien des vaccins contre des maladies infectueuses que la pasteurisation du lait. _____

_____

_____

13. Georg Friedrich Händel était un célèbre compositeur allemand qui créa aussi bien des opéras que des oratorios comme *Le Messie.* _____

_____

_____

14. Stéphane Mallarmé fut aussi bien professeur d'anglais que poète symboliste.

_____

15. A l'Opéra on a installé des machines modernes grâce auxquelles on peut produire de magiques effets; aussi devrait-on les employer davantage.

_____

_____

© 1987 Houghton Mifflin Company. All rights reserved.

Name_____ Section_____ Date_____

Subjunctive, possessive pronouns. Translate into English.

1. Tout est possible: il se peut même que Napoléon soit venu en Amérique après la bataille de Waterloo, mais ce n'est pas vraisemblable. _____

   _____

   _____

2. Arthur Rimbaud, poète symboliste par excellence, écrivit de la poésie exquise jusqu'à ce qu'il soit parti de la France à l'âge de dix-neuf ans pour mener une vie d'aventurier en Éthiopie. _____

   _____

   _____

3. Les poèmes de Walt Whitman sont parmi les plus longs que j'aie jamais lus.

   _____

   _____

4. Nos physiciens étudient ce problème depuis six mois: les vôtres n'ont pas encore commencé à l'examiner. _____

   _____

   _____

5. Peut-on douter que les soldats français se soient attendus à une résistance militaire du côté russe plutôt qu'à trouver la capitale en flammes? _____

   _____

   _____

6. Nous regrettons vivement que cet acteur veuille aller à Hollywood; nous doutons qu'il revienne à New York. _____

   _____

   _____

7. Vos programmes sont les meilleurs qu'on puisse imaginer; les nôtres sont moins ambitieux. _____

   _____

   _____

© 1987 Houghton Mifflin Company. All rights reserved.

8. M. Levêque craint que nous ne finissions pas notre travail avant que l'heure ne sonne. _____

_____

_____

9. Votre avion part d'Orly; le mien part de Roissy. _____

_____

_____

10. Est-il possible que le mouvement de ce train rapide soit parfaitement uniforme? _____

_____

_____

11. Il faut que vous sachiez la vérité: nous nous sommes servis de votre ordinateur. _____

_____

_____

12. D'habitude, pendant que je dors la nuit, mon camarade de chambre Pierre se trouve à la bibliothèque où il se sert des encyclopédies. _____

_____

_____

© 1987 Houghton Mifflin Company. All rights reserved.

Name_____ Section_____ Date_____

A. *Reflexive verbs.* Translate the following sentences into natural-sounding English.

1. Les étudiants se demandent souvent si la psychologie est une science. Est-ce qu'elle ressemble beaucoup aux autres sciences?_____

    _____

    _____

2. L'existence de la gravitation se déduit de la première loi de Kepler, n'est-ce pas?_____

    _____

    _____

3. Rousseau doute que les enfants comprennent ce qu'ils étudient; il se doutait que l'ancienne méthode d'enseignement n'était pas efficace. _____

    _____

    _____

4. Jean-Jacques se passe de la société: il préfère s'occuper des charmes de la nature en s'installant dans l'île de la Motte, près de Neuchâtel. _____

    _____

    _____

5. L'astrologue se doutait de ce que le roi avait l'intention de faire, mais il ne pouvait pas s'enfuir._____

    _____

    _____

6. D'après les résultats des tests, ces individus se sont montrés très doués pour la musique. _____

    _____

    _____

© 1987 Houghton Mifflin Company. All rights reserved.

B. *Interrogation.* Translate the following questions.

7. Quel est le but que l'auteur s'est proposé en écrivant une histoire du sacré chez les Arabes? _____

_____

_____

8. Comment est-ce que le voyageur a obtenu une bonne place près du feu en arrivant à l'auberge? _____

_____

_____

9. D'où viennent les principaux minerais de thorium? _____

_____

_____

10. Pourquoi Candide a-t-il dû quitter le château du baron? _____

_____

_____

11. Qu'est-ce que les prisonniers russes ont fait pour défendre Moscou? _____

_____

_____

12. Qui a inventé la machine à calculer au 17ᵉ siècle? _____

_____

_____

13. Pourquoi Mme de Staël admirait-elle la ville de Berne? _____

_____

_____

14. Les héros de Thomas Wolfe étaient obsédés par l'idée de la solitude. Etes-vous comme eux, ou bien avez-vous le goût de la solitude? _____

_____

_____

© 1987 Houghton Mifflin Company. All rights reserved.

Vocabulary

The following abbreviations are used:

abbr.	abbreviation	*inf.*	infinitive
Acad.	academic	*lit.*	literally
adj.	adjective	*m.*	masculine
adv.	adverb	*Math.*	mathematics
Arch.	architecture	*Mech.*	mechanics
art.	article	*Met.*	meteorology
Astron.	astronomy	*Mil.*	military
Biol.	biology	*Naut.*	nautical
Bot.	botany	*Phys.*	physics
C.	conditional	*pl.*	plural
Chem.	chemistry	*Pol.*	politics
conj.	conjunction	*pp.*	past participle
Elec.	electrical	*prep.*	preposition
f.	feminine	*pres.*	present tense
F.	future	*pres. p.*	present participle
fig.	figuratively	*pron.*	pronoun
fr.	from	*sth.*	something
Geog.	geography	*subj.*	subjunctive
Geol.	geology	*vb.*	verb
Geom.	geometry	*vst.*	verb stem
imperf.	imperfect		

To understand the entries, you must say the head-word each time the sign ~ appears. The entry under the head-word **part** for example, is

d'une ~ ... d'autre ~ ...

This means that you should read

d'une part (*intervening words*) **d'autre part** (*more words*)

The definition is

on the one hand (*something is the case*) and on the other hand (*something else is the case*)

Even more cryptic is the entry after the head-word **soit**, which is

~ ... ~

This is read

soit (*intervening words*) **soit**

It is important to notice whether the word you are seeking is a noun (which would be accompanied by an article in the text), a verb, or some other part of speech. In looking for a definition of **critique,** for example, you should note before using the vocabulary whether the word you want to translate is a noun or

253

so that you may select the correct entry. If the word appears *after* a
ok for an adjective. If, on the other hand, you determine that the
un, it helps to notice the gender before looking in the vocabulary.
wo nouns, **le critique** and **la critique**, which have different meanings.)

An asterisk (*) following the main entry indicates that the word is an irregular
verb. Irregular verb stems, such as **acquier-** and **aill-**, are also separate main
entries. Section references and references to Irregular Verb Tables are shown in
brackets.

à *prep.* to; at, in (*a place, a city*); with (*a characteristic*);
  un animal ~ quatre pattes a four-footed animal
à cause de because of, on account of
à côté de beside
à droite on the right
à gauche on the left
à peu près about, approximately
abaisser to lower; to drop; to be reduced
abolir to abolish
abondant, -e *adj.* abundant
abord: d'abord first of all; at first
aborder to approach
aboutir (à) to end (at), to conclude (with)
abréger* to shorten, to abridge, to condense
abri *m.* shelter
absolu, -e *adj.* absolute
absorber to absorb
abstrait, -e *adj.* abstract
abyssal, -e *adj.* abyssal
accélérateur, accélératrice *adj.* accelerating
accélérateur *m.* accelerator; (*Phys.*) ~ **linéaire** linear accelerator
accélératrice *adj.* accelerating
accélérer *v.* to accelerate, to speed up
accident *m.* (*Geog.*) irregularity
accidenté *adj.* irregular
accompagné de *pp.* accompanied by
accompagner to accompany
accomplir to accomplish
accord *m.* agreement;
  (*Phys.*) ~ **en phase** phasing
accorder to grant (*a request*)

accroissement *m.* increase, augmentation
accroître* to increase; to add to
accru *pp.* (accroître) increased; **s'étant ~** having increased
accumulateur *m.* storage battery
acheter* to buy
achever to finish
acier *m.* steel; ~ **inoxydable** stainless steel
Açores (*Geog.*) Azores
acquérir* to acquire, to obtain
acquier- (*vst. of* **acquérir**)
acquis *m.* knowledge, experience
acquis *pp.* acquired
actuel, -le *adj.* current, present-day
actuellement *adv.* currently, these days, now, at present
admet: on admet que it is admitted that
admettre* to admit [vb. 14]
afin: afin de in order to; ~ **que** in order that, so that
agent (de police) *m.* police officer
agir to act
agit: il s'agit de it's about, it concerns, it's a matter of
agréer to accept
aider to aid, to help
aïeul (*pl.* aïeux) *m.* ancestor
aigu, -ë *adj.* sharp, acute, high
aill- (*vst. of* **aller**)
ailleurs *adv.* elsewhere; **d'~** moreover, anyway, besides; **par ~** on the other hand
aimant *m.* magnet
aimantation *f.* magnetism
aimer to like, to love

aîné *m.* oldest, eldest

ainsi *adv.* thus, in this way; ~ **que** and, as well as; ~ **de suite** and so on, etc.; **pour ~ dire** so to speak

air *m.* air; **avoir l' ~** to appear, to seem

aire *f.* (*Geom.*) area

aisé, -e *adj.* easy

ait (*fr.* avoir) has; **qu'il y ~** that there are, will be

ajouter to add

algue *f.* alga, seaweed

Allemagne *f.* Germany

allemand, -e *adj.* German

aller* to go (*uses auxiliary* être); **s'en ~** to go away [vb. 1]

allongé *pp.* elongated

allumer to light, to ignite

alors *adv.* then, at that time; ~ **que** whereas, even though

âme *f.* soul; mind

aménagé *pp.* arranged

aménagement *m.* utilization

amené (à) *pp.* constrained (to)

amener* to bring; to get; to produce; to lead; to attract

ami *m.* friend

amie *f.* friend

amiante *m.* asbestos

amiral *m.* admiral

amour *m.* love (*pl. is f.*)

an *m.* year; **tous les ans** every year

ancien, -ne *adj.* old, ancient; (*before a noun*) former

anglais, -e *adj.* English

anglais *m.* English (*language*)

Angleterre *f.* England

anneau *m.* ring

année *f.* year

anse *f.* (*Geog.*) small bay; handle (*of a cup*)

antérieur, -e *adj.* anterior; prior (*time*)

août August

s'apercevoir* (de) to notice, to perceive

aplati *pp.* flattened

apparaître* to appear [vb. 18]

appareil *m.* apparatus, equipment; instrument; ~ **photographique** camera

apparition *f.* appearance

appartenir* to belong to [vb. 28]

appeler* to call; **s' ~** to be called, to be named

appelle: il s'appelle his name is

application *f.* diligence, zeal, careful attention; (*Math.*) mapping

appliquer to apply

apporter to bring

appréciation *f.* increase

apprendre* to learn; to teach [vb. 21]

apprentissage *m.* apprenticeship

apprit (*fr.* apprendre) learned

s'approcher (de) to approach

appuyé *pp.* supported

s'appuyer sur to rely on

après *prep.* after; ~ **quoi** after which; **d' ~** according to

après-midi *m.* or *f.* afternoon

arbre *m.* tree

arc *m.* arch, arc

arête *f.* edge (*of a knife*); ~ **vive** sharp edge

argent *m.* silver; money

arme *f.* arm, weapon

armé *pp.* reinforced

armée *f.* army

armure *f.* armor

arrachement *m.* stripping off

arracher to strip off

s'arranger to arrange

arrêt *m.* stop; **sans ~** ceaselessly, without stopping

arrêter to stop; **s' ~** to halt, to stop

arrière: en arrière behind, toward the rear, astern

arriver to arrive; to happen (*uses auxiliary* être)

as *m.* ace

assemblage *m.* assembly

assembleur: programme assembleur assembly program (*computer*)

s'asseoir* to sit down

assez *adv.* enough; (*before an adj.*) rather, fairly; ~ **peu considérable** rather small

assidu, -e *adj.* industrious; constant

assis *pp.* seated

assise *f.*   (*Geol.*) layer, stratum;
une ~ **de briques**   a course of bricks
assoupissement *m.*   indolence
assurer   to assure
astre *m.*   star
astrologue *m.*   astrologer
astrophysicien *m.*   astrophysicist
atelier *m.*   workshop, studio
atmosphère *f.*   atmosphere
atome *m.*   atom
attacher   to attach; to tie
atteign-   (*vst. of* **atteindre**)
atteindre*   to reach, to attain
atteint *pp.*   reached, attained
attendre   to wait for;   s'~ **à**   to expect
attente *f.*   wait, waiting; expectation
attirer   to attract;
~ **l'attention sur**   to draw attention to;
s'~   to be attracted
attraction *f.*   attraction; (*Phys.*)
gravitation
au (*contraction* à + le)   to the, at the, in
the;   ~ **bout de**   after (*time*);
~ **milieu de**   in the middle of
aucun, -e *adj.*   no, none
au-delà de *prep.*   beyond, past
au-dessous de *prep.*   below
au-dessus de *prep.*   above
augmentation *f.*   increase
aujourd'hui *adv.*   today
auprès de *prep.*   beside, at the side of;
close to, near
aur- (*FC vst. of* **avoir**)   will (would) have
aussi *adv.*   also; (*at the beginning of a
clause*) therefore;   ~ **bien ... que**
both ... and;   ~ **... que**   as ... as
(Sec. 81)
aussitôt *adv.*   immediately
autant *adv.*   as much, as many;
~ **de ... que**   as much (many) ... as;
d'~ plus que   all the more ... because;
~ **que**   as long as
auteur *m.*   author
automne *m.*   autumn, fall
automoteur, automotrice *adj.*   self-
propelled
autour de *adv.*   around
autre *adj.*   other;   ~ **part**   elsewhere;
d'une part ... d'~ part   on the one
hand ... on the other hand

autrefois *adv.*   formerly
autrement *adv.*   otherwise; in another
way;   ~ **dit**   in other words;
il en est (tout) ~   it is (quite) otherwise
autrichien, -ne *adj.*   Austrian
autrui *pron.*   others, other people
aux   (*contraction* à + **les**) (Sec. 19)
avait (*imperf. of* **avoir**)   had
avance: en avance   ahead of schedule,
early;   **par avance**   beforehand, in
advance
avant *prep.*   before;   **bien** ~   long
before;   **en** ~   forward;   ~ **que**
(+ *subj.*)   before
avant-garde *f.*   advance guard, vanguard
avec *prep.*   with
avenir *m.*   future
avertir   to warn
avertissement *m.*   warning; notice
aveugle *adj.*   blind
avion *m.*   airplane;   ~ **à réaction**   jet
plane;   ~ **en remorque**   glider
avis *m.*   opinion
avoir*   to have;   ~ **besoin de**   to
need;   ~ **chaud**   to be hot;
~ **envie de** (+ *inf.*)   to feel like;
~ **l'air**   to seem, to look;
~ **lieu**   to take place;   ~ **raison**
to be right;   ~ **tort**   to be
wrong [*vb.* 1]
avouer   to admit
axe *m.*   axis
ayant (*pres. p. of* **avoir**)   having
ayons   let us have
azote *m.*   nitrogen

baie *f.*   bay
baigner   to bathe; to be immersed
baisse *f.*   reduction
baisser   to lower; to reduce
balancer   to weigh
banc *m.*   bench; school (*of fish*)
bande *f.*   (*Phys.*) wave band;
~ **de fréquence**   frequency band
barbiche *f.*   beard
bas, -se *adj.*   low;   **en bas**   below, in the
lower part
base: de base   basic
basilique *f.*   basilica, church
basse-cour *f.*   farmyard

bataille *f.*   battle
bateau *m.*   boat
bâti *pp.*   built
bâtiment *m.*   building; (*rare*) ship
bâtir   to build
bâton *m.*   stick
battre   to beat
beau, bel, belle (*m.pl.* **beaux**) *adj.*
   beautiful, handsome;   **les beaux arts**
   fine arts;   **il fait beau**   the weather is
   nice, it's a nice day
beaucoup (de) *adv.*   much, many, a lot
   (of); (*after a verb*) greatly, very much
beaux *adj.* (*pl. of* beau)   beautiful,
   handsome
bel, belle *adj.* (*fr.* beau)   beautiful
besoin *m.*   need;   **avoir ~**   to need
béton *m.*   concrete;   **~ armé**
   reinforced concrete
bibliothèque *f.*   library; bookcase
bien *adv.*   well; (*before an adj. or adv.*)
   very; (*after some verbs*) indeed;
   ~ des   many;   **~ que**   although
biens *m.pl.*   property, possessions
bientôt *adv.*   soon
bijouterie *f.*   jewelry shop
bilan *m.*   schedule; statistics
billion *m.*   trillion (U.S.)
binocle *m.*   pince-nez glasses
biologique *adj.*   biological
blanc, blanche *adj.*   white
blesser   to hurt, to injure; to wound
bleu, -e *adj.*   blue
blindage *m.*   shielding; (*Mil.*) armor;
   ~ protecteur   protecting shield
bloc *m.*   block
blocage *m.*   freeze; block
boire   to drink
bois *m.*   wood; forest;   **en (de) ~**
   made of wood
boîte *f.*   box, can (*of food*);   **~ étanche**
   watertight box, airtight box
bon, -ne *adj.*   good;   **à quoi bon?**
   what's the use?
bond *m.*   leap; jump;   **d'un ~**
   suddenly
bonheur *m.*   happiness
bord *m.*   edge; border;   **à ~**   on
   board, aboard ship;   **au ~ de**   on the
   edge of

bore *m.*   (*Chem.*) boron
bouche *f.*   mouth
bougie *f.*   candle
boule *f.*   ball
bouleversement *m.*   upset; distress
bouleverser   to upset; to overthrow
bourgeois *m.*   middle class; one
   belonging to the middle class
bout *m.*   end; piece;   **au ~ de**   at the
   end of
bouteille *f.*   bottle
bouton *m.*   button; doorknob
branche *f.*   branch, limb
bras *m.*   arm; (*Geog.*) sound
bref, brève *adj.*   brief
brièvement *adv.*   briefly
brique *f.*   brick
brisé *pp.*   broken
briser   to break
bruit *m.*   noise; rumor
brûlé *pp.*   burned
brûler   to burn
brusquement *adv.*   suddenly
bureau *m.*   office; desk
but *m.*   purpose, goal; aim

ça (= **cela**) *pron.*   that
cacher (à)   to hide (from)
c.-à-d. (*abbr. of* c'est-à-dire)   that is (to
   say), i.e.
cadet *m.*   (the) younger, youngest
Caire: le Caire   Cairo
calcaire *adj.*   calcareous
calcaire *m.*   limestone ($CaCo_3$)
calcul *m.*   calculus; calculation
calculer   to calculate
cambriolage *m.*   burglary
cambrioleur *m.*   burglar
camion *m.*   truck
camp: ficher le camp   (*slang*) to beat it,
   to take off
campagne *f.*   country, countryside;
   à la ~   in the country
canal *m.*   channel, canal; (*Biol.*) duct
cap *m.*   (*Geol.*) cape
car *conj.*   for, because
caractère *m.*   character; characteristic
caractéristique *m.*   characteristic,
   (typical) feature
carbone *m.*   (*Chem.*) carbon

carbonique: gaz carbonique   carbon
  dioxide
carré *adj., m.*   square
carrefour *m.*   crossroads, junction
carrière *f.*   career
carte *f.*   card, map;
  jouer aux cartes   to play cards
cas *m.*   case
casser   to break
cause *f.*   cause;   **à ~ de**   because
  of;   **mettre en ~**   to involve
causer   to chat, to converse; to cause
ce, cet, cette (*pl.* **ces**) *adj.*   this, that;
  ce ...-ci   this ...;   **ce ...-là**   that ...
ce que *pron.*   what
ce qui *pron.*   what
ceci *pron.*   this (*as opposed to* **cela**)
cela *pron.*   that
célèbre *adj.*   famous
céleste *adj.*   celestial
célibataire *adj., m.*   bachelor
celle *f.sing. pron.*   the one, that
celle-ci *f. pron.*   the latter, this one
celles *f.pl. pron.*   the ones, those
cellule *f.*   cell
celui *m.sing. pron.*   the one;   **~-ci**
  the latter;   **~-là**   the former
cendre *f.*   cinder
cent   hundred
centaines   hundreds;   **plusieurs ~ (de)**
  several hundred
cependant *adv., conj.*   nevertheless,
  however
certain, -e *adj.*   certain
certes *adv.*   certainly
certitude *f.*   certainty
cerveau *m.*   brain
ces (*pl. of* **ce**)   these, those
cesse: sans cesse   incessantly
cesser   to cease
c'est   it is, he is, she is
c'est-à-dire *conj.*   i.e. (id est); that is
cet *adj.* (*alternate form of* **ce**)   this, that
cette *adj.* (*f. of* **ce**)   this, that
ceux *m.pl. pron.*   the ones, those;
  ~-ci   the latter;   **~-là**   the former
chacun *m. pron.*   each one, everyone
chacune *f. pron.*   each one, everyone
chair *f.*   flesh
chaleur *f.*   heat

chambre *f.*   bedroom
chameau *m.*   camel
champ *m.*   field
chance *f.*   luck, chance;   **avoir de la ~**
  to be lucky
changer (de)   to change
chantier *m.*   (*Arch.*) building site
chapitre *m.*   chapter
chaque *adj.*   each, every
charbon *m.*   coal
chargé (de) *pp.*   charged (with), loaded
  (with)
charger   to charge, to load;   **se ~ de**
  to take the responsibility for
charpente *f.*   carpentry, framing;   **à ~**
  timber, made of wood
chassant: en chassant   by forcing out
chasse *f.*   hunt, chase;   **aller à la ~**   to
  go hunting;   **faire la ~**   to hunt
chat *m.*   cat
château fort *m.*   castle
chaud, -e *adj.*   warm, hot;
  avoir chaud   to be hot (*person*);
  il fait chaud   it is hot (*weather*)
chauffage *m.*   heating
chauffer   to heat, to warm up
chauve-souris *f.*   bat
chef *m.*   chief, leader;   **~ d'état**   head
  of state
chemin *m.*   road;   **~ de fer**   railroad
cheminée *f.*   fireplace
cher, chère *adj.*   (*before noun*) dear;
  (*after noun*) expensive
chercher   to seek, to look for, to attempt;
  to get
chercheur *m.*   researcher
cheval *m.*   horse
chevelure *f.*   tail, coma (*of a comet*);
  (head of) hair
cheveu *m.*   hair
chez *prep.*   at the home of; at the place of
  business of; in the case of;   **~ eux**
  among them; in their case; at their
  house
chien *m.*   dog
chiffre *m.*   figure, number
chimie *f.*   chemistry
chimique *adj.*   chemical
chimiste *m. or f.*   chemist
chirurgie *f.*   surgery

chlorure *f.* chloride
choc *m.* shock
choisir to select, to choose
choix *m.* choice
chose *f.* thing; **quelque** ~ something; **peu de** ~ trivial, a trivial matter
christianisme *m.* Christianity
chute *f.* fall, decline, drop, decrease
cible *f.* target
ci-dessus *adv.* above
ciel *m.* (*pl.* **cieux**) sky, heavens
ciment *m.* cement, concrete
cinéma *m.* movie theater
cinq five
circonférence *f.* circumference
circonstance *f.* circumstance
circuit *m.* circumference; circuit
ciselé *pp.* chiseled
cité *f.* city
cité *pp.* quoted, mentioned
citer to quote, to cite
citoyen *m.* citizen
classer to classify
clé or **clef** *f.* key, wrench; ~ **anglaise** monkey wrench; ~ **de voûte** keystone; **fermé(e) à** ~ locked
climatisation (**de l'air**) *f.* air conditioning
cloche *f.* bell
cloison *f.* (*Arch.*) partition wall
cloître *m.* cloister; (*Arch.*) **arc de** ~ square vault
clou *m.* nail
cœur *m.* heart
coffre-fort *m.* safe, bank vault
coin *m.* corner; **au** ~ **de** at the corner of
colère *f.* anger; **se mettre en** ~ to become angry
colline *f.* hill
colon *m.* colonist
combien (**de**) how much, how many
combinaison *f.* combination
combustible *m.* fuel
comité *m.* committee
commander to control
comme *adv.* like, as; ~ **il faut** properly
commencer to begin

comment how; (*exclamation*) what!
commode *adj.* convenient; easy
commodité *f.* convenience
commun, -e *adj.* common
communauté *f.* community
communément *adv.* ordinarily
communiqué *pp.* reported
communiquer to connect; ~ **à** to give to, to report to
compensateur *adj.* compensating
compilateur, compilatrice *adj.* compiler
complet, complète *adj.* complete, full
complètement *adv.* completely
compliquer to complicate
comportement *m.* behavior
comporter to consist of, to include, to comprise; to entail; **se** ~ to behave
composante *f.* component part
composé *m.* (*Chem.*) compound
composé *pp.* composed; compound
composer to compose; **se** ~ **de** to be composed of
comprendre* to understand; to include [vb. 21]
comprimé *pp.* compressed
comprimer to compress
compris *pp.* (**comprendre**) included, understood; **y** ~ included (in it)
compromis *m.* compromise
compte *m.* account; **se rendre** ~ (**de**) to realize, to understand; **tenir** ~ **de** ... to take ... into account
compter to count, to count on, to plan on
compte-rendu *m.* report, minutes (*of a meeting*)
concentrer to concentrate; **se** ~ **sur** to be concentrated on, to be focused on
concevoir* to conceive; to think, to imagine [vb. 23]
conclu *pp.* concluded
conclure to conclude
conclut: on en conclut one concludes from this
concours *m.* coexistence; competition
concurremment *adv.* simultaneously
concurrencer to compete with
concurrent, -e *adj.* competing, rival
conçut (*fr.* **concevoir**) conceived
condensé *pp.* condensed

conduire* to conduct, to lead [vb. 22]
conduis- (*vst. of* **conduire**)
conduit *pp.* conducted, led
conduite *f.* conduct, behavior
conférence *f.* lecture, conference
confiance *f.* confidence
confondu *pp.* confused
conforme (à) *adj.* in conformity (with), true (to)
connaiss- (*vst. of* **connaître**)
connaissance *f.* knowledge, acquaintance; **les premières connaissances** the fundamentals, the basic ideas
connaître* to know, to be acquainted with [vb. 2]
connu *pp.* known
conscient, -e *adj.* conscious
conseil *m.* advice; **conseils d'orientation** guidance
conseiller to advise
conseiller *m.* counselor, advisor
conséquent, -e *adj.* consistent; important; **par ~** consequently; therefore
considérable *adj.* large, sizable; noteworthy, important
considéré *pp.* under consideration
considérer to consider; to contemplate
consigner to set down; to record; to confine
consommation *f.* consumption, using up
consommer to consume
constamment *adv.* constantly
constatation *f.* observation; verification
constater to verify, to ascertain; to establish
constituant *adj., m.* component
constituer to constitute, to consist of, to make up; **se ~** to be developed
constitution *f.* composition, makeup
construire* to construct [vb. 3]
construit *pp.* constructed
conte *m.* short story
contenir* to contain [vb. 28]
content, -e *adj.* happy, glad; satisfied
contient (*pres. of* **contenir**) contains
continu, -e *adj.* continuous
continuer to continue
continûment *adv.* continuously

contour *m.* outline
contourner to skirt, to follow along (closely)
contradictoire *adj.* contradictory
contraint *pp.* (**contraindre**) compelled, constrained
contraire *adj.* contrary
contraire *m.* contrary; **au ~** on the contrary
contrarier to contradict
contre *prep.* against
contredire* to contradict; to deny
contredit *pp.* contradicted
contrôle *m.* control, management; testing
contrôler to test; to supervise
contusionné *pp.* contused, bruised
convaincant *pres. p.* convincing
convaincre* to convince
convenable *adj.* appropriate
convenance *f.* propriety, appropriateness
convenir* to be appropriate, to be suitable; to agree, to suit, to fit [vb. 30]
convient: il convient it is appropriate
convoi *m.* convoy
copier to copy
coque *f.* shell, hull
coquille *f.* shell
corps *m.* body; substance; (*Chem.*) **~ simple** element
correspondre to correspond
corriger to correct
cosmique *adj.* cosmic
côte *f.* coast, shore
côté *m.* side; **à ~ de** beside; **~ cible** target; (*Elec.*) **~ haute fréquence, ~ H.F.** high-frequency side; **laisser de ~** to disregard
côtier, côtière *adj.* (*Geog.*) coastal
couche *f.* layer, stratum
se coucher to go to bed
coude *m.* elbow
couler to flow; to pour (*cement*)
couleur *f.* color; suit (*of cards*)
coulisser to slide
coup *m.* blow; stroke; toss (*of coins*); **~ d'état** revolution; **~ de foudre** thunderbolt; (*fig.*) love at first sight;

~ **de grâce**   finishing or decisive blow;
~ **de pied**   kick;   ~ **de sifflet**   blast
of a whistle;   ~ **de téléphone**
telephone call
coupable *adj.*   guilty
coupe *f.*   cut; division;   (*Arch.*)
~ **verticale**   cross section
couper   to cut
coupole *f.*   (*Arch.*) cupola, dome
cour *f.*   courtyard, yard; court (*royal*)
couramment *adv.*   commonly, fluently;
currently, at present
courant *m.*   current (*water, electricity*);
~ **alternatif**   alternating current;
~ **continu**   direct current;
~ **d'électrons**   electron stream
courbe *f.*   curve
courber   to bend;   **se ~ sur**   to bend
over
courir*   to run [vb. 4]
couronne *f.*   ring, annulus, corona
couronner   to crown
cours *m.*   **au ~ de**   in the course of,
during;   **au long ~**   of long
duration;   **en ~**   in progress;
~ **d'eau**   watercourse, waterway
course *f.*   course; journey, trip;
race;   **faire des courses**   to go
shopping
court, -e *adj.*   short
couru *pp.* (courir)   run
coût *m.*   cost
coûter   to cost
coûte: coûte que coûte   at all costs, no
matter what
coûteux, coûteuse *adj.*   expensive, costly
coutumier, coutumière *adj.*   usual,
customary
couvercle *m.*   cover
couvert *pp.*   covered
couvrir*   to cover [vb. 17]
craie *f.*   chalk
crain-   (*vst. of* **craindre**)
crainte *f.*   fear
crânien, -ne *adj.*   cranial
crédit *m.*   credit; support
créé *pp.*   created
créer   to create
creuser   to dig
creux, creuse *adj.*   hollow

crier   to shout, to cry out
critique *adj.*   critical
critique *f.*   criticism
critique *m.*   critic
critiquer   to criticize
croire*   to believe [vb. 5]
croiser   to cross; to pass (*in the opposite
direction*)
croissance *f.*   growth
croissant *pres. p.*   growing
croît (*pres. of* **croître**)   grows, increases
croyez   believe
croyons   let us believe
crut (*fr.* **croire**)   believed
cuir *m.*   leather
cuisine *f.*   kitchen; cooking
cultivateur *m.*   farmer
cultiver   to cultivate; to grow
curieux, curieuse *adj.*   curious; strange
cuve *f.*   basin, vat;
(*Phys.*) ~ **à réaction**   reaction
chamber

d'abord *adv.*   first, first of all; at first
d'ailleurs *adv.*   besides, moreover;
anyway
dalle *f.*   paving stone; (*Arch.*) plate
dame *f.*   lady
dangereux, dangereuse *adj.*   dangerous
dans *prep.*   in
d'après   according to; (adapted) from
daté *pp.*   dated
dauphin *m.*   dolphin; crown prince
davantage *adv.*   more, still more
de *prep.*   of, from, about; (*before inf.*)
to, with;   ~ [x] **à** [y]   from [x] to [y]
débarrassé *pp.*   relieved of, stripped of
débarrasser   to clear (off, out);
se ~ de   to get rid of
debout *adv.*   standing (up)
se débrouiller   to manage
début *m.*   beginning, start, origin;
au ~   at the beginning
deçà: en deçà (de)   below that, (on) this
side
décelable *adj.*   discoverable
déchirer   to tear, to rip
décider   to decide;   **se ~**   to make up
one's mind, to decide
décliner   to decline, to deteriorate

décontenancer   to disconcert, to upset, to perturb

décorer   to decorate

découler (de)   to be derived (from); to ensue; to pour (from)

découvert *pp.*   discovered

découverte *f.*   discovery

découvrir*   to discover [vb. 17]

décret *m.*   decree

décrire*   to describe [vb. 6]

décrit *pp.*   described

décroissance *f.*   decrease

décroître*   to decrease, to shrink

dedans *adv.*   inside

déduire*   to deduce

déduit: on déduit   it is deduced

déduit *pp.*   deduced

défavorable *adj.*   unfavorable

défectueux, défectueuse *adj.*   defective

défendre   to defend; to forbid, to prohibit

défini *pp.*   defined, definite, specific;   **mal ~**   poorly defined, unclear

définir   to define;   **se ~**   to be defined

définitive: en définitive   finally, in short, in a word, after all

définitivement   definitely

dégagé *pp.*   released

dégagement *m.*   release, disengagement

dégager (de)   to draw (from); to bring out

degré *m.*   degree; step

dehors *adv.*   outside;   **en ~ de**   in addition to, beyond

déjà *adv.*   already

délai *m.*   delay

demain *adv.*   tomorrow

demander   to ask (for), to request;   **se ~**   to wonder

démesuré *adj.*   unusually large, enormous

demeure *f.*   dwelling

demeurer   to remain; to reside, to live

demi, -e *adj.*   half;   **à demi-voix**   in a low tone (of voice)

demi-tour *m.*   about-turn;   **faire ~**   to turn around and go back;   **faire un ~**   to make an about-turn

démocratie *f.*   democracy

démolir   to demolish

démonter   to dismount; to disassemble

démontrer   to demonstrate

dent *f.*   tooth

départ *m.*   departure; starting point;   **au ~ de**   at the exit of;   **dès le ~**   from the outset

départagé *pp.*   divided; settled

dépasser   to exceed, to surpass

se dépêcher (de)   to hurry (*to do sth.*)

dépendre   to depend

dépens *m.*   expense;   **au ~ de**   at the expense of

dépenser   to spend

dépit: en dépit de   in spite of

se déplaçant *pres. p.*   moving

déployer   to deploy, to exhibit

déposé *pp.*   deposited

dépôt *m.*   deposit

depuis *adv.*   since

depuis *prep.*   since; for (a time) (Sec. 67B); from;   **~ l'antiquité**   since ancient times;   **~ lors**   since that time, since then

depuis que *conj.*   since

déranger   to disturb, to upset

dériver   (*Math.*) to derive; to divert (*river*)

dernier, dernière *adj.*   last, final, latest, most recent

dernier *m.*   the latter; the last

dernièrement *adv.*   recently

dérobé *pp.*   stolen;   **à la dérobée**   secretly, furtively

derrière *prep.*   behind, in back of

derviche *m.*   dervish (*member of a Moslem religious order*)

des   some, of the; from the; with the; any

dès *prep.*   starting with, since

dès que *conj.*   as soon as, when

descendre   to come down, descend; to get off (*a vehicle*); to stop at (*a hotel*) (*uses auxiliary* **être**)

désert, -e *adj.*   deserted

désigner   to designate

désincarné, -e *adj.*   disembodied

désirer   to desire

désobéir (à)   to disobey

désormais *adv.*   henceforth

dessin *m.*   sketch, plan

dessinateur *m.* sketcher, designer
dessiner to sketch, to draw; **se ~** to stand out, to be outlined
dessous *adv.* below
dessus *adv.* above, over
destiné (à) *pp.* intended (for)
déterminé *pp.* specified, determined
détroit *m.* (*Geog.*) narrows, strait
détruit *pp.* destroyed
deuton *m.* (*Phys.*) deuteron
deux two
deuxième second
devait (+ *inf.*) was supposed to, was to have (*done sth.*)
devancier *m.* predecessor
devant *prep.* in front of
développer to develop
devenir* to become (*uses auxiliary* être) [vb. 30]
dévié *pp.* deviated
devien- (*vst. of* **devenir**)
deviendr- (*vst. of* **devenir**)
devinrent (*pres. of* **devenir**) (they) became
dévoiler to reveal
devoir* to be obligated to
devoir *m.* duty; **devoirs** homework
diable *m.* devil
diamètre *m.* diameter
Dieu *m.* God
différence: à la différence de unlike
différencier to differentiate
difficile *adj.* difficult
difficulté *f.* difficulty
diffus, -e *adj.* diffuse, vague
digérer to digest
digne *adj.* worthy
dilatation *f.* dilation; expansion
diminuer to diminish, to decrease
diminution *f.* decrease, reduction
dîner to dine
dîner *m.* dinner
dire* to say, to tell; **à vrai ~** in fact; **c'est-à-~** i.e., that is; **pour ainsi ~** so to speak
directeur *m.* director
directrice *adj.* steering, directing
directrice *f.* director
se diriger (vers) to move (toward)
diriger to direct

disant (*pres. p. of* **dire**) saying; **en ~ que** by saying that
discernement *m.* judgment; distinction
discours *m.* speech; language
discuter to discuss
disparaissent (*pres. of* **disparaître**) (they) disappear
disparaître* to disappear [vb. 18]
disparition *f.* disappearance
disparu *pp.* disappeared
dispenser (de) to obviate, to make unnecessary
disponible *adj.* available
disposer to arrange, to place; **~ de** to have (sth.) at one's disposal
dispositif *m.* device; arrangement
disposition *f.* arrangement
disque *m.* record, disc
dissemblable *adj.* dissimilar, different
dissous *pp.* (**dissoudre**) dissolved
distinguer to discern, to distinguish
dit: l'on dit it is said
dit *pp.* (**dire**) said, told; named, called; **autrement ~** in other words
divers, -e *adj.* various
diviser to divide
dix ten
dix-huit eighteen
dix-sept seventeen
dizaine about ten, ten or so; **dizaines** dozens of, (*lit.*) tens of
docteur *m.* doctor
doigt *m.* finger
doit (*pres. of* **devoir**) must, should; owes
doiv- (*vst. of* **devoir**)
domaine *m.* domain, field
dominer to dominate
don *m.* gift, talent
donc *conj.* therefore, then; (*emphasis after imperative*) **parlez ~!** do speak!
donnée *f.* datum; **données** data
donner to give
dont *pron.* whose, of which, of whom [Sec. 28]
doré *pp.* gilded
dormir* to sleep
d'où whence, from where, from which
douleur *f.* pain
doute *m.* doubt; **sans ~** certainly, doubtless

doux, douce *adj.*   sweet, gentle, soft
douze   twelve
drame *m.*   drama
dresser   to raise, to put up, to erect;
se ~ sur   to rise on
droit, -e *adj.*   straight, just;
une ligne droite   a straight line
droit *m.*   right; fee (*legal*), tax, duty
(*import, etc.*)
droite *f.*   right (side);   à ~ de   on the
right of
drôle *adj.*   funny; strange
du (*contraction* de + le)   of the, from
the; some, any
dû *pp.* (**devoir**)   due;   il a ~   he had
to; he must have [Sec. 60, 64]
duc *m.*   duke
duquel (*contraction* de + lequel)   of
which
dur *adj., adv.*   hard
durée *f.*   duration
durer   to last, to endure
dureté *f.*   hardness

eau *f.*   water;   **entre deux eaux**
slightly below the surface;   ~ **lourde**
heavy water
écart *m.*   deviation
échantillon *m.*   sample, specimen
échantillonnage *m.*   sampling
échapper (à)   to escape (from)
échauffer   to warm
échelle *f.*   scale; ladder
éclairement *m.*   lighting
éclairer   to light, to illuminate
éclat *m.*   brilliance
éclater   to explode; to break out (*war*)
écliptique *m.*   (*Astron.*) ecliptic
école *f.*   school
écolier *m.*   schoolboy
écorce *f.*   crust;   ~ **terrestre**   earth's
crust
s'écouler   to flow; to pass by (*years, time*)
écoute: à l'écoute   listening
écouter   to listen
écran *m.*   screen
écraser   to crush
s'écrier   to exclaim; to shout
écrire*   to write [vb. 6]
écrit *pp.*   written;   **par** ~   in writing

s'écrouler   to fall (down), to collapse
éditeur *m.*   publisher
effacer   to erase, to efface, to obliterate
effectuer   to execute (*plan*); to achieve;
to carry out; to produce;   s' ~   to
occur, to take place
effet *m.*   effect, result;   **avoir pour** ~
to have as a result;   **en** ~   in fact,
indeed
efficace *adj.*   effective
s'effiler   to become tapered
effondré *pp.*   sunken, engulfed
effondrement *m.*   engulfment
s'efforcer (**de**)   to make an effort (to),
strive (to)
égal, -e *adj.* (*pl.* **égaux**)   equal
également *adv.*   also; equally
égaler   to equal
égalité *f.*   equality;
à ~ de distance   equidistant
égard *m.*   regard;   à son ~   toward it
(him, her);   **eu** ~ **à**   considering, by
comparison with
s'égarer   to stray, to wander
égaux *adj.* (*pl. of* **égal**)   equal
église *f.*   church
s'élancer   to thrust upward
électroaimant *m.*   electromagnet
élève *m.* or *f.*   pupil, student
élevé, -e *pp.*   raised; high;   **peu** ~   low
élever   to raise;   s' ~   to be raised, to be
built
éliminer   to eliminate
éloigné *pp.*   removed, distant
éloignement *m.*   separation; distance
s'éloigner   to move away, to go away, to
become more distant
émanation *f.*   emission
émaner   to emanate
embranchement *m.*   class, branch
embrasser   to include; to embrace, to kiss
émetteur *m.*   transmitter; source;
~ **de haute fréquence**   high-frequency
transmitter
émettre*   to emit [vb. 14]
émis *pp.*   emitted
empêcher   to prevent, to hinder
empire *m.*   dominance, control
empirique *adj.*   empirical
emplir   to fill

emploi *m.*   employment, job

employé *m.*   employee

employer   to use

emporter   to remove; to carry away, to take away; **l' ~ (sur)**   to prevail (over)

emprunter (à)   to borrow (from)

émule *m.*   imitator

en *prep.*   in, into;   **~ effet**   in fact, indeed;   **~ ce qui**   insofar as;   **~ dehors de**   outside of;   **~ être** to be advanced (to a certain point);   **~ face de**   opposite, across from;   **~ passant**   in passing

en *pron.*   some

enceinte *f.*   enclosure

encore *adv.*   still, again;   **pas ~**   not yet;   **~ une fois**   once again, once more

encre *f.*   ink

endommagé *pp.*   damaged

endroit *m.*   place, location;   **par endroits**   in places

énergie *f.*   energy;   **faible ~**   low energy

enfant *m.* or *f.*   child

enfanter   to create, to produce

enfermer   to include; to shut in

enfin *adv.*   finally

enfoncement *m.*   penetration, encroachment, inroad, indentation

s'enfoncer   to sink

engin *m.*   machine

englobé *pp.*   embodied, embraced

engrais *m.*   fertilizer

enjeu *m.*   wager, stake

enlèvement *m.*   removal

enlever   to remove

ennemi *m.*   enemy

énoncer   to state

énorme *adj.*   enormous

enregistrer   to record

enrichir   to enrich

enseignement *m.*   instruction, teaching

enseigner   to teach

ensemble *adv.*   together

ensemble *m.*   whole; (*Math*) set;   **d' ~**   overall, comprehensive, general;   **tout l' ~**   the whole of

s'ensuit (*pres. of* s'ensuivre)   results;   **il ~ que**   it follows logically that

ensuite *adv.*   then, next

s'ensuivre*   to follow

entendre   to hear; to understand

entendu *pp.*   heard; understood;   **bien ~**   of course

enterrer   to bury

entier, entière *adj.*   entire;   **dans son entier**   in its entirety;   **tout entier**   total, entire

entièrement *adv.*   entirely

entouré (de) *pp.*   surrounded (by)

entourer   to surround

entraider   to help each other

entraîné *pp.*   driven

entraîner   to be accompanied by; to entail

entre *prep.*   between; among;   **~ eux**   among themselves

entrée *f.*   entrance

entrefer *m.*   gap (*of a magnet*)

entrepris *pp.*   undertaken

entreprise *f.*   undertaking

entre: il entre pour [x] dans   it makes up [x] of

entrer   to enter (*uses auxiliary* être)

entretenir*   to maintain, to keep up; to support [vb. 28]

entretien *m.*   maintenance

entretient (*pres. of* entretenir)   supports

envahir   to invade

enverr- (*FC vst. of* envoyer)   will (would) send

envie *f.*   desire;   **avoir ~ de**   to want to, to have a desire to

environ *adv.*   about, approximately;   **d' ~**   by about, of about

envisagé *pp.*   contemplated, considered

envoi- (*vst. of* envoyer)

envoyer*   to send;   **~ chercher**   to send for [vb. 10]

épais, -se *adj.*   thick

épaisseur *f.*   thickness

épaule *f.*   shoulder

épineux, épineuse *adj.*   troublesome; spiny

époque *f.*   time, era, epoch;   **à cette ~**   at that (this) time;   **dès cette ~**   since that (this) time, from that time on

épreuve *f.*   test

éprouver   to experience, to feel; to test

épuiser   to exhaust
épure *f.*   final plan; (*Arch.*) design
s'équilibrer   to keep in balance; to sustain
équipe *f.*   team
erreur *f.*   error, mistake
escalier *m.*   stairs
espace *m.*   space
espèce *f.*   species, kind
espérer   to hope; **les gains à ~**   the benefits to be hoped for
espoir *m.*   hope, aspiration
esprit *m.*   mind; wit; spirit
essai *m.*   test, try, attempt; essay
essayer   to try
essence *f.*   gasoline
essuyer   to wipe off, to clean
est (*pres. of* **être**)   is
est *m.*   east
estimé *pp.*   estimated; esteemed
estimer   to consider
estomac *f.*   stomach
et *conj.*   and;   **et** [x] **et** [y]   both [x] and [y]
établir   to establish
établissement *m.*   establishment; construction;   **~ de crédit**   bank
étage *m.*   floor (*level of a building*); stage; phase
étagé *pp.*   in stages
étain *m.*   tin
était (*imperf. of* **être**)   was, used to be
s'étaler   to display, to spread out
étanche *adj.*   watertight;   **~ à l'air**   airtight
étant (*pres. p. of* **être**)   being;   **~ arrivé**   having arrived; having happened
étape *f.*   step, stage
état *m.*   state; condition
état-major *m.*   (*Mil.*) general staff
États-Unis *m. pl.* (*abbr.* **É-U.**)   United States
été *m.*   summer
été *pp.* (**être**)   been
éteign- (*vst. of* **éteindre**)
éteindre*   to extinguish;   **s' ~**   to die out, to become extinct [vb. 11]
étendre   to extend;   **s' ~ (sur)**   to expand (upon), to extend
étendue *f.*   extent, expanse; area

étoile *f.*   star
étoilé *adj.*   starlit, starry
étonner   to astonish
étrange *adj.*   strange
étranger, étrangère *adj.*   foreign
étranger: à l'étranger   abroad
être*   to be; (*as auxiliary*) to have;   **~ de retour**   to be back
être *m.*   a being, creature
étroit, -e *adj.*   narrow
étude *f.*   study, investigation
étudier   to study
eu *pp.* (**avoir**)   had
eurent (*fr.* **avoir**)   had
européen, -ne *adj.*   European
eut (*fr.* **avoir**)   had
eût (*fr.* **avoir**)   had
eux *pron.*   them
eV (*abbr.*)   electron-volts
évaluer   to evaluate
s'évanouir   to faint; to fade away
événement *m.*   event
évidemment *adv.*   obviously
évidence: mise en évidence *f.*   demonstration, proof
éviter   to avoid
évoluer   to evolve, to develop
examen *m.*   examination;   **passer un ~**   to take an examination
examiner   to examine
excès *m.*   excess
exécuter   to carry out (*a task*); to execute;   **s' ~**   to be carried out
exemple *m.*   example;   **par ~**   for example;   **par ~!**   for Pete's sake!
exerçant *pres. p.*   exercising
exercer   to exercise; to exert
exiger   to require
exogène *adj.*   exogenous
expérience *f.*   experiment; experience
expérimentateur *m.*   experimenter
s'expérimenter   to become adjusted; to become experienced
explication *f.*   explanation
explicitation *f.*   clarification, elucidation
expliqué *pp.*   explained
expliquer   to explain
exposant *m.*   (*Math*) exponent
exposer   to explain

exprimer to express; **s'~** to express oneself; **s'~ par** to be expressed by

expulsé *pp.* ejected

exquis, -e *adj.* exquisite

extraire* to extract; to draw out

extrait *m.* extract

extrait *pp.* extracted

extrémité *f.* end; extremity

face: en face (de) opposite

facile *adj.* easy

facilement *adv.* easily

facilité *f.* ease

faciliter to facilitate

façon *f.* way, manner; **de cette ~** in this way; **de ~ ou d'autre** one way or the other; **de ~ que** in such a way that; **de toute ~** anyhow

facultatif, facultative *adj.* optional

faculté *f.* college

faible *adj.* weak, poor; low; **à ~ distance** a short distance away; **à ~ vitesse** at low velocity

faiblesse *f.* weakness

faim *f.* hunger; **avoir ~** to be hungry

faire* to make, to do; (+ *inf.*) to cause (*sth. to be done*) [Sec. 55]; **~ partie de** to be part of; **~ remarquer** to point out; **~ semblant de** to pretend to; **~ son possible** to do one's best; **~ signe de** to give the signal to; **~ voir** to show [vb. 12]

faisant *pres. p.* making, doing

faisceau: ~ d'électrons stream of electrons

fait *m.* fact; **du ~ que** from the fact that; **en ~** in fact

fait *pp.* (**faire**) made, done

falaise *f.* cliff

fallait: il fallait it was necessary [vb. 13]

falloir* to be necessary

fallu *pp.* (**falloir**) **il a ~** it was necessary [vb. 13]

famille *f.* family

fantaisiste *adj.* imaginary

fass- (*subj. vst. of* **faire**)

fatigué *adj.* tired

faudra: il faudra it will be necessary [vb. 13]

faudrait: il faudrait it would be necessary [vb. 13]

faut: il faut it is necessary; **il ne faut pas** one must not [vb. 13]

faute *f.* mistake; **~ de mieux** for lack of something better

faux, fausse *adj.* false; wrong

faveur: en faveur de in favor of

favorisant, -e *adj.* favorable

fécond, -e *adj.* fruitful; profitable

femme *f.* woman; wife

fenêtre *f.* window; (*Arch.*) **~ coulissante** sash window; **~ à guillotine** sliding window

fer *m.* iron; **chemin de ~** railroad

fer- (*FC vst. of* **faire**) will (would) do

ferme *f.* farm

fermer to close

fermier *m.* farmer

fête *f.* holiday

feu *m.* fire; (*Mil.*) firing, action

feuille *f.* leaf; sheet (*paper*); foil

fibreux, fibreuse *adj.* fibrous

fidèlement *adv.* faithfully

se fier (à) to rely (on)

fier, fière *adj.* proud

figure *f.* face

fil *m.* thread; **~ de fer** wire

filiation *f.* affiliation, connection

fille *f.* daughter; girl; **jeune ~** girl

fils *m.* son

filtre *m.* filter

fin, -e *adj.* fine; detailed; **réglage fin** fine adjustment

fin *f.* end; **à cette ~** for this purpose; **mettre ~ à** to put an end to

finir to finish

fissible *adj.* fissionable

fixe *adj.* fixed, stationary

fixer to stabilize

se fixer to decide upon; to set for oneself

flacon *m.* flask

fleur *f.* flower

flottant *pres. p.* floating

flux *m.* flow, flux

focalisation *f.* focus

focaliser to focus

foi *f.*   faith, trust
fois *f.*   time; **à la ~**   at the same time; **mille ~**   a thousand times; **une ~ pour toutes**   once and for all; **une seule ~**   a single time; **encore une ~**   again, once more
folie *f.*   folly; madness
foncé, -e *adj.*   dark colored; **bleu foncé**   dark blue
fonction *f.*   function, duty; **en ~ de**   as a function of
fonctionner   to function
fond *m.*   bottom; background; (*Naut.*) sea floor; depths; **à ~**   thoroughly; (*Met.*) **un ~ froid**   a cold front
se fonder (sur)   to be based (on)
fondre   to melt
fondu *pp.*   melted; cast (*foundry*)
font (*pres. of* **faire**) (they) make, do; (+ *inf.*) cause
force: à force de   by dint of, by means of
forêt *f.*   forest
formation *f.*   training
forme *f.*   form; **sous ~ de**   in the form of
former   to form, to train
formule *f.*   formula; equation
fort, -e *adj.*   strong
fort *adv.*   (*before an adj. or adv.*) very
fortement *adv.*   strongly, sharply
fortifier   to strengthen
fosse *f.*   depression, hole; (*Arch.*) moat
foudre *f.*   lightning
four *m.*   furnace, oven
fournir   to furnish
fournissant *pres. p.*   furnishing
foyer: foyer solaire   sun's atmosphere
fractionnaire *adj.*   fractional
frais, fraîche *adj.*   cool
français, -e *adj.*   French; **le français**   French (language)
Français *m.*   Frenchman
Française *f.*   French woman
franchir   to cross; to pass (through or over)
frappant *pres. p.*   striking
frapper   to strike; to knock
frayer   to spawn
freiner   to brake; to slow down
frénateur, frénatrice *adj.*   braking; damping; checking

fréquemment *adv.*   frequently
fréquence *f.*   frequency; **~ d'inversion**   number of cycles (A.C.)
frère *m.*   brother
froid, -e *adj.*   cold
froid *m.*   cold; **avoir ~**   to be cold (*person*); **il fait ~**   it's cold (*weather*)
front *m.*   forehead; (*Mil.*) front
frontière *f.*   frontier
frottement *m.*   friction
fructueux, fructueuse *adj.*   fruitful, profitable
fuir*   to flee
fumée *f.*   smoke
fumer   to smoke
fur: au fur et à mesure   as
furent (*fr.* **être**) (they) were
fusée *f.*   rocket
fusse (*subj.* of **être**)   was, were
fut (*fr.* **être**)   was

gageure *f.*   wager
gagner   to gain; to earn; to increase; to win
galerie *f.*   gallery; **~ de peinture**   art gallery
garçon *m.*   boy; waiter
garder   to keep, to retain
garni (de) *pp.*   equipped (with)
gauche: à gauche   to the left
gaz *m.*   gas
géant, -e *adj.*   giant
gênant *pres. p.*   annoying, troublesome
gêne *f.*   discomfort
gêner   to annoy
génie *m.*   genius; spirit; **~ civil**   engineering
genou *m.*   knee
genre *m.*   kind; species; (*literary*) genre
gens *f.pl.*   people
gisement *m.*   (*Min.*) deposit
glace *f.*   ice; mirror; ice cream
glissement *m.*   sliding
glisser   to slip; to slide
golfe *m.*   (*Geog.*) gulf
goût *m.*   taste
goutte *f.*   drop (of water, etc.)
gouvernail *m.*   rudder
gouvernants: les gouvernants   (*Pol.*) government officials
gouverné *m.*   governed (*person*); citizen

grâce *f.* pardon; ~ **à** because of, thanks to

gradin *m.* step; **à gradins** in the form of steps

graine *f.* seed

grammaire *f.* grammar

grand, -e *adj.* big, tall; **un grand homme** a great man; **un homme grand** a tall man

grand *m.* (*Hist.*) a nobleman

grandeur *f.* size; greatness; quantity

grave *adj.* (*Music*) low, deep

grec, grecque *adj.* Greek

Grèce *f.* Greece

grenier *m.* attic

grenu, -e *adj.* granular

grimper to climb, to clamber

gris, -e *adj.* gray

Groenland *m.* Greenland

gros, -se *adj.* thick, fat

grossi *pp.* enlarged

guère: ne . . . guère scarcely, hardly

guérir to heal, to cure

guerre *f.* war

guetter to watch attentively; to stalk (*prey*)

guidage *m.* guidance

Guinée *f.* Guinea

habile *adj.* talented, skillful

habileté *f.* skill, ability

habitant *m.* inhabitant

habiter to inhabit, to live

habitude *f.* habit; **d'habitude** usually

haine *f.* hate

haïssable *adj.* detestable, hateful

hardiesse *f.* boldness, daring

hasard *m.* chance; **les lois du** ~ the laws of chance

hasarder to risk

se hâter de to hasten to

haut, -e *adj.* high, tall; advanced; **haute en couleur** rosy-cheeked; **plus haut** above, above mentioned, stated earlier (*in text*)

haut *m.* height; upper part; **de** ~ in height

hauteur *f.* height; (*Music*) pitch

herbe *f.* grass; **mauvaise** ~ weed

hérissé (de) *pp.* bristling (with)

heure *f.* hour; o'clock; **à l'** ~ on time; **de bonne** ~ early; **tout à l'** ~ just now, a short while ago; in a little while, shortly

heureusement *adv.* fortunately

heureux, heureuse *adj.* happy, fortunate

se heurter à to collide with

hier *adv.* yesterday

histoire *f.* history; story

hiver *m.* winter

homme *m.* man

homogène *adj.* homogeneous

horloge *f.* clock

hors (de) *prep.* out of; outside (of); **hors d'usage** out of service; **hors programme** unplanned; unexpected

hôtel *m.* hotel; ~ **particulier** mansion, private house

huile *f.* oil

huit eight; ~ **jours** a week

huître *f.* oyster

hypothèse *f.* hypothesis

ici *adv.* here

idée *f.* idea

identique *adj.* identical

ignorer to be unaware of; not to know

il y a there is, there are

il y avait there was, there were

île *f.* island

illimité, -e *adj.* unlimited

image *f.* picture

imaginé *pp.* invented

imaginer to imagine; to invent

imitateur, imitatrice *adj.* imitative

immerger to sink, to submerge

immeuble: immeuble locatif apartment building

immuable *adj.* immutable, unchangeable

impair, -e *adj.* odd-numbered

imparfait, -e *adj.* imperfect

impasse *f.* blind alley

s'impatienter to lose patience

important, -e *adj.* large, important

importe: il importe de it is important to; **n'importe** it doesn't matter; no matter; **n'importe quel** any; **n'importe qui** anybody, anyone (at all); **n'importe quoi** anything

importer   to matter
imposant *pres. p.*   imposing, impressive
s'imposer   to become necessary
impressionant *pres. p.*   impressive
imprévisible *adj.*   unforeseeable, unpredictable
imprimé *pp.*   printed; impressed
imprimer   to print; to impart; to exert
impuissant, -e *adj.*   powerless
impureté *f.*   impurity
imputer   to attribute
inattendu, -e *adj.*   unexpected
incendie *m.*   fire, conflagration
incessant, -e *adj.*   ceaseless
inclination: inclination à   inclination toward
incliné *pp.*   inclined
incolore *adj.*   colorless
incomber (à)   to be the responsibility (of)
incommodé *pp.*   inconvenienced
inconnu *adj.*   unknown
inconnu *m.*   stranger
inconvénient *m.*   disadvantage
incorporé *pp.*   incorporated
inculquer   to instill
inculte *adj.*   uncultivated
incurvé, -e *adj.*   curved
indice *m.*   index
indiscutable *adj.*   indisputable
indium *m.*   indium
individu *m.*   individual
inégal, -e *adj.*   unequal
inférieur, -e (à) *adj.*   inferior; less (than); lower
infime *adj.*   tiny
infini: à l'infini   endlessly
infini, -e *adj.*   infinite
informatique *f.*   computer science, data processing
infrason *m.*   infrasonic vibration
ingénieur *m.*   engineer
ingénieux, ingénieuse *adj.*   ingenious
innombrable *adj.*   countless
inodore *adj.*   odorless
inoxydable *adj.*   stainless
inquiet, inquiète *adj.*   worried; restless; uneasy
s'inquiéter   to worry
insaisissable *adj.*   evasive
inscrire* (*Acad.*) to register
inscrit *pp.*   registered, enrolled

insensiblement *adv.*   imperceptibly
s'insinuer   to creep in; to penetrate
insonorisation *f.*   soundproofing
s'installer   to settle down
instituer   to establish
instruit *pp.*   instructed; learned
insuffisant, -e *adj.*   insufficient
insupportable *adj.*   unbearable
intelligence *f.*   understanding; knowledge
interdit *pp.*   prohibited
intéressé *pp.*   concerned; involved
intéresser   to interest; to concern;
   s' ~ (à)   to be interested (in)
intérêt *m.*   interest; self-interest
intérieur *m.*   interior; inside
intermédiaire *adj.*   intermediate
interprète *m.* or *f.*   interpreter
s'interroger   to wonder; to ask oneself
interrompu *pp.*   interrupted
intervenir*   to intervene; to take effect [vb. 30]
intime *adj.*   very close
intimement *adv.*   closely, intimately, thoroughly
introduit *pp.*   introduced
inusable *adj.*   inexhaustible
inversant: en inversant   by reversing; by inverting
inverse: à l'inverse de   contrary to
inverse *adj.*   inverse; **sens inverse** opposite direction
s'inverser   to be reversed; to reverse; to invert
investir   to invest
invraisemblable *adj.*   incredible; improbable
iode *m.*   iodine
ioniser   to ionize
ir- (*FC vst. of* **aller**)   will (would) go
irradiant *pres. p.*   radiating
isocèle *adj.*   isosceles
isolant *pres. p.*   insulating
isoler   to isolate
isotope *m.*   isotope
issu (de) *pp.*   originating (from); derived (from)

jamais: ne ... jamais   never;   **à jamais** forever
japonais, -e *adj.*   Japanese

jardin *m.*   garden

jeter   to throw;   ~ **un soupir**   to heave a sigh

jette: que l'on jette   which is thrown

jeu *m.*   game; action; set;   ~ **de cartes**   deck of cards

jeune *adj.*   young

joie *f.*   joy

joli, -e *adj.*   pretty

jouant *pres. p.*   playing

jouer   to play

jouir de   to enjoy, to have

jour *m.*   day;   (*Arch.*) **à** ~   in openwork;   **au** ~ **le** ~   from day to day;   **au grand** ~ (*lit.*)   in broad daylight; (*fig.*) in the open

journal *m.* (*pl.* **journaux**)   newspaper

journée *f.*   day

jugement *m.*   judgment

juger   to judge

juillet   July

juin   June

jusqu'à   until; up to;   ~ **nos jours**   up to the present

jusqu'à ce que   until

jusqu'ici   until now, thus far

juste *adj.*   just, exact

se justifier   to be confirmed, to be substantiated

kilomètre *m.*   kilometer (1000 meters) (= .62137 mile, or about 5/8 of a mile)

la *art.*   the

la *pron.*   (*before verb*) it, her

là *adv.*   there;   ~ **-bas**   over there;   ~ **-dedans**   in it

laborieux, laborieuse *adj.*   hard-working, industrious

laissant *pres. p.*   allowing; leaving;   ~ **subsister**   allowing to remain

laisser   to allow; to leave;   ~ **de côté**   to disregard;   **ne pas** ~ (**de**)   not to cease

laiton *m.*   brass

lame *f.*   blade

lancer   to throw; to launch

langue *f.*   tongue; language

laquelle *f.sing. pron.*   which (*see* **lequel**)

larcin *m.*   larceny

large *adj.*   wide

largement *adv.*   greatly

largeur *f.*   width

laver   to wash

le *art.*   the

le *pron.*   (*before verb*) it, him

leçon *f.*   lesson

lecteur *m.*   reader

lecture *f.*   reading

léger, légère *adj.*   light; slight

légèrement *adv.*   slightly

lendemain *m.*   the next day

lent, -e *adj.*   slow

lentement *adv.*   slowly

lenteur *f.*   slowness

lequel *m.sing. pron.*   who, whom, which; (*interrogative*) which one(s) [Sec. 61]

les *art.*   the;   ~ **uns** ~ **autres**   each other; both

lesquels *m.pl. pron.*   which (Sec. 61)

lesquelles *f.pl. pron.*   which (Sec. 61)

leur *adj.*   their

leur *pron.*   (*before a verb*) to them

lever   to raise, to lift;   **se** ~   to get up, to rise

liaison *f.*   bond, linking, connection;   **énergie de** ~   bonding force

libre *adj.*   free

lié *pp.*   connected, related

lier   to link, to connect, to relate; to tie

lieu *m.*   place;   **avoir** ~   to take place;   **donner** ~ **à**   to cause;   **au** ~ **de**   instead of

lieue *f.*   league (*distance measure*)

ligne *f.*   line

linéaire *adj.*   linear

lingot *m.*   ingot

lire*   to read

lit (*pres. of* **lire**)   reads

lit *m.*   bed

littéraire *adj.*   literary

littoral *m.*   shore

livre *f.*   pound (*weight*)

livre *m.*   book

livrer   to deliver

locuteur *m.*   speaker

logé *pp.*   lodged

logement *m.*   lodging; (*Mil.*) quarters

loi *f.*   law

loin *adv.*   far;   **voir plus** ~   see below, see further on (*in text*) lointain, -e *adj.*   distant, remote

loisir *m.*   leisure

Londres   London

long: le long de   along

long, -ue *adj.*   long

longue: à la longue   in the long run

longtemps *adv.*   for a long time;
   il y a ~   a long time ago

longueur *f.*   length;   ~ d'onde
   wavelength

lors   then;   ~ de   at the time of;
   ~ même que   even though, even if

lorsque *conj.*   when

louer   to rent; to praise

Louisiane *f.*   Louisiana

lourd, -e *adj.*   heavy

lu *pp.* (lire)   read

lui *pron.*   (*before a verb*) to him, to her;
   (*after a preposition*) him;
   lui-même   himself

lumière *f.*   light; enlightenment;
   knowledge

lune *f.*   moon

lutte *f.*   battle, struggle

lutter   to struggle, to fight

luxe *m.*   luxury

lycée *m.*   lycée (*French secondary
   school*)

M. (*abbr. of* Monsieur)   Mr.

MM. (*abbr. of* Messieurs)   Messrs.

magasin *m.*   store

magie *f.*   magic

magique *adj.*   magical

main *f.*   hand

maintenant *adv.*   now

maintenir*   to maintain, to keep, to
   preserve;   se ~   to persist; to hold
   one's own

mais *conj.*   but

maison *f.*   house

maître *m.*   master;   ~ d'œuvre
   foreman

maîtrise *f.*   mastery

mal *adv.*   badly

mal *m.*   evil; difficulty

malade *adj.*   sick;   *m.*   sick person

malfaiteur *m.*   criminal, evildoer

malgré   in spite of

malheur *m.*   misfortune

malheureusement *adv.*   unfortunately

malhonnête *adj.*   dishonest

mammifère *m.*   mammal

manche *f.*   channel; sleeve;
   la Manche   the English Channel

manger   to eat

manière *f.*   manner, way;   à la ~   in
   the way

manifester   to show

manquer   to miss; to fail; to be lacking
   in;   ~ le train   to miss the train

marais *m.*   swamp

marbre *m.*   marble

marchandise *f.*   merchandise;
   train de marchandises   freight train

marche *f.*   progress; operation; motion;
   march; step (*of stairs*)

marché *m.*   market

marcher   to walk; to march; to run
   (*machinery*)

maréchal *m.*   (*Mil.*) marshal

marqué *pp.*   obvious; marked

marquer   to mark;   ~ un but   to score
   a goal

mars   March; Mars

marteau *m.*   hammer

masse *f.*   mass

massif, -ive *adj.*   solid, massive

massif *m.*   mountain range

matériel (*pl.* matériaux) *m.*   material

matière *f.*   matter; (*Acad.*) subject;
   ~ première   raw material

matin *m.*   morning

matinée *f.*   morning

mauvais, -e *adj.*   bad; poor (*quality*)

mécanique *m.*   mechanics;   ~
   quantique   quantum mechanics

méchant, -e *adj.*   wicked, bad, evil

médecin *m.*   doctor (M.D.)

médical, -e *adj.* (*m.pl.* médicaux)
   medical

médicament *m.*   medicine, medication

médiocre *adj.*   mediocre, small

se méfier de   to beware of

meilleur, -e *adj.*   better (*comparative of
   bon*);   le (la, les) meilleur(e)(s)   the
   best

mélange *m.*   mixture

mélanger   to mix

même *adj.*   (*before noun*) same; (*after
   noun*) very, itself; (*at beginning of*

clause) even; **de ~ que** the same
as; **il en est de ~ de** the same holds
true for

mémoire *f.* memory; *m.* (*Acad.*) article,
paper

ménagé *pp.* arranged, provided

mener* to lead

mentir to lie

mer *f.* sea

mère *f.* mother

méridienne *f.* (*Geog.*) meridian

méridional, -e *adj.* (*m.pl.*
méridionaux) southern, from the
south of France (**le Midi**)

merveille *f.* wonder, marvel

mesure *f.* measure; **à ~ que** as

mesurer to measure

métaux *m.* (*pl. of* **métal**) metals

méthode *f.* method

mètre *m.* meter (= 39.3701 inches, or
about 1.1 yards)

mettre* to put; to place; to spend
(*time*); **~ au point** to perfect;
~ en doute to cast doubt upon;
~ en état de put in a position to;
~ en évidence to demonstrate;
~ en jeu to produce; **se ~ à**
to begin [Sec. 56]

meurt (*pres. of* **mourir**) dies

meuvent (*pres. of* **mouvoir**) (they) move

midi *m.* noon, midday; **le Midi** the
south of France

mieux *adv.* better; **faute de ~** for
lack of something better

milieu *m.* environment; medium,
substance; **au ~ de** in the middle of,
in the midst of

mille thousand

milliard *m.* a billion (= 1000 million)

milliardième a billionth

millier *m.* thousand

mince *adj.* thin, delicate

minerai *m.* ore

minéral *m.* mineral

minime *adj.* slight, minimum

minuit *m.* midnight

minuscule *adj.* slight, tiny

minutieusement *adv.* minutely, in
detail, painstakingly

mirent (*fr.* **mettre**) (they) put

miroir *m.* mirror

mis *pp.* (**mettre**) put, placed;
~ à part excepted, set aside;
~ au point perfected; **~ en
évidence** demonstrated, shown;
~ en œuvre put into operation;
~ en question challenged, questioned

mise en évidence *f.* demonstration,
proof

mise en œuvre *f.* operation

Mlle (*abbr. of* **Mademoiselle**) Miss

modérateur, modératrice *adj.*
moderating

modérer to moderate, to modify, to
damp

moindre *adj.* less; **le ~** the
least; **~ que** less than

moins *adv.* less; **à ~ que** unless;
au ~ at least; **de ~ en ~** less and
less; **du ~** at least; **~ de** less
than

mois *m.* month

moitié *f.* half

monde *m.* world; **tout le ~**
everybody

montagne *f.* mountain

montagneux, montagneuse *adj.*
mountainous

montée *f.* climb, rise

monter to climb; to rise; to go upstairs;
to board (*a vehicle*) (*uses auxiliary* **être**
when intransitive)

montrer to show, to demonstrate;
se ~ to appear, to occur, to happen

morceau *m.* piece, portion

mordre to bite

mort *f.* death

mort *m.* the deceased

mort *pp.* (**mourir**) dead; **il est ~** he
died

mortier *m.* (*Mil.*) mortar, cannon;
~ de liaison mortar, cement

Moscou Moscow

moteur, motrice *adj.* motor;
installations motrices engine
installations

motif *m.* motive, purpose; (*Music*)
theme

mou, molle *adj.* soft

mouche *f.* housefly

moule *m.* mold; matrix

mouler to mold, to shape

mourir* to die (*uses auxiliary* être)

mourr- (*FC vst. of* **mourir**) will (would) die

mourut (*fr.* **mourir**) died

mouvement *m.* movement, motion

mouvoir* to move

moyen, -ne *adj.* average; medium; middle

moyen *m.* means, way; **au ~ de** by means of; **les moyens** the means, the resources

moyen-âge *m.* Middle Ages

muet, -te *adj.* mute, silent

mur *m.* wall; (*Arch.*) **~ mitoyen** common wall (*dividing adjoining properties*)

muraille *f.* wall

musée *m.* museum

musique *f.* music

mystère *m.* mystery

mythique *adj.* mythical

naissance *f.* birth; beginning; **après avoir pris ~** after originating; **donner ~ à** to produce

naître* to be born (*uses auxiliary* être) [vb. 16]

narguer to scoff at

naviguer to sail, to navigate

navire *m.* ship

ne not, no; **ne ... jamais** never; **ne ... pas encore** not yet; **ne ... plus** no longer; **ne ... que** only [Sec. 33]

né *pp.* (**naître**) born

néanmoins *adv.* nevertheless

nef *m.* nave (*of a church*)

néfaste *adj.* disastrous

négatif, négative *adj.* negative

négociant *m.* merchant

nerf *m.* nerve

net, -te *adj.* clear, distinct

nettement *adv.* clearly

nettoyer* to clean

neuf nine

neuf, neuve *adj.* new

neutre *adj.* neutral

nez *m.* nose

ni ... ni neither ... nor

nier to deny, to negate

n'importe it does not matter (*see* **importe**)

niveau *m.* level; **~ de la mer** sea level

nœud *m.* knot

noir, -e *adj.* black

nom *m.* name; **sous le ~ de** by the name of

nombre *m.* number; **~ atomique** atomic number

nombreux, nombreuse *adj.* numerous

nommer to name

non *adv.* no; **~ plus** either

nord *m.* north

Norvège *f.* Norway

notamment *adv.* especially

noter to note, to notice

nôtre: le nôtre, la nôtre ours

notre *adj.* our

nourrir to feed, to nourish

nourriture *f.* food, nourishment

nouveau, nouvel, nouvelle *adj.* (*m.pl.* **nouveaux**) new; **de nouveau** again

noyau *m.* nucleus

nu, -e *adj.* bare, naked; stripped

nuage *m.* cloud

nuancé *pp.* discerning; specific

nucléaire *adj.* nuclear

nuit *f.* night; **la ~** at night, every night; **la ~ se fait** night is falling

nul, -le *adj.* no; nil; zero

nulle part *adv.* nowhere

numéroter to number

nutritif, nutritive *adj.* nutritious

obéir (à) to obey

objectif *m.* objective

s'objectiver to be demonstrated

objet *m.* object

obliger to require, to oblige

observateur *m.* observer

observer to observe

obtenir* to obtain; **s'~** to be obtained [vb. 28]

obtenu *pp.* obtained

obtien- (*vst. of* **obtenir**) [vb. 28]

occasionner to cause

occidental, -e *adj.* western

occuper to occupy; **s' ~ de** to devote oneself to, to be busy with

océanographie *f.* oceanography

odorat *m.* sense of smell, olfaction

œil *m.* (*pl.* **yeux**) eye; **à l' ~** by eye, with the eye; **coup d' ~** glance; overall comprehensive view

œuf *m.* egg

œuvre *f.* work; work of art

œuvrer to work

offert *pp.* offered, presented

offrir* to offer, to give [vb. 17]

ogival, -e *adj.* (*Arch.*) gothic

oiseau *m.* bird

oiseau-lyre *m.* lyrebird

ombre *f.* shadow

ombré *pp.* shaded

on *pron.* one; we; they [Sec. 26]

onde *f.* (*Phys.*) wave

ondulatoire *adj.* undulatory, wave; **mécanique ~** wave mechanics

opère (*pres. of* **opérer**) operates

opérer to operate; **s' ~** to take place, to occur

opposé *pp.* opposite

s'opposer (à) to be contrasted (with)

or *conj.* now; but; now we know that …

or *m.* gold

orbite *f.* orbit

ordinaire: d'ordinaire usually

ordinaire *adj.* ordinary

ordinateur *m.* computer

ordonner to order, to command

ordre *m.* order; **de l' ~ de** on the order of

oreille *f.* ear

orgueil *m.* pride

s'orienter to be directed, to be oriented toward

orifice *m.* orifice, opening

origine *f.* origin

ôté *pp.* eliminated, removed

ou *conj.* or

où *adv.* where; when

oublier to forget

ouest *m.* west

oui *adv.* yes

outre: en outre further

outre *prep.* besides, in addition to

ouvert *pp.* (**ouvrir**) opened; **étant ~** being open

ouverture *f.* opening, aperture

ouvrage *m.* work, production

ouvrir* to open [vb. 17]

ovation *f.* acclaim, reception

oxygène *m.* oxygen

pair *adj.* even-numbered

palais *m.* palace

palier *m.* landing (*stairs*)

palpe *f.* feeler; antenna (*insects*)

panne *f.* breakdown

papier: papier à lettres writing paper, stationery

paquet *m.* pack, packet; group

par *prep.* by; per; **~ exemple** for example; **~ exemple!** for Pete's sake!

paradis *m.* paradise

paraiss- (*vst. of* **paraître**)

paraître* to appear, to seem [vb. 18]

parce que *conj.* because

parcourir* to traverse; to travel through [vb. 4]

parcours *m.* path; travel

pareil, -le *adj.* such (a)

parenté *f.* relationship, kinship

parfait, -e *adj.* perfect

parfois *adv.* sometimes

parisien, -ne *adj.* Parisian

parler to speak, to talk

parmi *prep.* among

parole *f.* word; speech

part *f.* part, share; **d'une ~ … d'autre ~ …** on the one hand … on the other hand …; **de ~ et d'autre** on both sides; **de toutes parts** from everywhere; **nulle ~** nowhere; **quelque ~** somewhere

partage *m.* dividing up, division

partager to divide, to share

partant (de) *pres. p.* starting (with) (at)

parti *m.* (*Pol.*) party

parti *pp.* left, departed

particularité *f.* characteristic

particule *f.* particle

particulier, particulière *adj.* individual,

unique, special;   **maison particuliére**
private house;   **en particulier**
in particular
partie *f.*   part; game;   **faire ~ de**   to be
a part of, to belong
partiellement *adv.*   partially
partir* to depart, to leave (*uses auxiliary*
être);   **à ~ de**   beginning with [vb.
19]
partout *adv.*   everywhere;   **un peu ~**
almost everywhere
paru *pp.* (**paraître**)   appeared
parut (*fr.* **paraître**)   appeared
parvenir* (à)   to succeed (in); to reach, to
attain [vb. 30]
parvien-   (*vst. of* **parvenir**)
parviendr-   (*FC vst. of* **parvenir**)   will
(would) succeed; will (would) reach
pas *adv.*   not
pas *m.*   pace, step; (*Geog.*) pass, strait
passer   to pass; to take (*an exam*); to
spend (*time*);   **~ de** [x] **à** [y]   to make
the transition from [x] to [y];   **se ~**   to
happen;   **se ~ de**   to do without
passion *f.*   enthusiasm, emotion
patrimoine *m.*   inheritance, patrimony
patte *f.*   foot (*of an animal*)
pauvre *adj.*   poor; (*after noun*) poverty-
stricken; (*before noun*) deserving of pity
pauvreté *f.*   poverty
payer   to pay (for)
pays *m.*   country
pêche *f.*   fishing
péché *m.*   sin
pêcher   to fish
pédagogique *adj.*   pedagogical
peindre*   to paint
peine *f.*   difficulty;   **à ~**   hardly;
sans ~   easily, without difficulty;
sous ~ de mort   at the risk of death
peintre *m.*   painter
peinture *f.*   painting
pellicule *f.*   film, layer
se pencher (sur)   to bend down; to lean
over
pendant *prep.*   during; for (*a time*);
~ que   while
pendentif *m.*   (*Arch.*) pendentive
pendre   to hang, to suspend
pendule *f.*   clock
pendule *m.*   pendulum

pénétrant *pres. p.*   penetrating;
peu ~   nonpenetrating
pensée *f.*   thought
penser   to think;   **~ à**   to think about
(*give attention to*);   **~ de**   to think
about (*opinion*)
pente *f.*   slope
percement *m.*   piercing
percevoir*   to perceive; to be aware of;
to hear
perdre   to lose
père *m.*   father
perfectionné *pp.*   perfected
périlleux, périlleuse *adj.*   dangerous
période *f.*   period; (*Phys.*) half-life
périr   to perish
permettre*   to permit, to allow [vb. 14]
perse *adj.*   Persian
personnage *m.*   character
personne *f.*   person;   **ne … ~**   nobody
perte *f.*   loss
pesanteur *f.*   weight; gravity;
~ universelle   gravity
pesée *f.*   evaluation; weighing
peser   to weigh
petit, -e *adj.*   small;   **moins ~**   not so
small, larger;   **plus ~**   smaller
pétrole *m.*   oil;   **moteur à ~**   diesel
engine
peu *adv.*   little; (+ *adj.*) *translate by the*
antonym of the adj.;   **à ~ près**
approximately;   **~ à ~**   little by
little;   **~ profond**   shallow, not so
deep;   **~ marqué**   negligible;
pour ~ que   if on top of that;
un ~   a little
peuple *m.*   people, nation
peuplement *m.*   populating; population
peut (*pres. of* **pouvoir**)   can;
il se ~ (que)   it is possible (that)
peut-être *adv.*   perhaps
peuvent (*pres. of* **pouvoir**)   (they) can
phénomène *m.*   phenomenon
phonologie *f.*   phonology
physicien *m.*   physicist
physique *adj.*   physical
physique *f.*   physics
pièce *f.*   piece, part; room; play;
document; coin;   **~ polaire**   pole (*of*
a magnet)   **pièces de recharge**
pl.   spare parts

pied *m.*   foot (= 12.7892 U.S. inches);
  (*Geom.*) base;   **à ~**   on foot
pierre *f.*   stone
Pierre le Grand   Peter the Great, Czar of
  Russia (1682–1725)
pile *f.*   reactor (*atomic*);
  ~ autorégeneratrice   (*Phys.*)
  "breeder" pile
pinceau *m.*   beam, pencil of light
piquer   to sting (*insect*); to prick (*with a
  sharp instrument*); (*Med.*) to give an
  injection to
pire *adj.*   worse
piscine *f.*   swimming pool
pitre: faire le pitre   to clown, to fool
  around
place *f.*   place; seat
placer   to place
se plaindre*   to complain
plaire* (à)   to please
plaît: on se plaît   one enjoys;
  s'il vous plaît (*abbr.* **s.v.p.**)   please
plan *m.*   map, plan; (*Arch.*) floor plan;
  (*Geom.*) plane;   **~ horizontal**
  (vertical)   horizontal (vertical)
  plane;   **~ médian**   midplane;
  au premier ~   in the foreground
planche *f.*   plank, board
plancher *m.*   floor
plaque *f.*   plate
plat, -e *adj.*   flat
plateau *m.*   plateau; platform (*of a scale*)
plein, -e *adj.*   full;   **en pleine mer**   on
  the high seas
pleurer   to weep, to cry
plier   to fold; to bend;   **se ~** (à)   to
  adapt (to), to adjust (to)
plomb *m.*   lead (*metal*)
plongée *f.*   dive
plonger   to dive; to plunge
pluie *f.*   rain
plume *f.*   pen; feather
plupart: la plupart de   most of the
plus *adv.*   more;   **de ~**   moreover;
  de ~ en ~   more and more;
  en ~ de   in addition to, besides;
  ~ grand que   bigger than;   **~ … ~**
  the more … the more;   **~ que jamais**
  more than ever
plusieurs *adv.*   several
plutôt (que) *adv.*   rather (than)

poche *f.*   pocket
poésie *f.*   poetry
poids *m.*   weight
point: ne … point (= **ne … pas**)   not
poisson *m.*   fish
polissage *m.*   polishing
pompe *f.*   pump;   **~ à vide**   vacuum
  pump
ponctuel, -le *adj.*   punctual
pondérable *adj.*   weighable
pont *m.*   bridge; deck (*of a ship*)
poreux, poreuse *adj.*   porous
portail *m.*   portal
porte *f.*   door
porte-plume *m.*   penholder
porte: que l'on porte   which is brought;
  qui porte à   which leads to
porter   to carry; to wear
porteur *m.*   bearer
portique *m.*   (*Arch.*) porch
posé *pp.*   asked, posed
poser   to place; to propose;
  ~ une question   to ask a question
positif, positive *adj.*   positive
posséder*   to have, to possess
poste *m.*   station, post;
  ~ de haute fréquence   high-frequency
  generator;   **~ émetteur**   transmitting
  station, transmitter;   **~ de**
  T.S.F.   radio
poteau *m.*   (*Arch.*) pile; post, pole
poudre *f.*   powder
pour *prep.*   for; to; (+ *inf.*) in order
  to;   **~ cent, ~ 100**   percent;
  ~ effet   as a result;   **~ que**   so that
pourchasser   to hunt, to pursue
pourquoi *adv.*   why
pourr-   (*FC vst. of* **pouvoir**)   will
  (would) be able to
poursuivant *pres. p.*   continuing
poursuivre*   to pursue
pourtant *adv.*   however
pourvu *pp.*   provided;   **~ de**
  provided with;   **~ que**   provided
  that
poussé *pp.*   developed;   **vide ~**   high
  vacuum
poussée *f.*   (*Arch.*) thrust; push
pousser   to push;   **~ un cri**   to cry out,
  to shout;   **~ un soupir**   to heave a
  sigh

poussière *f.*   dust
poutre *f.*   (*Arch.*) beam
pouvant *pres. p.*   being able to; capable of
pouvoir*   to be able [vb. 20]
pouvoir *m.*   power
praticien *m.*   practitioner
pratique *adj.*   practical
pratique *f.*   practice
pratiqué *pp.*   practiced, exercised
pratiquement *adv.*   practically
pratiquer   to carry out, to execute
préalable *adj.*   prerequisite
précéder   to precede
précis, -e *adj.*   precise
préciser   to determine, to specify
précision *f.*   detail
préconisé *pp.*   highly praised
premier, première *adj.*   first
prenant *pres. p.*   taking
prendre*   to take;   ~ naissance to originate;   ~ garde   to be careful;   ~ en compte   to take into account [vb. 21]
prenn-   (*vst. of* prendre)
préparer   to prepare
près *adv.*   near;   à peu ~   approximately, nearly;   au (millième) ~   within about (a thousand);   ~ de   near (*location*); about to (*do an action*);   tout ~ (de)   very near (to)
se présenter   to appear
presque *adv.*   almost
se presser   to hurry
pression *f.*   pressure
présumé *pp.*   presumed, assumed
prêt, -e *adj.*   ready
prétendre   to claim, to allege
prétendu *pp.*   alleged, claimed
prétention *f.*   claim
prêter   to lend;   se ~ à   to lend itself to ...
preuve *f.*   proof;   faire ~ de   to give proof of
prévenir*   to forewarn, to warn, to alert [vb. 30]
prévoir*   to foresee; to anticipate [vb. 31]
prévu *pp.*   anticipated, foreseen, predicted

prière *f.*   prayer
primaire *m.*   primary
primitif, primitive *adj.*   original
principe *m.*   principle; basis; element
printemps *m.*   spring (*season*)
pris *pp.* (prendre)   taken, caught;   ~ pour   taken as;   ~ sur   taken from; hardened (*cement*)
prix *m.*   prize; price;   au ~ de   at the price of
procédé *m.*   process, procedure
procéder*   to proceed;   ~ de   to stem from
prochain, -e *adj.*   next
proche (de) *adv.*   near
produire*   to produce
se produisant *pres. p.*   occurring
produit *m.*   product, material
produit *pp.*   produced
professer   to teach, to profess
profil *m.*   cross-section
profond, -e *adj.*   deep;   peu profond   shallow
profondeur *f.*   depth
programmation *f.*   programming
progrès *m.*   progress
proie *f.*   prey
projet *m.*   plan, project;   à l'état de ~   in the planning stage
promeneur *m.*   stroller, person out for a walk
promettre*   to promise [vb. 14]
se propager   to be propagated
se proposer de   to set out to; to intend to
propre *adj.*   clean; appropriate; (*before noun*) own;   ~ à   peculiar to
proprement: à proprement parler   actually, really;   proprement dit   per se; proper, itself
propriété *f.*   property; characteristic
prospection *f.*   prospecting
protection *f.*   shield
protéger*   to protect
protéide *f.*   protein
prouver   to prove
provenance *f.*   source, origin
provenant *pres. p.*   resulting
provenir*   to originate [vb. 30]
provisoirement *adv.*   tentatively
provoquer   to cause; to produce
psycholinguistique *f.*   psycholinguistics

pu *pp.* (**pouvoir**) been able
public, publique *adj.* public
public *m.* public; **le grand ~** the general public
publié *pp.* published
puis *adv.* then, next
puiser to derive, to get
puisque *conj.* since, inasmuch as
puiss- (*subj. vst. of* **pouvoir**) can; will be able to
puissamment *adv.* greatly, powerfully
puissance *f.* power; **de faible ~** low power(ed)
puissant, -e *adj.* powerful
puisse (*fr.* **pouvoir**) may, can
puits *m.* well
punir to punish
pupitre *m.* (school) desk
pur, -e *adj.* pure

quadrilatère *m.* quadrilateral
qualité: en qualité de in the status of
quand *conj.* when; **~ même** nevertheless, anyway
quant à as for, with regard to
quantique *adj.* quantum
quantité *f.* quantity; **une toute petite ~** a very small quantity
quarante forty
quart *m.* quarter, fourth
quatre four
que *conj.* that; (*in comparisons*) as, than
que *pron.* which, whom; that
quel, quelle *adj.* (*pl.* **quels, quelles**) what, which; **quel que soit ...** whatever ... may be
quelconque *adj.* ordinary; any; whatever
quelque *adj.* some; **quelques** a few, several; **~ chose** something
quelquefois *adv.* sometimes
quelques-unes *f.pl. pron.* some
quelques-uns *m.pl. pron.* some
quelqu'un *pron.* somebody, someone
qu'est-ce que (qui) ... ? what ... ?
queue *f.* tail; line
qui *pron.* who; which; that
quitte à even if it means

quitter to leave
quoi *pron.* what; **après ~** after which
quoique *conj.* although
quotidien, -ne *adj.* daily
quotidien *m.* daily (*paper*)

racine *f.* root
raconter to relate, to tell (*a story*)
rade *f.* harbor; (*Naval*) roads
radio-élément *m.* radioactive element
raide *adj.* steep, stiff
raie *f.* ray; (*Phys.*) **~ spectrale** spectral band
raison *f.* reason; proportion; **à ~ de** at a rate of; **avec ~** rightly; **avoir ~** to be right; **en ~ de** as a result of; **en ~ directe (inverse)** in direct (inverse) proportion
raisonnement *m.* reasoning
ralentir to slow down; to decelerate
ramasser to pick up; to gather, to collect
rameau *m.* branch
ramener* to bring back, to lead back
ramifier to ramify; to branch out
rang *m.* rank
ranger to arrange; to line up
rapide: train rapide express train
se rappeler* to remember, to recall
rappelons let us remember
rapport *m.* relationship, connection; ratio; **par ~ à** in relation to; compared to
rapporter to report; **se ~ à** to refer to, to relate to
rapprocher to approach; to compare; **se ~ de** to draw nearer
rassembler to assemble, to gather together; to collect
rattacher to reattach; to connect; **se ~ à** to be related to; to deal with
se raviser to change one's mind
ravitaillement *m.* (*Mil.*) supplies
rayon *m.* ray; beam; shelf; (*Geom.*) radius; **~ d'action** operating range; **~ lumineux** light ray; **rayons X** x-rays
rayonnement *m.* radiation
réacteur *m.* reactor
réactif *m.* (*Chem.*) reagent

réaction: réaction en chaîne chain reaction
réagir to react
réalisation *f.* accomplishment
réaliser to accomplish; to create
réalité: en réalité in reality, really
récemment *adv.* recently; **tout ~** quite recently
recevoir* to receive [vb. 23]
réchauffer to warm, to heat
recherche *f.* search; **à la ~** seeking, looking for; **faire des recherches** to do research
rechercher to seek, to seek out, to search for
récipient *m.* container
reçoi- (*vst. of* **recevoir**) [vb. 23]
recommander to entrust
recommencer to begin again
reconnaître* to recognize; to realize; **se ~** to recognize oneself [vb. 2]
recours *m.* recourse
recouvert (de) *pp.* covered (with)
recouvrir* (**de**) to cover (with)
rectitude *f.* accuracy
recueillir* to collect, to gather
récupéré *pp.* recovered
reçut (*fr.* **recevoir**) received
redescendre to go (come) back down again
redevable *adj.* indebted
redevenir to become again
redresseur *m.* (*Elec.*) commutator
réduire* to reduce
réduit *pp.* reduced; **~ à néant** reduced to nothing; destroyed [vb. 22]
réel, -e *adj.* real, actual
réfectoire *m.* dining hall
se référer (à) to refer (to)
réfléchir to reflect
réflexion *f.* reflection
réfractaire *adj.* fireproof; refractory; **~ à** resistant to
se réfracter to be refracted
refroidi *pp.* cooled
refroidir to cool (down)
refroidissement *m.* cooling
refroidisseur *m.* cooling element
regarde: cela ne vous regarde pas that does not concern you

regarder to look at; to watch; to view; to concern
règle *f.* rule
réglé (sur) *pp.* based (on)
règne *m.* reign, rule
régner to reign; to exist
réitérer to repeat, to reiterate
rejeter* to throw away, to reject
rejoign- (*vst. of* **rejoindre**)
rejoindre to join
relâcher to release
relai *m.* relay
relatif, relative *adj.* relative
relation *f.* relationship; friend, acquaintance
relativité *f.* relativity
reliant *pres. p.* relating; connecting
relié *pp.* related, connected
relier to connect, to join; to tie
remarquer to notice, to observe
remarquons let us notice, let us observe
remettre* to put back; to postpone [vb. 14]
remis *pp.* given back; **~ à neuf** renovated
remonter to go back up; to wind (*a clock*); **~ le courant** to go upstream; **~ à** to go back to
remorquer to pull; to tow
remous *m.* eddy; **~ atmosphériques** atmospheric eddies
remplaçant: en remplaçant by replacing
remplacement *m.* replacement, substitute
remplacer to replace
remplir (de) to fill (with)
remporter to win (*a victory*); to achieve
remuer to move, to be in motion; to stir
rencontrer to meet, to encounter
rendre (+ *adj.*) to render, to make; (+ *noun*) to give back, return; **~ raison de** to give an explanation for; **se ~ compte** to realize
rendu *pp.* rendered
renfermer to contain; to include
renommé *pp.* famous
renouvellement *m.* renewal; replenishment
renseignements *m.pl.* information
renseigner to inform

rentrer to return home
répandre to spread
répandu *pp.* spread; widespread
reparaît (*pres. of* **reparaître**) reappears
réparation *f.* repair
repartir* to depart again
répartir to divide, to distribute
répartition *f.* distribution
repérer to locate
répéter to repeat
repli *m.* fold, crease
répliquer to reply
répondre (à) to answer, to reply; to respond (to); to correspond (to)
repos *m.* rest; **au ~** at rest
reposer (sur) to depend (on)
repousser to push back
reprendre* to take up again, to resume; to take back
représenter to represent; **se ~** to imagine; to picture
reprise: à plusieurs reprises several times, on several occasions
requis *pp.* required
resserrer to constrict
résolu *pp.* resolved; solved
résolution *f.* solution (*of a problem*)
résoudre* to solve, to resolve
respirer to breathe
ressembler to resemble
ressortir à to come under the jurisdiction of; to be the domain of
restant *m.* remainder
restant *pres. p.* remaining
reste (*pres. of* **rester**) remains; **il en ~** there remain(s)
reste *m.* remainder; **du ~** moreover, however
rester to stay, to remain (*uses auxiliary* **être**)
restreint *pp.* limited, restrained
résultant (de) *pres. p.* resulting (from)
résultat *m.* result
résumer to summarize
retard *m.* delay; **en ~** late
retardé *pp.* delayed, retarded
retenir* to retain, to keep; to remember; to detain [vb. 28]
retentissement: avoir retentissement to have repercussions

retien- (*vst. of* **retenir**)
rétine *f.* retina
retirer to withdraw; to remove
retour *m.* return; **être de ~** to be back
retourner to return, to go back (*uses auxiliary* **être**); **se ~** to turn round
retrouver to find; to rediscover
réunion *f.* meeting
réunir to assemble, to bring together; to coexist
réunissent (*pres. of* **réunir**) (they) meet
réussir (à, dans) to succeed (in); **~ à un examen** to pass an exam
revanche: en revanche on the other hand
rêve *m.* dream
réveiller to awaken
révélateur, révélatrice *adj.* revealing
révéler to reveal
revenir* to come back, to return; to reappear (*uses auxiliary* **être**) [vb. 30]
revêtement *m.* casing, revetment
revêtir to cover
rêveur, rêveuse *adj.* dreamer
revien- (*vst. of* **revenir**)
revoir* to see again; to revise, to go over again [vb. 31]
revue *f.* magazine; review
rien *pron.* nothing; **ne ... ~** nothing, not anything; **il n'en est ~** it's nothing of the sort
rigoureusement *adv.* strictly
rigoureux, rigoureuse *adj.* strict; complete; harsh
rire* to laugh
risquer (de) to risk, to run the risk (of); to threaten (to)
rivage *m.* shore; bank (*of a body of water*)
rive *f.* shore, bank (*river*)
roche *f.* rock
romain, -e *adj.* Roman
roman, -e *adj.* (*Arch.*) Romanesque
roman *m.* novel
rompre to break
roue *f.* wheel; **~ directrice** steering wheel; **~ motrice** drive wheel
rouge *adj.* red; **porter au ~ vif** to bring to red-hot

rougir   to blush
rouler   to roll
royal, -e   (*m.pl.* **royaux**) *adj.* royal
rue *f.*   street
Russie *f.*   Russia

sa *adj.*   his, her, its
sable *m.*   sand
sach-   (*subj. vst. of* **savoir**)   know(s),
will know
sagesse *f.*   wisdom, sagacity
sais (*pres. of* **savoir**)   know
saisir   to grasp, to seize
saison *f.*   season
sait (*pres. of* **savoir**)   know;   **on ~**   it is
known
salé *pp.*   saline, salty
salle *f.*   room;   **~ de théâtre**
auditorium
sans *prep.*   without
satisfaire*   to satisfy [vb. 12]
satisfaisant, -e *adj.*   satisfactory
saur-   (*FC vst. of* **savoir**)   will (would)
know
sauter   to jump; to skip; to explode
sauvage *adj.*   wild
sauver   to save
savant, -e *adj.*   scholarly, learned
saveur *f.*   taste, flavor
savoir*   to know; to know how to;
à ~   namely [vb. 24]
savoir *m.*   knowledge
schéma *m.*   schematic drawing
scindé *pp.*   split
scruter   to scrutinize
sec, sèche *adj.*   dry
sécher   to dry
secours *m.*   help
sécurité *f.*   safety
seigneur *m.*   lord, master
sein: au sein de   in the midst of, at the
heart of (*a machine, etc.*)
seize   sixteen
séjour *m.*   visit, stay; habitat
sel *m.*   salt
selon *prep.*   according to; depending on
semaine *f.*   week
sémantique *f.*   semantics
semblable *adj.*   similar
sembler   to seem

sens *m.*   sense, meaning; opinion;
direction;   **en ce ~ que**   in the sense
that;   **~ inverse**   opposite direction
sensibilité *f.*   sensitivity
sensible *adj.*   sensitive; noticeable;
perceptible
sensiblement *adv.*   obviously, noticeably
sentiment *m.*   feeling
sentir*   to feel; to smell
séparer   to separate
sept   seven
ser-   (*FC vst. of* **être**)   will (would) be
sériation *f.*   sequence, serialization,
placing in serial form
série *f.*   series
sérieux, sérieuse *adj.*   serious; marked;
important;   **prendre au sérieux**   to
take seriously
serment *m.*   vow, promise
serpentin *m.*   coil
serrer   to squeeze, to press, to tighten; to
hold (press) tightly
sert (*pres. of* **servir**)   serves
servir* (**de**)   to serve (as);   **se ~ de**   to
make use of [vb. 25]
serviteur *m.*   servant
ses *adj.* (*pl.*)   his, her, its
seuil *m.*   threshold
seul, -e *adj.*   alone; (*before noun*) only,
lone, single;   **tout ~**   by oneself
seulement *adv.*   only
sévèrement *adv.*   strictly
si *adv.*   so
si *conj.*   if, whether;
~ ce n'est (que)   except (that)
siècle *m.*   century
sien: le sien   his
sienne: la sienne *pron.*   his, hers
sifflet *m.*   whistle
signaler   to point out
silice *f.*   silica
sillonner   to furrow
singe *m.*   monkey
singulier, singulière *adj.*   singular,
individual
sinon *adv.*   if not; otherwise
sinueux, sinueuse *adj.*   winding
social, -e   (*m.pl.* **sociaux**) *adj.*   social
société *f.*   society; company,
organization

sœur *f.*   sister
soi *pron.*   oneself; **en** ~   in itself
soi- (*vst. of* être)
soient (*without subject* ils)   let there be
soigner   to care for, to take care of
soin *m.*   care
soir *m.*   evening
soit (*subj.* of être)   that is, i.e.; be, will
  be; (*Math*) let;   ~ ... ~   either ... or
soixante   sixty
soixante-dix   seventy
sol *m.*   soil, ground
soldat *m.*   soldier
soleil *m.*   sun
sombre *adj.*   dark
sommairement *adv.*   briefly
somme *f.*   (*Math*) sum
sommier *m.*   (*Arch.*) beam
son *adj.*   his, her, its
son *m.*   sound
sonner   to ring (*bell*); to strike (*clock*); to
  sound
sonore *adj.*   sonorous; sound-
  transmitting
sonorité *f.*   sound
sont (*pres. of* être)   (they) are
sorte *f.*   kind, sort, species; **de la** ~   in
  that way; **en** ~ **que**   so that;
  en quelque ~   in a way
sortie *f.*   exit; outlet; leaving
sortir*   to leave, to go out of (*uses
  auxiliary* être) [vb. 26]
se soucier (**de**)   to be concerned (with)
  (about)
soudaine, -e *adj.*   sudden
soudé *pp.*   fused, joined, attached
souffler   to blow; to breathe (*a word*), to
  whisper
souffrir   to suffer
soulever*   to raise
souligner   to emphasize; to underline
soumettre*   to submit; to subject [vb. 14]
soumis (à) *pp.*   subjected (to)
soupape *f.*   valve
soupçonner   to suspect
souplesse *f.*   flexibility
sourire*   to smile
souris *f.*   mouse
sous *prep.*   under
sous-entendu *m.*   implication

sous-marin *m.*   submarine
soustrayant *pres. p.*   subtracting
soutenir*   to sustain; to support
soutien *m.*   support
souvent *adv.*   often
souverain *m.*   sovereign, king
spectre *m.*   spectrum
spirituel, -le *adj.*   witty
stationner   to park (*a vehicle*)
statuaire *f.*   statuary
structuralisme *m.*   structuralism
subir   to undergo; to experience
subsister   to remain, to subsist; to exist
subtil, -e *adj.*   subtle; discerning; thin,
  rarefied
successif, successive *adj.*   successive
sud *m.*   south
Suède *f.*   Sweden
suffire*   to suffice
suffisamment *adv.*   enough, sufficiently
suffisant *pres. p.*   sufficient
suggérer*   to suggest
suisse *adj.*   Swiss
suite *f.*   continuity, continuation;
  coherence; **à la** ~ **de**   following; as a
  result of
suivant *pres. p.*   following; ~ **que**
  depending on whether, according as
suivre*   to follow [vb. 27]
sujet *m.*   subject
superficie *f.*   area, surface
supérieur, -e (à) *adj.*   greater (than);
  superior (to); upper, top (*part*)
suppléer: suppléer à ... **par**   to
  compensate for ... by
supporter   to endure
supposer   to suppose
supposons   let us suppose, let us presume,
  let us postulate
supprimer   to cancel
sur *prep.*   on; by (*dimensions*)
sûr, -e *adj.*   sure, certain; bien ~!
  sure! of course!
surbaissé: (*Arch.*) voûte surbaissée
  segmental arch
surcroît: par surcroît   in addition,
  moreover
surélevée: (*Arch.*) voûte surélevée   stilted
  arch
sur-le-champ *adv.*   immediately

surnommé *pp.*   named
surtout *adv.*   especially, primarily, above all
surveiller   to watch closely; to supervise
survenir*   to happen suddenly; to arrive
survient (*pres. of* survenir)   arrives, comes along; along comes
susceptible (de) *adj.*   capable (of) ...
susciter   to arouse, to excite
système *m.*   system;   ~ **de référence** system used as an example

tableau *m.*   picture; panel;   ~ **noir** blackboard
tacitement *adv.*   implied
taille *f.*   size, stature, dimensions
tailler   to trim
se taire*   to be silent, to remain quiet; to stop talking
tandis que *conj.*   whereas, while
tant *adv.*   so much, so many;
    ~ **à ... que**   as much in ... as;
    en ~ de   insofar as
tard *adv.*   late
tarder   to delay
tâtonnement *m.*   groping
tel, -le *adj.*   like, such;   **tel que**   such as
tellement *adv.*   so much, so
témérité *f.*   audacity
témoigner   to testify; to substantiate, to attest; to witness
témoin *m.*   witness; evidence;
    comme ~   as a guide
temps *m.*   time; weather;
    de ~ à autre, de ~ en ~   from time to time, occasionally
tendre   to stretch tight, to make taut
tenir*   to hold;   ~ **à**   to be anxious to;
    ~ **compte de**   to keep an account of;
    ~ **lieu de**   to take the place of;
    se ~   to remain, to stay [vb. 28]
tension *f.*   (*Elec.*) voltage, potential, gradient;   **à haute ~**   high tension;
    ~ **redressée**   direct current;
    ~ **superficielle**   surface tension
tente *f.*   tent
tenter (de)   to attempt (to)
tenu *pp.* (tenir)   held, bound
terme: au terme de   at the end of

terminer   to terminate, to end
terrain *m.*   (*Arch.*) building site
terre *f.*   earth, world; soil;   **par ~**   on the ground;   ~ **cuite**   terra cotta, ceramic clay
terrestre *adj.*   terrestrial
tête *f.*   head; face
théâtre *m.*   theater;   **salle de ~** auditorium
théorie *f.*   theory
tien- (*vst. of* tenir)
tiendr- (*FC vst. of* tenir)   will (would) hold
tiers *m.*   one-third
tige *f.*   stem; trunk (*tree*); (*Mech.*) shaft, rod
timbre *m.*   (*Music*) tone
tir *m.*   shooting, fire
tirer   to pull; to draw; to shoot;
    d'en ~   to obtain from it
titre *m.*   title; composition;   **à juste ~** with good reason
toit *m.*   roof
toiture *f.*   roof, roofing
tomber   to fall (*uses auxiliary* être);
    ~ **sur**   to happen upon
ton *m.*   tone;   **d'un ~**   in a tone
tonne *f.*   ton
tort *m.*   wrong;   **à ~**   wrongly;
    avoir ~   to be wrong
tortue *f.*   turtle
toucher   to touch
toucher *m.*   sense of touch
toujours *adv.*   always, still
tour *f.*   tower
tour *m.*   turn;   **à son ~**   in his turn, by turns
tourner   to rotate, to turn;
    ~ **sur elle-même**   to rotate on its own axis
tous, toutes *adj.* (*pl. of* tout, toute)   all; everybody;   ~ **les deux**   both
tout, toute *adj.* (*pl.* tous, toutes)   all, every; quite;
    du tout, pas du tout   not at all;
    tout à fait   entirely, completely;
    tout à l'heure   recently, just now;
    tout au plus   at the very most;
    tout autre   quite otherwise;
    tout ce qui ..., tout ce que ...

everything that …;
tout de suite   immediately;
tout le monde   everybody;
un tout petit peu   just a little [Sec. 72]
toutefois *adv.*   nevertheless, in any case
tracé *m.*   (*Arch.*) layout, plan
traduire* to translate;   **se ~**   to be reflected
traité *m.*   .article, treatise
traitement *m.*   treatment;   **usine de ~**   processing plant
traiter (de)   to deal (with)
traître *m.*   traitor
trajet *m.*   travel
tranche *f.*   slice; (*Arch.*) slab
tranquillement *adv.*   quietly, calmly
se transformer (en)   to be changed (into)
transporter   to transport
trapèze *m.*   (*Geom.*) trapezoid
travail *m.* (*pl.* **travaux**)   work, study
travailler   to work
travailleur *m.*   worker
travers: à travers   through; across
traversée *f.*   crossing; sweep
traverser   to cross; to go through
très *adv.*   very
triste *adj.*   sad
trois   three
se tromper (de)   to be mistaken (about); to have the wrong (*sth.*)
trop *adv.* too;   **~ de** too much
trou *m.*   hole
trouver   to find; to discover, to invent;   **se ~**   to be (located), to find oneself (*sth.*)
T.S.F. (*abbr. of* **télégraphie** *or* **téléphonie sans fil**)   radio;   **poste de ~** *m.*   radio receiver;   **poste émetteur de ~**   radio broadcasting transmitter
tuer   to kill
tuile *f.*   tile
tympan *m.*   eardrum

ultérieurement *adv.*   later, subsequently
ultime *adj.*   final, ultimate
ultrason *m.*   ultrasound
un, -e *art.*   a, an;   **un à un**   one by one;   **l'un … l'autre**   one … the other;   **l'un par rapport à l'autre**   with relation to each other

uni, -e *adj.*   smooth; joined, united
uniquement *adj.*   only
unir   to unite, to join; to unify; to smooth
unité *f.*   unit;   **~ de masse**   unit of mass
univers *m.*   universe
universitaire *adj.*   relating to the university; of higher learning; university
usine *f.*   factory, plant;   **~ de traitement**   processing plant
usuel, -le *adj.*   usual
utile (à) *adj.*   useful (for)
utilement *adv.*   profitably, usefully
utilisant: en utilisant   by using
utiliser   to use, to utilize
utopique *adj.*   utopian

va (*pres. of* **aller**)   goes
vaincre*   to overcome
vaincu *pp.*   vanquished, beaten, overcome
vainqueur *m.*   victor
vaisseau *m.*   ship, vessel; (*Bot.*) duct
valable *adj.*   valid; reliable; valuable
valeur *f.*   value
valoir*   to be worth;   **~ mieux**   to be preferable
vapeur *f.*   steam; vapor;   **~ de l'eau**   water vapor
vapeur *m.*   (*abbr. of* **machine à vapeur**)   steamship
varier   to vary
vase *f.*   mud, slime
vase *m.*   vase
vaudr- (*FC vst. of* **valoir**)   it will (would) be worth (*sth.*)
vaut: il vaut   it is worth
vécu *pp.*   lived, experienced
véhiculé *pp.*   transmitted
veille *f.*   eve
vendre   to sell
venir*   to come (*uses auxiliary* **être**);   (+ *inf.*) to happen to (*do sth.*);   **en ~ à** (+ *inf.*)   to go so far as to …;   **venir de**   to have just (*done sth.*) [vb. 30]
vent *m.*   wind
venu *pp.* (**venir**)   come
verdâtre *adj.*   greenish

véritable *adj.*   actual; correct

vérité *f.*   truth

verr-   (*FC vst. of* **voir**)   will (would) see

verre *m.*   glass

vers *prep.*   toward; about (*with time*)

vert, -e *adj.*   green

vertu *f.*   virtue; quality; courage;
   en ~ de   by virtue of, in accordance
   with

veuill-   (*vst. of* **vouloir**)

veut dire (*pres. of* **vouloir dire**)   means,
   signifies

vibratoire *adj.*   vibrating

vide *m.*   vacuum; emptiness;
   ~ parfait   perfect vacuum;
   ~ poussé   high vacuum

vider   to empty

vie *f.*   life

vieil, -le *adj.*   old, aged [Sec. 15]

vien-   (*vst. of* **venir**)

viendr-   (*FC vst. of* **venir**)   will (would)
   come

vierge *f., adj.*   virgin

vieux, vieil, vieille *adj.*   old [Sec. 15]

vif, vive *adj.*   lively, turbulent;
   rouge vif   red-hot, glowing red

vil, -e *adj.*   vile, base

ville *f.*   city;   **petite ~**   town

virtuel, -le *adj.*   theoretical

viser à   aim at

visiblement *adv.*   obviously, visibly

visière *f.*   visor

vit (*pres. of* **vivre**)   lives

vite *adv.*   quickly, fast;   **moins ~**
   slower

vitesse *f.*   speed; velocity

vitrage *m.*   windows

vitre *f.*   windowpane

vivant *pres. p.*   living

vivre*   to live

voi-   (*vst. of* **voir**)

voici *adv.*   here is (are)

voie *f.*   way; road; path (*of action*);
   ~ ferrée   railroad (right-of-way);

~ respiratoire   respiratory tract;
   en ~ de   in the process of

voilà *adv.*   there is (are)

voir*   to see; to understand [vb. 31]

voisin, -e *adj.*   neighboring; nearby,
   near, in the neighborhood

voisinage *m.*   neighborhood, vicinity

voiture *f.*   car; vehicle

voix *f.*   voice;   **à demi-voix**   in a low
   tone

volcan *m.*   volcano

voler   to fly; to steal

vorace *adj.*   voracious

voudr- (*FC vst. of* **vouloir**)   will want to
   (would like to)

vouloir*   to want, to wish; to insist on;
   ~ dire   to mean, to signify [vb. 32]

voulu *pp.*   wanted

voûte *f.*   (*Arch.*) vault

voûté, -e *adj.*   vaulted, arched

voy-   (*vst. of* **voir**)

voyage *m.*   trip; voyage;   **~ de retour**
   return trip

voyager   to travel

voyageur *m.*   traveller

voyant *pres. p.* (**voir**)   seeing;   **en ~**
   upon seeing

vrai, -e *adj.*   true;   **à vrai dire**   to tell
   the truth, in fact

vraiment   truly

vraisemblable *adj.*   probable, likely

vu *pp.* (**voir**)   seen

vue *f.*   view; vision; sight;   **à courte ~**
   shortsighted

y *adv.*   there;   **il ~ a**   there is (are);
   il ~ avait   there was (were);
   il ~ aura   there will be;
   il ~ aurait   there would be;
   ~ penser   to think of it (them);
   ~ obéir   to obey it

yeux (*pl. of* **œil**)   eyes

Index

Numbers refer to pages of the text.

Permissions and Credits

The author and editors would like to thank the following authors, publishers, and companies for their generous permission to use copyrighted material:

"Les Circuits logiques," adapted from "Panorama des méthodes de test non-déterministes des circuits logiques," by R. David and P. Thevenod-Fosse in *Rairo-automatique, Systems Analysis and Control*, Vol. 13, pp. 5–38, 1979, © AFCET.

"Les Psychologues au travail," "Orientation et sélection professionnelles," and "Les Aptitudes musicales," from *Traité de psychologie*, by Norman L. Munn, © Editions Payot.

"Un Mystère mathématique," "Un Esprit vif," and "Qui va à la chasse perd sa place," from *The All in French Course*, by E. B. Crampton, © Thomas Nelson and Sons, Ltd.

"L'Islam" and "Sociologie," from *Introduction à la sociologie de l'Islam*, by M. Chelhod, © Editions G. P. Maisonneuve et Larose.

"La Statistique," from *Introduction à la statistique*, by Marcel Bertaud, © Presses de l'Université de Montréal.

"Contre la technocratie; jouer la connaissance," from *On ne change pas la société par décret*, by Michel Crozier, © Editions Bernard Grasset.

"Langue et société," from *Ce que parler veut dire*, by Pierre Bourdieu, © Librairie Fayard.

"La Guerre d'Amérique," "Les Sciences au XVIIe siècle," and "L'Architecture ogivale: XIIIe siècle," from *Histoire de France*, by Victor Duruy, © Hachette.

"Océanographie biologique," from *Cours d'océanographie physique: Théorie de la circulation générale*, by Henri Lacombe, © Editions Bordas.

"Les Dauphins," from *Les Dauphins et la liberté*, by Jacques-Yves Cousteau and Philippe Diolé, © Editions Flammarion.

"Mousse," from the *Collins-Robert French Dictionary* (*French-English/English-French*), © Collins Publishers.

"L'Etranger," from *L'Etranger*, by Albert Camus, © Editions Gallimard.

"Page d'écriture," from *Paroles*, by Jacques Prévert, © Editions Gallimard.

"Le Passe-muraille," from *Marcel Aymé: Le passe-muraille*, by Marcel Aymé, © Editions Gallimard.

"Les Radars," from the article "Ondes herziennes" by H. Portier, and "La Masse et l'énergie," from the article "Explorations de la matière," by Louis Leprince-Ringuet and André Astier, in *Grandes Découvertes du XXe Siècle*, © Librairie Larousse.

"La Linguistique générative," from the article, "Linguistique," by G. Provost-Chauveau, in *La Grande Encyclopédie*, Vol. 12, © Librairie Larousse.

"Température et constitution du soleil," from *Astronomie*, by L. Rudaux and G. de Vaucouleurs, © Librairie Larousse.

"Thorium et uranium 233," and "Sous-marins atomiques," from *L'Energie nucléaire*, by Maurice E. Nahmias, © Librairie Larousse.

"L'Oxygène," "L'Azote," "L'Air," "La Lumière," and "Le Son," from *Sciences physiques et naturelles*, by J. Dutilleul and E. Ramé, © Librairie Larousse.

"Une Critique de Thomas Wolfe," by Maurice Coindreau, from *Quadrille américain II, Etude littéraire: Les œuvres nouvelles*, © Maurice Coindreau.

"Généralités sur la perception du son," from the article "Prévision de la gêne due au bruit autour des aéroports," from *Anthropologie appliquée*, by Ariel Alexandre, © Université René Descartes.